"**A collection** of other men's writings should be an oasis, an arsenal, or, at the very least, a stimulating companion for the innumerable desert islands of this crowded world. So we present thirty more or less philosophical pieces, each unabridged and complete in itself, and each meeting Emerson's test for books to be included in a small library—readable, medicinal, and invigorating."

—HOUSTON PETERSON

Dr. Peterson graduated from Pomona College in California and took his A.M. and Ph.D. degrees in philosophy at Columbia University. He retired from Rutgers University in 1963, after a long and influential career as Professor of Philosophy. In 1964, he was the first Extension Professor in Residence at U.C.L.A. In 1966, he was the first Professor in Residence at the University of Hawaii Library. In 1968, he appeared in seminars at the School of Oriental and African Studies at the University of London.

Among the books Dr. Peterson has written are:

Huxley: Prophet of Science, Havelock Ellis: Philosopher of Love, and *The Melody of Chaos*. He has edited, among other works, *Great Teachers* and *A Treasury of the World's Great Speeches* and a paperback anthology, *Great Essays*, which has sold over 850,000 copies. Currently he is at work on several publishing projects.

Also by Houston Peterson

Great Essays

Published by Washington Square Press

ESSAYS IN
PHILOSOPHY

From David Hume to
George Santayana

EDITED AND WITH NOTES BY
HOUSTON PETERSON
WITH THE ASSISTANCE OF JAMES BAYLEY

WASHINGTON SQUARE PRESS
POCKET BOOKS • NEW YORK

ESSAYS IN PHILOSOPHY

WASHINGTON SQUARE PRESS edition published 1959

Enlarged WASHINGTON SQUARE PRESS edition
published December, 1974

Ł

Published by
POCKET BOOKS, a division of Simon & Schuster, Inc.,
630 Fifth Avenue, New York, N.Y.

WASHINGTON SQUARE PRESS editions are distributed
in the U.S. by Simon & Schuster, Inc., 630 Fifth Avenue,
New York, N.Y. 10020 and in Canada by Simon & Schuster of Canada, Ltd., Markham, Ontario, Canada.

ACKNOWLEDGMENTS

For material copyrighted by authors, publishers, and agents, the editor of *Essays in Philosophy* is indebted to the following:

GEORGE ALLEN & UNWIN LTD. (London) for "Logic As the Essence of Philosophy" from *Our Knowledge of the External World* and "Knowledge and Wisdom" from *Portraits from Memory and Other Essays* by Bertrand Russell.

BASIL BLACKWELL, PUBLISHER (London) for "Gods" from *Philosophy and Psychoanalysis* by John Wisdom.

BOLLINGEN FOUNDATION, INC. for "Dante's Innocence and Luck" from *Creative Intuition in Art and Poetry* by Jacques Maritain; copyright, 1953, by the Trustees of the National Gallery of Art, Washington, D.C.

COLUMBIA UNIVERSITY PRESS for "The Three-Dimensional Diagram" from *Process and Polarity* by Wilmon Henry Sheldon.

MARGOT CORY for "A Long Way Round to Nirvana, or, Much Ado About Dying" by George Santayana. Reprinted by permission of Margot Cory, Literary Executor of the Santayana estate.

J. M. DENT & SONS LTD. (London) for "A Discourse on the Moral Effects of the Arts and Sciences" from *The Social Contract* by Jean-Jacques Rousseau, translated by G. D. H. Cole.

ACKNOWLEDGMENTS

v

E. P. DUTTON & CO., INC. for "A Discourse on the Moral Effects of the Arts and Sciences" from *The Social Contract* by Jean-Jacques Rousseau. Everyman's Library Edition published by E. P. Dutton & Co., Inc. Reprinted by permission of the publishers.

THE FREE PRESS for "Naturalism Reconsidered" from *Logic Without Metaphysics* by Ernest Nagel.

HARPER & ROW, PUBLISHERS, INC. for "East and West" in *Lectures on Zen Buddhism* by D. T. Suzuki from *Zen Buddhism and Psychoanalysis* by Erich Fromm, D. T. Suzuki and Richard De Martino. Copyright, ©, 1960, by Erich Fromm. Reprinted by permission of Harper & Row, Publishers, Inc.

THE HOGARTH PRESS LTD. (London) for "A Philosophy of Life" from *New Introductory Lectures on Psychoanalysis* by Sigmund Freud.

INTERNATIONAL PUBLISHERS for "Theses on Feuerbach" from *The German Ideology* by Karl Marx and Friedrich Engels.

THE LIBERAL ARTS PRESS, INC. for the "Preface" to the *Prolegomena to Any Future Metaphysics* by Immanuel Kant, edited and with an Introduction by Lewis W. Beck (The Library of Liberal Arts No. 27, New York, 1950). Reprinted by permission of the publishers, The Liberal Arts Press, Inc.

MACMILLAN & CO. LTD. (London) for the two "Prefaces" to the *Critique of Pure Reason* by Immanuel Kant, translated by Norman Kemp Smith. Permission granted by Professor Norman Kemp Smith, Macmillan & Co. Ltd., and St. Martin's Press.

THE MACMILLAN COMPANY for "Foresight" from *Adventures of Ideas* by Alfred North Whitehead; copyright, 1933, by The Macmillan Company.

THE NEW YORK REVIEW OF BOOKS for "The Psychology of Being Powerless." Reprinted with permission from *The New York Review of Books*. Copyright, ©, 1966, by Nyrev, Inc.

W. W. NORTON & COMPANY, INC. for "A Philosophy of Life" from *New Introductory Lectures on Psychoanalysis* by Sigmund Freud; copyright, 1933, by Sigmund Freud.

OPEN COURT PUBLISHING COMPANY for "Philosophy As Vision" from *Great Visions of Philosophy* by William Pepperell Montague.

PRENTICE-HALL, INC. for "The Metaphysical Compass" from *The Ways of Things* by William Pepperell Montague; copyright, 1940, by Prentice-Hall, Inc., published by Prentice-Hall, Inc., Englewood Cliffs, New Jersey.

DR. JOSEPH RATNER and MRS. JOHN DEWEY for "The Unity of the Human Being" from *Intelligence in the Modern World: John Dewey's Philosophy*, edited and with an Introduction by Joseph Ratner; copyright, 1939, by Random House, Inc.

HENRY REGNERY COMPANY for "Aphorisms" from *Beyond Good and Evil* by Friedrich Nietzsche, translated by Marianne Cowan; copyright, ©, 1955, by Henry Regnery Company.

PAUL R. REYNOLDS & SON for "On a Certain Blindness in Human Beings" by William James.

RINEHART & COMPANY, INC. for "Selfishness, Self-Love, and Self-Interest" from *Man for Himself* by Erich Fromm; copyright, 1947, by Erich Fromm.

ROUTLEDGE & KEGAN PAUL LTD. (London) for "Selfishness, Self-Love, and Self-Interest" from *Man for Himself* by Erich Fromm.

GILBERT RYLE for "Ludwig Wittgenstein." First delivered as a Third Programme talk of the British Broadcasting Corporation and later printed in Volume XII of *Analysis* (1951).

SIMON & SCHUSTER, INC. for "Knowledge and Wisdom" from *Portraits from Memory and Other Essays* by Bertrand Russell; copyright, 1951, 1952, 1953, ©, 1956, by Bertrand Russell.

THE UNIVERSITY OF CHICAGO PRESS for "Philosophy As Vision" from *Great Visions of Philosophy* by William Pepperell Montague. Published originally in the October, 1933, issue of *The International Journal of Ethics*.

GILBERT RYLE for "Ludwig Wittgenstein." First delivered as a Third Programme talk of the British Broadcasting Corporation and later printed in Volume XII of *Analysis* (1951).

SIMON AND SCHUSTER, INC. for "Knowledge and Wisdom" from *Portraits from Memory and Other Essays* by Bertrand Russell; copyright, ©, 1951, 1952, 1953, 1956, by Bertrand Russell.

THE UNIVERSITY OF CHICAGO PRESS for "Philosophy As Vision" from *Great Visions of Philosophy* by William Pepperell Montague. Published originally in the October, 1933, issue of *The International Journal of Ethics*.

To

Helen Huss Parkhurst

Who taught Philosophy for many years

at Barnard College

and

In memory of

The late Dean Walter Taylor Marvin

of Rutgers

IN BRIEF

A philosophical problem has the form: "I don't know my way about."

—Ludwig Wittgenstein

Can a man disclaim speculation, can he disclaim theory, without disclaiming thought?

—Jeremy Bentham

Practical men, who believe themselves to be quite exempt from any intellectual influences, are usually the slaves of some defunct economist.

—John Maynard Keynes

Nothing is more terrible than ignorance in action.

—Goethe

It is the mark of an educated man to look for precision in each class of things just so far as the nature of the subject permits.

—Aristotle

TABLE OF CONTENTS

PREFACE

"Philosophy," the dictionary tells us, came from two Greek words for *love* and *wisdom* and hence meant "the love of wisdom," not a passion for platitudes or for miscellaneous information. Philosophy was not only a view of life but a way of living. Socrates talked wisely for years, wrote nothing and died nobly. Wherever we go in philosophy, however technical or toploftical we become, we should never forget that "there was once a man named Socrates" who was deeply involved in mankind.

As various conceptions of philosophy are to be encountered in this informal excursion, stern definitions at this point would be intimidating. But here is a recent comment by Bertrand Russell concerning the general value of philosophy: "On the theoretical side it is a help in understanding the universe as a whole, in so far as this is possible. On the side of feeling it is a help toward a just appreciation of the ends of life." William James said that "A man with no philosophy in him is the most inauspicious and unprofitable of all possible social mates," and Alfred North Whitehead added that "There can be no successful democratic society till general education conveys a philosophic outlook."

A collection of other men's writings should be an oasis, an arsenal, or, at the very least, a stimulating companion for the innumerable desert islands of this crowded world. So we present twenty-seven more or less philosophical pieces, each unabridged and complete in itself, and each meeting Emerson's test for books to be included in a small library—readable, medicinal and invigorating. There are some novelties, and some explosive pages by Blake, Marx and Nietzsche, but no eccentric selections made simply to get a big name into the table of contents; and there is no elaborate connective tissue designed to turn an informal treasury into a systematic text-book.

We begin with David Hume because he was a great philosopher and a delightful human being who wrote with verve and consideration for his reader. We begin with him also because he is being rediscovered and appreciated as never before. He is no longer the merely sceptical, corrosive Scotsman, but a bold, affirmative thinker, quietly critical before the overwhelming prestige of Newton. "His particular conception of philosophy as an empirical 'science of man,'" writes the brilliant Isaiah Berlin, "is the true beginning of modern philosophy, which, in essence, is the history of the development of, and opposition to, his thought." Far from being a low-minded speculator contemptuous of human nature, Hume was trying from the beginning, in spite of his so-called flippancy, to preserve the dignity of man which was being savagely belittled on one side and rashly overpraised on the other.

"The self-torturing sophist, wild Rousseau," in Byron's phrase, is also being rehabilitated. No longer the egomaniac or erotomaniac of popular rumor, he is being treated with a new seriousness as a moralist, a rationalist, and as a prophetic critic of *civilization* and the tyrannical idea of *inevitable* progress. We cannot elude him, for he has been an immeasurable influence in education, government, literature, and philosophy. So it would seem better to have a little firsthand contact with Rousseau, even through his too easily belittled First Discourse, rather than to meet him through his enemies.

As to a few other inclusions: The scholar may find it convenient to be able to carry around in his pocket three famous Prefaces by Immanuel Kant, and the general reader will at least be able to say that he has exchanged greetings with the giant of Königsberg. Jeremy Bentham, who had nothing in common with Kant except his celibacy, was so busy getting his thoughts down on thousands of pages that he had neither time nor inclination to be selective. And consequently the best introduction to that tireless old boy may well be Sydney

Smith's long book review, which is a kind of compressed anthology.

In the field of religion, there is a pioneer discussion of the nature of belief by John Henry Newman, a contemporary of Kierkegaard, and a recent essay by John Wisdom on the "Gods," which became a focus of lively controversy almost overnight. In the field of aesthetics it would have been possible to present a grave discourse on the principles of art or the nature of Beauty, but perhaps it is kinder to include Whistler's sparkling case for modern art and Maritain's timely study of Dante.

Bertrand Russell's highly influential essay on "Logic As the Essence of Philosophy" is followed immediately by William Pepperell Montague's "Philosophy As Vision," thus illustrating a perennial contrast or cleavage in the history of thought.

Charles Sanders Peirce, who has been called "the most original and versatile of American philosophers" but is still hardly a name to the general reader, is represented in one of his more daring speculative flights. Ludwig Wittgenstein, the mystery man of twentieth-century philosophy, appears in a brilliant sketch by Gilbert Ryle.

As for William James and John Dewey, they themselves called particular attention to their respective essays, "On a Certain Blindness in Human Beings" and "The Unity of the Human Being."

Perhaps it is a good rule to begin any book, even a collection, at the beginning. But at this moment in history one might find a special relevance in Alfred North Whitehead's reflections on "Foresight."

Bon voyage!

—HOUSTON PETERSON

Manhattan
April 19, 1958

PREFACE TO ENLARGED EDITION

With some thirty pages placed at my disposal, I have hopefully made three additions.

As the East has learned much, possibly too much, from the West, we Westerners have not learned enough from the East. I have therefore included a lecture on "East and West" by that almost-legendary Japanese expositor of Zen Buddhism, Daisetz Teitaro Suzuki. It was delivered at the Conference on Zen Buddhism and Psychoanalysis in Mexico in 1957.

"The Psychology of Being Powerless" was written at a time when more bombs were being rained on North Vietnam than had been dropped on Germany at the peak of World War II, and there was talk of sending a million men. The year was 1966, and the writer was the late Paul Goodman.

And now finally we close with an essay, a moving meditation, on dying. It has been said that philosophy is a learning to die. Four dialogues by Plato, "The Euthyphro," "The Apology," "The Crito," and "The Phaedo," which deal with the trial and death of Socrates, stand out as the most poignant drama in Western philosophy. Two thousand years later, the dying skeptic David Hume, in a final note of sympathy to a widowed lady, wrote: "I see death approach gradually, without any anxiety or regret. I salute you with affection and regard for the last time." Immanuel Kant, who was "awakened from his dogmatic slumber" by Hume, pitifully frail and incoherent in his last days, waited for his friend and doctor to take a seat before he himself sat down, and then muttered, "The sense of humanity has not yet left me." George Santayana's comments on death and dying provide a fitting ending to this collection of thoughts about life and living.

March 3, 1974   —H. P.

DAVID HUME

[1711–1776]

Hume, in the last year of his life, wrote the best foreword to Hume.

.   .   .

MY OWN LIFE

It is difficult for a man to speak long of himself without vanity; therefore, I shall be short. It may be thought an instance of vanity that I pretend at all to write my life, but this narrative shall contain little more than the history of my writings, as, indeed, almost all my life has been spent in literary pursuits and occupations. The first success of most of my writings was not such as to be an object of vanity.

I was born the 26th of April, 1711, old style, at Edinburgh. I was of a good family, both by father and mother. My father's family is a branch of the Earl of Home's or Hume's; and my ancestors had been proprietors of the estate, which my brother possesses, for several generations. My mother was daughter of Sir David Falconer, President of the College of Justice; the title of Lord Halkerton came by succession to her brother.

My family, however, was not rich; and, being myself a younger brother, my patrimony, according to the mode of my country, was of course very slender. My father, who passed for a man of parts, died when I was an infant, leaving me, with an elder brother and a sister, under the care of our mother, a woman of singular merit, who, though young and handsome, devoted herself entirely to the rearing and educating of her children. I passed through the ordinary course of education with success, and was seized very early with a passion for literature, which has been the ruling passion of my life and the great source of my enjoyments. My studious disposition, my sobriety, and my industry gave my family a notion that the law was a proper profession for me, but I found an unsurmountable aversion to everything but the pursuits of philosophy and general learning; and while they fancied I was poring upon Voet and Vinnius, Cicero and Vergil were the authors which I was secretly devouring.

My very slender fortune, however, being unsuitable to this plan of life, and my health being a little broken by my ardent application, I was tempted, or rather forced, to make a very feeble trial for entering into a more active scene of life. In 1734, I went to Bristol with some recommendations to eminent merchants, but in a few months found that scene totally unsuitable to me. I went over to France with a view of prosecuting my studies in a country retreat; and I there laid that plan of life which I have steadily and successfully pursued. I resolved to make a very rigid frugality supply my deficiency of fortune, to maintain unimpaired my independence, and to regard every object as contemptible except the improvement of my talents in literature.

During my retreat in France, first at Rheims, but chiefly at La Flèche, in Anjou, I composed my *Treatise of Human Nature*. After passing three years very agreeably in that country, I came over to London in 1737. In the end of 1738, I published my *Treatise*, and immediately went down to my mother and my brother, who lived at his country house, and was employing himself very judiciously and successfully in the improvement of his fortune.

Never literary attempt was more unfortunate than my *Treatise of Human Nature*. It fell *deadborn from the press*, without reaching such distinction as even to excite a murmur among the zealots. But being naturally of a cheerful and sanguine temper, I very soon recovered the blow and prosecuted with great ardor my studies in the country. In 1742, I printed at Edinburgh the first part of my essays; the work was favorably received, and soon made me entirely forget my former disappointment. I continued with my mother and brother in the country, and in that time recovered the knowledge of the Greek language, which I had too much neglected in my early youth.

In 1745, I received a letter from the Marquis of Annandale, inviting me to come and live with him in England; I found also that the friends and family of that young nobleman were desirous of putting him under my care and direction, for the state of his mind and health required it. I lived with him a twelvemonth. My appointments during that time made a considerable accession to my small fortune. I then received an invitation from General St. Clair to attend him as a secretary to his expedition which was at first meant against Canada, but ended in an incursion on the coast of France. Next year, to wit, 1747, I received an invitation from the General to attend him in the same station in his military embassy to the courts of Vienna and Turin. I then wore the uniform of an officer, and was introduced at these courts as aide-de-camp to the General, along with Sir Harry Erskine and Captain Grant, now General Grant. These two years were almost the only interruptions which my studies have received during the course of my life. I passed them agreeably and in good company; and my appointments, with my frugality, had made me reach a fortune which I called independent, though most of my friends were inclined to smile when I said so; in short, I was now master of near a thousand pounds.

I had always entertained a notion that my want of success in publishing the *Treatise of Human Nature* had proceeded more from the manner than the matter, and that I had been guilty of a very usual indiscretion in going to the press too early. I, therefore, cast the first part of that work anew in the *Inquiry Concerning Human Understanding*, which was published while I was at Turin. But this piece was at first little more successful than the *Treatise of Human Nature*. On my return from Italy, I had the mortification to find all England in a ferment on account of Dr. Middleton's *Free Inquiry*, while my performance was entirely overlooked and neglected. A new edition, which had been published at London, of my

Essays, Moral and Political met not with a much better reception.

Such is the force of natural temper that these disappointments made little or no impression on me. I went down in 1749, and lived two years with my brother at his country house, for my mother was now dead. I there composed the second part of my essays, which I called *Political Discourses*, and also my *Inquiry Concerning the Principles of Morals*, which is another part of my *Treatise* that I cast anew. Meanwhile my bookseller A. Millar informed me that my former publications (all but the unfortunate *Treatise*) were beginning to be the subject of conversation, that the sale of them was gradually increasing, and that new editions were demanded. Answers by Reverends and Right Reverends came out two or three in a year, and I found, by Dr. Warburton's railing, that the books were beginning to be esteemed in good company. However, I had fixed a resolution which I inflexibly maintained, never to reply to anybody; and not being very irascible in my temper, I have easily kept myself clear of all literary squabbles. These symptoms of a rising reputation gave me encouragement, as I was ever more disposed to see the favorable than unfavorable side of things—a turn of mind which it is more happy to possess than to be born to an estate of ten thousand a year.

In 1751, I removed from the country to the town, the true scene for a man of letters. In 1752 were published at Edinburgh, where I then lived, my *Political Discourses*, the only work of mine that was successful on the first publication. It was well received abroad and at home. In the same year was published at London my *Inquiry Concerning the Principles of Morals*, which in my own opinion (who ought not to judge on that subject) is of all my writings, historical, philosophical, or literary, incomparably the best. It came unnoticed and unobserved into the world.

In 1752, the Faculty of Advocates chose me their librarian, an office from which I received little or no emolument, but which gave me the command of a large library. I then formed the plan of writing the *History of England;* but being frightened with the notion of continuing a narrative through a period of 1700 years, I commenced with the accession of the House of Stuart, an epoch when, I thought, the misrepresentations of faction began chiefly to take place. I was, I own, sanguine in my expectations of the success of this work. I thought that I was the only historian that had at once neglected present power, interest, and authority, and the cry of popular prejudices; and as the subject was suited to every capacity, I expected proportional applause. But miserable was my disappointment: I was assailed by one cry of reproach, disapprobation, and even detestation; English, Scotch, and Irish, Whig and Tory, Churchman and Sectary, Freethinker and Religionist, Patriot and Courtier united in their rage against the man who had presumed to shed a generous tear for the fate of Charles I and the Earl of Strafford; and after the first ebullitions of their fury were over, what was still more mortifying, the book seemed to sink into oblivion. Mr. Millar told me that in a twelvemonth he sold only forty-five copies of it. I scarcely, indeed, heard of one man in the three kingdoms, considerable for rank or letters, that could endure the book. I must only except the primate of England, Dr. Herring, and the primate of Ireland, Dr. Stone, which seem two odd exceptions. These dignified prelates separately sent me messages not to be discouraged.

I was however, I confess, discouraged; and had not the war been at that time breaking out between France and England, I had certainly retired to some provincial town of the former kingdom, have changed my name, and never more have returned to my native country. But as this scheme was not now practicable, and the subsequent volume was considerably advanced, I resolved to pick up courage and to persevere.

In this interval, I published at London my *Natural History of Religion*, along with some other small pieces. Its public entry was rather obscure, except only that Dr. Hurd wrote a pamphlet against it, with all the illiberal petulance, arrogance, and scurrility which distinguish the Warburtonian school. This pamphlet gave me some consolation for the otherwise indifferent reception of my performance.

In 1756, two years after the fall of the first volume, was published the second volume of my *History*, containing the period from the death of Charles I till the Revolution. This performance happened to give less displeasure to the Whigs, and was better received. It not only rose itself, but helped to buoy up its unfortunate brother.

But though I had been taught, by experience, that the Whig party were in possession of bestowing all places, both in the state and in literature, I was so little inclined to yield to their senseless clamor that in above a hundred alterations, which further study, reading or reflection engaged me to make in the reigns of the two first Stuarts, I have made all of them invariably to the Tory side It is ridiculous to consider the English constitution before that period as a regular plan of liberty.

In 1759, I published my History of the House of Tudor. The clamor against this performance was almost equal to that against the History of the two first Stuarts The reign of Elizabeth was particularly obnoxious. But I was now callous against the impressions of public folly, and continued very peaceably and contentedly in my retreat at Edinburgh to finish, in two volumes, the more early part of the English history, which I gave to the public in 1761, with tolerable, and but tolerable, success.

But, notwithstanding this variety of winds and seasons to which my writings had been exposed, they had still been making such advances that the copy-money given me by the booksellers much exceeded anything formerly known in England; I was become not only independent, but opulent I retired to my native country of Scotland, determined never more to set my foot out of it, and retaining the satisfaction of never having preferred a request to one great man, or even making advances of friendship to any of them. As I was now turned to fifty, I thought of passing all the rest of my life in this philosophical manner, when I received, in 1763, an invitation from the Earl of Hertford, with whom I was not in the least acquainted, to attend him on his embassy to Paris, with a near prospect of being appointed secretary to the embassy, and, in the meanwhile, of performing the functions of that office. This offer, however inviting, I at first declined, both because I was reluctant to begin connections with the great, and because I was afraid that the civilities and gay company of Paris would prove disagreeable to a person of my age and humor; but on his Lordship's repeating the invitation, I accepted of it. I have every reason, both of pleasure and interest, to think myself happy in my connections with that nobleman, as well as afterwards with his brother, General Conway.

Those who have not seen the strange effects of modes will never imagine the reception I met with at Paris from men and women of all ranks and stations. The more I resiled from their excessive civilities, the more I was loaded with them. There is, however, a real satisfaction in living at Paris, from the great number of sensible, knowing, and polite company with which that city abounds above all places in the universe. I thought once of settling there for life.

I was appointed secretary to the embassy; and, in summer 1765, Lord Hertford left me, being appointed Lord Lieutenant of Ireland. I was *chargé d'affaires* till the arrival of the Duke of Richmond, toward the end of the year. In the beginning of 1766, I left Paris, and next summer went to Edinburgh, with the same view as formerly, of burying myself in a philosophical retreat. I returned to that place, not richer, but with much more money and a much larger income, by means of Lord Hertford's friendship, than I left it; and I was desirous of trying what superfluity could produce, as I had formerly made an experiment of a competency. But, in 1767, I received from Mr. Conway an invitation to be Undersecretary; and this invitation, both the character of the person, and my connections with Lord Hertford, prevented me from declining. I returned to Edinburgh in 1769, very opulent (for I possessed a revenue of £1000 a year), healthy and, though somewhat stricken in years, with the prospect of enjoying long my ease and of seeing the increase of my reputation.

In spring 1775, I was struck with a disorder in my bowels, which at first gave me no alarm, but has since, as I apprehend it, become mortal and incurable. I now reckon upon a speedy dissolution. I have suffered very little pain from my disorder and, what is more strange, have, notwithstanding the great decline of my person, never suffered a moment's abatement of my spirits, insomuch that were I to name the period of my life which I should most choose to pass over again, I might be tempted to point to this later period. I possess the same ardor as ever in study, and the same gaiety in company. I consider, besides, that a man of sixty-five, by dying, cuts off only a few years of infirmities; and though I see many symptoms of my literary reputation's breaking out at last with additional luster, I know that I could have but few years to enjoy it. It is difficult to be more detached from life than I am at present

To conclude historically with my own character. I am, or rather was (for that is the style I must now use in speaking of myself, which emboldens me the more to speak my sentiments)—I was, I say, a man of mild dispositions, of command of temper, of an open, social, and cheerful humor, capable of attachment, but little susceptible of enmity, and of great moderation in all my passions. Even my love of literary fame, my ruling passion, never soured my temper, notwithstanding my frequent disappointments. My company was not unacceptable to the young and careless, as well as to the studious and literary; and as I took a particular pleasure in the company of modest women, I had no reason to be displeased with the reception I met with from them. In a word, though most men anywise eminent have found reason to complain of calumny, I never was touched or even attacked by her baleful tooth; and though I wantonly exposed myself to the rage of both civil and religious factions, they seemed to be disarmed in my behalf of their wonted fury My friends never had occasion to vindicate any one circumstance of my character and conduct; not but that the zealots, we may well suppose, would have been glad to invent and propagate any story to my disadvantage, but they could never find any which they thought would wear the face of probability. I cannot say there is no vanity in making this funeral oration of myself, but I hope it is not a misplaced one; and this is a matter of fact which is easily cleared and ascertained.

April 18, 1776

• • •

Hume died just four months later. His good friend Adam Smith wrote his eulogy in a letter to William Strahan: "Thus died our most excellent, and never to be forgotten friend; concerning whose philosophical opinions men will, no doubt, judge variously, everyone approving, or condemning them, according as they happen to coincide or disagree with his own; but concerning whose character and conduct there can scarce be a difference of opinion. His temper, indeed, seemed to be more happily balanced, if I may be allowed such an expression, than that perhaps of any other man I have ever known. Even in the lowest state of his fortune, his great and necessary frugality never hindered him from exercising, upon proper occasions, acts both of charity and generosity. . . . And that gaiety of temper, so agreeable to society, but which is so often accompanied with frivolous and superficial qualities, was in him certainly attended with the most severe application, the most extensive learning, the greatest depth of thought, and a capacity in every respect the most comprehensive. Upon the whole, I have always considered him, both in his lifetime and since his death, as approaching as nearly to the idea of a perfectly wise and virtuous man, as perhaps the nature of human frailty will permit."

A Treatise of Human Nature: Being an attempt to Introduce the Experimental method of reasoning into moral subjects is divided into three books: Of the Understanding, Of the Passions, Of Morals. Volume one, Of the Understanding, and volume two, Of the Passions, were published in January, 1739; and volume three, Of Morals, appeared late in 1740. This separation was unfortunate, for Book III seems to have been written first, and that was where Hume's primary interest lay, as indicated by the subtitle (which is often omitted from modern editions), and by his belief that his later revision of part three as an independent work was of all his writings "incomparably the best."

Be that as it may, the complete *Treatise*, published before Hume was thirty, is undoubtedly one of the two or three crucial books in modern philosophy and perhaps the greatest in the English language.

In insisting that man arrives at certainty only in the relationships between the abstract propositions of logic and mathematics, Hume was able to intimate that even the conclusions of Newtonian physics are only probable; and therefore inquiries into nature and human nature are not basically different. He was using the weapons of the sceptic not merely negatively or flippantly but to clear the way for a science of man.

As Hume told us, the *Treatise* fell "deadborn from the press" (the reviews, rancorous or unperceptive, did not begin for nearly a year), and to revivify it he wrote and published anonymously as a pamphlet *An Abstract of a Treatise of Human Nature*. This pamphlet was identified and published by J. M. Keynes and P Sraffa in 1938, as virtually a new work by David Hume! It confidently stressed the originality and future influence of the author and "it remains as good a brief introduction to the essence and original genius of the *Treatise* as can be found."

•   •   •

AN ABSTRACT OF A TREATISE OF HUMAN NATURE

PREFACE

My expectations in this small performance may seem somewhat extraordinary when I declare that my intentions are to render a larger work more intelligible to ordinary capacities by abridging it. It is, however, certain that those who are not accustomed to abstract reasoning are apt to lose the thread of argument where it is drawn out to a great length, and each part fortified with all the arguments, guarded against all the objections, and illustrated with all the views which occur to a writer in the diligent survey of his subject. Such readers will more readily apprehend a chain of reasoning that is more single and concise where the chief propositions only are linked on to each other, illustrated by some simple examples, and confirmed by a few of the more forcible arguments. The parts lying nearer together can better be compared, and the connection be more easily traced from the first principles to the last conclusion.

The work of which I here present the reader with an abstract has been complained of as obscure and difficult to be comprehended, and I am apt to think that this proceeded as much from the length as from the abstractedness of the argument. If I have remedied this inconvenience in any degree I have attained my end. The book seemed to me to have such an air of singularity and novelty as claimed the attention of the public, especially if it be found—as the author seems to insinuate—that were his philosophy received we must alter from the foundation the greatest part of the sciences. Such bold attempts are always advantageous in the republic of letters because they shake off the yoke of authority, accustom men to think for themselves, give new hints which men of genius may carry further and, by the very opposition, illustrate points wherein no one before suspected any difficulty.

The author must be contented to wait with patience for some time before the learned world can agree in their sentiments of his performance. It is his misfortune that he cannot make an *appeal to the people,* who in all matters of common reason and eloquence are found so infallible a tribunal. He must be judged by the *few,* whose verdict is more apt to be corrupted by partiality and prejudice, especially as no one is a proper judge in these subjects who has not often thought of them, and *such* are apt to form to themselves systems of their own which they resolve not to relinquish. I hope the author will excuse me for intermeddling in this affair, since my aim is only to increase his auditory by removing some difficulties which have kept many from apprehending his meaning.

I have chosen one simple argument which I have carefully traced from the beginning to the end. This is the only point I have taken care to finish. The rest is only hints of particular passages which seemed to me curious and remarkable.

This book seems to be written upon the same plan with several other works that have had a great vogue of late years in

England. The philosophical spirit, which has been so much improved all over Europe within these last fourscore years, has been carried to as great a length in this kingdom as in any other. Our writers seem even to have started a new kind of philosophy which promises more both to the entertainment and advantage of mankind than any other with which the world has been yet acquainted. Most of the philosophers of antiquity who treated of human nature have shown more of a delicacy of sentiment, a just sense of morals, or a greatness of soul, than a depth of reasoning and reflection. They content themselves with representing the common sense of mankind in the strongest lights, and with the best turn of thought and expression, without following out steadily a chain of propositions, or forming the several truths into a regular science. But it is at least worth while to try if the science of *man* will not admit of the same accuracy which several parts of natural philosophy are found susceptible of. There seems to be all the reason in the world to imagine that it may be carried to the greatest degree of exactness. If in examining several phenomena we find that they resolve themselves into one common principle, and can trace this principle into another, we shall at last arrive at those few simple principles on which all the rest depend. And though we can never arrive at the ultimate principles, it is a satisfaction to go as far as our faculties will allow us.

This seems to have been the aim of our late philosophers and, among the rest, of this author. He proposes to anatomize human nature in a regular manner, and promises to draw no conclusions but where he is authorized by experience. He talks with contempt of hypotheses and insinuates that such of our countrymen as have banished them from moral philosophy have done a more signal service to the world than my Lord Bacon, whom he considers as the father of experimental physics. He mentions, on this occasion, Mr. Locke, my Lord Shaftesbury, Dr. Mandeville, Mr. Hutchison, Dr. Butler, who, though they differ in many points among themselves, seem all to agree in founding their accurate disquisitions of human nature entirely upon experience.

Besides the satisfaction of being acquainted with what most nearly concerns us, it may be safely affirmed that almost all the sciences are comprehended in the science of human nature, and are dependent on it. *The sole end of* logic *is to explain the principles and operations of our reasoning faculty, and the nature of our ideas;* morals and criticism *regard our tastes and sentiments; and* politics *consider men as united in society and dependent on each other.* This treatise, therefore, of human nature seems intended for a system of the sciences. The author has finished what regards logic, and has laid the foundation of the other parts in his account of the passions.

The celebrated Monsieur Leibniz has observed it to be a defect in the common systems of logic that they are very copious when they explain the operations of the understanding in the forming of demonstrations, but are too concise when they treat of probabilities and those other measures of evidence on which life and action entirely depend, and which are our guides even in most of our philosophical speculations. In this censure, he comprehends the *Essay on Human Understanding, Le* [sic] *Recherche de la verité,* and *L'art de penser.* The author of the *Treatise of Human Nature* seems to have been sensible of this defect in these philosophers and has endeavored, as much as he can, to supply it. As his book contains a great number of speculations very new and remarkable, it will be impossible to give the reader a just notion of the whole. We shall, therefore, chiefly confine ourselves to his explication of our reasonings from cause and effect. If we can make this intelligible to the reader, it may serve as a specimen of the whole.

Our author begins with some definitions. He calls a "perception" whatever can be present to the mind, whether we employ our senses or are actuated with passion, or exercise our thought and reflection. He divides our perceptions into two kinds, viz., "impressions" and "ideas." When we feel a passion or emotion of any kind, or have the images of external objects conveyed by our senses, the perception of the mind is what he calls an "impression"—which is a word that he employs in a new sense. When we reflect on a passion or an object which is not present, this perception is an "idea." "Impressions," therefore, are our lively and strong perceptions; "ideas" are the fainter and weaker. This distinction is evident —as evident as that betwixt feeling and thinking.

The first proposition he advances is that all our ideas, or weak perceptions, are derived from our impressions or strong perceptions, and that we can never think of anything which we have not seen without us or felt in our own minds. This proposition seems to be equivalent to that which Mr. Locke has taken such pains to establish, viz., "that no ideas are innate." Only it may be observed, as an inaccuracy of that famous philosopher, that he comprehends all our perceptions under the term of "idea," in which sense it is false that we have no innate ideas. For it is evident our stronger perceptions or impressions are innate, and that natural affection, love of virtue, resentment, and all the other passions arise immediately from nature. I am persuaded whoever would take the question in this light would be easily able to reconcile all parties. Father Malebranche would find himself at a loss to point out any thought of the mind which did not represent something antecedently felt by it, either internally or by means of the external senses, and must allow that however we may compound and mix and augment and diminish our ideas, that they are all derived from these sources. Mr. Locke, on the other hand, would readily acknowledge that all our passions are a kind of natural instincts, derived from nothing but the original constitution of the human mind.

Our author thinks—

that no discovery could have been made more happily for deciding all controversies concerning ideas than this, that impressions always take the precedence of them, and that every idea with which the imagination is furnished first makes its appearance in a correspondent impression. These latter perceptions are all so clear and evident that they admit of no controversy, though many of our ideas are so obscure that 'tis almost impossible even for the mind which forms them to tell exactly their nature and composition.

Accordingly, wherever any idea is ambiguous he has always recourse to the impression which must render it clear and precise. And when he suspects that any philosophical term has no idea annexed to it (as is too common), he always asks "from what impression that idea is derived?" And if no impression can be produced, he concludes that the term is altogether insignificant. It is after this manner he examines our idea of *substance* and *essence;* and it were to be wished that this rigorous method were more practiced in all philosophical debates.

It is evident that all reasonings concerning *matter of fact* are founded on the relation of cause and effect, and that we can never infer the existence of one object from another unless they be connected together, either mediately or immediately. In order, therefore, to understand these reasonings we must be perfectly acquainted with the idea of a cause; and in order to that, must look about us to find something that is the cause of another.

Here is a billiard ball lying on the table, and another ball moving toward it with rapidity. They strike; and the ball which was formerly at rest now acquires a motion. This is as perfect an instance of the relation of cause and effect as any which we know either by sensation or reflection. Let us therefore examine it. It is evident that the two balls touched one another before the motion was communicated, and that there was no interval betwixt the shock and the motion. *Contiguity* in time and place is therefore a requisite circumstance to the operation of all causes. It is evident, likewise, that the motion which was the cause is prior to the motion which was the effect. *Priority* in time is, therefore, another requisite circumstance in every cause. But this is not all. Let us try any other balls of the same kind in a like situation, and we shall always find that the impulse of the one produces motion in the other. Here, therefore, is a *third* circumstance, viz., that of a *constant conjunction* betwixt the cause and effect. Every object like the cause produces always some object like the effect. Beyond these three circumstances of contiguity, priority, and constant conjunction I can discover nothing in this cause. The first ball is in motion, touches the second, immediately the second is in motion—and when I try the experiment with the same or like balls, in the same or like circumstances, I find that upon the motion and touch of the one ball motion always follows in the other. In whatever shape I turn this matter, and however I examine it, I can find nothing further.

This is the case when both the cause and effect are present to the senses. Let us now see upon what our inference is founded when we conclude from the one that the other has existed or will exist. Suppose I see a ball moving in a straight line toward another—I immediately conclude that they will shock, and that the second will be in motion. This is the inference from cause to effect, and of this nature are all our reasonings in the conduct of life; on this is founded all our belief in history, and from hence is derived all philosophy excepting only geometry and arithmetic. If we can explain the inference from the shock of the two balls we shall be able to account for this operation of the mind in all instances.

Were a man such as Adam created in the full vigor of understanding, without experience, he would never be able to infer motion in the second ball from the motion and impulse of the first. It is not anything that reason sees in the cause which makes us *infer* the effect. Such an inference, were it possible, would amount to a demonstration, as being founded merely on the comparison of ideas. But no inference from cause to effect amounts to a demonstration. Of which there is this evident proof. The mind can always *conceive* any effect to follow from any cause, and indeed any event to follow upon another; whatever we *conceive* is possible, at least in a metaphysical sense; but wherever a demonstration takes place the contrary is impossible and implies a contradiction. There is no demonstration, therefore, for any conjunction of cause and effect. And this is a principle which is generally allowed by philosophers.

It would have been necessary, therefore, for Adam (if he was not inspired) to have had *experience* of the effect which followed upon the impulse of these two balls. He must have seen in several instances that when the one ball struck upon the other, the second always acquired motion. If he had seen a sufficient number of instances of this kind, whenever he saw the one ball moving toward the other, he would always conclude without hesitation that the second would acquire motion. His understanding would anticipate his sight and form a conclusion suitable to his past experience.

It follows, then, that all reasonings concerning cause and effect are founded on experience, and that all reasonings from experience are founded on the supposition that the course of nature will continue uniformly the same. We conclude that like causes, in like circumstances, will always produce like effects. It may now be worth while to consider what determines us to form a conclusion of such infinite consequence.

It is evident that Adam, with all his science, would never have been able to *demonstrate* that the course of nature must continue uniformly the same, and that the future must be conformable to the past. What is possible can never be demonstrated to be false; and it is possible the course of nature may change, since we can conceive such a change. Nay, I will go further and assert that he could not so much as prove by any *probable* arguments that the future must be conformable to the past. All probable arguments are built on the supposition that there is this conformity betwixt the future and the past, and therefore [he] can never prove it. This conformity is a *matter of fact,* and if it must be proved will admit of no proof but from experience. But our experience in the past can be a proof of nothing for the future but upon a supposition that there is a resemblance betwixt them. This, therefore, is a point which can admit of no proof at all, and which we take for granted without any proof.

We are determined by *custom* alone to suppose the future conformable to the past. When I see a billiard ball moving toward another, my mind is immediately carried by habit to the usual effect, and anticipates my sight by conceiving the second ball in motion. There is nothing in these objects—abstractly considered, and independent of experience—which leads me to form any such conclusion: and even after I have had experience of many repeated effects of this kind, there is no argument which determines me to suppose that the effect will be conformable to past experience. The powers by which bodies operate are entirely unknown. We perceive only their sensible qualities—and what *reason* have we to think that the same powers will always be conjoined with the same sensible qualities?

It is not, therefore, reason which is the guide of life, but custom. That alone determines the mind in all instances to suppose the future conformable to the past. However easy this step may seem, reason would never, to all eternity, be able to make it.

This is a very curious discovery, but leads us to others that are still more curious. *When I see a billiard ball moving toward another, my mind is immediately carried by habit to the usual effect, and anticipates my sight by conceiving the second ball in motion.* But is this all? Do I nothing but *conceive* the motion of the second ball? No, surely. I also *believe* that it will move. What then is this "belief"? And how does it differ from the simple conception of anything? Here is a new question unthought of by philosophers.

When a demonstration convinces me of any proposition, it not only makes me conceive the proposition, but also makes me sensible that it is impossible to conceive anything contrary. What is demonstratively false implies a contradiction, and what implies a contradiction cannot be conceived. But with regard to any matter of fact, however strong the proof may be from experience, I can always conceive the contrary though I cannot always believe it. The belief, therefore, makes some difference betwixt the conception to which we assent and that to which we do not assent.

To account for this there are only two hypotheses. It may be said that belief joins some new idea to those which we may conceive without assenting to them. But this hypothesis is false. For, *first,* no such idea can be produced. When we simply conceive an object, we conceive it in all its parts. We conceive it as it might exist, though we do not believe it to exist. Our belief of it would discover no new qualities. We may paint out the entire object in imagination without believing it. We may set it, in a manner, before our eyes, with every circumstance of time and place. It is the very object conceived as it might exist; and when we believe it, we can do no more.

Secondly, the mind has a faculty of joining all ideas together which involve not a contradiction, and therefore, if belief consisted in some idea which we add to the simple conception, it would be in a man's power, by adding this idea to it, to believe anything which he can conceive.

Since, therefore, belief implies a conception and yet is something more, and since it adds no new idea to the conception, it follows that it is a different *manner* of conceiving an object— *something* that is distinguishable to the feeling and depends not upon our will, as all our ideas do. My mind runs by habit from the visible object of one ball moving toward another to the usual effect of motion in the second ball. It not only conceives that motion but *feels* something different in the conception of it from a mere reverie of the imagination. The presence of this visible object, and the constant conjunction of that particular effect, render the idea different to the *feeling* from those loose ideas which come into the mind without any introduction. This conclusion seems a little surprising, but we are led into it by a chain of propositions which admit of no doubt. To ease the reader's memory I shall briefly resume them: No matter of fact can be proved but from its cause or effect. Nothing can be known to be the cause of another but by experience. We can give no reason for extending to the future our experience in the past, but are entirely determined by custom when we conceive an effect to follow from its usual cause. But we also believe an effect to follow, as well as conceive it. This belief joins no new idea to the conception. It only varies the manner of conceiving and makes a difference to the feeling or sentiment. Belief, therefore, in all matters of fact arises only from custom and is an idea conceived in a peculiar *manner.*

Our author proceeds to explain the manner or feeling which renders belief different from a loose conception. He seems sensible that it is impossible by words to describe this feeling which everyone must be conscious of in his own breast. He calls it sometimes a *stronger* conception, sometimes a more *lively*, a more *vivid*, a *firmer*, or a more *intense* conception. And indeed, whatever name we may give to this feeling which constitutes belief, our author thinks it evident that it has a more forcible effect on the mind than fiction and mere conception. This he proves by its influence on the passions and on the imagination, which are only moved by truth or what is taken for such. Poetry with all its art can never cause a passion like one in real life. It fails in the original conception of its objects which never *feel* in the same manner as those which command our belief and opinion.

Our author, presuming that he had sufficiently proved that the ideas we assent to are different to the feeling from the other ideas, and that this feeling is more firm and lively than our common conception, endeavors in the next place to explain the cause of this lively feeling by an analogy with other acts of the mind. His reasoning seems to be curious, but could scarce be rendered intelligible, or at least probable, to the reader without a long detail which would exceed the compass I have prescribed to myself.

I have likewise omitted many arguments which he adduces to prove that belief consists merely in a peculiar feeling or sentiment. I shall only mention one: our past experience is not always uniform. Sometimes one effect follows from a cause, sometimes another, in which case we always believe that that will exist which is most common. I see a billiard ball moving toward another. I cannot distinguish whether it moves upon its axis or was struck so as to skim along the table. In the first case I know it will not stop after the shock. In the second it may stop. The first is most common, and therefore I lay my account with that effect. But I also conceive the other effect, and conceive it as possible and as connected with the cause. Were not the one conception different in the feeling or sentiment from the other there would be no difference betwixt them.

We have confined ourselves in this whole reasoning to the relation of cause and effect, as discovered in the motions and operations of matter. But the same reasoning extends to the operations of the mind. Whether we consider the influence of the will in moving our body or in governing our thought, it may safely be affirmed that we could never foretell the effect merely from the consideration of the cause, without experience. And even after we have experience of these effects, it is custom alone, not reason, which determines us to make it the standard of our future judgments. When the cause is presented, the mind, from habit, immediately passes to the conception and belief of the usual effect. This belief is something different from the conception. It does not, however, join any new idea to it. It only makes it be felt differently, and renders it stronger and more lively.

Having dispatched this material point concerning the nature of the inference from cause and effect, our author returns upon his footsteps and examines anew the idea of that relation. In the considering of motion communicated from one ball to another we could find nothing but contiguity, priority in the cause, and constant conjunction. But, besides these circumstances, it is commonly supposed that there is a necessary connection betwixt the cause and effect, and that the cause possesses something which we call a "power," or "force," or "energy." The question is, what idea is annexed to these terms? If all our ideas or thoughts be derived from our impressions, this power must either discover itself to our senses or to our internal feeling. But so little does any *power* discover itself to the senses in the operations of matter that the Cartesians have made no scruple to assert that matter is utterly deprived of energy, and that all its operations are performed merely by the energy of the Supreme Being. But the question still recurs, *What idea have we of energy or power even in the Supreme Being?* All our idea of a deity (according to those who deny innate ideas) is nothing but a composition of those ideas which we acquire from reflecting on the operations of our own minds. Now our own minds afford us no more notion of energy than matter does. When we consider our will or volition *a priori*, abstracting from experience, we should never be able to infer any effect from it. And when we take the assistance of experi-

ence it only shows us objects contiguous, successive, and constantly conjoined. Upon the whole, then, either we have no
idea at all of force and energy, and these words are altogether
insignificant, or they can mean nothing but that determination
of the thought, acquired by habit, to pass from the cause to
its usual effect. But whoever would thoroughly understand
this must consult the author himself. It is sufficient if I can
make the learned world apprehend that there is some difficulty
in the case, and that whoever solves the difficulty must say
something very new and extraordinary—as new as the difficulty
itself.

By all that has been said the reader will easily perceive that
the philosophy contained in this book is very skeptical and
tends to give us a notion of the imperfections and narrow limits of human understanding. Almost all reasoning is there reduced to experience, and the belief which attends experience
is explained to be nothing but a peculiar sentiment or lively
conception produced by habit. Nor is this all; when we believe
anything of *external* existence or suppose an object to exist a
moment after it is no longer perceived, this belief is nothing
but a sentiment of the same kind. Our author insists upon several other skeptical topics; and upon the whole concludes that
we assent to our faculties and employ our reason only because
we cannot help it. Philosophy would render us entirely Pyrrho-
nian, were not nature too strong for it.

I shall conclude the logics of this author with an account of
two opinions which seem to be peculiar to himself, as indeed
are most of his opinions. He asserts that the soul, as far as we
can conceive it, is nothing but a system or train of different
perceptions—those of heat and cold, love and anger, thoughts
and sensations—all united together but without any perfect
simplicity or identity. Descartes maintained that thought was
the essence of the mind—not this thought or that thought, but
thought in general. This seems to be absolutely unintelligible,
since everything that exists is particular; and therefore it must
be our several particular perceptions that compose the mind.
I say *compose* the mind, not *belong* to it. The mind is not a
substance in which the perceptions inhere. That notion is as

unintelligible as the Cartesian, that thought or perception in general is the essence of the mind. We have no idea of substance of any kind since we have no idea but what is derived from some impression, and we have no impression of any substance either material or spiritual. We know nothing but particular qualities and perceptions. As our idea of any body, a peach, for instance, is only that of a particular taste, color, figure, size, consistency, etc., so our idea of any mind is only that of particular perceptions without the notion of anything we call substance, either simple or compound.

The second principle which I propose to take notice of is with regard to geometry. Having denied the infinite divisibility of extension, our author finds himself obliged to refute those mathematical arguments which have been adduced for it—and these, indeed, are the only ones of any weight. This he does by denying geometry to be a science exact enough to admit of conclusions so subtile as those which regard infinite divisibility. His arguments may be thus explained: All geometry is founded on the notions of equality and inequality, and therefore, according as we have or have not an exact standard of that relation, the science itself will or will not admit of great exactness. Now there is an exact standard of equality, if we suppose that quantity is composed of indivisible points. Two lines are equal when the numbers of the points that compose them are equal, and when there is a point in one corresponding to a point in the other. But though this standard be exact, it is useless, since we can never compute the number of points in any line. It is, besides, founded on the supposition of finite divisibility, and therefore can never afford any conclusion against it. If we reject this standard of equality we have none that has any pretensions to exactness. I find two that are commonly made use of. Two lines above a yard, for instance, are said to be equal when they contain any inferior quantity, as an inch, an equal number of times. But this runs in a circle. For the quantity we call an inch in the one is supposed to be *equal* to what we call an inch in the other: and the question still is, by what standard we proceed when we judge them to be equal or, in other words, what we mean when we say they are equal.

If we take still inferior quantities, we go on *in infinitum*. This, therefore, is no standard of equality. The greatest part of philosophers, when asked what they mean by "equality," say that the word admits of no definition, and that it is sufficient to place before us two equal bodies, such as two diameters of a circle, to make us understand that term. Now this is taking the *general appearance* of the objects for the standard of that proportion, and renders our imagination and senses the ultimate judges of it. But such a standard admits of no exactness, and can never afford any conclusion contrary to the imagination and senses. Whether this question be just or not must be left to the learned world to judge. It were certainly to be wished that some expedient were fallen upon to reconcile philosophy and common sense, which with regard to the question of infinite divisibility have waged most cruel wars with each other.

We must now proceed to give some account of the second volume of this work, which treats of the *Passions*. It is of more easy comprehension than the first, but contains opinions that are altogether as new and extraordinary. The author begins with *pride* and *humility*. He observes that the objects which excite these passions are very numerous and seemingly very different from each other. Pride or self-esteem may arise from the qualities of the mind—wit, good sense, learning, courage, integrity; from those of the body—beauty, strength, agility, good mien, address in dancing, riding, fencing; from external advantages—country, family, children, relations, riches, houses, gardens, horses, dogs, clothes. He afterward proceeds to find out that common circumstance in which all these objects agree, and which causes them to operate on the passions. His theory likewise extends to love and hatred and other affections. As these questions, though curious, could not be rendered intelligible without a long discourse, we shall here omit them.

It may perhaps be more acceptable to the reader to be informed of what our author says concerning *free will*. He has laid the foundation of his doctrine in what he said concerning cause and effect, as above explained.—

It is universally acknowledged that the operations of external bodies are necessary, and that in the communication of their motion, in their attraction and mutual cohesion, there are not the least traces of indifference or liberty. . . . Whatever, therefore, is in this respect on the same footing with matter must be acknowledged to be necessary. That we may know whether this be the case with the actions of the mind, we may examine matter and consider on what the idea of a necessity in its operations is founded, and why we conclude one body or action to be the infallible cause of another.

It has been observed already that in no single instance the ultimate connection of any object is discoverable either by our senses or reason, and that we can never penetrate so far into the essence and construction of bodies as to perceive the principle on which their mutual influence is founded. It is their constant union alone with which we are acquainted; and it is from the constant union the necessity arises, when the mind is determined to pass from one object to its usual attendant and infer the existence of one from that of the other Here, then, are two particulars which we are to regard as essential to *necessity,* viz., the constant *union* and the *inference* of the mind, and wherever we discover these we must acknowledge a necessity.

Now nothing is more evident than the constant union of particular actions with particular motives. If all actions be not constantly united with their proper motives, this uncertainty is no more than what may be observed every day in the actions of matter, where by reason of the mixture and uncertainty of causes the effect is often variable and uncertain Thirty grains of opium will kill any man that is not accustomed to it, though thirty grains of rhubarb will not always purge him. In like manner the fear of death will always make a man go twenty paces out of his road, though it will not always make him do a bad action.

And as there is often a constant conjunction of the actions of the will with their motives, so the inference from the one to the other is often as certain as any reasoning concerning bodies; and there is always an inference proportioned to the

constancy of the conjunction. On this is founded our belief in
witnesses, our credit in history, and indeed all kinds of moral
evidence, and almost the whole conduct of life.

Our author pretends that this reasoning puts the whole controversy in a new light by giving a new definition of necessity.
And, indeed, the most zealous advocates for free will must allow this union and inference with regard to human actions.
They will only deny that this makes the whole of necessity.
But then they must show that we have an idea of something
else in the actions of matter, which according to the foregoing
reasoning is impossible.

Through this whole book there are great pretensions to new
discoveries in philosophy; but if anything can entitle the
author to so glorious a name as that of an "inventor," it is the
use he makes of the principle of the association of ideas, which
enters into most of his philosophy. Our imagination has a great
authority over our ideas, and there are no ideas that are different from each other which it cannot separate and join and
compose into all the varieties of fiction. But notwithstanding
the empire of the imagination, there is a secret tie or union
among particular ideas which causes the mind to conjoin them
more frequently together and makes the one, upon its appearance, introduce the other. Hence arises what we call the
apropos of discourse; hence the connection of writing; and
hence that thread or chain of thought which a man naturally
supports even in the loosest *reverie* These principles of association are reduced to three, viz., "resemblance"—a picture
naturally makes us think of the man it was drawn for; "contiguity"—when St. Dennis is mentioned, the idea of Paris naturally occurs; "causation"—when we think of the son we are
apt to carry our attention to the father. It will be easy to conceive of what vast consequence these principles must be in
the science of human nature if we consider that so far as regards the mind these are the only links that bind the parts of
the universe together or connect us with any person or object
exterior to ourselves. For as it is by means of thought only
that anything operates upon our passions, and as these are the
only ties of our thoughts, they are really *to us* the cement of

the universe, and all the operations of the mind must, in a great measure, depend on them.

FINIS

•   .   •

The *Abstract* did not appear to stimulate the sales or the appreciation of the *Treatise*—that is, Books I and II; nor did it build up even a meager public for Book III.

However, "such is the force of natural temper," said Hume, "that these disappointments made little or no impression on me." He went down to the country to visit his mother and brother and started to compose what was to become two volumes of *Essays Moral and Political,* which did catch on with that generation of essay readers. "Of the Dignity or Meanness of Human Nature" seems to be totally forgotten but it is Hume at his essential best and it has relevance for our day of furious psychologizing.

The title seems to be a deliberate echo of Pascal, who hung at times like a threatening shadow over the sanguine thinkers of the Enlightenment. Briefly, but with indelible eloquence, Pascal spoke again and again of the greatness and littleness of man·

"It is dangerous to show man too clearly how near he stands to the beasts without showing him his greatness. It is equally dangerous to show him his greatness too clearly, and not his lowness. It is yet more dangerous to leave him in ignorance of either. But it is very good to show him both"

"Man must not think he is equal to the beasts or to the angels, nor must he remain ignorant of either truth; he must know both."

"Man is neither angel nor beast, and the mischief is that he who would play the angel plays the beast."

Hume says much the same thing in a modulated voice. Yet one might suggest that Hume was a second Montaigne come to plague the ghost of Pascal.

•   •   •

OF THE DIGNITY OR MEANNESS
OF HUMAN NATURE

There are certain sects which secretly form themselves in the learned world, as well as factions in the political; and though sometimes they come not to an open rupture, they give a different turn to the ways of thinking of those who have taken part on either side. The most remarkable of this kind are the sects founded on the different sentiments with regard to the *dignity of human nature;* which is a point that seems to have divided philosophers and poets, as well as divines, from the beginning of the world to this day. Some exalt our species to the skies, and represent man as a kind of human demigod, who derives his origin from heaven, and retains evident marks of his lineage and descent. Others insist upon the blind sides of human nature, and can discover nothing, except vanity, in which man surpasses the other animals, whom he affects so much to despise. If an author possess the talent of rhetoric and declamation, he commonly takes part with the former: if his turn lie towards irony and ridicule, he naturally throws himself into the other extreme.

I am far from thinking that all those who have depreciated our species have been enemies to virtue, and have exposed the frailties of their fellow-creatures with any bad intention. On the contrary, I am sensible that a delicate sense of morals, especially when attended with a splenetic temper, is apt to give a man a disgust of the world, and to make him consider the common course of human affairs with too much indignation. I must, however, be of opinion, that the sentiments of those who are inclined to think favorably of mankind, are more advantageous to virtue than the contrary principles, which give us a mean opinion of our nature When a man is prepossessed with a high notion of his rank and character in the creation, he will naturally endeavor to act up to it, and will scorn to do a base or vicious action which might sink him below that figure which he makes in his own imagination. Accordingly we find, that all our polite and fashionable moralists insist upon this topic, and endeavor to represent vice unworthy of man, as well as odious in itself.[1]

---

[1] Women are generally much more flattered in their youth than men, which may proceed from this reason among others, that their chief point of honor is considered as much more difficult than ours, and requires to be supported by all that decent pride which can be instilled into them.

We find few disputes that are not founded on some ambiguity in the expression; and I am persuaded that the present dispute, concerning the dignity or meanness of human nature, is not more exempt from it than any other. It may therefore be worth while to consider what is real, and what is only verbal, in this controversy.

That there is a natural difference between merit and demerit, virtue and vice, wisdom and folly, no reasonable man will deny: yet it is evident that, in affixing the term, which denotes either our approbation or blame, we are commonly more influenced by comparison than by any fixed unalterable standard in the nature of things. In like manner, quantity, and extension, and bulk, are by every one acknowledged to be real things: but when we call any animal *great* or *little*, we always form a secret comparison between that animal and others, of the same species; and it is that comparison which regulates our judgment concerning its greatness. A dog and a horse may be of the very same size, while the one is admired for the greatness of its bulk, and the other for the smallness. When I am present, therefore, at any dispute, I always consider with myself whether it be a question of comparison or not that is the subject of controversy; and if it be, whether the disputants compare the same objects together, or talk of things that are widely different.

In forming our notions of human nature, we are apt to make a comparison between men and animals, the only creatures endowed with thought that fall under our senses. Certainly this comparison is favorable to mankind. On the one hand, we see a creature whose thoughts are not limited by any narrow bounds, either of place or time; who carries his researches into the most distant regions of this globe, and beyond this globe, to the planets and heavenly bodies; looks backward to consider the first origin, at least the history of the human race; casts his eye forward to see the influence of his actions upon posterity, and the judgments which will be formed of his character a thousand years hence; a creature, who traces causes and effects to a great length and intricacy;

extracts general principles from particular appearances; improves upon his discoveries; corrects his mistakes; and makes his very errors profitable. On the other hand, we are presented with a creature the very reverse of this; limited in its observations and reasonings to a few sensible objects which surround it; without curiosity, without foresight; blindly conducted by instinct, and attaining, in a short time, its utmost perfection, beyond which it is never able to advance a single step. What a wide difference is there between these creatures! And how exalted a notion must we entertain of the former, in comparison of the latter.

There are two means commonly employed to destroy this conclusion: *First*, By making an unfair representation of the case, and insisting only upon the weakness of human nature. And, *secondly*, By forming a new and secret comparison between man and beings of the most perfect wisdom. Among the other excellences of man, this is one, that he can form an idea of perfections much beyond what he has experience of in himself; and is not limited in his conception of wisdom and virtue. He can easily exalt his notions, and conceive a degree of knowledge, which, when compared to his own, will make the latter appear very contemptible, and will cause the difference between that and the sagacity of animals, in a manner, to disappear and vanish. Now this being a point in which all the world is agreed, that human understanding falls infinitely short of perfect wisdom, it is proper we should know when this comparison takes place, that we may not dispute where there is no real difference in our sentiments. Man falls much more short of perfect wisdom, and even of his own ideas of perfect wisdom, than animals do of man; yet the latter difference is so considerable, that nothing but a comparison with the former can make it appear of little moment.

It is also usual to *compare* one man with another; and finding very few whom we can call *wise* or *virtuous*, we are apt to entertain a contemptible notion of our species in general. That we may be sensible of the fallacy of this way of reasoning, we may observe, that the honorable appellations of wise and virtuous are not annexed to any particular degree of those qualities of *wisdom* and *virtue,* but arise altogether from the comparison we make between one man and another. When we find a man who arrives at such a pitch of wisdom as is very uncommon, we pronounce him a wise man: so that to say there are few wise men in the world, is really to say nothing; since it is only by their scarcity that they merit that appellation. Were the lowest of our species as wise as Tully or Lord Bacon, we should still have reason to say that there are few wise men. For in that case we should exalt our notions of wisdom, and should not pay a singular homage to any one who was not singularly distinguished by his talents. In like manner, I have heard it observed by thoughtless people, that there are few women possessed of beauty in comparison of those who want it; not considering that we bestow the epithet of *beautiful* only on such as possess a degree of beauty that is common to them with a few. The same degree of beauty in a woman is called deformity, which is treated as real beauty in one of our sex.

As it is usual, in forming a notion of our species, to *compare* it with the other species above or below it, or to compare the individuals of the species among themselves; so we often compare together the different motives or actuating principles of human nature, in order to regulate our judgment concerning it. And, indeed, this is the only kind of comparison which is worth our attention, or decides any thing in the present question. Were our selfish and vicious principles so much predominant above our social and virtuous, as is asserted by some philosophers, we ought undoubtedly to entertain a contemptible notion of human nature.[2]

There is much of a dispute of words in all this controversy. When a man denies the sincerity of all public spirit or affec-

---

[2] I may perhaps treat more fully of this subject in some future Essay. In the mean time I shall observe, what has been proved beyond question by several great moralists of the present age, that the social passions are by far the most powerful of any, and that even all the other passions receive from them their chief force and influence. Whoever desires to see this question treated at large, with the greatest force of argument and eloquence, may consult my Lord Shaftesbury's *Enquiry Concerning Virtue.*

tion to a country and community, I am at a loss what to think
of him. Perhaps he never felt this passion in so clear and
distinct a manner as to remove all his doubts concerning its
force and reality. But when he proceeds afterwards to reject
all private friendship, if no interest or self-love intermix itself;
I am then confident that he abuses terms, and confounds the
ideas of things; since it is impossible for any one to be so selfish, or rather so stupid, as to make no difference between
one man and another, and give no preference to qualities
which engage his approbation and esteem. Is he also, say I,
as insensible to anger as he pretends to be to friendship? And
does injury and wrong no more affect him than kindness or
benefits? Impossible: he does not know himself: he has forgotten the movements of his heart; or rather, he makes use
of a different language from the rest of his countrymen, and
calls not things by their proper names. What say you of
natural affection? (I subjoin), Is that also a species of self-
love? Yes; all is self-love. *Your* children are loved only because they are yours: *your* friend for a like reason: and *your*
country engages you only so far as it has a connection with
yourself. Were the idea of self removed, nothing would affect
you: you would be altogether unactive and insensible: or, if
you ever give yourself any movement, it would only be from
vanity, and a desire of fame and reputation to this same self.
I am willing, reply I, to receive your interpretation of human
actions, provided you admit the facts. That species of self-
love which displays itself in kindness to others, you must
allow to have great influence over human actions, and even
greater, on many occasions, than that which remains in its
original shape and form. For how few are there, having a
family, children, and relations, who do not spend more on
the maintenance and education of these than on their own
pleasures? This, indeed, you justly observe, may proceed from
their self-love, since the prosperity of their family and friends
is one, or the chief, of their pleasures, as well as their chief
honor. Be you also one of these selfish men, and you are
sure of every one's good opinion and good-will; or, not to

shock your ears with these expressions, the self-love of every one, and mine among the rest, will then incline us to serve you, and speak well of you.

In my opinion, there are two things which have led astray those philosophers that have insisted so much on the selfishness of man. In the *first* place, they found that every act of virtue or friendship was attended with a secret pleasure; whence they concluded, that friendship and virtue could not be disinterested. But the fallacy of this is obvious. The virtuous sentiment or passion produces the pleasure, and does not arise from it. I feel a pleasure in doing good to my friend, because I love him; but do not love him for the sake of that pleasure.

In the *second* place, it has always been found, that the virtuous are far from being indifferent to praise; and therefore they have been represented as a set of vainglorious men, who had nothing in view but the applauses of others. But this also is a fallacy. It is very unjust in the world, when they find any tincture of vanity in a laudable action, to depreciate it upon that account, or ascribe it entirely to that motive. The case is not the same with vanity, as with other passions. Where avarice or revenge enters into any seemingly virtuous action, it is difficult for us to determine how far it enters, and it is natural to suppose it the sole actuating principle. But vanity is so closely allied to virtue, and to love the fame of laudable actions approaches so near the love of laudable actions for their own sake, that these passions are more capable of mixture, than any other kinds of affection; and it is almost impossible to have the latter without some degree of the former. Accordingly we find, that this passion for glory is always warped and varied according to the particular taste or disposition of the mind on which it falls. Nero had the same vanity in driving a chariot, that Trajan had in governing the empire with justice and ability. To love the glory of virtuous deeds is a sure proof of the love of virtue.

JEAN-JACQUES ROUSSEAU
[1712-1778]

Hume and Rousseau were born only a year apart, Hume in Calvinist Scotland and Rousseau in Calvinist Geneva, and in their ways they were both rebels against Calvinist backgrounds. But there the comparison stops, for Hume, starting from a comfortable home, led an amazingly serene life, while the motherless Rousseau, brought up for ten years by an affectionate though irresponsible father, led one of the most eccentric and disturbed lives in the history of genius. Hume's brief autobiography is an excellent portrait of the man and a good introduction to his work. On the other hand, Rousseau's autobiography, the famous and notorious *Confessions*, some six or eight hundred pages in length, was written in his last troubled decade by a broken man, miserably suspicious. Consequently the *Confessions*, however fascinating, is an unfair introduction to Rousseau himself and the worst possible introduction to the social, political and educational works of his central period. No, even worse is the approach to Rousseau through his latter-day enemies.

At the sound of his name, even those who have not read him—or read perhaps only the *Confessions*—are apt to turn red with anger, or white with fear, or only a little pink with shameful thoughts. Wasn't he an envious neurotic trying to take revenge on his social superiors? Wasn't he an egomaniac who frequently preferred solitude instead of the constant companionship of his witty contemporaries? In fact, wasn't Rousseau the original primitivist, or rather nudist, who was anxious to remove man's clothes and restore him to the happy freedom of the primeval forest? Didn't the enormously learned Professor Irving Babbitt show that Rousseau was the father of romanticism and therefore the source of practically every evil in modern times? But didn't Havelock Ellis say, in a more sympathetic voice, that Rousseau was "the

34

most important and influential force to appear in our western world since Jesus"?

Rousseau's unpromising decades have been neatly captioned by F. J. C. Hearnshaw as "the undisciplined boy" (1712-1728), "the super-tramp" (1728-1742) and "the would-be man of the world" (1742-1749). His temperament unfitted him for the society of Parisian wits and ladies of fashion but it did fit him all too well to perceive the extravagant artificiality of that society and the misery of masses of people. For the time being, he was on good terms with the Encyclopedists, and their leader, Diderot, was his closest friend. One day in August, 1749, while walking from Paris to Vincennes to visit his imprisoned friend, who had rather carelessly ignored the laws of censorship, Rousseau noticed in a journal he was carrying the announcement of a prize to be awarded by the Academy of Dijon for the best answer to the question: "Has the restoration of the arts and sciences had a purifying effect upon morals?" According to the *Confessions,* he was at once overwhelmed with excitement, rushed on to talk with Diderot and wrote out his answer with frenzied speed.

•   •   •

A DISCOURSE

WHICH WON THE PRIZE AT THE ACADEMY OF DIJON IN 1750, ON THIS QUESTION PROPOSED BY THE ACADEMY:

HAS THE RESTORATION OF THE ARTS AND SCIENCES HAD A PURIFYING EFFECT UPON MORALS?

———

Barbarus hic ego sum, qui non intelligor illis.[1]—OVID

PREFACE

The following pages contain a discussion of one of the most sublime and interesting of all moral questions. It is not concerned, however, with those metaphysical subtleties

---

[1] [Here I am, a barbarian, because men understand me not.]

which of late have found their way into every department of
literature, and from which even our academic curricula are
not always free. We have now to do with one of those truths
on which the happiness of mankind depends.

I foresee that I shall not readily be forgiven for having
taken up the position I have adopted. Setting myself up
against all that is nowadays most admired, I can expect no
less than a universal outcry against me: nor is the approbation
of a few sensible men enough to make me count on that of
the public. But I have taken my stand, and I shall be at no
pains to please either intellectuals or men of the world. There
are in all ages men born to be in bondage to the opinions of
the society in which they live. There are not a few, who to-
day play the free-thinker and the philosopher, who would, if
they had lived in the time of the League, have been no more
than fanatics. No author, who has a mind to outlive his own
age, should write for such readers.

A word more and I have done. As I did not expect the
honour conferred on me, I had, since sending in my Discourse, so altered and enlarged it as almost to make it a new
work; but in the circumstances I have felt bound to publish
it just as it was when it received the prize. I have only added
a few notes, and left two alterations which are easily recognisable, of which the Academy possibly might not have approved. The respect, gratitude and even justice I owe to that
body seemed to me to demand this acknowledgment.

A DISCOURSE ON THE MORAL EFFECTS
OF THE ARTS AND SCIENCES

Decipimur specie recti.[1]—HORACE

The question before me is, "Whether the restoration of
the arts and sciences has had the effect of purifying or cor-

---

[1] [We are deceived by an appearance of right.]

rupting morals." Which side am I to take? That, gentlemen, which becomes an honest man, who is sensible of his own ignorance, and thinks himself none the worse for it.

I feel the difficulty of treating this subject fittingly, before the tribunal which is to judge of what I advance. How can I presume to belittle the sciences before one of the most learned assemblies in Europe, to commend ignorance in a famous Academy, and reconcile my contempt for study with the respect due to the truly learned?

I was aware of these inconsistencies, but not discouraged by them. It is not science, I said to myself, that I am attacking; it is virtue that I am defending, and that before virtuous men—and goodness is even dearer to the good than learning to the learned.

What then have I to fear? The sagacity of the assembly before which I am pleading? That, I acknowledge, is to be feared; but rather on account of faults of construction than of the views I hold. Just sovereigns have never hesitated to decide against themselves in doubtful cases; and indeed the most advantageous situation in which a just claim can be, is that of being laid before a just and enlightened arbitrator, who is judge in his own case.

To this motive, which encouraged me, I may add another which finally decided me. And this is, that as I have upheld the cause of truth to the best of my natural abilities, whatever my apparent success, there is one reward which cannot fail me. That reward I shall find in the bottom of my heart.

THE FIRST PART

It is a noble and beautiful spectacle to see man raising himself, so to speak, from nothing by his own exertions; dissipating, by the light of reason, all the thick clouds in which he was by nature enveloped; mounting above himself; soaring in thought even to the celestial regions; like the sun, encompassing with giant strides the vast extent of the universe; and, what is still grander and more wonderful, going back into himself, there to study man and get to know his own nature, his duties and his end. All these miracles we have seen renewed within the last few generations.

Europe had relapsed into the barbarism of the earliest ages; the inhabitants of this part of the world, which is at present so highly enlightened, were plunged, some centuries ago, in a state still worse than ignorance. A scientific jargon, more despicable than mere ignorance, had usurped the name of knowledge, and opposed an almost invincible obstacle to its restoration.

Things had come to such a pass, that it required a complete revolution to bring men back to common sense. This came at last from the quarter from which it was least to be expected. It was the stupid Mussulman, the eternal scourge of letters, who was the immediate cause of their revival among us. The fall of the throne of Constantine brought to Italy the relics of ancient Greece; and with these precious spoils France in turn was enriched. The sciences soon followed literature, and the art of thinking joined that of writing: an order which may seem strange, but is perhaps only too natural. The world now began to perceive the principal advantage of an intercourse with the Muses, that of rendering mankind more sociable by inspiring them with the desire to please one another with performances worthy of their mutual approbation.

The mind, as well as the body, has its needs: those of the body are the basis of society, those of the mind its ornaments.

So long as government and law provide for the security and well-being of men in their common life, the arts, literature and the sciences, less despotic though perhaps more powerful, fling garlands of flowers over the chains which weigh them down. They stifle in men's breasts that sense of original liberty, for which they seem to have been born; cause them to love their own slavery, and so make of them what is called a civilised people.

Necessity raised up thrones; the arts and sciences have made them strong. Powers of the earth, cherish all talents and protect those who cultivate them.[2] Civilised peoples, cultivate such pursuits: to them, happy slaves, you owe that delicacy and exquisiteness of taste, which is so much your boast, that sweetness of disposition and urbanity of manners which make intercourse so easy and agreeable among you —in a word, the appearance of all the virtues, without being in possession of one of them.

It was for this sort of accomplishment, which is by so much the more captivating as it seems less affected, that Athens and Rome were so much distinguished in the boasted times of their splendour and magnificence: and it is doubtless in the same respect that our own age and nation will excel all periods and peoples. An air of philosophy without pedantry; an address at once natural and engaging, distant equally from Teutonic clumsiness and Italian pantomime; these are the effects of a taste acquired by liberal studies and improved by conversation with the world. What happiness would it be for those who live among us, if our external appearance were always a true mirror of our hearts; if decorum were but virtue; if the maxims we professed were the rules of our conduct; and if real philosophy were inseparable from the title of a philosopher! But so many good qualities too seldom go together; virtue rarely appears in so much pomp and state.

Richness of apparel may proclaim the man of fortune, and elegance the man of taste; but true health and manliness are known by different signs. It is under the homespun of the labourer, and not beneath the gilt and tinsel of the courtier, that we should look for strength and vigour of body.

External ornaments are no less foreign to virtue, which

---

[2] Sovereigns always see with pleasure a taste for the arts of amusement and superfluity, which do not result in the exportation of bullion, increase among their subjects. They very well know that, besides nourishing that littleness of mind which is proper to slavery, the increase of artificial wants only binds so many more chains upon the people. Alexander, wishing to keep the Ichthyophages in a state of dependence, compelled them to give up fishing, and subsist on the customary food of civilised nations. The American savages, who go naked, and live entirely on the products of the chase, have been always impossible to subdue. What yoke, indeed, can be imposed on men who stand in need of nothing?

is the strength and activity of the mind. The honest man is an athlete, who loves to wrestle stark naked; he scorns all those vile trappings, which prevent the exertion of his strength, and were, for the most part, invented only to conceal some deformity.

Before art had moulded our behaviour, and taught our passions to speak an artificial language, our morals were rude but natural; and the different ways in which we behaved proclaimed at the first glance the difference of our dispositions. Human nature was not at bottom better then than now; but men found their security in the ease with which they could see through one another, and this advantage, of which we no longer feel the value, prevented their having many vices.

In our day, now that more subtle study and a more refined taste have reduced the art of pleasing to a system, there prevails in modern manners a servile and deceptive conformity; so that one would think every mind had been cast in the same mould. Politeness requires this thing; decorum that; ceremony has its forms, and fashion its laws, and these we must always follow, never the promptings of our own nature.

We no longer dare seem what we really are, but lie under a perpetual restraint; in the meantime the herd of men, which we call society, all act under the same circumstances exactly alike, unless very particular and powerful motives prevent them. Thus we never know with whom we have to deal; and even to know our friends we must wait for some critical and pressing occasion; that is, till it is too late; for it is on those very occasions that such knowledge is of use to us.

What a train of vices must attend this uncertainty! Sincere friendship, real esteem, and perfect confidence are banished from among men. Jealousy, suspicion, fear, coldness, reserve, hate and fraud lie constantly concealed under that uniform and deceitful veil of politeness; that boasted candour and urbanity, for which we are indebted to the light and leading of this age. We shall no longer take in vain by our oaths the name of our Creator; but we shall insult Him with our blasphemies, and our scrupulous ears will take no offence. We have grown too modest to brag of our own deserts; but we do not scruple to decry those of others. We do not grossly outrage even our enemies, but artfully calumniate them. Our hatred of other nations diminishes, but patriotism dies with it. Ignorance is held in contempt; but a dangerous scepticism has succeeded it. Some vices indeed are condemned and others grown dishonourable; but we have still many that are honoured with the names of virtues, and it is become necessary that we should either have, or at least pretend to have them. Let who will extol the moderation of our modern sages, I see nothing in it but a refinement of intemperance as unworthy of my commendation as their artificial simplicity.[3]

Such is the purity to which our morals have attained; this is the virtue we have made our own. Let the arts and sciences claim the share they have had in this salutary work. I shall add but one reflection more; suppose an inhabitant of some distant country should endeavour to form an idea of European morals from the state of the sciences, the perfection of the arts, the propriety of our public entertainments, the politeness of our behaviour, the affability of our conversation, our constant professions of benevolence, and from those tumultuous assemblies of people of all ranks, who seem, from morning till night, to have no other care than to oblige one another. Such a stranger, I maintain, would arrive at a totally false view of our morality.

Where there is no effect, it is idle to look for a cause: but here the effect is certain and the depravity actual; our minds have been corrupted in proportion as the arts and sciences have improved. Will it be said, that this is a misfortune peculiar to the present age? No, gentlemen, the evils resulting from our vain curiosity are as old as the world.

---

[3] "I love," said Montaigne, "to converse and hold an argument; but only with very few people, and that for my own gratification. For to do so, by way of affording amusement for the great, or of making a parade of one's talents, is, in my opinion, a trade very ill-becoming a man of honour." It is the trade of all our intellectuals, save one.

The daily ebb and flow of the tides are not more regularly influenced by the moon, than the morals of a people by the progress of the arts and sciences. As their light has risen above our horizon, virtue has taken flight, and the same phenomenon has been constantly observed in all times and places.

Take Egypt, the first school of mankind, that ancient country, famous for its fertility under a brazen sky; the spot from which Sesostris once set out to conquer the world. Egypt became the mother of philosophy and the fine arts; soon she was conquered by Cambyses, and then successively by the Greeks, the Romans, the Arabs, and finally the Turks.

Take Greece, once peopled by heroes, who twice vanquished Asia. Letters, as yet in their infancy, had not corrupted the disposition of its inhabitants; but the progress of the sciences soon produced a dissoluteness of manners, and the imposition of the Macedonian yoke: from which time Greece, always learned, always voluptuous and always a slave, has experienced amid all its revolutions no more than a change of masters. Not all the eloquence of Demosthenes could breathe life into a body which luxury and the arts had once enervated.

It was not till the days of Ennius and Terence that Rome, founded by a shepherd, and made illustrious by peasants, began to degenerate. But after the appearance of an Ovid, a Catullus, a Martial, and the rest of those numerous obscene authors, whose very names are enough to put modesty to the blush, Rome, once the shrine of virtue, became the theatre of vice, a scorn among the nations, and an object of derision even to barbarians. Thus the capital of the world at length submitted to the yoke of slavery it had imposed on others, and the very day of its fall was the eve of that on which it conferred on one of its citizens the title of Arbiter of Good Taste.

What shall I say of that metropolis of the Eastern Empire, which, by its situation, seemed destined to be the capital of the world; that refuge of the arts and sciences, when they

were banished from the rest of Europe, more perhaps by
wisdom than barbarism? The most profligate debaucheries,
the most abandoned villainies, the most atrocious crimes,
plots, murders and assassinations form the warp and woof of
the history of Constantinople. Such is the pure source from
which have flowed to us the floods of knowledge on which
the present age so prides itself.

But wherefore should we seek, in past ages, for proofs of
a truth, of which the present affords us ample evidence?
There is in Asia a vast empire, where learning is held in
honour, and leads to the highest dignities in the state. If the
sciences improved our morals, if they inspired us with
courage and taught us to lay down our lives for the good of
our country, the Chinese should be wise, free and invincible.
But, if there be no vice they do not practise, no crime with
which they are not familiar; if the sagacity of their ministers,
the supposed wisdom of their laws, and the multitude of inhabitants who people that vast empire, have alike failed to
preserve them from the yoke of the rude and ignorant
Tartars, of what use were their men of science and literature?
What advantage has that country reaped from the honours
bestowed on its learned men? Can it be that of being peopled
by a race of scoundrels and slaves?

Contrast with these instances the morals of those few
nations which, being preserved from the contagion of useless knowledge, have by their virtues become happy in themselves and afforded an example to the rest of the world. Such
were the first inhabitants of Persia, a nation so singular that
virtue was taught among them in the same manner as the
sciences are with us. They very easily subdued Asia, and
possess the exclusive glory of having had the history of their
political institutions regarded as a philosophical romance.
Such were the Scythians, of whom such wonderful eulogies
have come down to us. Such were the Germans, whose simplicity, innocence and virtue, afforded a most delightful contrast to the pen of an historian, weary of describing the base-
ness and villainies of an enlightened, opulent and voluptuous
nation. Such had been even Rome in the days of its poverty

and ignorance. And such has shown itself to be, even in our own times, that rustic nation, whose justly renowned courage not even adversity could conquer, and whose fidelity no example could corrupt.[4]

It is not through stupidity that the people have preferred other activities to those of the mind. They were not ignorant that in other countries there were men who spent their time in disputing idly about the sovereign good, and about vice and virtue. They knew that these useless thinkers were lavish in their own praises, and stigmatised other nations contemptuously as barbarians. But they noted the morals of these people, and so learnt what to think of their learning.[5]

Can it be forgotten that, in the very heart of Greece, there arose a city as famous for the happy ignorance of its inhabitants, as for the wisdom of its laws; a republic of demigods rather than of men, so greatly superior their virtues seemed to those of mere humanity? Sparta, eternal proof of the vanity of science, while the vices, under the conduct of the fine arts, were being introduced into Athens, even while its tyrant was carefully collecting together the works of the prince of poets, was driving from her walls artists and the arts, the learned and their learning!

The difference was seen in the outcome. Athens became the seat of politeness and taste, the country of orators and philosophers. The elegance of its buildings equalled that of its language; on every side might be seen marble and canvas, animated by the hands of the most skilful artists. From Athens

---

[4] I dare not speak of those happy nations, who did not even know the name of many vices, which we find it difficult to suppress; the savages of America, whose simple and natural mode of government Montaigne preferred, without hesitation, not only to the laws of Plato, but to the most perfect visions of government philosophy can ever suggest. He cites many examples, striking for those who are capable of appreciating them. But, what of all that, says he, they can't run to a pair of breeches!

[5] What are we to think was the real opinion of the Athenians themselves about eloquence, when they were so very careful to banish declamation from that upright tribunal, against whose decision even their gods made no appeal? What did the Romans think of physicians, when they expelled medicine from the republic? And when the relics of humanity left among the Spaniards induced them to forbid their lawyers to set foot in America, what must they have thought of jurisprudence? May it not be said that they thought, by this single expedient, to make reparation for all the outrages they had committed against the unhappy Indians?

we derive those astonishing performances, which will serve as models to every corrupt age. The picture of Lacedæmon is not so highly coloured. There, the neighbouring nations used to say, "men were born virtuous, their native air seeming to inspire them with virtue." But its inhabitants have left us nothing but the memory of their heroic actions: monuments that should not count for less in our eyes than the most curious relics of Athenian marble.

It is true that, among the Athenians, there were some few wise men who withstood the general torrent, and preserved their integrity even in the company of the muses. But hear the judgment which the principal, and most unhappy of them, passed on the artists and learned men of his day.

"I have considered the poets," says he, "and I look upon them as people whose talents impose both on themselves and on others; they give themselves out for wise men, and are taken for such; but in reality they are anything sooner than that.

"From the poets," continues Socrates, "I turned to the artists. Nobody was more ignorant of the arts than myself; nobody was more fully persuaded that the artists were possessed of amazing knowledge. I soon discovered, however, that they were in as bad a way as the poets, and that both had fallen into the same misconception. Because the most skilful of them excel others in their particular jobs, they think themselves wiser than all the rest of mankind. This arrogance spoilt all their skill in my eyes, so that, putting myself in the place of the oracle, and asking myself whether I would rather be what I am or what they are, know what they know, or know that I know nothing, I very readily answered, for myself and the god, that I had rather remain as I am.

"None of us, neither the sophists, nor the poets, nor the orators, nor the artists, nor I, know what is the nature of the *true*, the *good*, or the *beautiful*. But there is this difference between us; that, though none of these people know anything, they all think they know something; whereas for my part, if I know nothing, I am at least in no doubt of my ignorance. So the superiority of wisdom, imputed to me by

the oracle, is reduced merely to my being fully convinced that
I am ignorant of what I do not know."

Thus we find Socrates, the wisest of men in the judgment of the god, and the most learned of all the Athenians
in the opinion of all Greece, speaking in praise of ignorance.
Were he alive now, there is little reason to think that our
modern scholars and artists would induce him to change his
mind. No, gentlemen, that honest man would still persist in
despising our vain sciences. He would lend no aid to swell
the flood of books that flows from every quarter: he would
leave to us, as he did to his disciples, only the example and
memory of his virtues; that is the noblest method of instructing mankind.

Socrates had begun at Athens, and the elder Cato proceeded at Rome, to inveigh against those seductive and subtle
Greeks, who corrupted the virtue and destroyed the courage
of their fellow-citizens: culture, however, prevailed. Rome
was filled with philosophers and orators, military discipline
was neglected, agriculture was held in contempt, men formed
sects, and forgot their country. To the sacred names of liberty,
disinterestedness and obedience to law, succeeded those of
Epicurus, Zeno and Arcesilaus. It was even a saying among
their own philosophers that since learned men appeared
among them, honest men had been in eclipse. Before that
time the Romans were satisfied with the practice of virtue;
they were undone when they began to study it.

What would the great soul of Fabricius have felt, if it had
been his misfortune to be called back to life, when he saw
the pomp and magnificence of that Rome, which his arm
had saved from ruin, and his honourable name made more
illustrious than all its conquests. "Ye gods!" he would have
said, "what has become of those thatched roofs and rustic
hearths, which were formerly the habitations of temperance
and virtue? What fatal splendour has succeeded the ancient
Roman simplicity? What is this foreign language, this effem-
inacy of manners? What is the meaning of these statues, paintings and buildings? Fools, what have you done? You, the
lords of the earth, have made yourselves the slaves of the

frivolous nations you have subdued. You are governed by rhetoricians, and it has been only to enrich architects, painters, sculptors and stage-players that you have watered Greece and Asia with your blood. Even the spoils of Carthage are the prize of a flute-player. Romans! Romans! make haste to demolish those amphitheatres, break to pieces those statues, burn those paintings; drive from among you those slaves who keep you in subjection, and whose fatal arts are corrupting your morals. Let other hands make themselves illustrious by such vain talents; the only talent worthy of Rome is that of conquering the world and making virtue its ruler. When Cyneas took the Roman senate for an assembly of kings, he was not struck by either useless pomp or studied elegance. He heard there none of that futile eloquence, which is now the study and the charm of frivolous orators. What then was the majesty that Cyneas beheld? Fellow citizens, he saw the noblest sight that ever existed under heaven, a sight which not all your riches or your arts can show; an assembly of two hundred virtuous men, worthy to command in Rome, and to govern the world."

But let pass the distance of time and place, and let us see what has happened to our own time and country; or rather let us banish odious descriptions that might offend our delicacy, and spare ourselves the pains of repeating the same things under different names. It was not for nothing that I invoked the Manes of Fabricius; for what have I put into his mouth, that might not have come with as much propriety from Louis the Twelfth or Henry the Fourth? It is true that in France Socrates would not have drunk the hemlock, but he would have drunk of a potion infinitely more bitter, of insult, mockery and contempt a hundred times worse than death.

Thus it is that luxury, profligacy and slavery, have been, in all ages, the scourge of the efforts of our pride to emerge from that happy state of ignorance, in which the wisdom of providence had placed us. That thick veil with which it has covered all its operations seems to be a sufficient proof that it never designed us for such fruitless researches. But is there, indeed, one lesson it has taught us, by which we have rightly profited, or which we have neglected with impunity? Let men learn for once that nature would have preserved them from science, as a mother snatches a dangerous weapon from the hands of her child. Let them know that all the secrets she hides are so many evils from which she protects them, and that the very difficulty they find in acquiring knowledge is not the least of her bounty towards them. Men are perverse; but they would have been far worse, if they had had the misfortune to be born learned.

How humiliating are these reflections to humanity, and how mortified by them our pride should be! What! it will be asked, is uprightness the child of ignorance? Is virtue inconsistent with learning? What consequences might not be drawn from such suppositions? But to reconcile these apparent contradictions, we need only examine closely the emptiness and vanity of those pompous titles, which are so liberally bestowed on human knowledge, and which so blind our judgment. Let us consider, therefore, the arts and sciences in themselves. Let us see what must result from their advancement, and let us not hesitate to admit the truth of all those points on which our arguments coincide with the inductions we can make from history.

THE SECOND PART

An ancient tradition passed out of Egypt into Greece, that some god, who was an enemy to the repose of mankind, was the inventor of the sciences.[6] What must the Egyptians, among whom the sciences first arose, have thought of them? And they beheld, near at hand, the sources from which they sprang. In fact, whether we turn to the annals of the world, or eke out with philosophical investigations the uncertain

---

[6] It is easy to see the allegory in the fable of Prometheus: and it does not appear that the Greeks, who chained him to the Caucasus, had a better opinion of him than the Egyptians had of their god Theutus. The Satyr, says an ancient fable, the first time he saw a fire, was going to kiss and embrace it; but Prometheus cried out to him to forbear, or his beard would rue it. It burns, says he, everything that touches it.

chronicles of history, we shall not find for human knowledge an origin answering to the idea we are pleased to entertain of it at present. Astronomy was born of superstition, eloquence of ambition, hatred, falsehood and flattery; geometry of avarice; physics of an idle curiosity; and even moral philosophy of human pride. Thus the arts and sciences owe their birth to our vices; we should be less doubtful of their advantages, if they had sprung from our virtues.

Their evil origin is, indeed, but too plainly reproduced in their objects. What would become of the arts, were they not cherished by luxury? If men were not unjust, of what use were jurisprudence? What would become of history, if there were no tyrants, wars, or conspiracies? In a word, who would pass his life in barren speculations, if everybody, attentive only to the obligations of humanity and the necessities of nature, spent his whole life in serving his country, obliging his friends, and relieving the unhappy? Are we then made to live and die on the brink of that well at the bottom of which Truth lies hid? This reflection alone is, in my opinion, enough to discourage at first setting out every man who seriously endeavours to instruct himself by the study of philosophy.

What a variety of dangers surrounds us! What a number of wrong paths present themselves in the investigation of the sciences! Through how many errors, more perilous than truth itself is useful, must we not pass to arrive at it? The disadvantages we lie under are evident; for falsehood is capable of an infinite variety of combinations; but the truth has only one manner of being. Besides, where is the man who sincerely desires to find it? Or even admitting his good will, by what characteristic marks is he sure of knowing it? Amid the infinite diversity of opinions where is the criterion⁷ by which we may certainly judge of it? Again, what is still more difficult, should we even be fortunate enough to discover it, who among us will know how to make right use of it?

---

⁷ The less we know, the more we think we know. The peripatetics doubted of nothing. Did not Descartes construct the universe with cubes and vortices? And is there in all Europe one single physicist who does not boldly explain the inexplicable mysteries of electricity, which will, perhaps, be for ever the despair of real philosophers?

If our sciences are futile in the objects they propose, they
are not less dangerous in the effects they produce. Being the
effect of idleness, they generate idleness in their turn; and
an irreparable loss of time is the first prejudice which they
must necessarily cause to society. To live without doing some
good is a great evil as well in the political as in the moral
world; and hence every useless citizen should be regarded as
a pernicious person. Tell me then, illustrious philosophers, of
whom we learn the ratios in which attraction acts in vacuo;
and in the revolution of the planets, the relations of spaces
traversed in equal times; by whom we are taught what
curves have conjugate points, points of inflexion, and cusps;
how the soul and body correspond, like two clocks, without
actual communication; what planets may be inhabited; and
what insects reproduce in an extraordinary manner. Answer
me, I say, you from whom we receive all this sublime information, whether we should have been less numerous, worse
governed, less formidable, less flourishing, or more perverse,
supposing you had taught us none of all these fine things.

Reconsider therefore the importance of your productions;
and, since the labours of the most enlightened of our learned
men and the best of our citizens are of so little utility, tell
us what we ought to think of that numerous herd of obscure writers and useless littérateurs, who devour without
any return the substance of the State.

Useless, do I say? Would God they were! Society would be
more peaceful, and morals less corrupt. But these vain and
futile declaimers go forth on all sides, armed with their fatal
paradoxes, to sap the foundations of our faith, and nullify
virtue. They smile contemptuously at such old names as
patriotism and religion, and consecrate their talents and philosophy to the destruction and defamation of all that men
hold sacred. Not that they bear any real hatred to virtue or
dogma; they are the enemies of public opinion alone; to bring
them to the foot of the altar, it would be enough to banish
them to a land of atheists. What extravagancies will not the
rage of singularity induce men to commit!

The waste of time is certainly a great evil; but still greater evils attend upon literature and the arts. One is luxury, produced like them by indolence and vanity. Luxury is seldom unattended by the arts and sciences; and they are always attended by luxury. I know that our philosophy, fertile in paradoxes, pretends, in contradiction to the experience of all ages, that luxury contributes to the splendour of States. But, without insisting on the necessity of sumptuary laws, can it be denied that rectitude of morals is essential to the duration of empires, and that luxury is diametrically opposed to such rectitude? Let it be admitted that luxury is a certain indication of wealth; that it even serves, if you will, to increase such wealth: what conclusion is to be drawn from this paradox, so worthy of the times? And what will become of virtue if riches are to be acquired at any cost? The politicians of the ancient world were always talking of morals and virtue; ours speak of nothing but commerce and money. One of them will tell you that in such a country a man is worth just as much as he will sell for at Algiers: another, pursuing the same mode of calculation, finds that in some countries a man is worth nothing, and in others still less than nothing; they value men as they do droves of oxen. According to them, a man is worth no more to the State, than the amount he consumes; and thus a Sybarite would be worth at least thirty Lacedæmonians. Let these writers tell me, however, which of the two republics, Sybaris or Sparta, was subdued by a handful of peasants, and which became the terror of Asia.

The monarchy of Cyrus was conquered by thirty thousand men, led by a prince poorer than the meanest of Persian Satraps: in like manner the Scythians, the poorest of all nations, were able to resist the most powerful monarchs of the universe. When two famous republics contended for the empire of the world, the one rich and the other poor, the former was subdued by the latter. The Roman empire in its turn, after having engulfed all the riches of the universe, fell a prey to peoples who knew not even what riches were. The Franks conquered the Gauls, and the Saxons England, without any other treasures than their bravery and their poverty. A band of poor mountaineers, whose whole cupidity was

confined to the possession of a few sheep-skins, having first
given a check to the arrogance of Austria, went on to crush
the opulent and formidable house of Burgundy, which at that
time made the potentates of Europe tremble. In short, all the
power and wisdom of the heir of Charles the Fifth, backed
by all the treasures of the Indies, broke before a few herring-
fishers. Let our politicians condescend to lay aside their calculations for a moment, to reflect on these examples; let them
learn for once that money, though it buys everything else,
cannot buy morals and citizens. What then is the precise
point in dispute about luxury? It is to know which is most
advantageous to empires, that their existence should be brilliant and momentary, or virtuous and lasting? I say brilliant,
but with what lustre! A taste for ostentation never prevails in
the same minds as a taste for honesty. No, it is impossible that
understandings, degraded by a multitude of futile cares,
should ever rise to what is truly great and noble; even if they
had the strength, they would want the courage.

Every artist loves applause. The praise of his contemporaries is the most valuable part of his recompense. What
then will he do to obtain it, if he have the misfortune to be
born among a people, and at a time, when learning is in
vogue, and the superficiality of youth is in a position to lead
the fashion; when men have sacrificed their taste to those who
tyrannise over their liberty, and one sex dare not approve
anything but what is proportionate to the pusillanimity of the
other;[8] when the greatest masterpieces of dramatic poetry
are condemned, and the noblest of musical productions neglected? This is what he will do. He will lower his genius to
the level of the age, and will rather submit to compose mediocre works, that will be admired during his life-time, than

---

[8] I am far from thinking that the ascendancy which women have obtained
over men is an evil in itself. It is a present which nature has made them
for the good of mankind. If better directed, it might be productive of as
much good, as it is now of evil. We are not sufficiently sensible of what
advantage it would be to society to give a better education to that half of
our species which governs the other. Men will always be what women
choose to make them. If you wish then that they should be noble and
virtuous, let women be taught what greatness of soul and virtue are. The
reflections which this subject arouses, and which Plato formerly made,
deserve to be more fully developed by a pen worthy of following so great a
master, and defending so great a cause.

labour at sublime achievements which will not be admired till long after he is dead. Let the famous Voltaire tell us how many nervous and masculine beauties he has sacrificed to our false delicacy, and how much that is great and noble, that spirit of gallantry, which delights in what is frivolous and petty, has cost him.

It is thus that the dissolution of morals, the necessary consequence of luxury, brings with it in its turn the corruption of taste. Further, if by chance there be found among men of average ability, an individual with enough strength of mind to refuse to comply with the spirit of the age, and to debase himself by puerile productions, his lot will be hard. He will die in indigence and oblivion. This is not so much a prediction, as a fact already confirmed by experience! Yes, Carle and Pierre Vanloo, the time is already come when your pencils, destined to increase the majesty of our temples by sublime and holy images, must fall from your hands, or else be prostituted to adorn the panels of a coach with lascivious paintings. And you, inimitable Pigal, rival of Phidias and Praxiteles, whose chisel the ancients would have employed to carve them gods, whose images almost excuse their idolatry in our eyes; even your hand must condescend to fashion the belly of an ape, or else remain idle.

We cannot reflect on the morality of mankind without contemplating with pleasure the picture of the simplicity which prevailed in the earliest times. This image may be justly compared to a beautiful coast, adorned only by the hands of nature; towards which our eyes are constantly turned, and which we see receding with regret. While men were innocent and virtuous and loved to have the gods for witnesses of their actions, they dwelt together in the same huts; but when they became vicious, they grew tired of such inconvenient onlookers, and banished them to magnificent temples. Finally, they expelled their deities even from these, in order to dwell there themselves; or at least the temples of the gods were no longer more magnificent than the palaces of the citizens. This was the height of degeneracy; nor could vice ever be carried to greater lengths than when it was seen, supported, as it were,

at the doors of the great, on columns of marble, and graven
on Corinthian capitals.

As the conveniences of life increase, as the arts are brought
to perfection, and luxury spreads, true courage flags, the virtues disappear; and all this is the effect of the sciences and
of those arts which are exercised in the privacy of men's dwell-
ings. When the Goths ravaged Greece, the libraries only
escaped the flames owing to an opinion that was set on foot
among them, that it was best to leave the enemy with a
possession so calculated to divert their attention from military exercises, and keep them engaged in indolent and
sedentary occupations.

Charles the Eighth found himself master of Tuscany and
the kingdom of Naples, almost without drawing sword; and
all his court attributed this unexpected success to the fact
that the princes and nobles of Italy applied themselves with
greater earnestness to the cultivation of their understandings
than to active and martial pursuits. In fact, says the sensible
person who records these characteristics, experience plainly
tells us, that in military matters and all that resemble them
application to the sciences tends rather to make men effeminate and cowardly than resolute and vigorous.

The Romans confessed that military virtue was extin-
guished among them, in proportion as they became con-
noisseurs in the arts of the painter, the engraver and the
goldsmith, and began to cultivate the fine arts. Indeed, as if
this famous country was to be for ever an example to other
nations, the rise of the Medici and the revival of letters has
once more destroyed, this time perhaps for ever, the martial
reputation which Italy seemed a few centuries ago to have
recovered.

The ancient republics of Greece, with that wisdom which
was so conspicuous in most of their institutions, forbade their
citizens to pursue all those inactive and sedentary occupations,
which by enervating and corrupting the body diminish also
the vigour of the mind. With what courage, in fact, can it be
thought that hunger and thirst, fatigues, dangers and death,
can be faced by men whom the smallest want overwhelms

and the slightest difficulty repels? With what resolution can soldiers support the excessive toils of war, when they are entirely unaccustomed to them? With what spirits can they make forced marches under officers who have not even the strength to travel on horseback? It is no answer to cite the reputed valour of all the modern warriors who are so scientifically trained. I hear much of their bravery in a day's battle; but I am told nothing of how they support excessive fatigue, how they stand the severity of the seasons and the inclemency of the weather. A little sunshine or snow, or the want of a few superfluities, is enough to cripple and destroy one of our finest armies in a few days. Intrepid warriors! permit me for once to tell you the truth, which you seldom hear. Of your bravery I am fully satisfied. I have no doubt that you would have triumphed with Hannibal at Cannæ, and at Trasimene: that you would have passed the Rubicon with Cæsar, and enabled him to enslave his country; but you never would have been able to cross the Alps with the former, or with the latter to subdue your own ancestors, the Gauls.

A war does not always depend on the events of battle: there is in generalship an art superior to that of gaining victories. A man may behave with great intrepidity under fire, and yet be a very bad officer. Even in the common soldier, a little more strength and vigour would perhaps be more useful than so much courage, which after all is no protection from death. And what does it matter to the State whether its troops perish by cold and fever, or by the sword of the enemy?

If the cultivation of the sciences is prejudicial to military qualities, it is still more so to moral qualities. Even from our infancy an absurd system of education serves to adorn our wit and corrupt our judgment. We see, on every side, huge institutions, where our youth are educated at great expense, and instructed in everything but their duty. Your children will be ignorant of their own language, when they can talk others which are not spoken anywhere. They will be able to compose verses which they can hardly understand; and, without being capable of distinguishing truth from error, they will possess the art of making them unrecognisable by specious arguments. But magnanimity, equity, temperance, humanity and courage will be words of which they know not the meaning. The dear name of country will never strike on their ears; and if they ever hear speak of God,[9] it will be less to fear, than to be frightened of, Him. I would as soon, said a wise man, that my pupil had spent his time in the tennis court as in this manner; for there his body at least would have got exercise.

I well know that children ought to be kept employed, and that idleness is for them the danger most to be feared. But what should they be taught? This is undoubtedly an important question. Let them be taught what they are to practise when they come to be men;[10] not what they ought to forget.

Our gardens are adorned with statues and our galleries with pictures. What would you imagine these masterpieces of art, thus exhibited to public admiration, represent? The great

---

[9] *Pensées philosophiques* (Diderot).

[10] Such was the education of the Spartans with regard to one of the greatest of their kings. It is well worthy of notice, says Montaigne, that the excellent institutions of Lycurgus, which were in truth miraculously perfect, paid as much attention to the bringing up of youth as if this were their principal object, and yet, at the very seat of the Muses, they make so little mention of learning that it seems as if their generous-spirited youth disdained every other restraint, and required, instead of masters of the sciences, instructors in valour, prudence and justice alone.

Let us hear next what the same writer says of the ancient Persians. Plato, says he, relates that the heir to the throne was thus brought up. At his birth he was committed, not to the care of women, but to eunuchs in the highest authority and near the person of the king, on account of their virtue. These undertook to render his body beautiful and healthy. At seven years of age they taught him to ride and go hunting. At fourteen he was placed in the hands of four, the wisest, the most just, the most temperate and the bravest persons in the kingdom. The first instructed him in religion, the second taught him to adhere inviolably to truth, the third to conquer his passions, and the fourth to be afraid of nothing. All, I may add, taught him to be a good man; but not one taught him to be learned.

Astyages, in Xenophon, desires Cyrus to give him an account of his last lesson It was this, answered Cyrus, one of the big boys of the school having a small coat, gave it to a little boy and took away from him his coat, which was larger. Our master having appointed me arbiter in the dispute, I ordered that matters should stand as they were, as each boy seemed to be better suited than before. The master, however, remonstrated with me, saying that I considered only convenience, whereas justice ought to have been the first concern, and justice teaches that no one should suffer forcible interference with what belongs to him. He added that he was punished for his wrong decision, just as boys are punished in our country schools when they forget the first aorist of τύπτω. My tutor must make me a fine harangue, *in genere demonstrativo*, before he will persuade me that his school is as good as this.

men, who have defended their country, or the still greater men who have enriched it by their virtues? Far from it. They are the images of every perversion of heart and mind, carefully selected from ancient mythology, and presented to the early curiosity of our children, doubtless that they may have before their eyes the representations of vicious actions, even before they are able to read.

Whence arise all those abuses, unless it be from that fatal inequality introduced among men by the difference of talents and the cheapening of virtue? This is the most evident effect of all our studies, and the most dangerous of all their consequences. The question is no longer whether a man is honest, but whether he is clever. We do not ask whether a book is useful, but whether it is well-written. Rewards are lavished on wit and ingenuity, while virtue is left unhonoured. There are a thousand prizes for fine discourses, and none for good actions. I should be glad, however, to know whether the honour attaching to the best discourse that ever wins the prize in this Academy is comparable with the merit of having founded the prize.

A wise man does not go in chase of fortune; but he is by no means insensible to glory, and when he sees it so ill distributed, his virtue, which might have been animated by a little emulation, and turned to the advantage of society, droops and dies away in obscurity and indigence. It is for this reason that the agreeable arts must in time everywhere be preferred to the useful; and this truth has been but too much confirmed since the revival of the arts and sciences. We have physicists, geometricians, chemists, astronomers, poets, musicians, and painters in plenty; but we have no longer a citizen among us; or if there be found a few scattered over our abandoned countryside, they are left to perish there unnoticed and neglected. Such is the condition to which we are reduced, and such are our feelings towards those who give us our daily bread, and our children milk.

I confess, however, that the evil is not so great as it might have become. The eternal providence, in placing salutary simples beside noxious plants, and making poisonous animals contain their own antidote, has taught the sovereigns of the earth, who are its ministers, to imitate its wisdom. It is by following this example that the truly great monarch, to whose glory every age will add new lustre, drew from the very bosom of the arts and sciences, the very fountains of a thousand lapses from rectitude, those famous societies, which, while they are depositaries of the dangerous trust of human knowledge, are yet the sacred guardians of morals, by the attention they pay to their maintenance among themselves in all their purity, and by the demands which they make on every member whom they admit.

These wise institutions, confirmed by his august successor and imitated by all the kings of Europe, will serve at least to restrain men of letters, who, all aspiring to the honour of being admitted into these Academies, will keep watch over themselves, and endeavour to make themselves worthy of such honour by useful performances and irreproachable morals. Those Academies also, which, in proposing prizes for literary merit, make choice of such subjects as are calculated to arouse the love of virtue in the hearts of citizens, prove that it prevails in themselves, and must give men the rare and real pleasure of finding learned societies devoting themselves to the enlightenment of mankind, not only by agreeable exercises of the intellect, but also by useful instructions.

An objection which may be made is, in fact, only an additional proof of my argument. So much precaution proves but too evidently the need for it. We never seek remedies for evils that do not exist. Why, indeed, must these bear all the marks of ordinary remedies, on account of their inefficacy? The numerous establishments in favour of the learned are only adapted to make men mistake the objects of the sciences, and turn men's attention to the cultivation of them. One would be inclined to think, from the precautions everywhere taken, that we are overstocked with husbandmen, and are afraid of a shortage of philosophers. I will not venture here to enter into a comparison between agriculture and philosophy, as they would not bear it. I shall only ask What is philosophy? What is contained in the writings of the most celebrated philosophers? What are the lessons of these friends of wisdom? To hear them, should we not take them for so many mountebanks, exhibiting themselves in public, and crying out, *Here, Here, come to me, I am the only true doctor?* One of them teaches that there is no such thing as matter, but that everything exists only in representation. Another declares that there is no other substance than matter, and no other God than the world itself. A third tells you that there are no such things as virtue and vice, and that moral good and evil are chimeras; while a fourth informs you that men are only beasts of prey, and may conscientiously devour one another. Why, my great philosophers, do you not reserve these wise and profitable lessons for your friends and children? You would soon reap the benefit of them, nor should we be under any apprehension of our own becoming your disciples.

Such are the wonderful men, whom their contemporaries held in the highest esteem during their lives, and to whom immortality has been attributed since their decease. Such are the wise maxims we have received from them, and which are transmitted, from age to age, to our descendants. Paganism, though given over to all the extravagances of human reason, has left nothing to compare with the shameful monuments which have been prepared by the art of printing, during the reign of the gospel. The impious writings of Leucippus and Diagoras perished with their authors. The world, in their days, was ignorant of the art of immortalising the errors and extravagancies of the human mind. But thanks to the art of printing[11] and the use we make of it, the pernicious reflections of Hobbes and Spinoza will last for ever. Go, famous writings,

---

[11] If we consider the frightful disorders which printing has already caused in Europe, and judge of the future by the progress of its evils from day to day, it is easy to foresee that sovereigns will hereafter take as much pains to banish this dreadful art from their dominions, as they ever took to encourage it. The Sultan Achmet, yielding to the importunities of certain pretenders to taste, consented to have a press erected at Constantinople; but it was hardly set to work before they were obliged to destroy it, and throw the plant into a well.

It is related that the Caliph Omar, being asked what should be done with

of which the ignorance and rusticity of our forefathers would
have been incapable. Go to our descendants, along with
those still more pernicious works which reek of the corrupted
manners of the present age! Let them together convey to posterity a faithful history of the progress and advantages of
our arts and sciences. If they are read, they will leave not a
doubt about the question we are now discussing, and unless
mankind should then be still more foolish than we, they will
lift up their hands to Heaven and exclaim in bitterness of
heart: "Almighty God! thou who holdest in Thy hand the
minds of men, deliver us from the fatal arts and sciences of
our forefathers; give us back ignorance, innocence and poverty, which alone can make us happy and are precious in
Thy sight."

But if the progress of the arts and sciences has added
nothing to our real happiness; if it has corrupted our morals,
and if that corruption has vitiated our taste, what are we to
think of the herd of text-book authors, who have removed
those impediments which nature purposely laid in the way
to the Temple of the Muses, in order to guard its approach
and try the powers of those who might be tempted to seek
knowledge? What are we to think of those compilers who
have indiscreetly broken open the door of the sciences, and
introduced into their sanctuary a populace unworthy to approach it, when it was greatly to be wished that all who
should be found incapable of making a considerable progress
in the career of learning should have been repulsed at the
entrance, and thereby cast upon those arts which are useful
to society. A man who will be all his life a bad versifier, or a
third-rate geometrician, might have made nevertheless an
excellent clothier. Those whom nature intended for her disciples have not needed masters. Bacon, Descartes and New-

---

the library at Alexandria, answered in these words: "If the books in the
library contain anything contrary to the Alcoran, they are evil and ought
to be burnt; if they contain only what the Alcoran teaches, they are
superfluous." This reasoning has been cited by our men of letters as the
height of absurdity; but if Gregory the Great had been in the place of
Omar, and the Gospel in the place of the Alcoran, the library would
still have been burnt, and it would have been perhaps the finest action of
his life.

ton, those teachers of mankind, had themselves no teachers. What guide indeed could have taken them so far as their sublime genius directed them? Ordinary masters would only have cramped their intelligence, by confining it within the narrow limits of their own capacity. It was from the obstacles they met with at first, that they learned to exert themselves, and bestirred themselves to traverse the vast field which they covered. If it be proper to allow some men to apply themselves to the study of the arts and sciences, it is only those who feel themselves able to walk alone in their footsteps and to outstrip them. It belongs only to these few to raise monuments to the glory of the human understanding. But if we are desirous that nothing should be above their genius, nothing should be beyond their hopes. This is the only encouragement they require. The soul insensibly adapts itself to the objects on which it is employed, and thus it is that great occasions produce great men. The greatest orator in the world was Consul of Rome, and perhaps the greatest of philosophers Lord Chancellor of England. Can it be conceived that, if the former had only been a professor at some University, and the latter a pensioner of some Academy, their works would not have suffered from their situation. Let not princes disdain to admit into their councils those who are most capable of giving them good advice. Let them renounce the old prejudice, which was invented by the pride of the great, that the art of governing mankind is more difficult than that of instructing them; as if it was easier to induce men to do good voluntarily, than to compel them to it by force. Let the learned of the first rank find an honourable refuge in their courts; let them there enjoy the only recompense worthy of them, that of promoting by their influence the happiness of the peoples they have enlightened by their wisdom. It is by this means only that we are likely to see what virtue, science and authority can do, when animated by the noblest emulation, and working unanimously for the happiness of mankind.

But so long as power alone is on one side, and knowledge and understanding alone on the other, the learned will seldom make great objects their study, princes will still more rarely do great actions, and the peoples will continue to be, as they are, mean, corrupt and miserable.

As for us, ordinary men, on whom Heaven has not been pleased to bestow such great talents; as we are not destined to reap such glory, let us remain in our obscurity. Let us not covet a reputation we should never attain, and which, in the present state of things, would never make up to us for the trouble it would have cost us, even if we were fully qualified to obtain it. Why should we build our happiness on the opinions of others, when we can find it in our own hearts? Let us leave to others the task of instructing mankind in their duty, and confine ourselves to the discharge of our own. We have no occasion for greater knowledge than this.

Virtue! sublime science of simple minds, are such industry and preparation needed if we are to know you? Are not your principles graven on every heart? Need we do more, to learn your laws, than examine ourselves, and listen to the voice of conscience, when the passions are silent?

This is the true philosophy, with which we must learn to be content, without envying the fame of those celebrated men, whose names are immortal in the republic of letters. Let us, instead of envying them, endeavour to make, between them and us, that honourable distinction, which was formerly seen to exist between two great peoples, that the one knew how to speak, and the other how to act, aright.

　　　　　•　　　　　•　　　　　•

This *Discourse* not only won the prize but it made a tremendous sensation among the arrogantly complacent elite, and it made Rousseau famous, or rather notorious, overnight. He was judged a blind man, a mad man, an enemy of the human race. Lessing, almost alone, praised him as a courageous, penetrating thinker, in spite of his excesses.

More in tune with the times was an eloquent, optimistic lecture on the inevitability of progress, "On the Successive Advances of the Human Mind," delivered at the Sorbonne in December, 1750, by a gentleman of twenty-four who was to become known as a great economist and administrator, Turgot. That lecture was repeated again and again in one form or another until the beginning of the First World War.

Rousseau's second discourse presented to the Academy of Dijon, on the question: "What is the origin of inequality among men, and is it authorized by natural law?" did not win the prize, although it was much more coherent and profound than the first, as well as five times longer. In spite of the common interpretation, Rousseau did not argue for the return to the original "state of nature," which he regarded as ignorant and bestial, but he did argue for the organization of a more equitable society. His hopes, however, were not unclouded, for he feared that intellectual progress might be fatally warped by the self-interest of human nature—with catastrophe the result. Anyone who questions this reading may turn to that superb essay on "The Supposed Primitivism of Rousseau's Discourse on Inequality," by Arthur O. Lovejoy, the great pioneer in the study of the history of ideas.

In 1761-1762 Rousseau saw through the press three epoch-making books: the novel *Julie, or The New Héloïse,* which seems to have given a new color to human sentiment, for better or for worse; *The Social Contract,* in which political thinkers of all shades have found their justification; and *Émile, or Education,* which has been a basic factor in discussions of education during the past two centuries. Lessing, Kant, Herder, Goethe and Schiller admired him—but so did Robespierre.

In his last sixteen years Rousseau was both a hunted and a haunted man. *Émile* was condemned by ecclesiastical, legal and academic authorities in Paris and Geneva. His patrons were afraid of being compromised by his presence. Playful gentlemen such as Horace Walpole wrote anonymous letters about him. He began to see enemies everywhere—even among his friends. Yet before the shadows had deepened, Hume met Rousseau in Paris and wrote of him in a letter: "I find him mild, and gentle and modest and good humoured; and he has more of the behaviour of a Man of the World than any of the Learned here, except M. de Buffon. . . . I think Rousseau in many things very much resembles Socrates: The Philosopher of Geneva seems only to have more Genius than he of Athens, who never wrote anything; and less Sociableness and Temper." Hume tried to protect Rousseau in a haven in England but failed pitifully because of malicious gossip and the fugitive's terrible suspicions.

Yet in the last year or so of his life, Rousseau found a kind of serenity and wrote some of the loveliest pages in the French language in *The Reveries of a Solitary Walker*. To Romain Rolland they were like "the beautiful song of an old and melancholy nightingale in the silence of the forest."

IMMANUEL KANT
[1724–1804]

One cannot resist Heine's sharp etchings of famous men. For example: "It is hard to write the story of Immanuel Kant's life, for he had neither life nor story. He led a mechanically ordered, almost abstract, old bachelor's existence, in a quiet, retired alley in Königsberg, an old town on the northeastern border of Germany. I do not believe that the great clock of the cathedral there did its day's work more regularly and impassively than its compatriot, Immanuel Kant. Rising, coffee drinking, writing, lecturing at the university, eating, walking—all had their fixed time, and the neighbors knew that it was exactly half past three when Immanuel Kant in his gray coat, malacca cane in hand, stepped from his house and strolled in the direction of the small avenue of lime trees which is still called, in memory, the Philosopher's Walk. There he promenaded down, in every season, and when bad weather threatened, or gray clouds foretold rain, his old servant Lampe was seen walking anxiously behind him with a long umbrella under his arm, like an image of Providence. What a strange contrast between the man's external life and his destructive, world-convulsing thoughts!" And so on, and so on, toward cynicism, toward malice.

Right or wrong, Kant may well have been the greatest philosopher of modern times and, with the exception of Spinoza, the most completely dedicated. Thanks to the Pietism which swept across Germany in his youth, as Methodism swept across England, his mind was of a deep religious cast. He had an invincible sense of duty. He was the soul of courtesy. Ten days before his death the emaciated, half-blind old man struggled to his feet when his doctor came in for a visit. Of course the doctor remonstrated and heard the muttered answer: "The sense of humanity has not yet left me."

65

Yet this man of immense learning and world-wide sympathies (although he never traveled more than a hundred miles from Königsberg), who lived the mechanically ordered life described by Heine and taught traditional philosophy successfully for years, experienced two profound shocks in mid-career and as a result changed the whole direction of his thinking—and to some extent the Western world's thinking.

He was about forty when he wrote: "I am myself by inclination a seeker after truth. I feel a consuming thirst for knowledge and a restless passion to advance in it, as well as satisfaction in every forward step. There was a time when I thought that this alone could constitute the honor of mankind, and I despised the common man who knows nothing. Rousseau set me right. This blind prejudice vanished; I learned to respect human nature, and I should consider myself far more useless than the ordinary workingman if I did not believe that this view could give worth to all others to establish the rights of man." In Kant's austere study there was but one ornament, a portrait of Rousseau.

He was about fifty when he ran across some lengthy quotations from Hume's *Treatise* and suddenly realized that he had long been philosophizing "dogmatically"—that is, "without any previous investigation of the ability or inability of reason' to ascend philosophy's traditional heights. Hence the oft-quoted phrase: "Hume awakened me from my dogmatic slumber"

As a result of these two crises, what might be called Kant's "Kantian" contributions did not begin until he was approaching sixty, with the publication of the *Critique of Pure Reason*, soon to be followed by a less technical work, *Prolegomena to Any Future Metaphysics*.

As this is not a textbook, we shall not be tempted to present large excerpts from these works and add suitable background and connective tissue. Nor shall we include such an interesting though tangential article as the "Idea for a Universal History with a Cosmopolitan Intent" nor the noble and now well-known discourse "On Perpetual Peace." Rather we will recall to the reader Charles Lamb's curt remark to his publishers: "The *Essays* want no Preface: they are all Preface. A Preface is nothing but a talk with the reader."

So we give you, with Lamb's authority, Kant's Prefaces: to the

Critique of Pure Reason (1781); to the *Prolegomena* (1783); and to the second edition of the *Critique* (1787). This will not be exactly casual talk—but perhaps 'twill serve.

.   .   .

CRITIQUE OF PURE REASON

PREFACE TO FIRST EDITION

Human reason has this peculiar fate that in one species of its knowledge it is burdened by questions which, as prescribed by the very nature of reason itself, it is not able to ignore, but which, as transcending all its powers, it is also not able to answer.

The perplexity into which it thus falls is not due to any fault of its own. It begins with principles which it has no option save to employ in the course of experience, and which this experience at the same time abundantly justifies it in using. Rising with their aid (since it is determined to this also by its own nature) to ever higher, ever more remote, conditions, it soon becomes aware that in this way—the questions never ceasing—its work must always remain incomplete; and it therefore finds itself compelled to resort to principles which overstep all possible empirical employment, and which yet seem so unobjectionable that even ordinary consciousness readily accepts them. But by this procedure human reason precipitates itself into darkness and contradictions; and while it may indeed conjecture that these must be in some way due to concealed errors, it is not in a position to be able to detect them. For since the principles of which it is making use transcend the limits of experience, they are no longer subject to any empirical test. The battle-field of these endless controversies is called metaphysics.

Time was when metaphysics was entitled the Queen of all the sciences; and if the will be taken for the deed, the pre-eminent importance of her accepted tasks gives her every right to this title of honour. Now, however, the changed fashion of the time brings her only scorn; a matron outcast

and forsaken, she mourns like Hecuba: *Modo maxima rerum,
tot generis natisque potens—nunc trahor exul, inops.*[1]

Her government, under the administration of the *dogmatists,* was at first *despotic.* But inasmuch as the legislation still bore traces of the ancient barbarism, her empire gradually through intestine wars gave way to complete anarchy; and the *sceptics,* a species of nomads, despising all settled modes of life, broke up from time to time all civil society. Happily they were few in number, and were unable to prevent its being established ever anew, although on no uniform and self-consistent plan. In more recent times, it has seemed as if an end might be put to all these controversies and the claims of metaphysics receive final judgment, through a certain *physiology* of the human understanding—that of the celebrated Locke. But it has turned out quite otherwise. For however the attempt be made to cast doubt upon the pretensions of the supposed Queen by tracing her lineage to vulgar origins in common experience, this genealogy has, as a matter of fact, been fictitiously invented, and she has still continued to uphold her claims. Metaphysics has accordingly lapsed back into the ancient time-worn dogmatism, and so again suffers that depreciation from which it was to have been rescued. And now, after all methods, so it is believed, have been tried and found wanting, the prevailing mood is that of weariness and complete *indifferentism*—the mother, in all sciences, of chaos and night, but happily in this case the source, or at least the prelude, of their approaching reform and restoration. For it at least puts an end to that ill-applied industry which has rendered them thus dark, confused, and unserviceable.

But it is idle to feign indifference to such enquiries, the object of which can never be indifferent to our human nature. Indeed these pretended *indifferentists,* however they may try to disguise themselves by substituting a popular tone for the language of the Schools, inevitably fall back, in so far as they think at all, into those very metaphysical assertions which they profess so greatly to despise. None the less this

---

[1] Ovid, *Metam[orphoses.* xiii. 508-510].

indifference, showing itself in the midst of flourishing sciences, and affecting precisely those sciences, the knowledge of which, if attainable, we should least of all care to dispense with, is a phenomenon that calls for attention and reflection. It is obviously the effect not of levity but of the matured judgment[2] of the age, which refuses to be any longer put off with illusory knowledge. It is a call to reason to undertake anew the most difficult of all its tasks, namely, that of self-knowledge, and to institute a tribunal which will assure to reason its lawful claims, and dismiss all groundless pretensions, not by despotic decrees, but in accordance with its own eternal and unalterable laws. This tribunal is no other than the *critique of pure reason.*

I do not mean by this a critique of books and systems, but of the faculty of reason in general, in respect of all knowledge after which it may strive *independently of all experience*. It will therefore decide as to the possibility or impossibility of metaphysics in general, and determine its sources, its extent, and its limits—all in accordance with principles.

I have entered upon this path—the only one that has remained unexplored—and flatter myself that in following it I have found a way of guarding against all those errors which have hitherto set reason, in its non-empirical employment, at variance with itself. I have not evaded its questions by pleading the insufficiency of human reason. On the contrary, I have specified these questions exhaustively, according to principles; and after locating the point at which, through misunderstanding, reason comes into conflict with itself, I have

---

[2] We often hear complaints of shallowness of thought in our age and of the consequent decline of sound science. But I do not see that the sciences which rest upon a secure foundation, such as mathematics, physics, etc., in the least deserve this reproach. On the contrary, they merit their old reputation for solidity, and, in the case of physics, even surpass it. The same spirit would have become active in other kinds of knowledge, if only attention had first been directed to the determination of their principles. Till this is done, indifference, doubt, and, in the final issue, severe criticism, are themselves proofs of a profound habit of thought. Our age is, in especial degree, the age of criticism, and to criticism everything must submit. Religion through its sanctity, and law-giving through its majesty, may seek to exempt themselves from it. But they then awaken just suspicion, and cannot claim the sincere respect which reason accords only to that which has been able to sustain the test of free and open examination.

solved them to its complete satisfaction. The answer to these
questions has not, indeed, been such as a dogmatic and visionary insistence upon knowledge might lead us to expect—that
can be catered for only through magical devices, in which I
am no adept. Such ways of answering them are, indeed, not
within the intention of the natural constitution of our reason;
and inasmuch as they have their source in misunderstanding,
it is the duty of philosophy to counteract their deceptive influence, no matter what prized and cherished dreams may
have to be disowned. In this enquiry I have made completeness my chief aim, and I venture to assert that there is not a
single metaphysical problem which has not been solved, or
for the solution of which the key at least has not been sup-
plied. Pure reason is, indeed, so perfect a unity that if its
principle were insufficient for the solution of even a single
one of all the questions to which it itself gives birth we should
have no alternative but to reject the principle, since we
should then no longer be able to place implicit reliance
upon it in dealing with any one of the other questions.

While I am saying this I can fancy that I detect in the
face of the reader an expression of indignation, mingled with
contempt, at pretensions seemingly so arrogant and vain-glori-
ous. Yet they are incomparably more moderate than the
claims of all those writers who on the lines of the usual programme profess to prove the simple nature of the soul or the
necessity of a first beginning of the world. For while such
writers pledge themselves to extend human knowledge beyond all limits of possible experience, I humbly confess that
this is entirely beyond my power. I have to deal with
nothing save reason itself and its pure thinking; and to obtain complete knowledge of these, there is no need to go far
afield, since I come upon them in my own self. Common logic
itself supplies an example, how all the simple acts of reason
can be enumerated completely and systematically. The subject of the present enquiry is the [kindred] question, how
much we can hope to achieve by reason, when all the material and assistance of experience are taken away.

So much as regards *completeness* in our determination of

each question, and *exhaustiveness* in our determination of all the questions with which we have to deal. These questions are not arbitrarily selected; they are prescribed to us, by the very nature of knowledge itself, as being the subject-matter of our critical enquiry.

As regards the *form* of our enquiry, *certainty* and *clearness* are two essential requirements, rightly to be exacted from anyone who ventures upon so delicate an undertaking.

As to *certainty*, I have prescribed to myself the maxim, that in this kind of investigation it is in no wise permissible to hold *opinions*. Everything, therefore, which bears any manner of resemblance to an hypothesis is to be treated as contraband; it is not to be put up for sale even at the lowest price, but forthwith confiscated, immediately upon detection. Any knowledge that professes to hold *a priori* lays claim to be regarded as absolutely necessary. This applies still more to any *determination* of all pure *a priori* knowledge, since such determination has to serve as the measure, and therefore as the [supreme] example, of all apodeictic (philosophical) certainty. Whether I have succeeded in what I have undertaken must be left altogether to the reader's judgment; the author's task is solely to adduce grounds, not to speak as to the effect which they should have upon those who are sitting in judgment. But the author, in order that he may not himself, innocently, be the cause of any weakening of his arguments, may be permitted to draw attention to certain passages, which, although merely incidental, may yet occasion some mistrust. Such timely intervention may serve to counteract the influence which even quite undefined doubts as to these minor matters might otherwise exercise upon the reader's attitude in regard to the main issue.

I know no enquiries which are more important for exploring the faculty which we entitle understanding, and for determining the rules and limits of its employment, than those which I have instituted in the second chapter of the Transcendental Analytic under the title *Deduction of the Pure Concepts of Understanding*. They are also those which have cost me the greatest labour—labour, as I hope, not unrewarded. This enquiry, which is somewhat deeply grounded, has two sides. The one refers to the objects of pure understanding, and is intended to expound and render intelligible the objective validity of its *a priori* concepts. It is therefore essential to my purposes. The other seeks to investigate the pure understanding itself, its possibility and the cognitive faculties upon which it rests; and so deals with it in its subjective aspect. Although this latter exposition is of great importance for my chief purpose, it does not form an essential part of it. For the chief question is always simply this:—what and how much can the understanding and reason know apart from all experience? not:—how is the faculty of thought itself possible? The latter is, as it were, the search for the cause of a given effect, and to that extent is somewhat hypothetical in character (though, as I shall show elsewhere, it is not really so); and I would appear to be taking the liberty simply of expressing an *opinion*, in which case the reader would be free to express a different *opinion*. For this reason I must forestall the reader's criticism by pointing out that the objective deduction with which I am here chiefly concerned retains its full force even if my subjective deduction should fail to produce that complete conviction for which I hope.

As regards *clearness*, the reader has a right to demand, in the first place, a *discursive* (logical) clearness, through *concepts*, and secondly, an *intuitive* (aesthetic) clearness, through *intuitions,* that is, through examples and other concrete illustrations. For the first I have sufficiently provided. That was essential to my purpose; but it has also been the incidental cause of my not being in a position to do justice to the second demand, which, if not so pressing, is yet still quite reasonable. I have been almost continuously at a loss, during the progress of my work, how I should proceed in this matter. Examples and illustrations seemed always to be necessary, and so took their place, as required, in my first draft. But I very soon became aware of the magnitude of my task and of the multiplicity of matters with which I should have to deal; and as I perceived that even if treated in dry, purely *scholastic* fashion, the outcome would by itself be already quite sufficiently large in bulk, I found it inadvisable to enlarge it yet further through examples and illustrations. These are necessary only from a *popular* point of view; and this work can never be made suitable for popular consumption. Such assistance is not required by genuine students of the science, and, though always pleasing, might very well in this case have been self-defeating in its effects. Abbot Terrasson has remarked that if the size of a volume be measured not by the number of its pages but by the time required for mastering it, it can be said of many a book, *that it would be much shorter if it were not so short.* On the other hand, if we have in view the comprehensibility of a whole of speculative knowledge, which, though wide-ranging, has the coherence that follows from unity of principle, we can say with equal justice *that many a book would have been much clearer if it had not made such an effort to be clear.* For the aids to clearness, though they may be of assistance in regard to details, often interfere with our grasp of the whole. The reader is not allowed to arrive sufficiently quickly at a conspectus of the whole; the bright colouring of the illustrative material intervenes to cover over and conceal the articulation and organisation of the system, which, if we are to be able to judge of its unity and solidity, are what chiefly concern us.

The reader, I should judge, will feel it to be no small inducement to yield his willing co-operation, when the author is thus endeavouring, according to the plan here proposed, to carry through a large and important work in a complete and lasting manner. Metaphysics, on the view which we are adopting, is the only one of all the sciences which dares promise that through a small but concentrated effort it will attain, and this in a short time, such completion as will leave no task to our successors save that of adapting it in a *didactic* manner according to their own preferences, without their being able to add anything whatsoever to its content. For it is nothing but the *inventory* of all our possessions through *pure* reason, systematically arranged. In this field nothing can escape us. What reason produces entirely out of itself cannot be concealed, but is brought to light by reason itself immediately the common principle has been discovered. The complete unity of this kind of knowledge, and the fact that it is derived solely from pure concepts, entirely unin-fluenced by any experience or by *special* intuition, such as might lead to any determinate experience that would enlarge and increase it, make this unconditioned completeness not only practicable but also necessary. *Tecum habita, et noris quam sit tibi curta supellex.*[3]

Such a system of pure (speculative) reason I hope myself to produce under the title *Metaphysics of Nature.* It will be not half as large, yet incomparably richer in content than this present *Critique,* which has as its first task to discover the sources and conditions of the possibility of such criticism, clearing, as it were, and levelling what has hitherto been wasteground. In this present enterprise I look to my reader for the patience and impartiality of a *judge;* whereas in the other I shall look for the benevolent assistance of a *fellow-worker.* For however completely all the *principles* of the system are presented in this *Critique,* the completeness of the system itself likewise requires that none of the *derivative* concepts be lacking. These cannot be enumerated by any *a priori* computation, but must be discovered gradually. Whereas, therefore, in this *Critique* the entire *synthesis* of the concepts has been exhausted, there will still remain the further work of making their *analysis* similarly complete, a task which is rather an amusement than a labour.

PROLEGOMENA TO ANY FUTURE METAPHYSICS

PREFACE

These *Prolegomena* are for the use, not of mere learners, but of future teachers, and even the latter should not expect that they will be serviceable for the systematic exposition of

---

[3] Persius [*Satires.* iv. 52].

a ready-made science, but merely for the discovery of the science itself.

There are scholarly men to whom the history of philosophy (both ancient and modern) is philosophy itself; for these the present *Prolegomena* are not written. They must wait till those who endeavor to draw from the fountain of reason itself have completed their work; it will then be the turn of these scholars to inform the world of what has been done. Unfortunately, nothing can be said which, in their opinion, has not been said before, and truly the same prophecy applies to all future time; for since the human reason has for many centuries speculated upon innumerable objects in various ways, it is hardly to be expected that we should not be able to discover analogies for every new idea among the old sayings of past ages.

My purpose is to persuade all those who think metaphysics worth studying that it is absolutely necessary to pause a moment and, regarding all that has been done as though undone, to propose first the preliminary question, "Whether such a thing as metaphysics be even possible at all?"

If it be science, how is it that it cannot, like other sciences, obtain universal and lasting recognition? If not, how can it maintain its pretensions and keep the human mind in suspense with hopes never ceasing, yet never fulfilled? Whether then we demonstrate our knowledge or our ignorance in this field, we must come once for all to a definite conclusion respecting the nature of this so-called science, which cannot possibly remain on its present footing. It seems almost ridiculous, while every other science is continually advancing, that in this, which pretends to be wisdom incarnate, for whose oracle everyone inquires, we should constantly move round the same spot, without gaining a single step. And so its votaries having melted away, we do not find men confident of their ability to shine in other sciences venturing their reputation here, where everybody, however ignorant in other matters, presumes to deliver a final verdict, because in this domain there is actually as yet no standard weight and measure to distinguish sound knowledge from shallow talk.

After all it is nothing extraordinary in the elaboration of a science that, when men begin to wonder how far it has advanced, the question should at last occur whether and how such a science is possible at all. Human reason so delights in building that it has several times built up a tower and then razed it to see how the foundation was laid. It is never too late to become reasonable and wise; but if the knowledge comes late, there is always more difficulty in starting a reform.

The question whether a science be possible presupposes a doubt as to its actuality. But such a doubt offends the men whose whole fortune consists of this supposed jewel; hence he who raises the doubt must expect opposition from all sides. Some, in the proud consciousness of their possessions, which are ancient and therefore considered legitimate, will take their metaphysical compendia in their hands and look down on him with contempt; others, who never see anything except it be identical with what they have elsewhere seen before, will not understand him, and everything will remain for a time as if nothing had happened to excite the concern or the hope for an impending change.

Nevertheless, I venture to predict that the independent reader of these *Prolegomena* will not only doubt his previous science, but ultimately be fully persuaded that it cannot exist unless the demands here stated on which its possibility depends be satisfied; and, as this has never been done, that there is, as yet, no such thing as metaphysics. But as it can never cease to be in demand[1]—since the interests of common sense are so intimately interwoven with it—he must confess that a radical reform, or rather a new birth of the science, after a new plan, is unavoidable, however men may struggle against it for a while.

---

[1] Says Horace:

> *Rusticus expectat, dum defluat amnis, at ille*
> *Labitur et labetur in omne volubilis aevum.*

> ["A rustic fellow waiteth on the shore
> For the river to flow away,
> But the river flows, and flows on as before,
> And it flows forever and aye".]
>   —*Epistle* I, 2, 42f.

Since the *Essays* of Locke and Leibniz, or rather since the origin of metaphysics so far as we know its history, nothing has ever happened which could have been more decisive to its fate than the attack made upon it by David Hume. He threw no light on this species of knowledge, but he certainly struck a spark by which light might have been kindled had it caught some inflammable substance and had its smouldering fire been carefully nursed and developed.

Hume started chiefly from a single but important concept in metaphysics, namely, that of the connection of cause and effect (including its derivatives force and action, and so on). He challenged reason, which pretends to have given birth to this concept of herself, to answer him by what right she thinks anything could be so constituted that if that thing be posited, something else also must necessarily be posited; for this is the meaning of the concept of cause. He demonstrated irrefutably that it was perfectly impossible for reason to think *a priori* and by means of concepts such a combination, for it implies necessity. We cannot at all see why, in consequence of the existence of one thing, another must necessarily exist or how the concept of such a combination can arise *a priori*. Hence he inferred that reason was altogether deluded with reference to this concept, which she erroneously considered as one of her own children, whereas in reality it was nothing but a bastard of imagination, impregnated by experience, which subsumed certain representations under the law of association and mistook a subjective necessity (habit) for an objective necessity arising from insight. Hence he inferred that reason had no power to think such combinations, even in general, because her concepts would then be purely fictitious and all her pretended *a priori* cognitions nothing but common experiences marked with a false stamp. In plain language, this means that there is not and cannot be any such thing as metaphysics at all.[2]

[2] Nevertheless Hume called this destructive science metaphysics and attached to it great value. "Metaphysics and morals," he declares, "are the most considerable branches of science. Mathematics and natural philosophy are not half so valuable" ["Of the Rise and Progress of the Arts and Sciences," *Essays Moral, Political, and Literary*, XIV]. But the acute man

However hasty and mistaken Hume's inference may appear, it was at least founded upon investigation, and this investigation deserved the concentrated attention of the brighter spirits of his day as well as determined efforts on their part to discover, if possible, a happier solution of the problem in the sense proposed by him, all of which would have speedily resulted in a complete reform of the science.

But Hume suffered the usual misfortune of metaphysicians, of not being understood. It is positively painful to see how utterly his opponents, Reid, Oswald, Beattie, and lastly Priestley, missed the point of the problem; for while they were ever taking for granted that which he doubted, and demonstrating with zeal and often with impudence that which he never thought of doubting, they so misconstrued his valuable suggestion that everything remained in its old condition, as if nothing had happened. The question was not whether the concept of cause was right, useful, and even indispensable for our knowledge of nature, for this Hume had never doubted; but whether that concept could be thought by reason *a priori*, and consequently whether it possessed an inner truth, independent of all experience, implying a perhaps more extended use not restricted merely to objects of experience. This was Hume's problem. It was solely a question concerning the *origin*, not concerning the *indispensable* need of using the concept. Were the former decided, the conditions of the use and the sphere of its valid application would have been determined as a matter of course.

But to satisfy the conditions of the problem, the opponents of the great thinker should have penetrated very deeply into the nature of reason, so far as it is concerned with pure thinking—a task which did not suit them. They found a more convenient method of being defiant without any insight, namely, the appeal to *common sense*. It is indeed a great gift of God

---

merely regarded the negative use arising from the moderation of extravagant claims of speculative reason, and the complete settlement of the many endless and troublesome controversies that mislead mankind. He overlooked the positive injury which results if reason be deprived of its most important prospects, which can alone supply to the will the highest aim for all its endeavors.

to possess right or (as they now call it) plain common sense. But this common sense must be shown in action by well-considered and reasonable thoughts and words, not by appealing to it as an oracle when no rational justification for one's position can be advanced. To appeal to common sense when insight and science fail, and no sooner—this is one of the subtle discoveries of modern times, by means of which the most superficial ranter can safely enter the lists with the most thorough thinker and hold his own. But as long as a particle of insight remains, no one would think of having recourse to this subterfuge. Seen clearly, it is but an appeal to the opinion of the multitude, of whose applause the philosopher is ashamed, while the popular charlatan glories and boasts in it. I should think that Hume might fairly have laid as much claim to common sense as Beattie and, in addition, to a critical reason (such as the latter did not possess), which keeps common sense in check and prevents it from speculating, or, if speculations are under discussion, restrains the desire to decide because it cannot satisfy itself concerning its own premises. By this means alone can common sense remain sound. Chisels and hammers may suffice to work a piece of wood, but for etching we require an etcher's needle. Thus common sense and speculative understanding are each serviceable, but each in its own way: the former in judgments which apply immediately to experience; the latter when we judge universally from mere concepts, as in metaphysics, where that which calls itself, in spite of the inappropriateness of the name, sound common sense, has no right to judge at all.

I openly confess my recollection of David Hume was the very thing which many years ago first interrupted my dogmatic slumber and gave my investigations in the field of speculative philosophy a quite new direction. I was far from following him in the conclusions at which he arrived by regarding, not the whole of his problem, but a part, which by itself can give us no information. If we start from a well-founded, but undeveloped, thought which another has bequeathed to us, we may well hope by continued reflection to advance farther than the acute man to whom we owe the first spark of light.

I therefore first tried whether Hume's objection could not be put into a general form, and soon found that the concept of the connection of cause and effect was by no means the only concept by which the understanding thinks the connection of things *a priori*, but rather that metaphysics consists altogether of such concepts. I sought to ascertain their number; and when I had satisfactorily succeeded in this by starting from a single principle, I proceeded to the deduction of these concepts, which I was now certain were not derived from experience, as Hume had attempted to derive them, but sprang from the pure understanding. This deduction (which seemed impossible to my acute predecessor, which had never even occurred to anyone else, though no one had hesitated to use the concepts without investigating the basis of their objective validity) was the most difficult task which ever could have been undertaken in the service of metaphysics; and the worst was that metaphysics, such as it is, could not assist me in the least because this deduction alone can render metaphysics possible. But as soon as I had succeeded in solving Hume's problem, not merely in a particular case, but with respect to the whole faculty of pure reason, I could proceed safely, though slowly, to determine the whole sphere of pure reason completely and from universal principles, in its boundaries as well as in its contents. This was required for metaphysics in order to construct its system according to a safe plan.

But I fear that the execution of Hume's problem in its widest extent (namely, my *Critique of Pure Reason*) will fare as the problem itself fared when first proposed. It will be misjudged because it is misunderstood, and misunderstood because men choose to skim through the book and not to think through it—a disagreeable task, because the work is dry, obscure, opposed to all ordinary notions, and moreover long-winded. I confess, however, I did not expect to hear from philosophers complaints of want of popularity, entertainment, and facility when the existence of highly prized and indispensable knowledge is at stake, which cannot be established otherwise than by the strictest rules of a scholastic precision. Popularity may follow, but is inadmissible at the beginning. Yet as regards a certain obscurity, arising partly from the diffuseness of the plan, owing to which the principal points of the investigation are easily lost sight of, the complaint is just, and I intend to remove it by the present *Prolegomena*.

The first-mentioned work, which discusses the pure faculty of reason in its whole compass and bounds, will remain the foundation, to which the *Prolegomena*, as a preliminary exercise, refer; for critique as a science must first be established as complete and perfect before we can think of letting metaphysics appear on the scene or even have the most distant hope of attaining it.

We have been long accustomed to seeing antiquated knowledge produced as new by taking it out of its former context and fitting it into a systematic garment of any fancy pattern with new titles. Most readers will set out by expecting nothing else from the *Critique;* but these *Prolegomena* may persuade him that it is a perfectly new science, of which no one has ever even thought, the very idea of which was unknown, and for which nothing hitherto accomplished can be of the smallest use, except it be the suggestion of Hume's doubts. Yet even he did not suspect such a formal science, but ran his ship ashore, for safety's sake, landing on scepticism, there to let it lie and rot; whereas my object is rather to give it a pilot, who, by means of safe principles of navigation drawn from a knowledge of the globe, and provided with a complete chart and compass, may steer the ship safely whither he listeth.

If in a new science which is wholly isolated and unique in its kind, we started with the prejudice that we can judge of things by means of alleged knowledge previously acquired —though this is precisely what has first to be called in question—we should only fancy we saw everywhere what we had already known, because the expressions have a similar sound. But everything would appear utterly metamorphosed, senseless, and unintelligible, because we should have as a foundation our own thoughts, made by long habit a second nature, instead of the author's. But the long-windedness of the work, so far as it depends on the subject and not on the exposition, its consequent unavoidable dryness and its scholastic precision, are qualities which can only benefit the science, though they may discredit the book.

Few writers are gifted with the subtlety and, at the same time, with the grace of David Hume, or with the depth, as well as the elegance, of Moses Mendelssohn. Yet I flatter myself I might have made my own exposition popular had my object been merely to sketch out a plan and leave its completion to others, instead of having my heart in the welfare of the science to which I had devoted myself so long; in truth, it required no little constancy, and even self-denial, to postpone the sweets of an immediate success to the prospect of a slower, but more lasting, reputation.

Making plans is often the occupation of an opulent and boastful mind, which thus obtains the reputation of a creative genius by demanding what it cannot itself supply, by censuring what it cannot improve, and by proposing what it knows not where to find. And yet something more should belong to a sound plan of a general critique of pure reason than mere conjectures if this plan is to be other than the usual declamations of pious aspirations. But pure reason is a sphere so separate and self-contained that we cannot touch a part without affecting all the rest. We can do nothing without first determining the position of each part and its relation to the rest; for, as our judgment within this sphere cannot be corrected by anything without, the validity and use of every part depends upon the relation in which it stands to all the rest within the domain of reason. As in the structure of an organized body, the end of each member can only be deduced from the full conception of the whole. It may, then, be said of such a critique that it is never trustworthy except it be perfectly complete, down to the most minute elements of pure reason. In the sphere of this faculty you can determine and define either everything or nothing.

But although a mere sketch preceding the *Critique of Pure Reason* would be unintelligible, unreliable, and useless, it is all the more useful as a sequel. It enables us to grasp the whole, to examine in detail the chief points of importance in the science, and to improve in many respects our exposition, as compared with the first execution of the work.

With that work complete, I offer here a sketch based on an *analytical* method, while the *Critique* itself had to be executed in the *synthetical* style, in order that the science may present all its articulations, as the structure of a peculiar cognitive faculty, in their natural combination. But should any reader find this sketch, which I publish as the *Prolegomena to Any Future Metaphysics*, still obscure, let him consider that not everyone is bound to study metaphysics; that many minds will succeed very well in the exact and even in deep sciences more closely allied to the empirical, while they cannot succeed in investigations dealing exclusively with abstract concepts. In such cases men should apply their talents to other subjects. But he who undertakes to judge or, still more, to construct a system of metaphysics must satisfy the demands here made, either by adopting my solution or by thoroughly refuting it and substituting another. To evade it is impossible.

In conclusion, let it be remembered that this much abused obscurity (frequently serving as a mere pretext under which people hide their own indolence or dullness) has its uses, since all who in other sciences observe a judicious silence speak authoritatively in metaphysics and make bold decisions, because their ignorance is not here contrasted with the knowledge of others. Yet it does contrast with sound critical principles, which we may therefore commend in the words of Virgil:

Ignavum, fucos, pecus a praesepibus arcent.[3]

---

[3] ["They defend the hives against drones, those indolent creatures." —*Georgics* IV, 168.]

CRITIQUE OF PURE REASON

PREFACE TO SECOND EDITION

Whether the treatment of such knowledge as lies within the province of reason does or does not follow the secure path of a science, is easily to be determined from the outcome. For if after elaborate preparations, frequently renewed, it is brought to a stop immediately it nears its goal; if often it is compelled to retrace its steps and strike into some new line of approach; or again, if the various participants are unable to agree in any common plan of procedure, then we may rest assured that it is very far from having entered upon the secure path of a science, and is indeed a merely random groping. In these circumstances, we shall be rendering a service to reason should we succeed in discovering the path upon which it can securely travel, even if, as a result of so doing, much that is comprised in our original aims, adopted without reflection, may have to be abandoned as fruitless.

That logic has already, from the earliest times, proceeded upon this sure path is evidenced by the fact that since Aristotle it has not required to retrace a single step, unless, indeed, we care to count as improvements the removal of certain needless subtleties or the clearer exposition of its recognised teaching, features which concern the elegance rather than the certainty of the science. It is remarkable also that to the present day this logic has not been able to advance a single step, and is thus to all appearance a closed and completed body of doctrine. If some of the moderns have thought to enlarge it by introducing *psychological* chapters on the different faculties of knowledge (imagination, wit, etc.), *metaphysical* chapters on the origin of knowledge or on the different kinds of certainty according to difference in the objects (idealism, scepticism, etc.), or *an-*

thropological chapters on prejudices, their causes and remedies, this could only arise from their ignorance of the peculiar
nature of logical science. We do not enlarge but disfigure
sciences, if we allow them to trespass upon one another's
territory. The sphere of logic is quite precisely delimited;
its sole concern is to give an exhaustive exposition and a
strict proof of the formal rules of all thought, whether it be
a priori or empirical, whatever be its origin or its object,
and whatever hindrances, accidental or natural, it may encounter in our minds.

That logic should have been thus successful is an advantage which it owes entirely to its limitations, whereby it is
justified in abstracting—indeed, it is under obligation to do
so—from all objects of knowledge and their differences, leaving the understanding nothing to deal with save itself and its
form. But for reason to enter on the sure path of science is,
of course, much more difficult, since it has to deal not with
itself alone but also with objects. Logic, therefore, as a propaedeutic, forms, as it were, only the vestibule of the sciences;
and when we are concerned with specific modes of knowledge, while logic is indeed presupposed in any critical
estimate of them, yet for the actual acquiring of them we
have to look to the sciences properly and objectively so called.

Now if reason is to be a factor in these sciences, something
in them must be known *a priori*, and this knowledge may be
related to its object in one or other of two ways, either as
merely *determining* it and its concept (which must be sup-
plied from elsewhere) or as also *making it actual*. The former
is *theoretical*, the latter *practical* knowledge of reason. In
both, that part in which reason determines its object completely *a priori*, namely, the *pure* part—however much or little
this part may contain—must be first and separately dealt with,
in case it be confounded with what comes from other sources.
For it is bad management if we blindly pay out what comes
in, and are not able, when the income falls into arrears, to
distinguish which part of it can justify expenditure, and in
which line we must make reductions.

Mathematics and physics, the two sciences in which reason

yields theoretical knowledge, have to determine their objects
a priori, the former doing so quite purely, the latter having
to reckon, at least partially, with sources of knowledge other
than reason.

In the earliest times to which the history of human reason
extends, *mathematics,* among that wonderful people, the
Greeks, had already entered upon the sure path of science.
But it must not be supposed that it was as easy for mathematics as it was for logic—in which reason has to deal with
itself alone—to light upon, or rather to construct for itself,
that royal road. On the contrary, I believe that it long remained, especially among the Egyptians, in the groping stage,
and that the transformation must have been due to a *revolution* brought about by the happy thought of a single man,
the experiment which he devised marking out the path
upon which the science must enter, and by following which,
secure progress throughout all time and in endless expansion
is infallibly secured. The history of this intellectual revolution
—far more important than the discovery of the passage round
the celebrated Cape of Good Hope—and of its fortunate
author, has not been preserved. But the fact that Diogenes
Laertius, in handing down an account of these matters,
names the reputed author of even the least important among
the geometrical demonstrations, even of those which, for
ordinary consciousness, stand in need of no such proof, does
at least show that the memory of the revolution, brought
about by the first glimpse of this new path, must have seemed
to mathematicians of such outstanding importance as to
cause it to survive the tide of oblivion. A new light flashed
upon the mind of the first man (be he Thales or some other)
who demonstrated the properties of the isosceles triangle.
The true method, so he found, was not to inspect what he
discerned either in the figure, or in the bare concept of it,
and from this, as it were, to read off its properties; but to
bring out what was necessarily implied in the concepts that
he had himself formed *a priori,* and had put into the figure
in the construction by which he presented it to himself. If
he is to know anything with *a priori* certainty he must not

ascribe to the figure anything save what necessarily follows from what he has himself set into it in accordance with his concept.

Natural science was very much longer in entering upon the highway of science. It is, indeed, only about a century and a half since Bacon, by his ingenious proposals, partly initiated this discovery, partly inspired fresh vigour in those who were already on the way to it. In this case also the discovery can be explained as being the sudden outcome of an intellectual revolution. In my present remarks I am referring to natural science only in so far as it is founded on *empirical* principles.

When Galileo caused balls, the weights of which he had himself previously determined, to roll down an inclined plane; when Torricelli made the air carry a weight which he had calculated beforehand to be equal to that of a definite column of water; or in more recent times, when Stahl changed metal into lime, and lime back into metal, by withdrawing something and then restoring it,[1] a light broke upon all students of nature. They learned that reason has insight only into that which it produces after a plan of its own, and that it must not allow itself to be kept, as it were, in nature's leading-strings, but must itself show the way with principles of judgment based upon fixed laws, constraining nature to give answer to questions of reason's own determining. Accidental observations, made in obedience to no previously thought-out plan, can never be made to yield a necessary law, which alone reason is concerned to discover. Reason, holding in one hand its principles, according to which alone concordant appearances can be admitted as equivalent to laws, and in the other hand the experiment which it has devised in conformity with these principles, must approach nature in order to be taught by it. It must not, however, do so in the character of a pupil who listens to everything that the teacher chooses to say, but of an appointed judge who

---

[1] I am not, in my choice of examples, tracing the exact course of the history of the experimental method; we have indeed no very precise knowledge of its first beginnings.

compels the witnesses to answer questions which he has himself formulated. Even physics, therefore, owes the beneficent revolution in its point of view entirely to the happy thought, that while reason must seek in nature, not fictitiously ascribe to it, whatever as not being knowable through reason's own resources has to be learnt, if learnt at all, only from nature, it must adopt as its guide, in so seeking, that which it has itself put into nature. It is thus that the study of nature has entered on the secure path of a science, after having for so many centuries been nothing but a process of merely random groping.

Metaphysics is a completely isolated speculative science of reason, which soars far above the teachings of experience, and in which reason is indeed meant to be its own pupil. Metaphysics rests on concepts alone—not, like mathematics, on their application to intuition. But though it is older than all other sciences, and would survive even if all the rest were swallowed up in the abyss of an all-destroying barbarism, it has not yet had the good fortune to enter upon the secure path of a science. For in it reason is perpetually being brought to a stand, even when the laws into which it is seeking to have, as it professes, an *a priori* insight are those that are confirmed by our most common experiences. Ever and again we have to retrace our steps, as not leading us in the direction in which we desire to go. So far, too, are the students of metaphysics from exhibiting any kind of unanimity in their contentions, that metaphysics has rather to be regarded as a battle-ground quite peculiarly suited for those who desire to exercise themselves in mock combats, and in which no participant has ever yet succeeded in gaining even so much as an inch of territory, not at least in such manner as to secure him in its permanent possession. This shows, beyond all questioning, that the procedure of metaphysics has hitherto been a merely random groping, and, what is worst of all, a groping among mere concepts.

What, then, is the reason why, in this field, the sure road to science has not hitherto been found? Is it, perhaps, impossible of discovery? Why, in that case, should nature have visited our reason with the restless endeavour whereby it is ever searching for such a path, as if this were one of its most important concerns. Nay, more, how little cause have we to place trust in our reason, if, in one of the most important domains of which we would fain have knowledge, it does not merely fail us, but lures us on by deceitful promises, and in the end betrays us! Or if it be only that we have thus far failed to find the true path, are there any indications to justify the hope that by renewed efforts we may have better fortune than has fallen to our predecessors?

The examples of mathematics and natural science, which by a single and sudden revolution have become what they now are, seem to me sufficiently remarkable to suggest our considering what may have been the essential features in the changed point of view by which they have so greatly benefited. Their success should incline us, at least by way of experiment, to imitate their procedure, so far as the analogy which, as species of rational knowledge, they bear to metaphysics may permit. Hitherto it has been assumed that all our knowledge must conform to objects. But all attempts to extend our knowledge of objects by establishing something in regard to them *a priori*, by means of concepts, have, on this assumption, ended in failure. We must therefore make trial whether we may not have more success in the tasks of metaphysics, if we suppose that objects must conform to our knowledge. This would agree better with what is desired, namely, that it should be possible to have knowledge of objects *a priori*, determining something in regard to them prior to their being given. We should then be proceeding precisely on the lines of Copernicus' primary hypothesis. Failing of satisfactory progress in explaining the movements of the heavenly bodies on the supposition that they all revolved round the spectator, he tried whether he might not have better success if he made the spectator to revolve and the stars to remain at rest. A similar experiment can be tried in metaphysics, as regards the *intuition* of objects. If intuition must conform to the constitution of the objects, I do not see how we could know anything of the latter *a priori;* but if the object (as object of the senses) must conform to the consti-tution of our faculty of intuition, I have no difficulty in con-ceiving such a possibility. Since I cannot rest in these intu-itions if they are to become known, but must relate them as representations to something as their object, and determine this latter through them, either I must assume that the *con-cepts,* by means of which I obtain this determination, con-form to the object, or else I assume that the objects, or what is the same thing, that the *experience* in which alone, as given objects, they can be known, conform to the concepts. In the former case, I am again in the same perplexity as to how I can know anything *a priori* in regard to the objects. In the latter case the outlook is more hopeful. For experience is itself a species of knowledge which involves understanding; and understanding has rules which I must presuppose as being in me prior to objects being given to me, and therefore as being *a priori.* They find expression in *a priori* concepts to which all objects of experience necessarily conform, and with which they must agree. As regards objects which are thought solely through reason, and indeed as necessary, but which can never—at least not in the manner in which reason thinks them—be given in experience, the attempts at thinking them (for they must admit of being thought) will furnish an excellent touchstone of what we are adopting as our new method of thought, namely, that we can know *a priori* of things only what we ourselves put into them.[2]

This experiment succeeds as well as could be desired, and

---

[2] This method, modelled on that of the student of nature, consists in looking for the elements of pure reason in *what admits of confirmation or refutation by experiment* Now the propositions of pure reason, especially if they venture out beyond all limits of possible experience, cannot be brought to the test through any experiment with their *objects,* as in natural science. In dealing with those *concepts* and *principles* which we adopt *a priori,* all that we can do is to contrive that they be used for viewing objects from two different points of view—on the one hand, in connection with experience, as objects of the senses and of the understanding, and on the other hand, for the isolated reason that strives to transcend all limits of experience, as objects which are thought merely. If, when things are viewed from this twofold standpoint, we find that there is agreement with the principle of pure reason, but that when we regard them only from a single point of view reason is involved in unavoidable self-conflict, the experiment decides in favour of the correctness of this distinction.

promises to metaphysics, in its first part—the part that is occupied with those concepts *a priori* to which the corresponding objects, commensurate with them, can be given in experience—the secure path of a science. For the new point of view enables us to explain how there can be knowledge *a priori;* and, in addition, to furnish satisfactory proofs of the laws which form the *a priori* basis of nature, regarded as the sum of the objects of experience—neither achievement being possible on the procedure hitherto followed. But this deduction of our power of knowing *a priori,* in the first part of metaphysics, has a consequence which is startling, and which has the appearance of being highly prejudicial to the whole purpose of metaphysics, as dealt with in the second part. For we are brought to the conclusion that we can never transcend the limits of possible experience, though that is precisely what this science is concerned, above all else, to achieve. This situation yields, however, just the very experiment by which, indirectly, we are enabled to prove the truth of this first estimate of our *a priori* knowledge of reason, namely, that such knowledge has to do only with appearances, and must leave the thing in itself as indeed real *per se,* but as not known by us. For what necessarily forces us to transcend the limits of experience and of all appearances is the *unconditioned,* which reason, by necessity and by right, demands in things in themselves, as required to complete the series of conditions. If, then, on the supposition that our empirical knowledge conforms to objects as things in themselves, we find that the unconditioned *cannot be thought without contradiction,* and that when, on the other hand, we suppose that our representation of things, as they are given to us, does not conform to these things as they are in themselves, but that these objects, as appearances, conform to our mode of representation, *the contradiction vanishes;* and if, therefore, we thus find that the unconditioned is not to be met with in things, so far as we know them, that is, so far as they are given to us, but only so far as we do not know them, that is, so far as they are things in themselves, we are

justified in concluding that what we at first assumed for
the purposes of experiment is now definitely confirmed.[3] But
when all progress in the field of the supersensible has thus
been denied to speculative reason, it is still open to us to
enquire whether, in the practical knowledge of reason, data
may not be found sufficient to determine reason's transcendent concept of the unconditioned, and so to enable us, in
accordance with the wish of metaphysics, and by means of
knowledge that is possible *a priori,* though only from a practical point of view, to pass beyond the limits of all possible
experience. Speculative reason has thus at least made room
for such an extension; and if it must at the same time leave
it empty, yet none the less we are at liberty, indeed we are
summoned, to take occupation of it, if we can, by practical
data of reason.[4]

This attempt to alter the procedure which has hitherto
prevailed in metaphysics, by completely revolutionising it
in accordance with the example set by the geometers and
physicists, forms indeed the main purpose of this critique of
pure speculative reason. It is a treatise on the method, not
a system of the science itself. But at the same time it marks
out the whole plan of the science, both as regards its limits
and as regards its entire internal structure. For pure specula-

---

[3] This experiment of pure reason bears a great similarity to what in
chemistry is sometimes entitled the experiment of *reduction,* or more
usually the *synthetic* process. The *analysis of the metaphysician* separates
pure *a priori* knowledge into two very heterogeneous elements, namely, the
knowledge of things as appearances, and the knowledge of things in themselves; his *dialectic* combines these two again, in *harmony* with the necessary
idea of the *unconditioned* demanded by reason, and finds that this harmony
can never be obtained except through the above distinction, which must
therefore be accepted.

[4] Similarly, the fundamental laws of the motions of the heavenly bodies
gave established certainty to what Copernicus had at first assumed only
as an hypothesis, and at the same time yielded proof of the invisible force
(the Newtonian attraction) which holds the universe together. The latter
would have remained for ever undiscovered if Copernicus had not dared,
in a manner contradictory of the senses, but yet true, to seek the observed
movements, not in the heavenly bodies, but in the spectator. The change
in point of view, analogous to this hypothesis, which is expounded in the
Critique, I put forward in this preface as an hypothesis only, in order
to draw attention to the character of these first attempts at such a change,
which are always hypothetical. But in the *Critique* itself it will be proved,
apodeictically not hypothetically, from the nature of our representations
of space and time and from the elementary concepts of the understanding.

tive reason has this peculiarity, that it can measure its powers according to the different ways in which it chooses the objects of its thinking, and can also give an exhaustive enumeration of the various ways in which it propounds its problems, and so is able, nay bound, to trace the complete outline of a system of metaphysics. As regards the first point, nothing in *a priori* knowledge can be ascribed to objects save what the thinking subject derives from itself; as regards the second point, pure reason, so far as the principles of its knowledge are concerned, is a quite separate self-subsistent unity, in which, as in an organised body, every member exists for every other, and all for the sake of each, so that no principle can safely be taken in *any one* relation, unless it has been investigated in the *entirety* of its relations to the whole employment of pure reason. Consequently, metaphysics has also this singular advantage, such as falls to the lot of no other science which deals with objects (for *logic* is concerned only with the form of thought in general), that should it, through this critique, be set upon the secure path of a science, it is capable of acquiring exhaustive knowledge of its entire field. Metaphysics has to deal only with principles, and with the limits of their employment as determined by these principles themselves, and it can therefore finish its work and bequeath it to posterity as a capital to which no addition can be made. Since it is a fundamental science, it is under obligation to achieve this completeness. We must be able to say of it: *nil actum reputans, si quid superesset agendum.*

But, it will be asked, what sort of a treasure is this that we propose to bequeath to posterity? What is the value of the metaphysics that is alleged to be thus purified by criticism and established once for all? On a cursory view of the present work it may seem that its results are merely *negative*, warning us that we must never venture with speculative reason beyond the limits of experience. Such is in fact its primary use. But such teaching at once acquires a *positive* value when we recognise that the principles with which

speculative reason ventures out beyond its proper limits do
not in effect *extend* the employment of reason, but, as we
find on closer scrutiny, inevitably *narrow* it. These principles
properly belong [not to reason but] to sensibility, and when
thus employed they threaten to make the bounds of sensibility
coextensive with the real, and so to supplant reason in its
pure (practical) employment. So far, therefore, as our Critique limits speculative reason, it is indeed *negative;* but since
it thereby removes an obstacle which stands in the way of
the employment of practical reason, nay threatens to destroy
it, it has in reality a *positive* and very important use. At least
this is so, immediately we are convinced that there is an
absolutely necessary *practical* employment of pure reason—
the *moral*—in which it inevitably goes beyond the limits of
sensibility. Though [practical] reason, in thus proceeding,
requires no assistance from speculative reason, it must yet
be assured against its opposition, that reason may not be
brought into conflict with itself. To deny that the service
which the Critique renders is *positive* in character, would
thus be like saying that the police are of no positive benefit,
inasmuch as their main business is merely to prevent the
violence of which citizens stand in mutual fear, in order that
each may pursue his vocation in peace and security. That
space and time are only forms of sensible intuition, and so
only conditions of the existence of things as appearances;
that, moreover, we have no concepts of understanding, and
consequently no elements for the knowledge of things, save
in so far as intuition can be given corresponding to these
concepts; and that we can therefore have no knowledge of
any object as thing in itself, but only in so far as it is an
object of sensible intuition, that is, an appearance—all this is
proved in the analytical part of the Critique. Thus it does indeed follow that all possible speculative knowledge of reason
is limited to mere objects of *experience.* But our further contention must also be duly borne in mind, namely, that though
we cannot *know* these objects as things in themselves, we
must yet be in position at least to *think* them as things in

themselves;[5] otherwise we should be landed in the absurd conclusion that there can be appearance without anything that appears. Now let us suppose that the distinction, which our Critique has shown to be necessary, between things as objects of experience and those same things as things in themselves, had not been made. In that case all things in general, as far as they are efficient causes, would be determined by the principle of causality, and consequently by the mechanism of nature. I could not, therefore, without palpable contradiction, say of one and the same being, for instance the human soul, that its will is free and yet is subject to natural necessity, that is, is not free. For I have taken the soul in both propositions *in one and the same sense*, namely as a thing in general, that is, as a thing in itself; and save by means of a preceding critique, could not have done otherwise. But if our Critique is not in error in teaching that the object is to be taken *in a twofold sense*, namely as appearance and as thing in itself; if the deduction of the concepts of understanding is valid, and the principle of causality therefore applies only to things taken in the former sense, namely, in so far as they are objects of experience—these same objects, taken in the other sense, not being subject to the principle—then there is no contradiction in supposing that one and the same will is, in the appearance, that is, in its visible acts, necessarily subject to the law of nature, and so far *not free*, while yet, as belonging to a thing in itself, it is not subject to that law, and is therefore *free*. My soul, viewed from the latter standpoint, cannot indeed be known by means of speculative reason (and still less through empirical observation); and freedom as a property of a being to which I attribute effects in the sensible world, is therefore also not

---

[5] To *know* an object I must be able to prove its possibility, either from its actuality as attested by experience, or *a priori* by means of reason. But I can *think* whatever I please, provided only that I do not contradict myself, that is, provided my concept is a possible thought. This suffices for the possibility of the concept, even though I may not be able to answer for there being, in the sum of all possibilities, an object corresponding to it. But something more is required before I can ascribe to such a concept objective validity, that is, real possibility; the former possibility is merely logical. This something more need not, however, be sought in the theoretical sources of knowledge; it may lie in those that are practical.

knowable in any such fashion. For I should then have to know such a being as determined in its existence, and yet as not determined in time—which is impossible, since I cannot support my concept by any intuition. But though I cannot *know*, I can yet *think* freedom; that is to say, the representation of it is at least not self-contradictory, provided due account be taken of our critical distinction between the two modes of representation, the sensible and the intellectual, and of the resulting limitation of the pure concepts of understanding and of the principles which flow from them.

If we grant that morality necessarily presupposes freedom (in the strictest sense) as a property of our will; if, that is to say, we grant that it yields practical principles—original principles, proper to our reason—as *a priori data* of reason, and that this would be absolutely impossible save on the assumption of freedom; and if at the same time we grant that speculative reason has proved that such freedom does not allow of being thought, then the former supposition—that made on behalf of morality—would have to give way to this other contention, the opposite of which involves a palpable contradiction. For since it is only on the assumption of freedom that the negation of morality contains any contradiction; freedom, and with it morality, would have to yield to the mechanism of nature.

Morality does not, indeed, require that freedom should be understood, but only that it should not contradict itself, and so should at least allow of being thought, and that as thus thought it should place no obstacle in the way of a free act (viewed in another relation) likewise conforming to the mechanism of nature. The doctrine of morality and the doctrine of nature may each, therefore, make good its position. This, however, is only possible in so far as criticism has previously established our unavoidable ignorance of things in themselves, and has limited all that we can theoretically *know* to mere appearances.

This discussion as to the positive advantage of critical principles of pure reason can be similarly developed in regard to the concept of *God* and of the *simple nature* of our *soul;*

but for the sake of brevity such further discussion may be omitted. [From what has already been said, it is evident that] even the *assumption*—as made on behalf of the necessary practical employment of my reason—of *God, freedom,* and *immortality* is not permissible unless at the same time speculative reason be deprived of its pretensions to transcendent insight. For in order to arrive at such insight it must make use of principles which, in fact, extend only to objects of possible experience, and which, if also applied to what cannot be an object of experience, always really change this into an appearance, thus rendering all *practical extension* of pure reason impossible. I have therefore found it necessary to deny *knowledge,* in order to make room for *faith.* The dogmatism of metaphysics, that is, the preconception that it is possible to make headway in metaphysics without a previous criticism of pure reason, is the source of all that unbelief, always very dogmatic, which wars against morality.

Though it may not, then, be very difficult to leave to posterity the bequest of a systematic metaphysic, constructed in conformity with a critique of pure reason, yet such a gift is not to be valued lightly. For not only will reason be enabled to follow the secure path of a science, instead of, as hitherto, groping at random, without circumspection or self-criticism; our enquiring youth will also be in a position to spend their time more profitably than in the ordinary dogmatism by which they are so early and so greatly encouraged to indulge in easy speculation about things of which they understand nothing, and into which neither they nor anyone else will ever have any insight—encouraged, indeed, to invent new ideas and opinions, while neglecting the study of the better-established sciences. But, above all, there is the inestimable benefit, that all objections to morality and religion will be for ever silenced, and this in Socratic fashion, namely, by the clearest proof of the ignorance of the objectors. There has always existed in the world, and there will always continue to exist, some kind of metaphysics, and with it the dialectic that is natural to pure reason. It is therefore the first and most important task of philosophy to deprive metaphysics, once and for all, of its injurious influence, by attacking its errors at their very source.

Notwithstanding this important change in the field of the sciences, and the *loss* of its fancied possessions which speculative reason must suffer, general human interests remain in the same privileged position as hitherto, and the advantages which the world has hitherto derived from the teachings of pure reason are in no way diminished. The loss affects only the *monopoly of the schools*, in no respect the *interests of humanity*. I appeal to the most rigid dogmatist, whether the proof of the continued existence of our soul after death, derived from the simplicity of substance, or of the freedom of the will as opposed to a universal mechanism, arrived at through the subtle but ineffectual distinctions between subjective and objective practical necessity, or of the existence of God as deduced from the concept of an *ens realissimum* (of the contingency of the changeable and of the necessity of a prime mover), have ever, upon passing out from the schools, succeeded in reaching the public mind or in exercising the slightest influence on its convictions? That has never been found to occur, and in view of the unfitness of the common human understanding for such subtle speculation, ought never to have been expected. Such widely held convictions, so far as they rest on rational grounds, are due to quite other considerations. The hope of a *future life* has its source in that notable characteristic of our nature, never to be capable of being satisfied by what is temporal (as insufficient for the capacities of its whole destination); the consciousness of *freedom* rests exclusively on the clear exhibition of duties, in opposition to all claims of the inclinations; the belief in a wise and great *Author of the world* is generated solely by the glorious order, beauty, and providential care everywhere displayed in nature. When the schools have been brought to recognise that they can lay no claim to higher and fuller insight in a matter of universal human concern than that which is equally within the reach of the great mass of men (ever to be held by us in the highest esteem), and that, as Schools of philosophy, they should limit themselves to the study of those universally comprehensible, and, for moral purposes, sufficient grounds of proof, then not only do these latter possessions remain undisturbed, but through this very fact they acquire yet greater authority. The change affects only the arrogant pretensions of the Schools, which would fain be counted the sole authors and possessors of such truths (as, indeed, they can justly claim to be in many other branches of knowledge), reserving the key to themselves, and communicating to the public their use only—*quod mecum nescit, solus vult scire videri.* At the same time due regard is paid to the more moderate claims of the speculative philosopher. He still remains the sole authority in regard to a science which benefits the public without their knowing it, namely, the critique of reason. That critique can never become popular, and indeed there is no need that it should. For just as fine-spun arguments in favour of useful truths make no appeal to the general mind, so neither do the subtle objections that can be raised against them. On the other hand, both inevitably present themselves to everyone who rises to the height of speculation; and it is therefore the duty of the Schools, by means of a thorough investigation of the rights of speculative reason, once for all to prevent the scandal which, sooner or later, is sure to break out even among the masses, as the result of the disputes in which metaphysicians (and, as such, finally also the clergy) inevitably become involved to the consequent perversion of their teaching. Criticism alone can sever the root of *materialism, fatalism, atheism, free-thinking, fanaticism,* and *superstition,* which can be injurious universally; as well as of *idealism* and *scepticism,* which are dangerous chiefly to the Schools, and hardly allow of being handed on to the public. If governments think proper to interfere with the affairs of the learned, it would be more consistent with a wise regard for science as well as for mankind, to favour the freedom of such criticism, by which alone the labours of reason can be established on a firm basis, than to support the ridiculous despotism of the Schools, which raise a loud cry of public danger over the destruction of cobwebs to

which the public has never paid any attention, and the loss
of which it can therefore never feel.

This critique is not opposed to the *dogmatic procedure* of
reason in its pure knowledge, as science, for that must always be dogmatic, that is, yield strict proof from sure principles *a priori*. It is opposed only to *dogmatism,* that is, to the
presumption that it is possible to make progress with pure
knowledge, according to principles, from concepts alone
(those that are philosophical), as reason has long been in
the habit of doing; and that it is possible to do this without
having first investigated in what way and by what right
reason has come into possession of these concepts. Dogmatism
is thus the dogmatic procedure of pure reason, *without previous criticism of its own powers*. In withstanding dogmatism
we must not allow ourselves to give free rein to that loqua-
cious shallowness, which assumes for itself the name of popularity, nor yet to scepticism, which makes short work with
all metaphysics. On the contrary, such criticism is the necessary preparation for a thoroughly grounded metaphysics,
which, as science, must necessarily be developed dogmatically, according to the strictest demands of system, in such
manner as to satisfy not the general public but the requirements of the Schools. For that is a demand to which it stands
pledged, and which it may not neglect, namely, that it carry
out its work entirely *a priori,* to the complete satisfaction
of speculative reason. In the execution of the plan prescribed
by the critique, that is, in the future system of metaphysics,
we have therefore to follow the strict method of the celebrated Wolff, the greatest of all the dogmatic philosophers.
He was the first to show by example (and by his example he
awakened that spirit of thoroughness which is not extinct in
Germany) how the secure progress of a science is to be attained only through orderly establishment of principles, clear
determination of concepts, insistence upon strictness of proof,
and avoidance of venturesome, non-consecutive steps in our
inferences. He was thus peculiarly well fitted to raise metaphysics to the dignity of a science, if only it had occurred to
him to prepare the ground beforehand by a critique of the

organ, that is, of pure reason itself. The blame for his having failed to do so lies not so much with himself as with the dogmatic way of thinking prevalent in his day, and with which the philosophers of his time, and of all previous times, have no right to reproach one another. Those who reject both the method of Wolff and the procedure of a critique of pure reason can have no other aim than to shake off the fetters of *science* altogether, and thus to change work into play, certainty into opinion, philosophy into philodoxy.

Now, *as regards this second edition,* I have, as is fitting, endeavoured to profit by the opportunity, in order to remove, wherever possible, difficulties and obscurity which, not perhaps without my fault, may have given rise to the many misunderstandings into which even acute thinkers have fallen in passing judgment upon my book. In the propositions themselves and their proofs, and also in the form and completeness of the [architectonic] plan, I have found nothing to alter. This is due partly to the long examination to which I have subjected them, before offering them to the public, partly to the nature of the subject-matter with which we are dealing. For pure speculative reason has a structure wherein everything is an *organ,* the whole being for the sake of every part, and every part for the sake of all the others, so that even the smallest imperfection, be it a fault (error) or a deficiency, must inevitably betray itself in use. This system will, as I hope, maintain, throughout the future, this unchangeableness. It is not self-conceit which justifies me in this confidence, but the evidence experimentally obtained through the parity of the result, whether we proceed from the smallest elements to the whole of pure reason or reverse-wise from the whole (for this also is presented to reason through its final end in the sphere of the practical) to each part. Any attempt to change even the smallest part at once gives rise to contradictions, not merely in the system, but in human reason in general. As to the mode of *exposition,* on the other hand, much still remains to be done; and in this edition I have sought to make improvements which should help in removing, first, the misunderstanding in regard to the Aesthetic, especially concerning the concept of time; secondly, the obscurity of the deduction of the concepts of understanding; thirdly, a supposed want of sufficient evidence in the proofs of the principles of pure understanding; and finally, the false interpretation placed upon the paralogisms charged against rational psychology. Beyond this point, that is, beyond the end of the first chapter of the Transcendental Dialectic, I have made no changes in the mode of exposition.[6] Time was too short to allow of further changes; and besides, I have not found among competent and impartial critics any misapprehension in regard to the remaining sections. Though I shall not venture to name these critics with the praise that is their due, the attention which I have paid to their comments will easily be recognised in the [new] passages [above mentioned]. These improvements involve, however, a small loss, not to be prevented save by making the book too voluminous, namely, that I have had to omit or abridge certain passages, which, though not indeed essential to the completeness of the whole, may

---

[6] The only addition, strictly so called, though one affecting the method of proof only, is the new refutation of psychological *idealism*, and a strict (also, as I believe, the only possible) proof of the objective reality of outer intuition. However harmless idealism may be considered in respect of the essential aims of metaphysics (though, in fact, it is not thus harmless), it still remains a scandal to philosophy and to human reason in general that the existence of things outside us (from which we derive the whole material of knowledge, even for our inner sense) must be accepted merely on *faith*, and that if anyone thinks good to doubt their existence, we are unable to counter his doubts by any satisfactory proof. Since there is some obscurity in the expressions used in the proof, from the third line to the sixth line, I beg to alter the passage as follows: "*But this permanent cannot be an intuition in me. For all grounds of determination of my existence which are to be bc met with in me are representations; and as representations themselves require a permanent distinct from them, in relation to which their change, and so my existence in the time wherein they change, may be determined.*" To this proof it will probably be objected, that I am immediately conscious only of that which is in me, that is, of my *representation* of outer things; and consequently that it must still remain uncertain whether outside me there is anything corresponding to it, or not. But through inner *experience* I am conscious of *my existence* in time (consequently also of its determinability in time), and this is more than to be conscious merely of my representation. It is identical with the *empirical consciousness of my existence*, which is determinable only through relation to something which, while bound up with my existence, is outside me. This consciousness of my existence in time is bound up in the way of identity with the consciousness of a relation to something outside me, and it is therefore experience not invention, sense not imagination, which inseparably connects this outside something with my inner sense. For outer sense is already in itself a relation of intuition to something actual outside me, and the reality of outer sense, in its distinction from imagination, rests simply on that which is here found to take place, namely, its being in-

yet be missed by many readers as otherwise helpful. Only so could I obtain space for what, as I hope, is now a more intelligible exposition, which, though altering absolutely nothing in the fundamentals of the propositions put forward or even in their proofs, yet here and there departs so far from the previous method of treatment, that mere interpolations could not be made to suffice. This loss, which is small and can be remedied by consulting the first edition, will, I hope, be compensated by the greater clearness of the new text. I have observed, with pleasure and thankfulness, in various published works—alike in critical reviews and in independent treatises—that the spirit of thoroughness is not extinct in Germany, but has only been temporarily overshadowed by the prevalence of a pretentiously free manner of thinking; and that the thorny paths of the Critique have not discouraged courageous and clear heads from setting themselves to master my book—a work which leads to a methodical, and as such alone enduring, and therefore most necessary, science of pure

separably bound up with inner experience, as the condition of its possibility. If, with the *intellectual consciousness* of my existence, in the representation 'I am', which accompanies all my judgments and acts of understanding, I could at the same time connect a determination of my existence through *intellectual intuition*, the consciousness of a relation to something outside me would not be required. But though that intellectual consciousness does indeed come first, the inner intuition, in which my existence can alone be determined, is sensible and is bound up with the condition of time. This determination, however, and therefore the inner experience itself, depends upon something permanent which is not in me, and consequently can be only in something outside me, to which I must regard myself as standing in relation. The reality of outer sense is thus necessarily bound up with inner sense, if experience in general is to be possible at all; that is, I am just as certainly conscious that there are things outside me, which are in relation to my sense, as I am conscious that I myself exist as determined in time. In order to determine to which given intuitions objects outside me actually correspond, and which therefore belong to outer *sense* (to which, and not to the faculty of imagination, they are to be ascribed), we must in each single case appeal to the rules according to which experience in general, even inner experience, is distinguished from imagination—the proposition that there is such a thing as outer experience being always presupposed. This further remark may be added. The representation of something *permanent* in existence is not the same as *permanent representation*. For though the representation of [something permanent] may be very transitory and variable like all our other representations, not excepting those of matter, it yet refers to something permanent. This latter must therefore be an external thing distinct from all my representations, and its existence must be included in the *determination* of my own existence, constituting with it but a single experience such as would not take place even inwardly if it were not also at the same time, in part, outer. How this should be possible we are as little capable of explaining further as we are of accounting for our being able to think the abiding in time, the co-existence of which with the changing generates the concept of alteration.

reason. To these worthy men, who so happily combine thoroughness of insight with a talent for lucid exposition—which I cannot regard myself as possessing—I leave the task of perfecting what, here and there, in its exposition, is still somewhat defective; for in this regard the danger is not that of being refuted, but of not being understood. From now on, though I cannot allow myself to enter into controversy, I shall take careful note of all suggestions, be they from friends or from opponents, for use, in accordance with this propaedeutic, in the further elaboration of the system. In the course of these labours I have advanced somewhat far in years (this month I reach my sixty-fourth year), and I must be careful with my time if I am to succeed in my proposed scheme of providing a metaphysic of nature and of morals which will confirm the truth of my Critique in the two fields, of speculative and of practical reason. The clearing up of the obscurities in the present work—they are hardly to be avoided in a new enterprise—and the defence of it as a whole, I must therefore leave to those worthy men who have made my teaching their own. A philosophical work cannot be armed at all points, like a mathematical treatise, and may therefore be open to objection in this or that respect, while yet the structure of the system, taken in its unity, is not in the least endangered. Few have the versatility of mind to familiarise themselves with a new system; and owing to the general distaste for all innovation, still fewer have the inclination to do so. If we take single passages, torn from their contexts, and compare them with one another, apparent contradictions are not likely to be lacking, especially in a work that is written with any freedom of expression. In the eyes of those who rely on the judgment of others, such contradictions have the effect of placing the work in an unfavourable light; but they are easily resolved by those who have mastered the idea of the whole. If a theory has in itself stability, the stresses and strains which may at first have seemed very threatening to it serve only, in the course of time, to smooth away its inequalities; and if men of impartiality, insight, and true popularity devote themselves to its exposition, it may also, in a short time, secure for itself the necessary elegance of statement.

Königsberg, April, 1787

. . .

Although the complete layman may not find Kant's three prefaces utterly lucid and illuminating, he may get a better notion of Kant's point of view from them than from myopic concentration on a few technical sections of Kant's first mighty *Critique*.

"I have therefore found it necessary to deny *knowledge* in order to make room for *faith*." This famous sentence from the second preface sums up Kant's program which he elaborated in the *Critique of Practical Reason*, the *Critique of Judgment* and other works on morality. Kant had demonstrated to his own satisfaction that the human understanding can only know appearances, phenomena, and can never penetrate to ultimate reality—can never answer the final questions about the beginning and end of the world, about the human soul, about God. But Kant also demonstrated to his own satisfaction that the inescapable sense of duty, "the moral law within," does pierce the veil of appearance, does point "to the ultimate ground of all being and all existence." In short, the moral realm occupied by all human beings is deeper than the intellectual realm occupied by the elite.

If the moral life is paramount, then as moral beings we must be free; if our moral tasks are endless, we must be immortal; if justice is to be rewarded, then there must be a God. God, Freedom and Immortality are, of course, supersensible realities that cannot be proved by the theoretical reason. Then they must be implied or postulated by the practical reason, by the moral law within us. They must be objects of unconquerable faith. That is what Kant meant by the second half of his famous sentence—"to make room for faith."

What have been the reactions to this stupendous, two-leveled argument?

There have been those who accepted Kant's whole contention and wept with joy because he broke the chains both of scepticism and determinism. For Schiller and Beethoven, Kant was the supreme liberator, justifying man's highest endeavors. For Protestant theology Kant was a vast reservoir of new energy.

On the other hand, there were people who did not read beyond Kant's first *Critique,* or did not find his reversal or "somersault," as Unamuno called it, convincing. The argument for the denial of *knowledge* of supersensible realities they found all too impressive; the urge to go on to faith they did not feel. So Moses Mendelssohn, Kant's contemporary, called him *der alles Zermalmende,* the all-pulverizer. Heine, two generations later, described the movement in Kant's system as that from tragedy to farce. And still later Pater spoke of "the *désillusionné,* who had found in Kant's negations the last word concerning an unseen world."

However there were also bolder if not more able men who found ambiguities and difficulties in Kant's tremendous scheme, men who denied his denials, who affirmed the capacity of the human mind to penetrate into the heart of things. These were the famous post-Kantians—Hegel who worked mainly through dialectic and history, Fichte who combined logic, morality and nationalism into a dangerous amalgam, and Schopenhauer who looked darkly into his aimless, restless, insatiable will-to-live.

But these are men for other collections!

WILLIAM BLAKE
[1757–1827]

Sages down through the centuries have conveyed their wisdom in sayings and not in systems. Goethe carefully watched his own growing collection of "maxims and reflections," which finally formed one of his most precious books. Even that notoriously difficult metaphysician F. H. Bradley left at his death a hundred aphorisms, long carefully polished. In our own day many a flashing sentence by Alfred North Whitehead is taking its place in the anthology of civilization. Both books of the fabulous Ludwig Wittgenstein, *Tractatus Logico-Philosophicus* and *Philosophical Investigations*, are rich in aphorisms and highly condensed paragraphs.

William Blake, engraver, designer, painter, poet, mystic—a rebellious dreamer brought up in an England being uglified by the Industrial Revolution and later terrified by the French Revolution—was poor all his life and a failure by all worldly standards. A self-taught man, he no doubt often fell into errors of taste and obscurity, but he managed to write a number of lyrics that chime with perfection, a number of aphorisms more brilliantly compact than any in the English language and some prophetic poems with a high obscurity that challenges more than it repels. His central work, *The Marriage of Heaven and Hell* (circa 1793), is complicated by his special views of Milton and Swedenborg, but the section "Proverbs of Hell" is a unit in itself. Perhaps he called them "proverbs" because proverbs are supposed to originate with the common man. But whatever they are called, they warm or chill or search the heart. If, as Whitehead said, "the romantic reaction was a revolt in behalf of value," then William Blake was the romantic reaction in person.

PROVERBS OF HELL

In seed time learn, in harvest teach, in winter enjoy.

Drive your cart and your plow over the bones of the dead.

The road of excess leads to the palace of wisdom.

Prudence is a rich, ugly old maid, courted by Incapacity.

He who desires but acts not, breeds pestilence.

The cut worm forgives the plow.

Dip him in the river who loves water.

A fool sees not the same tree that a wise man sees.

He whose face gives no light, shall never become a star.

Eternity is in love with the productions of time.

The busy bee has no time for sorrow.

The hours of folly are measured by the clock; but of wisdom, no clock can measure.

All wholesome food is caught without a net or a trap.

Bring out number, weight & measure in a year of dearth.

No bird soars too high, if he soars with his own wings.

A dead body revenges not injuries.

The most sublime act is to set another before you.

If the fool would persist in his folly he would become wise.

Folly is the cloke of knavery.

Shame is Pride's cloke.

Prisons are built with stones of Law, Brothels with bricks of Religion.

The pride of the peacock is the glory of God.

The lust of the goat is the bounty of God.

The wrath of the lion is the wisdom of God.

The nakedness of woman is the work of God.

Excess of sorrow laughs. Excess of joy weeps.

The roaring of lions, the howling of wolves, the raging of the stormy sea, and the destructive sword, are portions of eternity, too great for the eye of man.

The fox condemns the trap, not himself.

Joys impregnate. Sorrows bring forth.

Let man wear the fell of the lion, woman the fleece of the sheep.

The bird a nest, the spider a web, man friendship.

The selfish, smiling fool, & the sullen, frowning fool shall be both thought wise, that they may be a rod.

What is now proved was once only imagined.

The rat, the mouse, the fox, the rabbet watch the roots; the lion, the tyger, the horse, the elephant watch the fruits.

The cistern contains: the fountain overflows.

One thought fills immensity.

Always be ready to speak your mind, and a base man will avoid you.

Every thing possible to be believed is an image of truth.

The eagle never lost so much time as when he submitted to learn of the crow.

The fox provides for himself, but God provides for the lion.

Think in the morning. Act in the noon. Eat in the evening. Sleep in the night.

He who has suffered you to impose on him, knows you.

As the plow follows words, so God rewards prayers.

The tygers of wrath are wiser than the horses of instruction.

Expect poison from the standing water.

You never know what is enough unless you know what is more than enough.

Listen to the fool's reproach! it is a kingly title!

The eyes of fire, the nostrils of air, the mouth of water, the beard of earth.

The weak in courage is strong in cunning.

The apple tree never asks the beech how he shall grow; nor the lion, the horse, how he shall take his prey.

The thankful receiver bears a plentiful harvest.

If others had not been foolish, we should be so.

The soul of sweet delight can never be defiled.

When thou seest an Eagle, thou seest a portion of Genius; lift up thy head!

As the caterpiller chooses the fairest leaves to lay her eggs on, so the priest lays his curse on the fairest joys.

To create a little flower is the labour of ages.

Damn braces. Bless relaxes.

The best wine is the oldest, the best water the newest.

Prayers plow not! Praises reap not!

Joys laugh not! Sorrows weep not!

The head Sublime, the heart Pathos, the genitals Beauty, the hands & feet Proportion.

As the air to a bird or the sea to a fish, so is contempt to the contemptible.

The crow wished every thing was black, the owl that every thing was white.

Exuberance is Beauty.

If the lion was advised by the fox, he would be cunning.

Improvement makes strait roads; but the crooked roads without Improvement are roads of Genius.

Sooner murder an infant in its cradle than nurse unacted desires.

Where man is not, nature is barren.

Truth can never be told so as to be understood, and not be believed.

Enough! or Too much.

JEREMY BENTHAM

[1748–1832]

"The French have already discovered that the blackness of the skin is no reason why a human being should be abandoned without redress to the caprice of a tormentor. (See Louis XIV's *Code Noir*.) It may come one day to be recognized that the number of the legs, the villosity of the skin, or the termination of the *os sacrum*, are reasons equally insufficient for abandoning a sensitive being to the same fate. What else is it that should trace the insuperable line? Is it the faculty of reason or perhaps the faculty of discourse? But a full-grown horse or dog is beyond comparison a more rational, as well as a more conversable animal, than an infant of a day, or a week, or even a month, old. But suppose the case were otherwise, what would it avail? The question is not, Can they *reason?* nor, Can they *talk?* but, Can they *suffer?*"

This passage closes a long footnote in the final chapter of the *Introduction to the Principles of Morals and Legislation,* by Jeremy Bentham, and it is infinitely more revealing than the out-of-context quotation, repeated for the nth time, that "quantity of pleasure being equal, pushpin is as good as poetry." As a matter of fact, Bentham was almost as much of a prodigy as his famous disciple John Stuart Mill, and he was far more original, witty and winning! Many of his projects are now being worked on by semanticists, logical empiricists and philosophical analysts—whether they realize it or not. The late C. K. Ogden's Bentham centenary lecture, "Jeremy Bentham 1832–2032," not only was a celebration of a score of legal reforms directly traceable to Bentham but, more, placed an emphasis on the unexploited treasures still left in Bentham's writings, of which hundreds or even thousands of pages are still unprinted!

In a way Bentham himself was responsible for this situation, for he was so busy during sixty years getting his ideas down on paper that he had little time to worry about their publication. For example, his first book, *Fragment on Government*, was published in 1776 but the complete work, *Comment on the Commentaries*, did not appear until 1928, having been discovered and edited by an American, Charles Warren Everett. *The Principles of Morals and Legislation* (1789) was apparently a complete book—but Mr. Everett discovered the manuscript of Part II, "The Limits of Jurisprudence Defined," and brought it out in 1940. Bentham's world fame was largely based on *Traités de Legislation*, a compilation made from his work and translated into French by a Swiss Protestant minister, Étienne Dumont, which was in turn translated into English by an American lawyer, Robert Hildreth, thirty-four years after Bentham's death!

As a hypersensitive child, Jeremy Bentham was continually frightened by the servants with stories of imps, ghosts and hobgoblins. After taking his bachelor's degree at Oxford at the age of sixteen, he heard Sir William Blackstone give some of the lectures which were to be published as *Commentaries on the Laws of England*, and even then Bentham detected fallacies, not to mention imperfections, in a code of law which provided corporal or capital punishment for several hundred crimes. It was unlikely that he would take up the practice of law with much enthusiasm or meet with much success. In what may have been his first case, he advised the litigants to settle out of court, for only the opposing attorneys would profit by a trial. In another case he lost, not because his interpretation of the code was wrong, but because he had not had access to judicial opinions now suddenly introduced as precedent. His career lay in another direction: to dispel imps, ghosts and hobgoblins from human life, to bring more clarity into language, to bring more reason and humanity into morals and legislation.

His brief experience with the practice of law in his early twenties was completely overshadowed by his excited reading of several volumes including Hume's *Essays*, Beccaria's pioneer work on penology, Helvétius' *De l'Esprit* and Priestley's *Essay on Government*. Rather than trying to be impossibly specific about their several influences on Bentham, we may say that he reached with their help the notion of a more or less plastic human nature deeply molded by circumstances, the notion of utility measured by pleasure and pain as an ethical standard, and the slogan "the greatest happiness of the greatest number." This was the core of all his thinking except for the principle of political democracy, which he adopted at sixty, under the arguments of James Mill.

If Bentham had been twitted about his ambition to be the Newton of social philosophy with his so-called "felicific calculus" and "moral arithmetic," he could have smiled and suggested that his principle of utility was at least in harmony with the doctrine that "by their fruits ye shall know them," more objective than "the arbitrary principle of sympathy and antipathy" and more suitable to human nature than "the ascetic principle," which by definition was a ceaseless check on human desire. In any case, before anyone indulges in condescending remarks about Bentham's naïve, over-simplified psychology he should ponder the long-out-of-print and almost entirely neglected *A Table of the Springs of Action*.

Sydney Smith (1771-1845) was an Anglican clergyman and a joyous liberal who finally became, at the age of sixty-one, in spite of his wit, not a bishop but a residential canon of St. Paul's, London—some months before the passage of the great Reform Bill of 1832, for which he had long helped to prepare the way. In 1802, he had been one of the chief founders of the liberal *Edinburgh Review;* in 1807-1808, he wrote the famous *Peter Plymley Letters* (published anonymously) in favor of Catholic emancipation; and he continued to write with polemical genius against the brutal Game Laws and various other abuses. And he had his own idea for editing Jeremy Bentham.

· · ·

FALLACIES OF ANTI-REFORMERS [1]

There are a vast number of absurd and mischievous fallacies, which pass readily in the world for sense and virtue, while in truth they tend only to fortify error and encourage crime. Mr. Bentham has enumerated the most conspicuous of these in the book before us.

Whether it be necessary there should be a middleman between the cultivator and the possessor, learned economists have doubted; but neither gods, men, nor booksellers can doubt the necessity of a middleman between Mr. Bentham

---

[1] A review of "The Book of Fallacies: from *Unfinished Papers of Jeremy Bentham*. By a Friend. London, 1824."

and the public. Mr. Bentham is long; Mr. Bentham is oc·
casionally involved and obscure; Mr. Bentham invents new
and alarming expressions; Mr. Bentham loves division and
subdivision—and he loves method itself, more than its consequences. Those only, therefore, who know his originality,
his knowledge, his vigor, and his boldness, will recur to the
works themselves. The great mass of readers will not purchase improvement at so dear a rate; but will choose rather
to become acquainted with Mr. Bentham through the medium of reviews—after that eminent philosopher has been
washed, trimmed, shaved, and forced into clean linen. One
great use of a review, indeed, is to make men wise in ten
pages, who have no appetite for a hundred pages; to con-
dense nourishment, to work with pulp and essence, and to
guard the stomach from idle burden and unmeaning bulk.
For half a page, sometimes for a whole page, Mr Bentham
writes with a power which few can equal; and by selecting
and omitting, an admirable style may be formed from the
text. Using this liberty, we shall endeavor to give an account
of Mr. Bentham's doctrines, for the most part in his own
words. Wherever an expression is particularly happy, let it
be considered to be Mr. Bentham's—the dulness we take to
ourselves.

OUR WISE ANCESTORS—*The Wisdom of Our Ancestors*—
*The Wisdom of Ages—Venerable Antiquity—Wisdom of Old
Times.* This mischievous and absurd fallacy springs from
the grossest perversion of the meaning of words. Experience
is certainly the mother of wisdom, and the old have, of course,
a greater experience than the young; but the question is who
are the old? and who are the young? Of *individuals* living at
the same period, the oldest has, of course, the greatest experience; but among *generations* of men the reverse of this
is true. Those who come first (our ancestors) are the young
people, and have the least experience. We have added to
their experience the experience of many centuries; and therefore, as far as experience goes, are wiser, and more capable
of forming an opinion than they were. The real feeling should

be, *not* can we be so presumptuous as to put our opinions in opposition to those of our ancestors? but can such young, ignorant, inexperienced persons as our ancestors necessarily were, be expected to have understood a subject as well as those who have seen so much more, lived so much longer, and enjoyed the experience of so many centuries? All this cant, then, about our ancestors is merely an abuse of words, by transferring phrases true of contemporary men to succeeding ages. Whereas (as we have before observed) of living men the oldest has, *cæteris paribus,*[2] the most experience; of generations, the oldest has, *cæteris paribus,* the least experience. Our ancestors, up to the Conquest, were children in arms; chubby boys in the time of Edward I; striplings under Elizabeth; men in the reign of Queen Anne; and *we* only are the white-bearded, silver-headed ancients, who have treasured up, and are prepared to profit by, all the experience which human life can supply. We are not disputing with our ancestors the palm of talent, in which they may or may not be our superiors, but the palm of experience in which it is utterly impossible they can be our superiors. And yet, whenever the Chancellor comes forward to protect some abuse, or to oppose some plan which has the increase of human happiness for its object, his first appeal is always to the wisdom of our ancestors; and he himself, and many noble lords who vote with him, are, to this hour, persuaded that all alterations and amendments on their devices are an unblushing controversy between youthful temerity and mature experience!—and so, in truth they are—only that much-loved magistrate mistakes the young for the old, and the old for the young—and is guilty of that very sin against experience which he attributes to the lovers of innovation.

We cannot of course be supposed to maintain that our ancestors wanted wisdom, or that they were necessarily mistaken in their institutions, because their means of information were more limited than ours. But we do confidently main-

---

[2] [Other things being equal.]

tain that when we find it expedient to change anything which
our ancestors have enacted, we are the experienced persons,
and not they. The quantity of talent is always varying in any
great nation. To say that we are more or less able than our
ancestors is an assertion that requires to be explained. All the
able men of all ages, who have ever lived in England, probably possessed, if taken altogether, more intellect than all
the able men England can now boast of. But if authority
must be resorted to rather than reason, the question is, What
was the wisdom of that single age which enacted the law,
compared with the wisdom of the age which proposes to
alter it? What are the eminent men of one and the other
period? If you say that our ancestors were wiser than us,
mention your date and year. If the splendor of names is equal,
are the circumstances the same? If the circumstances are the
same, we have a superiority of experience, of which the difference between the two periods is the measure. It is necessary to insist upon this; for upon sacks of wool, and on
benches forensic, sit grave men, and agricolous persons in
the Commons, crying out: "Ancestors, ancestors! *hodie non!*"
Saxons, Danes, save us! Fiddlefrig, help us! Howel, Ethelwolf,
protect us!" Any cover for nonsense—any veil for trash—any
pretext for repelling the innovations of conscience and of
duty!

"So long as they keep to vague generalities—so long as
the two objects of comparison are each of them taken in the
lump—wise ancestors in one lump, ignorant and foolish mob
of modern times in the other—the weakness of the fallacy
may escape detection. But let them assign for the period of
superior wisdom any determinate period whatsoever, not
only will the groundlessness of the notion be apparent (class
being compared with class in that period and the present
one), but unless the antecedent period be comparatively
speaking a very modern one, so wide will be the disparity,
and to such an amount in favor of modern times, that, in
comparison of the lowest class of the people in modern times

---

³ [Not to-day!]

(always supposing them proficient in the art of reading, and their proficiency employed in the reading of newspapers), the very highest and best-informed class of these wise ancestors will turn out to be grossly ignorant.

"Take, for example, any year in the reign of Henry VIII, from 1509 to 1546. At that time the House of Lords would probably have been in possession of by far the larger proportion of what little instruction the age afforded; in the House of Lords, among the laity, it might even then be a question whether, without exception, their lordships were all of them able so much as to read. But even supposing them all in the fullest possession of that useful art, political science being the science in question, what instruction on the subject could they meet with at that time of day?

"On no one branch of legislation was any book extant from which, with regard to the circumstances of the then present times, any useful instruction could be derived: distributive law, penal law, international law, political economy, so far from existing as sciences, had scarcely obtained a name: in all those departments under the head of *quid faciendum*, a mere blank: the whole literature of the age consisted of a meagre chronicle or two, containing short memorandums of the usual occurrences of war and peace, battles, sieges, executions, revels, deaths, births, processions, ceremonies, and other external events; but with scarce a speech or an incident that could enter into the composition of any such work as a history of the human mind—with scarce an attempt at investigation into causes, characters, or the state of the people at large. Even when at last, little by little, a scrap or two of political instruction came to be obtainable, the proportion of error and mischievous doctrine mixed up with it was so great, that whether a blank unfilled might not have been less prejudicial than a blank thus filled, may reasonably be matter of doubt.

"If we come down to the reign of James I, we shall find that Solomon of his time eminently eloquent as well as learned, not only among crowned but among uncrowned heads, marking out for prohibition and punishment the practices of devils and witches, and without the slightest objection on the part of the great characters of that day in their high situations, consigning men to death and torment for the misfortune of not being so well acquainted as he was with the composition of the Godhead.

"Under the name of exorcism the Catholic liturgy contains a form of procedure for driving out devils;—even with the help of this instrument, the operation cannot be performed with the desired success, but by an operator qualified by holy orders for the working of this as well as so many other wonders. In our days and in our country the same object is attained, and beyond comparison more effectually, by so cheap an instrument as a common newspaper; before this talisman, not only devils but ghosts, vampires, witches, and all their kindred tribes, are driven out of the land, never to return again! The touch of holy water is not so intolerable to them as the bare smell of printers' ink."

FALLACY OF IRREVOCABLE LAWS. A law, says Mr. Bentham (no matter to what effect) is proposed to a legislative assembly, who are called upon to reject it, upon the single ground that by those who in some former period exercised the same power, a regulation was made, having for its object to preclude forever, or to the end of an unexpired period, all succeeding legislators from enacting a law to any such effect as that now proposed.

Now it appears quite evident that, at every period of time, every legislature must be endowed with all those powers which the exigency of the times may require; and any attempt to infringe on this power is inadmissible and absurd. The sovereign power, at any one period, can only form a blind guess at the measures which may be necessary for any future period; but by this principle of immutable laws, the government is transferred from those who are necessarily the best judges of what they want, to others who can know little or nothing about the matter. The thirteenth century decides for the fourteenth. The fourteenth makes laws for the fifteenth. The fifteenth hermetically seals up the sixteenth, which tyrannizes over the seventeenth, which again tells the eighteenth how it is to act, under circumstances which cannot be foreseen, and how it is to conduct itself in exigencies which no human wit can anticipate.

"Men who have a century more experience to ground their judgments on, surrender their intellect to men who had a century less experience, and who, unless that deficiency constitutes a claim, have no claim to preference. If the prior generation were, in respect of intellectual qualification, ever so much superior to the subsequent generation—if it understood so much better than the subsequent generation itself the interest of that subsequent generation—could it have been in an equal degree anxious to promote that interest, and consequently equally attentive to those facts with which, though in order to form a judgment it ought to have been, it is impossible that it should have been, acquainted? In a word, will its love for that subsequent generation be quite so great as that same generation's love for itself?

"Not even here, after a moment's deliberate reflection, will the assertion be in the affirmative. And yet it is their prodigious anxiety for the welfare of their posterity that produces the propensity of these sages to tie up the hands of this same posterity forever more—to act as guardians to its perpetual and incurable weakness, and take its conduct forever out of its own hands.

"If it be right that the conduct of the nineteenth century should be determined not by its own judgment but by that of the eighteenth, it will be equally right that the conduct of the twentieth century should be determined not by its own judgment but by that of the nineteenth. And if the same principle were still pursued, what at length would be the consequence?—that in process of time the practice of legislation would be at an end. The conduct and fate of all men would be determined by those who neither knew nor cared anything about the matter; and the aggregate body of the living would remain forever in subjection to an inexorable tyranny, exercised as it were by the aggregate body of the Dead."

The despotism, as Mr. Bentham well observes, of Nero or Caligula would be more tolerable than an "irrevocable law."

The despot, through fear or favor, or in a lucid interval, might relent; but how are the Parliament who made the Scotch Union, for example, to be awakened from that dust in which they repose—the jobber and the patriot, the speaker and the doorkeeper, the silent voters and the men of rich allusions, Cannings and cultivators, Barings and beggars—making irrevocable laws for men who toss their remains about with spades, and use the relics of these legislators to give breadth to broccoli, and to aid the vernal eruption of asparagus?

If the law be good, it will support itself; if bad, it should not be supported by "irrevocable theory," which is never resorted to but as the veil of abuses. All living men must possess the supreme power over their own happiness at every particular period. To suppose that there is anything which a whole nation cannot do, which they deem to be essential to their happiness, and that they cannot do it, because *another* generation, long ago dead and gone, said it must not be done, is mere nonsense. While you are captain of the vessel, do what you please; but the moment you quit the ship I become as omnipotent as you. You may leave me as much *advice* as you please, but you cannot leave me *commands;* though, in fact, this is the only meaning which can be applied to what are called irrevocable laws. It appeared to the legislature for the time being to be of immense importance to make such and such a law. Great good was gained, or great evil avoided, by enacting it. Pause before you alter an institution which has been deemed to be of so much importance. This is prudence and common-sense; the rest is the exaggeration of fools, or the artifice of knaves, who eat up fools. What endless nonsense has been talked of our navigation laws! What wealth has been sacrificed to either before they were repealed! How impossible it appeared to Noodledom to repeal them! They were considered of the irrevocable class—a kind of law over which the dead only were omnipotent, and the living had no power. Frost, it is true, cannot be put off by act of Parliament, nor can spring be accelerated by any majority of both houses. It is, however, quite a mistake to suppose that any alteration of any of the articles of union is as much out of the jurisdiction of Parliament as these meteorological changes. In every year, and every day of that year, living men have a right to make their own laws and manage their own affairs; to break through the tyranny of the antespirants—the people who breathed before them—and to do what they please for themselves. Such supreme power cannot indeed be well exercised by the people at large; it must be exercised therefore by the delegates, or Parliament, whom the people choose; and such Parliament, disregarding the superstitious reverence for "irrevocable laws," can have no other criterion of wrong and right than that of public utility.

When a law is considered as immutable, and the immutable law happens at the same time to be too foolish and mischievous to be endured, instead of being repealed, it is clandestinely evaded, or openly violated; and thus the authority of all law is weakened.

Where a nation has been ancestorially bound by foolish and improvident treaties, ample notice must be given of their termination. Where the State has made ill-advised grants, or rash bargains with individuals, it is necessary to grant proper compensation. The most difficult case, certainly, is that of the union of nations, where a smaller number of the weaker nation is admitted into the larger senate of the greater nation, and will be overpowered if the question come to a vote; but the lesser nation must run this risk; it is not probable that any violation of articles will take place till they are absolutely called for by extreme necessity. But let the danger be what it may, no danger is so great, no supposition so foolish, as to consider any human law as irrevocable. The shifting attitude of human affairs would often render such a condition an intolerable evil to all parties. The absurd jealousy of our countrymen at the Union secured heritable jurisdiction to the owners; nine and thirty years afterward they were abolished, in the very teeth of the Act of Union, and to the evident promotion of the public good.

CONTINUITY OF A LAW BY OATH. The sovereign of England at his coronation takes an oath to maintain the laws of

God, the true profession of the Gospel, and the Protestant religion, as established by law, and to preserve to the bishops and clergy of this realm the rights and privileges which by law appertain to them, and to preserve inviolate the doctrine, discipline, worship, and the government of the Church. It has been suggested that by this oath the King stands precluded from granting those indulgences to the Irish Catholics which are included in the bill for their emancipation. The true meaning of these provisions is of course to be decided, if doubtful, by the same legislative authority which enacted them. But a different notion it seems is now afloat. The King for the time being (we are putting an imaginary case) thinks as an individual that he is not maintaining the doctrine, discipline, and rights of the Church of England, if he grant any extension of civil rights to those who are not members of that Church; that he is violating his oath by so doing. This oath, then, according to this reasoning, is the great palladium of the Church. As long as it remains inviolate the Church is safe. How, then, can any monarch who has taken it ever consent to repeal it? How can he, consistently with his oath, for the preservation of the privileges of the Church, contribute his part to throw down so strong a bulwark as he deems his oath to be! The oath, then, cannot be altered. It must remain under all circumstances of society the same. The King who has taken it is bound to continue it, and to refuse his sanction to any bill for its future alteration, because it prevents him, and, he must needs think, will prevent others, from granting dangerous immunities to the enemies of the Church.

Here, then, is an irrevocable law—a piece of absurd tyranny exercised by the rulers of Queen Anne's time upon the government of 1825—a certain art of potting and preserving a kingdom in one shape, attitude, and flavor—and in this way it is that an institution appears like old ladies' sweetmeats and made wines—Apricot Jam 1822—Currant Wine 1819—Court of Chancery 1427—Penal Laws against Catholics 1676. The difference is, that the ancient woman is a better judge of mouldy commodities than the illiberal part of his majesty's ministers. The potting lady goes sniffing about and admitting light and air to prevent the progress of decay; while to him of the wool-sack all seems doubly dear in proportion as it is antiquated, worthless, and unusable.

It ought not to be in the power of the sovereign to tie up his own hands, much less the hands of his successors. If the sovereign were to oppose his own opinion to that of the two other branches of the legislature, and himself to decide what he considers to be for the benefit of the Protestant Church, and what not, a king who has spent his whole life in the frivolous occupation of a court may by perversion of understanding conceive measures most salutary to the Church to be most pernicious, and, persevering obstinately in his own error, may frustrate the wisdom of his parliament, and perpetuate the most inconceivable folly! If Henry VIII had argued in this manner we should have had no Reformation. If George III had always argued in this manner the Catholic code would never have been relaxed. And thus a King, however incapable of forming an opinion upon serious subjects, has nothing to do but pronounce the word "Conscience," and the whole power of the country is at his feet.

Can there be greater absurdity than to say that a man is acting contrary to his conscience who surrenders his opinion upon any subject to those who must understand the subject better than himself? I think my ward has a claim to the estate; but the best lawyers tell me he has none. I think my son capable of undergoing the fatigues of a military life; but the best physicians say he is much too weak. My Parliament say this measure will do the Church no harm; but I think it very pernicious to the Church. Am I acting contrary to my conscience because I apply much higher intellectual powers than my own to the investigation and protection of these high interests?

"According to the form in which it is conceived, any such engagement is in effect either a check or a license:—a license under the appearance of a check, and for that very reason but the more efficiently operative.

"Chains to the man in power? Yes:—but only such as he figures with on the stage; to the spectators as imposing, to himself as light as possible. Modelled by the wearer to suit his own purposes, they serve to rattle but not to restrain.

"Suppose a king of Great Britain and Ireland to have expressed his fixed determination, in the event of any proposed law being tendered to him for his assent, to refuse such assent, and this not on the persuasion that the law would not be 'for the utility of the subjects,' but that by his coronation oath he stands precluded from so doing, the course proper to be taken by Parliament, the course pointed out by principle and precedent, would be a vote of abdication—a vote declaring the king to have abdicated his royal authority, and that, as in case of death or incurable mental derangement, now is the time for the person next in succession to take his place. In the celebrated case in which a vote to this effect was actually passed, the declaration of abdication was, in lawyers' language, a fiction—in plain truth, a falsehood, and that falsehood a mockery; not a particle of his power was it the wish of James to abdicate, to part with, but to increase it to a maximum was the manifest object of all his efforts. But in the case here supposed, with respect to a part, and that a principal part of the royal authority, the will and purpose to abdicate is actually declared; and this being such a part, without which the remainder cannot, 'to the utility of the subjects,' be exercised, the remainder must of necessity be, on their part and for their sake, added."

SELF-TRUMPETER'S FALLACY. Mr. Bentham explains the self-trumpeter's fallacy as follows:

"There are certain men in office who, in discharge of their functions, arrogate to themselves a degree of probity, which is to exclude all imputations and all inquiry. Their assertions are to be deemed equivalent to proof, their virtues are guaranties for the faithful discharge of their duties, and the most implicit confidence is to be reposed in them on all occasions. If you expose any abuse, propose any reform, call for securities, inquiry, or measures to promote publicity, they set up a cry of surprise, amounting almost to indignation, as if their integrity were questioned or their honor wounded. With all this, they dexterously mix up intimations that the most exalted patriotism, honor, and perhaps religion, are the only sources of all their actions."

Of course every man will try what he can effect by these means; but (as Mr. Bentham observes) if there be any one maxim in politics more certain than another, it is that no possible degree of virtue in the governor can render it expedient for the governed to dispense with good laws and good institutions. Madame De Staël (to her disgrace) said to the Emperor of Russia: "Sire, your character is a constitution for your country, and your conscience its guaranty." His reply was: *"Quand cela serait, je ne serais jamais qu'un accident heureux;"*[4] and this we think one of the truest and most brilliant replies ever made by monarch.

LAUDATORY PERSONALITIES. "The object of laudatory personalities is to effect the rejection of a measure on account of the alleged good character of those who oppose it, and the argument advanced is: 'The measure is rendered unnecessary by the virtues of those who are in power—their opposition is a sufficient authority for the rejection of the measure. The measure proposed implies a distrust of the members of his Majesty's Government; but so great is their integrity, so complete their disinterestedness, so uniformly do they prefer the public advantage to their own, that such a measure is altogether unnecessary. Their disapproval is sufficient to warrant an opposition; precautions can only be requisite where danger is apprehended; here the high character of the individuals in question is a sufficient guaranty against any ground of alarm.' "

The panegyric goes on increasing with the dignity of the lauded person. All are honorable and delightful men. The person who opens the door of the office is a person of approved fidelity; the junior clerk is a model of assiduity; all the clerks are models—seven years' models, eight years' models, nine years' models, and upward. The first clerk is a paragon, and ministers the very perfection of probity and intelligence; and as for the highest magistrate of the State,

---

[4] [If that were so, I should be only a happy accident.]

no adulation is equal to describe the extent of his various merits! It is too condescending, perhaps, to refute such folly as this. But we would just observe that, if the propriety of the measure in question be established by direct arguments, these must be at least as conclusive against the character of those who oppose it as their character can be against the measure.

The effect of such an argument is to give men of good or reputed good character the power of putting a negative on any question not agreeable to their inclinations.

"In every public trust the legislator should for the purpose of prevention, suppose the trustee disposed to break the trust in every imaginable way in which it would be possible for him to reap from the breach of it any personal advantage. This is the principle on which public institutions ought to be formed, and when it is applied to all men indiscriminately, it is injurious to none. The practical inference is to oppose to such possible (and what will always be probable) breaches of trust every bar that can be opposed consistently with the power requisite for the efficient and due discharge of the trust. Indeed, these arguments, drawn from the supposed virtues of men in power, are opposed to the first principles on which all laws proceed.

"Such allegations of individual virtue are never supported by specific proof, are scarce ever susceptible of specific disproof, and specific disproof, if offered, could not be admitted in either House of Parliament. If attempted elsewhere, the punishment would fall not on the unworthy trustee, but on him by whom the unworthiness has been proved."

FALLACIES OF PRETENDED DANGER—*Imputations of Bad Design; of Bad Character; of Bad Motives; of Inconsistency; of Suspicious Connections.* The object of this class of fallacies is to draw aside attention from the measure to the man, and this in such a manner that, for some real or supposed defect in the author of the measure, a corresponding defect shall be imputed to the measure itself. Thus "the author of the measure entertains a bad design; therefore the measure is bad. His character is bad, therefore the measure is bad; his motive is bad, I will vote against the measure. On former occasions this same person who proposed the measure was its enemy, therefore the measure is bad. He is on a footing of intimacy with this or that dangerous man, or has been seen in his company, or is suspected of entertaining some of his opinions, therefore the measure is bad. He bears a name that at a former period was borne by a set of men now no more, by whom bad principles were entertained, therefore the measure is bad!"

Now, if the measure be really inexpedient, why not at once show it to be so? If the measure be good, is it bad because a bad man is its author? If bad, is it good because a good man has produced it? What are these arguments but to say to the assembly who are to be the judges of any measure, that their imbecility is too great to allow them to judge of the measure by its own merits, and that they must have recourse to distant and feebler probabilities for that purpose?

"In proportion to the degree of efficiency with which a man suffers these instruments of deception to operate upon his mind, he enables bad men to exercise over him a sort of power, the thought of which ought to cover him with shame. Allow this argument the effect of a conclusive one, you put it into the power of any man to draw you at pleasure from the support of every measure which in your own eyes is good, to force you to give your support to any and every measure which in your own eyes is bad. Is it good?—the bad man embraces it, and by the supposition, you reject it. Is it bad?—he vituperates it, and that suffices for driving you into its embrace. You split upon the rocks because he has avoided them; you miss the harbor because he has steered into it! Give yourself up to any such blind antipathy, you are no less in the power of your adversaries than if, by a correspondingly irrational sympathy and obsequiousness, you put yourself into the power of your friends.

"Besides, nothing but laborious application and a clear and comprehensive intellect can enable a man on any given subject to employ successfully relevant arguments drawn from the subject itself. To employ personalities, neither labor nor intellect is required. In this sort of contest the most idle and the most ignorant are quite on a par with, if not superior to, the most industrious and the most highly gifted individuals. Nothing can be more convenient for those who would speak without the trouble of thinking. The same ideas are brought forward over and over again, and all that is required is to vary the turn of expression. Close and relevant arguments have very little hold on the passions, and serve rather to quell than to inflame them; while in personalities there is always something stimulant, whether on the part of him who praises or him who blames. Praise forms a kind of connection between the party praising and the party praised, and vituperation gives an air of courage and independence to the party who blames.

"Ignorance and indolence, friendship and enmity, concurring and conflicting interest, servility and independence, all conspire to give personalities the ascendency they so unhappily maintain. The more we lie under the influence of our own passions, the more we rely on others being affected in a similar degree. A man who can repel these injuries with dignity may often convert them into triumph: 'Strike me, but hear,' says he, and the fury of his antagonist redounds to his own discomfiture."

No INNOVATION! To say that all things new are bad is to say that all old things were bad in their commencement: for of all the old things ever seen or heard of there is not one that was not once new. Whatever is now establishment was once innovation. The first inventor of pews and parish clerks was no doubt considered as a Jacobin in his day. Judges, juries, criers of the court, are all the inventions of ardent spirits, who filled the world with alarm, and were considered as the great precursors of ruin and dissolution. No inoculation, no turnpikes, no reading, no writing, no popery! The fool sayeth in his heart and crieth with his mouth, "I will have nothing new!"

FALLACY OF DISTRUST!—*"What's at the Bottom?"*—This fallacy begins with a virtual admission of the propriety of the measure considered in itself, and thus demonstrates its own futility, and cuts up from under itself the ground which it endeavours to make. A measure is to be rejected for something that, by bare possibility, may be found amiss in some other measure! This is vicarious reprobation; upon this principle Herod instituted his massacre. It is the argument of a driveller to other drivellers, who says: "We are not able to decide upon the evil when it arises; our only safe way is to act upon the general apprehension of evil."

OFFICIAL MALEFACTOR'S SCREEN—"*Attack Us, You Attack Government.*" If this notion is acceded to, everyone who derives at present any advantage from misrule has it in fee-simple, and all abuses, present and future, are without remedy. So long as there is anything amiss in conducting the business of government, so long as it can be made better, there can be no other mode of bringing it nearer to perfection than the indication of such imperfections as at the time being exist.

"But so far is it from being true that a man's aversion or contempt for the hands by which the powers of government, or even for the system under which they are exercised, is a proof of his aversion or contempt toward government itself, that, even in proportion to the strength of that aversion or contempt, it is a proof of the opposite affection. What, in consequence of such contempt or aversion, he wishes for is not that there be no hands at all to exercise these powers, but that the hands may be better regulated; —not that those powers should not be exercised at all, but that they should be better exercised;—not that in the exercise of them no rules at all should be pursued, but that the rules by which they are exercised should be a better set of rules.

"All government is a trust, every branch of government is a trust, and immemorially acknowledged so to be; it is only by the magnitude of the scale that public differ from private trusts. I complain of the conduct of a person in the character of guardian, as domestic guardian, having the care of a minor or insane person. In so doing do I say that guardianship is a bad institution? Does it enter into the head of anyone to suspect me of so doing? I complain of an individual in the character of a commercial agent or assignee of the effects of an insolvent. In so doing do I say that commercial agency is a bad thing? that the practice of vesting in the hands of trustees or assignees the effects of an insolvent for the purpose of their being divided among his creditors is a bad practice? Does any such conceit ever enter into the head of man as that of suspecting me of so doing?"

There are no complaints against government in Turkey—no motions in Parliament, no "Morning Chronicles," and no "Edinburgh Reviews": yet of all countries in the world it is that in which revolts and revolutions are the most frequent.

It is so far from true that no good government can exist consistently with such disclosure, that no good government can exist without it. It is quite obvious to all who are capable of reflection that by no other means than by lowering the governors in the estimation of the people can there be hope or chance of beneficial change. To infer from this wise endeavor to lessen the existing rulers in the estimation of the people, a wish of dissolving the government, is either artifice or error. The physician who intentionally weakens the patient by bleeding him has no intention he should perish.

The greater the quantity of respect a man receives, independently of good conduct, the less good is his behavior likely to be. It is the interest, therefore, of the public in the case of each to see that the respect paid to him should, as completely as possible, depend upon the goodness of his behavior in the execution of his trust. But it is, on the contrary, the interest of the trustee that the respect, the money, or any other advantage he receives in virtue of his office, should be as great, as secure, and as independent of conduct as possible. Soldiers expect to be shot at; public men must expect to be attacked, and sometimes unjustly. It keeps up the habit of considering their conduct as exposed to scrutiny; on the part of the people at large it keeps alive the expectation of witnessing such attacks, and the habit of looking out for them. The friends and supporters of government have always greater facility in keeping and raising it up than its adversaries have for lowering it.

ACCUSATION-SCARER'S DEVICE—"*Infamy Must Attach Somewhere.*" This fallacy consists in representing the character of a calumniator as necessarily and justly attaching upon him who, having made a charge of misconduct against any person possessed of political power or influence, fails of producing evidence sufficient for their conviction.

"If taken as a general proposition, applying to all public accusations, nothing can be more mischievous as well as fallacious. Supposing the charge unfounded, the delivery of it may have been accompanied with *mala fides* (consciousness of its injustice), with *temerity* only, or it may have been perfectly blameless. It is in the first case alone that infamy can with propriety attach upon him who brings it forward. A charge really groundless may have been honestly *believed* to be well founded, *i.e.*, believed with a sort of provisional credence, sufficient for the purpose of engaging a man to do his part toward the bringing about an investigation, but without sufficient reasons. But a charge may be perfectly groundless without attaching the smallest particle of blame upon him who brings it forward. Suppose him to have heard from one or more, presenting themselves to him in the character of percipient witnesses, a story which, either *in toto*, or perhaps only in *circumstances*, though in circumstances of the most material importance, should prove false and mendacious, how is the person who hears this and acts accordingly to blame? What sagacity can enable a man previously to legal investigation, a man who has no power that can enable him to insure correctness or completeness on the part of this extrajudicial testimony, to guard against deception in such a case?"

FALLACY OF FALSE CONSOLATION—"*What is the Matter with You?—What Would You Have?—Look at the People There, and There; Think how much Better Off You Are than They Are—Your Prosperity and Liberty are Objects of Their Envy; Your Institutions, Models of Their Imitation.*"

It is not the desire to look to the bright side that is blamed, but when a particular suffering, produced by an assigned cause, has been pointed out, the object of many apologists is to turn the eyes of inquirers and judges into any other quarter in preference. If a man's tenants were to come with a general encomium on the prosperity of the country instead of a specified sum, would it be accepted? In a court of justice in an action for damages did ever any such device occur as that of pleading assets in the hands of a third person? There is in fact no country so poor and so wretched in every element of prosperity, in which matter for this argument might not be found. Were the prosperity of the country tenfold as great as at present, the absurdity of the argument would not in the least degree be lessened. Why should the smallest evil be endured which can be cured because others suffer patiently under greater evils? Should the smallest improvement attainable be neglected because others remain contented in a state of still greater inferiority?

"Seriously and pointedly in the character of a bar to any measure of relief, no, nor to the most trivial improvement, can it ever be employed. Suppose a bill brought in for converting an impassable road anywhere into a passable one, would any man stand up to oppose it who could find nothing better to urge against it than the multitude and goodness of the roads we have already? No: when in the character of a serious bar to the measure in hand, be that measure what it may, an argument so palpably inapplicable is employed, it can only be for the purpose of creating a diversion;—of turning aside the minds of men from the subject really in hand to a picture which, by its beauty, it is hoped, may engross the attention of the assembly, and make them forget for the moment for what purpose they came there."

THE QUIETEST, OR NO COMPLAINT. "A new law or measure being proposed in the character of a remedy for some incontestable abuse or evil, an objection is frequently started to the following effect:—'The measure is unnecessary. Nobody complains of disorder in that shape, in which it is the aim of your measure to propose a remedy to it. But even when *no* cause of complaint has been found to exist, especially under governments which admit of complaints, men have in general not been slow to complain; much less where any just cause of complaint has existed.' The argument amounts to this:—Nobody complains, therefore nobody suffers. It amounts to a veto on all measures of precaution or prevention, and goes to establish a maxim in legislation directly opposed to the most ordinary prudence of common life; it enjoins us to build no parapets to a bridge till the number of accidents has raised a universal clamor."

PROCRASTINATOR'S ARGUMENT—*"Wait a Little; This is Not the Time."* This is the common argument of men who, being in reality hostile to a measure, are ashamed or afraid of appearing to be so. *To-day* is the plea—*eternal exclusion* commonly the object. It is the same sort of quirk as a plea of abatement in law—which is never employed but on the side of a dishonest defendant, whose hope it is to obtain an ultimate triumph, by overwhelming his adversary with despair, impoverishment, and lassitude. Which is the properest day to do good? which is the properest day to remove a nuisance? We answer, the very first day a man can be found to propose the removal of it; and whoever opposes the removal of it on that day will (if he dare) oppose it on every other. There is in the minds of many feeble friends to virtue and improvement, an imaginary period for the removal of evils, which it would certainly be worth while to wait for, if there was the smallest chance of its ever arriving—a period of unexampled peace and prosperity, when a patriotic king and an enlightened mob unite their ardent efforts for the amelioration of human affairs; when the oppressor is as delighted to give up the oppression, as the oppressed is to be liberated from it; when the difficulty and the unpopularity would be to continue the evil, not to abolish it! These are the periods when fair-weather philosophers are willing to venture out and hazard a little for the general good. But the history of human nature is so contrary to all this, that almost all improvements are made after the bitterest resistance, and in the midst of tumults and civil violence—the worst period at which they can be made, compared to which any period is eligible, and should be seized hold of by the friends of salutary reform.

SNAIL'S PACE ARGUMENT—*"One Thing at a Time!—Not Too Fast!—Slow and Sure!*—Importance of the business—extreme difficulty of the business—danger of innovation—need of caution and circumspection—impossibility of foreseeing all consequences—danger of precipitation—everything should be gradual—one thing at a time—this is not the time—great occupation at present—wait for more leisure—people well satisfied—no petitions presented—no complaints heard—no such mischief has yet taken place—stay till it has taken place! Such is the prattle which the magpie in office, who, understanding nothing, yet understands that he must have something to say on every subject, shouts out among his auditors as a succedaneum to thought."

VAGUE GENERALITIES. Vague generalities comprehend a numerous class of fallacies resorted to by those who, in preference to the determinate expressions which they might use, adopt others more vague and indeterminate.

Take, for instance, the terms government, laws, morals, religion. Everybody will admit that there are in the world bad governments, bad laws, bad morals, and bad religions. The bare circumstance, therefore, of being engaged in exposing the defects of government, law, morals, and religion does not of itself afford the slightest presumption that a writer is engaged in anything blamable. If his attack be only directed against that which is bad in each, his efforts may be productive of good to any extent. This essential distinction, however, the defender of abuses uniformly takes care to keep out of sight; and boldly imputes to his antagonists an intention to subvert all *government, law, morals, and religion.* Propose anything with a view to the improvement of the existing practice, in relation to law, government, and religion, he will treat you with an oration upon the necessity and utility of law, government, and religion. Among the several cloudy appellatives which have been commonly employed as cloaks for misgovernment, there is none more conspicuous in this atmosphere of illusion than the word order. As often as any measure is brought forward which has for its object to lessen the sacrifice made by the many to the few, *social order* is the phrase commonly opposed to its progress.

"By a defalcation made from any part of the mass of fictitious delay, vexation, and expense, out of which, and in proportion to which, lawyers' profit is made to flow—by any defalcation made from the mass of needless and worse than useless emolument to office, with or without service or pretence of service—by any addition endeavored to be made to the quantity, or improvement in the quality of service rendered, or time bestowed in service rendered in return for such emolument—by every endeavor that has for its object the persuading the people to place their fate at the disposal of any other agents than those in whose hands breach of trust is certain, due fulfilment of it morally and physically impossible—*social order* is said to be endangered, and threatened to be destroyed."

In the same way "Establishment" is a word in use to protect the bad parts of establishments, by charging those who wish to remove or alter them, with a wish to subvert all good establishments.

Mischievous fallacies also circulate from the convertible use of what Mr. B. is pleased to call dyslogistic and eulogistic terms. Thus, a vast concern is expressed for the "liberty of the press," and the utmost abhorrence of its "licentiousness": but then, by the licentiousness of the press is meant every disclosure by which any abuse is brought to light and exposed to shame—by the "liberty of the press" is meant only publications from which no such inconvenience is to be apprehended; and the fallacy consists in employing the sham approbation of liberty as a mask for the real opposition to all free discussion. To write a pamphlet so ill that nobody will read it; to animadvert in terms so weak and insipid upon great evils, that no disgust is excited at the vice, and no apprehension in the evil-doer, is a fair use of the liberty of the press, and is not only pardoned by the friends of government, but draws from them the most fervent eulogium. The licentiousness of the press consists in doing the thing boldly and well, in striking terror into the guilty, and in rousing the attention of the public to the defence of their highest interests. This is the licentiousness of the press held in the greatest horror by timid and corrupt men, and punished by semi-animous, semi-cadaverous judges, with a captivity of many years. In the same manner the dyslogistic and eulogistic fallacies are used in the case of reform.

"Between all abuses whatsoever there exists that connection—between all persons who see, each of them, any one abuse in which an advantage results to himself, there exists, in point of interest, that close and sufficiently understood connection, of which intimation has been given already. To no one abuse can correction be administered without endangering the existence of every other.

"If, then, with this inward determination not to suffer, so far as depends upon himself, the adoption of any reform which he is able to prevent, it should seem to him necessary or advisable to put on for a cover the profession or appearance of a desire to contribute to such reform—in pursuance of the device or fallacy here in question, he will represent that which goes by the name of reform as distinguishable into two species; one of them a fit subject for approbation, the other for disapprobation. That which he thus professes to have marked for approbation, he will accordingly for the expression of such approbation, characterize by some adjunct of the *eulogistic* cast, such as moderate, for example, or temperate, or practical, or practicable.

"To the other of these nominally distinct species, he will, at the same time, attach some adjunct of the *dyslogistic* cast, such as violent, intemperate, extravagant, outrageous, theoretical, speculative, and so forth.

"Thus, then, in profession and to appearance, there are in his conception of the matter two distinct and opposite species of reform, to one of which his approbation, to the other his disapprobation, is attached. But the species to which his approbation is attached is an *empty* species—a species in which no individual is, or is intended to be, contained.

"The species to which his disapprobation is attached is, on the contrary, a crowded species, a receptacle in which the whole contents of the *genus*—of the *genus* 'Reform'—are intended to be included."

ANTI-RATIONAL FALLACIES. When reason is in opposition to a man's interests his study will naturally be to render the faculty itself, and whatever issues from it, an object of hatred and contempt. The sarcasm and other figures of speech employed on the occasion are directed not merely against reason but against thought, as if there were something in the faculty of thought that rendered the exercise of it incompatible with useful and successful practice. Sometimes a plan, which would not suit the official person's interest, is without more ado pronounced a speculative one; and, by this observation, all need of rational and deliberate discussion is considered to be superseded. The first effort of the corruptionist is to fix the epithet speculative upon any scheme which he thinks may cherish the spirit of reform. The expression is hailed with the greatest delight by bad and feeble men, and repeated with the most unwearied energy; and to the word "speculative," by way of reinforcement, are added: *theoretical, visionary, chimerical, romantic, Utopian.*

"Sometimes a distinction is taken, and thereupon a concession made. The plan is good in theory, but it would be bad in practice, *i.e.*, its being good in theory does not hinder its being bad in practice.

"Sometimes, as if in consequence of a further progress made in the art of irrationality, the plan is pronounced to be "too good to be practicable"; and its being so good as it is, is thus represented as the very cause of its being bad in practice.

"In short, such is the perfection at which this art is at length arrived, that the very circumstance of a plan's being susceptible of the appellation of a *plan*, has been gravely stated as a circumstance sufficient to warrant its being rejected—rejected, if not with hatred, at any rate with a sort of accompaniment which, to the million, is commonly felt still more galling—with contempt."

There is a propensity to push theory too far; but what is the just inference? not that theoretical propositions (*i.e.,* all propositions of any considerable comprehension or extent) should, from such their extent, be considered to be false *in toto,* but only that, in the particular case, should inquiry be made whether, supposing the proposition to be in the character of a rule generally true, an exception ought to be taken out of it. It might almost be imagined that there was something wicked or unwise in the exercise of thought; for everybody feels a necessity for disclaiming it. "I am not given to speculation, I am no friend to theories." Can a man disclaim theory, can he disclaim speculation, without disclaiming thought?

The description of persons by whom this fallacy is chiefly employed are those who, regarding a plan as adverse to their interests, and not finding it on the ground of general utility exposed to any preponderant objection, have recourse to this objection in the character of an instrument of contempt, in the view of preventing those from looking into it who might have been otherwise disposed. It is by the fear of seeing it practised that they are drawn to speak of it as impracticable. "Upon the face of it (exclaims some feeble or pensioned gentleman) it carries that air of plausibility, that, if you were not upon your guard, might engage you to bestow more or less attention upon it; but were you to take the trouble, you would find that (as it is with all these plans which promise so much) practicability would at last be wanting to it. To save yourself from this trouble, the wisest course you can take is to put the plan aside, and to think no more about the matter." This is always accompanied with a peculiar grin of triumph.

The whole of these fallacies may be gathered together in a little oration, which we will denominate the "Noodle's Oration":

"What would our ancestors say to this, Sir? How does

this measure tally with their institutions? How does it agree with their experience? Are we to put the wisdom of yesterday in competition with the wisdom of centuries? [*Hear! hear!*] Is beardless youth to show no respect for the decisions of mature age? [*Loud cries of hear! hear!*] If this measure be right, would it have escaped the wisdom of those Saxon progenitors to whom we are indebted for so many of our best political institutions? Would the Dane have passed it over? Would the Norman have rejected it? Would such a notable discovery have been reserved for these modern and degenerate times? Besides, Sir, if the measure itself is good, I ask the honorable gentleman if this is the time for carrying it into execution—whether, in fact, a more unfortunate period could have been selected than that which he has chosen? If this were an ordinary measure I should not oppose it with so much vehemence; but, Sir, it calls in question the wisdom of an irrevocable law—of a law passed at the memorable period of the Revolution. What right have we, Sir, to break down this firm column on which the great men of that age stamped a character of eternity? Are not all authorities against this measure—Pitt, Fox, Cicero, and the Attorney- and Solicitor-General? The proposition is new, Sir; it is the first time it was ever heard in this House. I am not prepared, Sir— this House is not prepared—to receive it. The measure implies a distrust of his Majesty's Government; their disapproval is sufficient to warrant opposition. Precaution only is requisite where danger is apprehended. Here the high character of the individuals in question is a sufficient guarantee against any ground of alarm. Give not, then, your sanction to this measure; for, whatever be its character, if you do give your sanction to it, the same man by whom this is proposed will propose to you others to which it will be impossible to give your consent. I care very little, Sir, for the ostensible measure; but what is there behind? What are the honorable gentleman's future schemes? If we pass this bill, what fresh concessions may he not require? What further degradation is he planning for his country? Talk of evil and inconvenience, Sir! look to other countries—study other aggregations and societies of men, and then see whether the laws of this country demand a remedy or deserve a panegyric. Was the honorable gentleman (let me ask him) always of this way of thinking? Do I not remember when he was the advocate, in this House, of very opposite opinions? I not only quarrel with his present sentiments, Sir, but I declare very frankly I do not like the party with which he acts. If his own motives were as pure as possible, they cannot but suffer contamination from those with whom he is politically associated. This measure may be a boon to the Constitution, but I will accept no favor to the Constitution from such hands. [*Loud cries of hear! hear!*] I profess myself, Sir, an honest and upright member of the British Parliament, and I am not afraid to profess myself an enemy to all change and all innovation. I am satisfied with things as they are; and it will be my pride and pleasure to hand down this country to my children as I received it from those who preceded me. The honorable gentleman pretends to justify the severity with which he has attacked the noble lord who presides in the Court of Chancery. But I say such attacks are pregnant with mischief to government itself. Oppose ministers, you oppose government; disgrace ministers, you disgrace government; bring ministers into contempt, you bring government into contempt; and anarchy and civil war are the consequences. Besides, sir, the measure is unnecessary. Nobody complains of disorder in that shape in which it is the aim of your measure to propose a remedy to it. The business is one of the greatest importance; there is need of the greatest caution and circumspection. Do not let us be precipitate, Sir; it is impossible to foresee all consequences. Everything should be gradual; the example of a neighboring nation should fill us with alarm! The honorable gentleman has taxed me with illiberality, Sir; I deny the charge. I hate innovation, but I love improvement. I am an enemy to the corruption of government, but I defend its influence. I dread reform, but I dread it only when it is intemperate. I consider the liberty of the press as the great palladium of the Constitution; but, at the same time, I hold the licentiousness of the press in the greatest abhorrence. Nobody is more conscious than I am of the splendid abilities of the honorable mover, but I tell him at once his scheme is too good to be practicable. It savors of Utopia. It looks well in theory, but it won't do in practice. It will not do, I repeat, Sir, in practice; and so the advocates of the measure will find, if, unfortunately, it should find its way through Parliament. [*Cheers.*] The source of that corruption to which the honorable member alludes is in the minds of the people; so rank and extensive is that corruption, that no political reform can have any effect in removing it. Instead of reforming others—instead of reforming the State, the Constitution, and everything that is most excellent, let each man reform himself! let him look at home, he will find there enough to do without looking abroad and aiming at what is out of his power. [*Loud cheers.*] And now, Sir, as it is frequently the custom in this House to end with a quotation, and as the gentleman who preceded me in the debate has anticipated me in my favorite quotation of the 'Strong pull and the long pull,' I shall end with the memorable words of the assembled barons: '*Nolumus leges Angliæ mutari.*' "[5]

"Upon the whole, the following are the characters which appertain in common to all the several arguments here distinguished by the name of fallacies:—

"1. Whatsoever be the measure in hand, they are, with relation to it, irrelevant.

"2. They are all of them such, that the application of these irrelevant arguments affords a presumption either of the weakness or total absence of relevant arguments on the side on which they are employed.

"3. To any good purpose they are all of them unnecessary.

"4. They are all of them not only capable of being applied, but actually in the habit of being applied, and with advantage, to bad purposes, viz.: to the obstruction and defeat of all such measures as have for their object the re-

---

[5] [We do not wish the laws of England to be changed.]

moval of the abuses or other imperfections still discernible
in the frame and practice of the government.

"5. By means of their irrelevancy, they all of them consume and misapply time, thereby obstructing the course
and retarding the progress of all necessary and useful business.

"6. By that irritative quality which, in virtue of their
irrelevancy, with the improbity or weakness of which it is
indicative, they possess, all of them, in a degree more or
less considerable, but in a more particular degree such of
them as consist in personalities, they are productive of ill-
humor, which in some instances has been productive of blood-
shed, and is continually productive, as above, of waste of
time and hindrance of business.

"7. On the part of those who, whether in spoken or
written discourses, give utterance to them, they are indicative either of improbity or intellectual weakness, or of a
contempt for the understanding of those on whose minds
they are destined to operate.

"8. On the part of those on whom they operate, they are
indicative of intellectual weakness; and on the part of those
in and by whom they are pretended to operate, they are
indicative of improbity, viz., in the shape of insincerity.

"The practical conclusion is, that in proportion as the acceptance, and thence the utterance, of them can be prevented,
the understanding of the public will be strengthened, the
morals of the public will be purified, and the practice of
government improved."

RICHARD WHATELY

[1787–1863]

Whately's once famous little book, *Historic Doubts Relative to Napoleon Buonaparte,* now seems to be quite forgotten. Indeed, Whately himself seems to be quite forgotten. In his own time, however, he was a leading figure in the Anglican Church and for years was Archbishop of Dublin. As a young man he was a vigorous, blustering, almost brutal teacher who loved to dangle his "young pups," since "the good dog does not whine." But he altered his methods for the awkward and sensitive John Henry Newman. It was Whately, Newman said, whose "gentle and encouraging instruction . . . opened my mind, and taught me to think and use my reason."

While teaching at Oxford, Whately wrote the articles on logic and rhetoric for the *Encyclopaedia Metropolitana.* When expanded in book form, they became standard texts for generations of students. But his greatest success was the early tour de force, *Historic Doubts Relative to Napoleon Buonaparte,* first published in 1819, two years before Napoleon's death, and reprinted many times after. It was a clever satire "directed against excessive scepticism as applied to the Gospel history." But Whately was often surprised and distressed to find that readers missed his point!

* * *

HISTORIC DOUBTS RELATIVE TO
NAPOLEON BUONAPARTE

Long as the public attention has been occupied by the extraordinary personage from whose ambition we are supposed to have so narrowly escaped, the subject seems to have lost scarcely anything of its interest. We are still occupied in recounting the exploits, discussing the character, inquiring into the present situation, and even conjecturing as to the future prospects of Napoleon Buonaparte.

Nor is this at all to be wondered at, if we consider the very extraordinary nature of those exploits, and of that character; their greatness and extensive importance, as well as the unexampled strangeness of the events, and also that strong additional stimulant, the mysterious uncertainty that hangs over the character of the man. If it be doubtful whether any history (exclusive of such as is confessedly fabulous) ever attributed to its hero such a series of wonderful achievements compressed into so small a space of time, it is certain that to no one were ever assigned so many dissimilar characters.

It is true, indeed, that party prejudices have drawn a favorable and an unfavorable portrait of almost every eminent man; but amidst all the diversities of coloring, something of the same general outline is always distinguishable. And even the virtues in the one description bear some resemblance to the vices of another. Rashness, for instance, will be called courage, or courage rashness; heroic firmness and obstinate pride will correspond in the two opposite descriptions; and in some leading features both will agree. Neither the friends nor the enemies of Philip of Macedon, or of Julius Cæsar, ever questioned their COURAGE or their MILITARY SKILL.

With Buonaparte, however, it has been otherwise. This obscure Corsican adventurer—a man, according to some, of extraordinary talents and courage, according to others, of very moderate abilities and a rank coward—advanced rapidly in the French army, obtained a high command, gained a series of important victories, and, elated by success, embarked in an expedition against Egypt; which was planned and conducted, according to some, with the most consummate skill, according to others, with the utmost wildness and folly. He was unsuccessful, however; and, leaving the army of Egypt in a very distressed situation, he returned to France, and found the nation, or at least the army, so favorably disposed towards him, that he was enabled, with the utmost ease, to overthrow the existing government, and obtain for himself the supreme power; at first under the modest appellation of consul, but afterwards with the more sounding title of Emperor. While in possession of this power, he overthrew the most powerful coalitions of the other European States against him, and, though driven from the sea by the British fleets, overran nearly the whole continent, triumphant. Finishing a war, not unfrequently, in a single campaign, he entered the capitals of most of the hostile potentates, deposed and created kings at his pleasure, and appeared the virtual sovereign of the chief part of the continent, from the frontiers of Spain to those of Russia. Even those countries we find him invading with prodigious armies, defeating their forces, penetrating to their capitals, and threatening their total subjugation. But at Moscow his progress is stopped; a winter of unusual severity, cooperating with the efforts of the Russians, totally destroys his enormous host; and the German sovereigns throw off the yoke, and combine to oppose him. He raises another vast army, which is also ruined at Leipsic; and again another, with which, like a second Antæus, he for some time maintains himself in France; but is finally defeated, deposed, and banished to the island of Elba, of which the sovereignty is conferred on him. Thence he returns, in about nine months, at the head of six hundred men, to attempt the deposition of King Louis, who had been peaceably recalled; the French nation declare in his favor, and he is reinstated without a struggle. He raises another great army to oppose the allied powers, which is totally defeated at Waterloo. He is a second time deposed, surrenders to the British, and is placed in confinement at the island of St. Helena. Such is the outline of the eventful history presented to us; in the detail of which, however, there is almost every conceivable variety of statement; while the motives and conduct of the chief actor are involved in still greater doubt, and the subject of still more eager controversy.

In the midst of these controversies, the preliminary question, concerning the *existence* of this extraordinary personage, seems never to have occurred to any one as a matter of doubt; and to show even the smallest hesitation in admitting it, would probably be regarded as an excess of scepticism, on the ground that this point has always been taken for granted by the disputants on all sides, being indeed implied by the very nature of their disputes.

But is it in fact found that *undisputed* points are always such as have been the most carefully examined as to the evidence on which they rest?—that facts or principles which are taken for granted, without controversy, as the common basis of opposite opinions, are always themselves established on sufficient grounds? On the contrary, is not any such fundamental point, from the very circumstance of its being taken for granted at once, and the attention drawn off to some other question, likely to be admitted on insufficient evidence, and the flaws in that evidence overlooked? Experience will teach us that such instances often occur. Witness the well-known anecdote of the Royal Society, to whom King Charles II proposed as a question, whence it is that a vessel of water receives no addition of weight from a live fish being put into it, though it does if the fish be dead. Various solutions, of great ingenuity, were proposed, discussed, objected to, and defended; nor was it till they had been long bewildered in the inquiry, that it occurred to them to *try the experiment;* by which they at once ascertained that the phenomenon which they were striving to account for- which was the acknowledged base and substratum, as it were, of their debates—had no existence but in the invention of the witty monarch.[1]

Another instance of the same kind is so very remarkable that I cannot forbear mentioning it. It was objected to the system of Copernicus when it was first brought forward, that if the earth turned on its axis, as he represented, a stone

---

[1] "A report is spread [says Voltaire in one of his works] that there is in some country or other a giant as big as a mountain; and men presently fall to hot disputing concerning the precise length of his nose, the breadth of his thumb, and other particulars, and anathematize each other for heterodoxy of belief concerning them. In the midst of all, if some bold sceptic ventures to hint a doubt as to the existence of this giant, all are ready to join against him and tear him to pieces." This looks almost like a prophetic allegory relating to the gigantic Napoleon.

dropped from the summit of a tower would not fall at the foot of it, but at a great distance to the west; *in the same manner as a stone dropped from the masthead of a ship in full sail does not fall at the foot of the mast, but towards the stern*. To this it was answered, that a stone, being a *part* of the earth, obeys the same laws, and moves with it; whereas, it is no part of the ship; of which, consequently, its motion is independent. This solution was admitted by some, but opposed by others, and the controversy went on with spirit; nor was it till *one hundred years* after the death of Copernicus that, the experiment being tried, it was ascertained that the stone thus dropped from the head of the mast *does* fall at the foot of it!

Let it be observed that I am not now impugning any one particular narrative; but merely showing generally, that what is *unquestioned* is not necessarily unquestionable; since men will often, at the very moment when they are accurately sifting the evidence of some disputed point, admit hastily, and on the most insufficient grounds, what they have been accustomed to see taken for granted.

The celebrated Hume[2] has pointed out, also, the readiness with which men believe, on very slight evidence, any story that pleases their imagination by its admirable and marvellous character. Such hasty credulity, however, as he well remarks, is utterly unworthy of a philosophical mind; which should rather suspend its judgment the more, in proportion to the strangeness of the account, and yield to none but the most decisive and unimpeachable proofs.

Let it, then, be allowed us, as is surely reasonable, just to inquire with respect to the extraordinary story I have been speaking of, on what evidence we believe it. We shall be told that it is *notorious;* that is, in plain English, it is very *much talked about*. But as the generality of those who talk about Buonaparte do not even pretend to speak from *their own authority*, but merely to repeat what they have casually

---

[2] "With what greediness are the miraculous accounts of travellers received, their descriptions of sea and land monsters, their relations of wonderful adventures, strange men, and uncouth manners!"—Hume's *Essay on Miracles*.

heard, we cannot reckon them as in any degree witnesses; but must allow, ninety-nine hundredths of what we are told to be mere hearsay, which would not be at all the more worthy of credit even if it were repeated by ten times as many more. As for those who profess to have *personally known* Napoleon Buonaparte, and to have *themselves witnessed* his transactions, I write not for them; *if any such there be,* who are inwardly conscious of the truth of all they relate, I have nothing to say to them, but to beg that they will be tolerant and charitable towards their neighbors, who have not the same means of ascertaining the truth, and who may well be excused for remaining doubtful about such extraordinary events, till most unanswerable proofs shall be adduced. "I would not have believed such a thing, if I had not seen it," is a common preface or appendix to a narrative of marvels; and usually calls forth from an intelligent hearer the appropriate answer, *"No more will I."*

Let us, however, endeavor to trace up some of this hearsay evidence as far towards its source as we are able. Most persons would refer to the *newspapers* as the authority from which their knowledge on the subject was derived; so that, generally speaking, we may say it is on the testimony of the newspapers that men believe in the existence and exploits of Napoleon Buonaparte.

It is rather a remarkable circumstance, that it is common to hear Englishmen speak of the impudent fabrications of foreign newspapers, and express wonder that any one can be found to credit them; while they conceive that, in this favored land, the liberty of the press is a sufficient security for veracity. It is true they often speak contemptuously of such "newspaper stories" as last but a short time; indeed, they continually see them contradicted within a day or two in the same paper, or their falsity detected by some journal of an opposite party; but still whatever is *long adhered to* and often *repeated,* especially if it also appear in *several different* papers (and this, though they notoriously copy from one another), is almost sure to be generally believed. Whence this high respect which is practically paid to newspaper authority? Do men think that because a witness has been perpetually detected in falsehood, he may therefore be the more safely believed whenever he is *not* detected? or does adherence to a story, and frequent repetition of it, render it the more credible? On the contrary, is it not a common remark in other cases, that a liar will generally stand to and reiterate what he has once said, merely because he *has* said it?

Let us, if possible, divest ourselves of this superstitious veneration for everything that appears "in print," and examine a little more systematically the evidence which is adduced.

I suppose it will not be denied, that the three following are among the most important points to be ascertained in deciding on the credibility of witnesses—first, whether they have the means of gaining correct *information;* secondly, whether they have any *interest* in concealing truth, or propagating falsehood; and, thirdly, whether they *agree* in their testimony. Let us examine the present witnesses upon all these points.

First, what means have the editors of newspapers for gaining correct information? We know not, except from their own statements. Besides what is copied from other journals, foreign or British (which is usually more than three fourths of the news published),² they profess to refer to the authority of certain "private correspondents" abroad; *who* these correspondents are, what means *they* have of obtaining information, or whether they exist at all, we have no way of ascer-

---

² "Suppose a fact to be transmitted through twenty persons; the first communicating it to the second, the second to the third, etc., and let the probability of each testimony be expressed by nine tenths (that is, suppose that of ten reports made by each witness, nine only are true), then, at every time the story passes from one witness to another, the evidence is reduced to nine tenths of what it was before. Thus, after it has passed through the whole twenty, the evidence will be found to be less than one eighth."—La Place, *Essai Philosophique sur les Probabilités.*

That is, the chances for the fact thus attested being true, will be, according to this distinguished calculator, less than one in eight. Very few of the common newspaper stories, however, relating to foreign countries, could be traced, if the matter were carefully investigated, up to an actual eye-witness, even through twenty intermediate witnesses; and many of the steps of our ladder would, I fear, prove but rotten; few of the reporters would deserve to have *one in ten* fixed as the proportion of their false accounts.

taining. We find ourselves in the condition of the Hindoos
who are told by their priests that the earth stands on an
elephant, and the elephant on a tortoise; but are left to find
out for themselves what the tortoise stands on, or whether it
stands on anything at all.

So much for our clear knowledge of the means of *information*
possessed by these witnesses; next for the grounds on
which we are to calculate on their *veracity*.

Have they not a manifest interest in circulating the wonderful accounts of Napoleon Buonaparte and his achievements,
whether true or false? Few would read newspapers if they
did not sometimes find wonderful or important news in them;
and we may safely say that no subject was ever found so
inexhaustibly interesting as the present.

It may be urged, however, that there are several adverse
political parties, of which the various public prints are respectively the organs, and who would not fail to expose each
other's fabrications.[4] Doubtless they would, if they could do
so without at the same time exposing *their own;* but identity
of interests may induce a community of operations up to a
certain point. And let it be observed that the object of contention between these rival parties is, *who* shall have the
administration of public affairs, the control of public expenditure, and the disposal of places: the question, I say,
is not, whether the people shall be governed or not, but *by
which party* they shall be governed; not whether the taxes
shall be paid or not, but *who* shall *receive* them. Now it
must be admitted, that Buonaparte is a political bugbear,
most convenient to *any* administration. "If you do not adopt
our measures and reject those of our opponents, Buonaparte
will be sure to prevail over you; if you do not submit to the
Government, at least under *our* administration, this formidable enemy will take advantage of your insubordination to

---

[4] "I did not mention the difficulty of detecting a falsehood in any private or
even public history, at the time and place where it is said to happen; much
more where the scene is removed to ever so small a distance. . . . But the
matter never comes to any issue, if trusted to the common method of alterca-
tion and debate and flying rumors."—Hume's *Essay on Miracles*.

conquer and enslave you. Pay your taxes cheerfully, or the tremendous Buonaparte will take all from you." Buonaparte, in short, was the burden of every song; his redoubted name was the charm which always succeeded in unloosing the purse-strings of the nation. And let us not be too sure, safe as we now think ourselves, that some occasion may not occur for again producing on the stage so useful a personage. It is not merely to naughty children in the nursery that the threat of being "given to Buonaparte" has proved effectual.

It is surely probable, therefore, that with an object substantially the same, all parties may have availed themselves of one common instrument. It is not necessary to suppose that for this purpose they secretly entered into a formal agreement; though, by the way, there are reports afloat, that the editors of the *Courier* and *Morning Chronicle* hold amicable consultations as to the conduct of their public warfare: I will not take upon me to say that this is incredible; but at any rate it is not necessary for the establishment of the probability I contend for. Neither, again, would I imply that *all* newspaper editors are utterers of forged stories, "knowing them to be forged;" most likely the great majority of them publish what they find in other papers with the same simplicity that their readers peruse it; and therefore, it must be observed, are not at all more proper than their readers to be cited as authorities.

Still it will be said, that unless we suppose a regularly preconcerted plan, we might at least expect to find great discrepancies in the accounts published. Though they might adopt the general outline of facts one from another, they would have to fill up the detail for themselves; and in this, therefore, we should meet with infinite and irreconcilable variety.

Now this is precisely the point I am tending to; for the fact exactly accords with the above supposition; the discordance and mutual contradictions of these witnesses being such as would alone throw a considerable shade of doubt over their testimony. It is not in minute circumstances alone that the discrepancy appears, such as might be expected to

appear in a narrative substantially true; but in very great
and leading transactions, and such as are very intimately
connected with the supposed hero. For instance, it is by no
means agreed whether Buonaparte led in person the celebrated charge over the bridge of Lodi (for *celebrated* it
certainly is, as well as the siege of Troy, whether either event
ever really took place or no), or was safe in the rear, while
Augereau performed the exploit. The same doubt hangs
over the charge of the French cavalry at Waterloo. The
peasant Lacoste, who professed to have been Buonaparte's
guide on the day of battle, and who earned a fortune by de-
tailing over and over again to visitors all the particulars of
what the great man said and did up to the moment of flight
—this same Lacoste has been suspected by others besides me
of having never even been near the great man, and having
fabricated the whole story for the sake of making a gain
of the credulity of travellers. In the accounts that are extant
of the battle itself, published by persons professing to have
been present, the reader will find that there is a discrepancy
of *three or four hours* as to the time when the battle began!
—a battle, be it remembered, not fought with javelins and
arrows, like those of the ancients, in which one part of a
large army might be engaged, while a distant portion of the
same army knew nothing of it, but a battle commencing
(if indeed it were ever fought at all) with the *firing of can-
non,* which would have announced pretty loudly what was
going on.

It is no less uncertain whether or no this strange personage
poisoned in Egypt an hospital full of his own soldiers, and
butchered in cold blood a garrison that had surrendered.
But, not to multiply instances, the battle of Borodino, which
is represented as one of the greatest ever fought, was un-
equivocally claimed as a victory by both parties; nor is the
question decided at this day. We have official accounts on
both sides, circumstantially detailed, in the names of supposed
respectable persons, professing to have been present on the
spot; yet totally irreconcilable. *Both* these accounts *may* be
false; but since *one* of them *must* be false, that one (it is no

matter *which,* we suppose) proves incontrovertibly this important maxim: that *it is possible for a narrative—however circumstantial—however steadily maintained—however public and however important the events it relates—however grave the authority on which it is published—to be nevertheless an entire fabrication!*

Many of the events which have been recorded were probably believed much the more readily and firmly from the apparent caution and hesitation with which they were at first published, the vehement contradiction in our papers of many pretended French accounts, and the abuse lavished upon them for falsehood, exaggeration, and gasconade. But is it not possible—is it not indeed perfectly natural?—that the publishers even of known falsehood should assume this cautious demeanor, and this abhorrence of exaggeration, in order the more easily to gain credit? Is it not also very possible that those who actually believed what they published, may have suspected mere *exaggeration* in stories which were entire *fictions?* Many men have that sort of simplicity, that they think themselves quite secure against being deceived, provided they believe only *part* of the story they hear, when perhaps the whole is equally false. So that perhaps these simple-hearted editors, who were so vehement against lying bulletins, and so wary in announcing their great news, were in the condition of a clown who thinks he has bought a great bargain because he has beat down the price perhaps from a guinea to a crown, for some article that is not really worth a groat.

With respect to the *character* of Buonaparte, the dissonance is, if possible, still greater. According to some, he was a wise, humane, magnanimous hero; others paint him as a monster of cruelty, meanness, and perfidy: some, even of those who are most inveterate against him, speak very highly of his political and military ability; others place him on the very verge of insanity. But allowing that all this may be the coloring of party prejudice (which surely is allowing a great deal), there is one point to which such a solution will hardly apply—if there be anything that can be clearly ascertained in

history, one would think it must be the *personal courage* of
a *military man;* yet here we are as much at a loss as ever;
at the very same times, and on the same occasions, he is
described by different writers as a man of undaunted intrepidity, and as an absolute poltroon.

What, then, are we to believe? If we are disposed to
credit all that is told us, we must believe in the existence
not only of one, but of two or three Buonapartes; if we admit
nothing but what is well authenticated, we shall be compelled to doubt of the existence of any.[5]

It appears, then, that those on whose testimony the
existence and actions of Buonaparte are generally believed,
fail in ALL the most essential points on which the credibility
of witnesses depends—first we have no assurance that they
have access to correct information; secondly, they have an
apparent interest in propagating falsehood; and, thirdly, they
palpably contradict each other in the most important points.

Another circumstance which throws additional suspicion
on these tales is, that the Whig party, as they are called—the
warm advocates of liberty, and opposers of the encroachments
of monarchical power—have for some time past strenuously
espoused the cause, and vindicated the character of Buonaparte, who is represented by all as having been, if not a
tyrant, at least an absolute despot. One of the most forward
in this cause is a gentleman who once stood foremost in
holding up this very man to public execration, who first
published, and long maintained against popular incredulity,
the accounts of his atrocities in Egypt. Now, that such a
course should be adopted for party purposes, by those who
are aware that the whole story is a fiction and the hero of
it imaginary, seems not very incredible; but if they believed
in the real existence of this despot, I cannot conceive how
they could so forsake their principles as to advocate his cause
and eulogize his character.

[5] We entertain a suspicion concerning any matter of fact "when the witnesses *contradict* each other; when they are of a *suspicious* character; when
they have an *interest* in what they affirm."—Hume's *Essay on Miracles.*

After all, it may be expected that many who perceive the force of these objections, will yet be loath to think it possible that they and the public at large can have been so long and so greatly imposed upon. And thus it is that the magnitude and boldness of a fraud becomes its best support; the millions who for so many ages have believed in Mahomet or Brahma, lean as it were on each other for support; and not having vigor of mind enough boldly to throw off vulgar prejudices, and dare be wiser than the multitude, persuade themselves that what so many have acknowledged must be true. But I call on those who boast their philosophical freedom of thought, and would fain tread in the steps of Hume and other inquirers of the like exalted and speculative genius, to follow up fairly and fully their own principles, and, throwing off the shackles of authority, to examine carefully the evidence of whatever is proposed to them before they admit its truth.

That even in this enlightened age, as it is called, a whole nation may be egregiously imposed upon, even in matters which intimately concern them, may be proved (if it has not been already proved) by the following instance: It was stated in the newspapers, that, a month after the battle of Trafalgar, an English officer who had been a prisoner of war, and was exchanged, returned to this country from France; and beginning to condole with his countrymen on the terrible *defeat* they had sustained, was infinitely astonished to learn that the battle of Trafalgar was a splendid victory: he had been assured, he said, that in that battle the English had been totally defeated; and the French were fully and universally persuaded that such was the fact. Now if this report of the belief of the French nation was *not* true, the British public were completely imposed upon; if it *was* true, then both nations were, at the same time, rejoicing in the event of the same battle, as a signal victory to themselves; and consequently one or other, at least, of these nations must have been the dupes of their Government; for if the battle was never fought at all, or was not decisive on either side, in that case *both* parties were deceived. This instance, I conceive, is absolutely demonstrative of the point in question.

"But what shall we say to the testimony of those many respectable persons who went to Plymouth, on purpose, and saw Buonaparte with their own eyes—must they not trust their senses?" I would not disparage either the eyesight or the veracity of these gentlemen. I am ready to allow that they went to Plymouth for the purpose of seeing Buonaparte; nay, more, that they actually rowed out into the harbor in a boat, and came alongside of a man-of-war, on whose deck they saw a man in a cocked hat, who, *they were told*, was Buonaparte. This is the utmost point to which their testimony goes; how they ascertained that this man in the cocked hat had gone through all the marvellous and romantic adventures with which we have so long been amused, we are not told. Did they perceive in his physiognomy his true name and authentic history? Truly this evidence is such as country people give one for a story of apparitions. If you discover any signs of incredulity, they triumphantly show the very house which the ghost haunted, the identical dark corner where it used to vanish, and perhaps even the tombstone of the person whose death it foretold. Jack Cade's nobility was supported by the same irresistible kind of evidence; having asserted that the eldest son of Edmond Mortimer, Earl of March, was stolen by a beggar-woman, "became a bricklayer when he came to age," and was the father of the supposed Jack Cade. One of his companions confirms the story by saying, "Sir, he made a chimney in my father's house, and the bricks are alive at this day to testify it; therefore deny it not."

Much of the same kind is the testimony of our brave countrymen, who are ready to produce the scars they received in fighting against this terrible Buonaparte. That they fought and were wounded, they may safely testify; and probably they no less firmly *believe* what they were *told* respecting the cause in which they fought: it would have been a high breach of discipline to doubt it; and they, I conceive, are men better skilled in handling a musket than in sifting evidence and detecting imposture. But I defy any one of them to come forward and declare, *on his own knowledge,* what was the cause in which he fought, under whose commands the opposed generals acted, and whether the person who issued those commands did really perform the mighty achievements we are told of.

Let those, then, who pretend to philosophical freedom of inquiry—who scorn to rest their opinions on popular belief, and to shelter themselves under the example of the unthinking multitude—consider carefully, each one for himself, what is the evidence, proposed to himself in particular, for the existence of such a person as Napoleon Buonaparte: I do not mean, whether there ever was a person bearing that *name,* for that is a question of no consequence; but whether any such person ever performed all the wonderful things attributed to him; let him, then, weigh well the objections to that evidence (of which I have given but a hasty and imperfect sketch), and if he then finds it amount to anything *more* than a probability, I have only to congratulate him on his easy faith.

But the same testimony which would have great weight in establishing a thing intrinsically probable, will lose part of this weight in proportion as the matter attested is improbable; and if adduced in support of anything that is at variance with uniform experience,[6] will be rejected at once by all sound reasoners. Let us, then, consider what sort of a story it is that is proposed to our acceptance. How grossly contradictory are the reports of the different authorities, I have already remarked: but consider by itself the story told by any one of them; it carries an air of fiction and romance on the very face of it. All the events are great, and splendid, and marvellous:[7] great armies, great victories, great frosts, great reverses, "hairbreadth 'scapes," empires subverted in a few days; everything happened in defiance of political calculations, and in opposi-

---

[6] "That testimony itself derives all its force from experience, seems very certain. . . . The first author, we believe, who stated fairly the connection between the evidence of testimony and the evidence of experience, was Hume, in his *Essay on Miracles;* a work . . . abounding in maxims of great use in the conduct of life."—*Edinburgh Review,* September, 1814, p. 328.

[7] "Suppose, for instance, that the fact which the testimony endeavors to establish partakes of the extraordinary and the marvellous; in that case, the evidence resulting from the testimony receives a diminution, greater or less in proportion as the fact is more or less unusual."—Hume's *Essay on Miracles.*

tion to the *experience* of past times; everything upon that grand scale so common in epic poetry, so rare in real life; and thus calculated to strike the imagination of the vulgar, and to remind the sober-thinking few of the Arabian Nights. Every event, too, has that *roundness* and completeness which is so characteristic of fiction; nothing is done by halves; we have *complete* victories, *total* overthrows, *entire* subversion of empires, *perfect* re-establishments of them, crowded upon us in rapid succession. To enumerate the improbabilities of each of the several parts of this history, would fill volumes; but they are so fresh in every one's memory, that there is no need of such a detail. Let any judicious man, not ignorant of history and of human nature, revolve them in his mind, and consider how far they are conformable to experience,[8] our best and only sure guide. In vain will he seek in history for something similar to this wonderful Buonaparte; "nought but himself can be his parallel."

Will the conquests of Alexander be compared with his? *They* were effected over a rabble of effeminate, undisciplined barbarians; else his progress would hardly have been so rapid. Witness his father, Philip, who was much longer occupied in subduing the comparatively insignificant territory of the warlike and civilized Greeks, notwithstanding their being divided into numerous petty states, whose mutual jealousy enabled him to contend with them separately. But the Greeks had never made such progress in arts and arms as the great and powerful states of Europe, which Buonaparte is represented as so speedily overpowering. His empire has been compared to the Roman. Mark the contrast: he gains in a few years that dominion, or at least control, over Germany, wealthy, civilized, and powerful, which the Romans, in the plenitude of their power, could not obtain, during a struggle of as many centuries, against the ignorant half-savages who then possessed it; of whom Tacitus remarks, that, up to his own time, they had been "triumphed over rather than conquered."

---

[8] "The ultimate standard by which we determine all disputes that may arise is always derived from experience and observation."—Hume's *Essay on Miracles.*

Another peculiar circumstance in the history of this extraordinary personage is, that when it is found convenient to represent him as defeated,—though he is by no means defeated by halves, but involved in much more sudden and total ruin than the personages of real history usually meet with,—yet, if it is thought fit he should be restored, it is done as quickly and completely as if Merlin's rod had been employed. He enters Russia with a prodigious army, which is totally ruined by an unprecedented hard winter (everything relating to this man is *prodigious* and *unprecedented*); yet in a few months we find him intrusted with another great army in Germany, which is also totally ruined at Leipsic; making, inclusive of the Egyptian, the third great army thus totally lost. Yet the French are so good-natured as to furnish him with another, sufficient to make a formidable stand in France. He is, however, *conquered, and presented with the sovereignty of Elba* (surely, by-the-by, some more *probable* way might have been found of disposing of him, till again wanted, than to place him thus on the very verge of his ancient dominions); thence he returns to France, where he is received with open arms, and enabled to lose a fifth great army, at Waterloo; yet so eager were these people to be a sixth time led to destruction, that it was found necessary to confine *him* in an island some thousand miles off, and to quarter foreign troops upon *them*, lest they make an insurrection in his favor! Does any one believe all this, and yet refuse to believe a miracle? Or, rather, what is this but a miracle? Is it not a violation of the laws of nature? for surely there are moral laws of nature as well as physical, which, though more liable to exceptions in this or that particular case, are no less *true as general rules* than the laws of matter, and therefore cannot be violated and contradicted *beyond a certain point,* without a miracle.[9]

---

[9] This doctrine, though hardly needing confirmation from authority, is supported by that of Hume; his eighth Essay is, throughout, an argument for the doctrine of "philosophical necessity," drawn entirely from the general uniformity observable in the course of nature with respect to the principles of *human conduct,* as well as those of the material universe; from which uniformity, he observes, it is that we are enabled, *in both cases,* to form our judgments by means of *experience;* and if, says he, "we would explode any forgery in history, we cannot make use of a more convincing argument, than to prove that

Nay, there is this additional circumstance which renders the contradiction of experience more glaring in this case than in that of the miraculous histories which ingenious sceptics have held up to contempt. All the advocates of miracles admit that they are rare exceptions to the course of nature; but contend that they must needs be so, on account of the rarity of those extraordinary *occasions* which are the *reason* of their being performed. "A miracle," they say, "does not happen every day, because a Revelation is not given every day." It would be foreign to the present purpose to seek for arguments against this answer; I leave it to those who are engaged in the controversy, to find a reply to it; but my present object is, to point out that this solution does not at all apply in the present case. Where is the peculiarity of the *occasion?* What sufficient *reason* is there for a series of events occurring in the eighteenth and nineteenth centuries, which never took place before? Was Europe at that period peculiarly weak, and in a state of barbarism, that one man could achieve such con-

the actions ascribed to any person are directly contrary to the course of nature. . . . The veracity of Quintus Curtius is as suspicious when he describes the supernatural courage of Alexander, by which he was hurried on singly to attack multitudes, as when he describes his supernatural force and activity, by which he was able to resist them. So readily and universally do we acknowledge a *uniformity in human motives and actions as well as in the operations of the body.*"—*Eighth Essay.*

Accordingly, in the tenth Essay, his use of the term "miracle," after having called it a "transgression of a law of nature," plainly shows that he meant to include *human* nature: "no testimony," says he, "is sufficient to establish a miracle, unless the testimony be of such a nature that its falsehood would be more miraculous than the fact which it endeavors to establish." The term "prodigy" also (which he all along employs as synonymous with "miracle") is applied to testimony, in the same manner, immediately after: "In the foregoing reasoning we have supposed . . . that the falsehood of that testimony would be a kind of *prodigy.*" Now had he meant to confine the meaning of "miracle," and "prodigy," to a violation of the laws of *matter,* the epithet *"miraculous,"* applied even thus hypothetically, to *false testimony,* would be as unmeaning as the epithets "green" or "square;" the only possible sense in which we can apply to it, even in imagination, the term "miraculous," is that of "highly improbable," "contrary to those laws of nature which respect human conduct;" and in this sense accordingly he uses the word in the very next sentence: "When any one tells me that he saw a dead man restored to life, I immediately consider with myself whether it be more *probable* that this person should either deceive or be deceived, or that the fact which he relates should really have happened. I weigh the one *miracle* against the other."—Hume's *Essay on Miracles.*

See also a passage above quoted from the same Essay, where he speaks of "the *miraculous* accounts of travellers;" evidently using the word in this sense.

Perhaps it was superfluous to cite authority for applying the term "miracle" to whatever is "highly improbable;" but it is important to the students of Hume, to be fully aware that *he* uses those two expressions as synonymous; since otherwise they would mistake the meaning of that passage which he justly calls "a general maxim worthy of our attention."

quests, and acquire such a vast empire? On the contrary, she was flourishing in the height of strength and civilization. Can the persevering attachment and blind devotedness of the French to this man be accounted for by his being the descendant of a long line of kings, whose race was hallowed by hereditary veneration? No: we are told he was a low-born usurper, and not even a Frenchman! Is it that he was a good and kind sovereign? He is represented not only as an imperious and merciless despot, but as most wantonly careless of the lives of his soldiers. Could the French army and people have failed to hear from the wretched survivors of his supposed Russian expedition, how they had left the corpses of above one hundred thousand of their comrades bleaching on the snow-drifts of that dismal country, whither his mad ambition had conducted him, and where his selfish cowardice had deserted them? Wherever we turn to seek for circumstances that may help to account for the events of this incredible story, we only meet with such as aggravate its improbability.[10] Had it been told of some distant country, at a remote period, we could not have told what peculiar circumstances there might have been to render probable what seems to us most strange; and yet in *that* case every philosophical sceptic, every free-thinking speculator, would instantly have rejected such a history as utterly unworthy of credit. What, for instance, would the great Hume, or any of the philosophers of his school, have said, if they had found, in the antique records of any nation, such a passage as this?—"There was a certain man of Corsica, whose name was Napoleon, and he was one of the chief captains of the host of the French; and he gathered together an army, and went and fought against Egypt; but when the king of Britain heard thereof, he sent ships of war and valiant men to fight against the French in Egypt. So they warred against them, and prevailed, and strengthened the hands of the rulers of the land

---

[10] "Events may be so extraordinary that they can hardly be established by testimony. We would not give credit to a man who would affirm that he saw a hundred dice thrown in the air, and that they all fell on the same faces." —*Edinburgh Review*, September, 1814, p. 327.

Let it be observed, that the instance here given is *miraculous* in no other sense than that of being highly *improbable*.

against the French, and drave away Napoleon from before the city of Acre. Then Napoleon left the captains and the army that were in Egypt, and fled, and returned back to France. So the French people took Napoleon, and made him ruler over them, and he became exceeding great, insomuch as there was none like him of all that had ruled over France before."

What, I say, would Hume have thought of this, especially if he had been told that it was at this day generally credited? Would he not have confessed that he had been mistaken in supposing there was a peculiarly blind credulity and prejudice in favor of everything that is accounted *sacred;*[11] for that, since even professed sceptics swallow implicitly such a story as this, it appears there must be a still blinder prejudice in favor of everything that is *not* accounted sacred?

Suppose, again, we found in this history such passages as the following: "And it came to pass after these things that Napoleon strengthened himself, and gathered together another host instead of that which he had lost, and went and warred against the Prussians, and the Russians, and the Austrians, and all the rulers of the north country, which were confederate against him. And the ruler of Sweden, also, which was a Frenchman, warred against Napoleon. So they went forth, and fought against the French in the plain of Leipsic. And the French were discomfited before their enemies, and fled and came to the rivers which are behind Leipsic, and essayed to pass over, that they might escape out of the hand of their enemies; but they could not; for Napoleon had broken down the bridges; so the people of the north countries came upon them, and smote them with a very grievous slaughter. . . .

"Then the ruler of Austria and all the rulers of the north countries sent messengers unto Napoleon to speak peaceably unto him, saying, Why should there be war between us any more? Now Napoleon had put away his wife, and taken the daughter of the ruler of Austria to wife. So all the counsellors

---

[11] "If the spirit of religion join itself to the love of wonder, there is an end of common sense; and human testimony in these circumstances loses all pretensions to authority."—Hume's *Essay on Miracles.*

of Napoleon came and stood before him, and said, Behold now these kings are merciful kings; do even as they say unto thee; knowest thou not yet that France is destroyed? But he spake roughly unto his counsellors, and drave them out from his presence, neither would he hearken unto their voice. And when all the kings saw that, they warred against France, and smote it with the edge of the sword, and came near to Paris, which is the royal city, to take it: so the men of Paris went out, and delivered up the city to them. Then those kings spake kindly unto the men of Paris, saying, Be of good cheer, there shall no harm happen unto you. Then were the men of Paris glad, and said, Napoleon is a tyrant; he shall no more rule over us: also all the princes, the judges, the counsellors, and the captains whom Napoleon had raised up even from the lowest of the people, sent unto Lewis the brother of King Lewis, whom he had slain, and made him king over France. . . .

"And when Napoleon saw that the kingdom was departed from him, he said unto the rulers which came against him, Let me, I pray you, give the kingdom unto my son; but they would not hearken unto him. Then he spake yet again, saying, Let me, I pray you, go and live in the island of Elba, which is over against Italy, nigh unto the coast of France; and ye shall give me an allowance for me and my household, and the land of Elba also for a possession. So they made him ruler of Elba. . . .

"In those days the Pope returned unto his own land. Now the French, and divers other nations of Europe, are servants of the Pope, and hold him in reverence; but he is an abomination unto the Britons, and to the Prussians, and to the Russians, and to the Swedes. Howbeit, the French had taken away all his lands, and robbed him of all that he had, and carried him away captive into France. But when the Britons, and the Prussians, and the Russians, and the Swedes, and the rest of the nations that were confederate against France, came thither, they caused the French to set the Pope at liberty, and to restore all his goods that they had taken; likewise they gave him back all his possessions; and he went home in peace, and ruled over his own city as in times past. . . .

"And it came to pass when Napoleon had not yet been a full year at Elba, that he said unto his men of war that clave unto him, Go to, let us go back to France, and fight against King Lewis, and thrust him out from being king. So he departed, he and six hundred men with him that drew the sword, and warred against King Lewis. Then all the men of Belial gathered themselves together, and said, God save Napoleon. And when Lewis saw that, he fled, and gat him into the land of Batavia; and Napoleon ruled over France," etc., etc., etc.

Now if a free-thinking philosopher—one of those who advocate the cause of unbiased reason, and despise pretended revelations—were to meet with such a tissue of absurdities as this in an old Jewish record, would he not reject it at once as too palpable an imposture[12] to deserve even any inquiry into its evidence? Is that credible, then, of the civilized Europeans now, which could not, if reported of the semi-barbarous Jews three thousand years ago, be established by any testimony? Will it be answered, that "there is nothing *supernatural* in all this"? Why is it, then, that you object to what is *supernatural*—that you reject every account of *miracles*—if not because they are *improbable?* Surely, then, a story equally or still more improbable is not to be implicitly received merely on the ground that it is *not* miraculous; though in fact, as I have already (in note 9) shown from Hume's authority, it really *is* miraculous. The opposition to experience has been proved to be as complete in this case as in what are commonly called miracles; and the reasons assigned for that contrariety by the defenders of *them,* cannot be pleaded in the present instance. If, then, philosophers who reject every wonderful story that is maintained by priests are yet found ready to be-

---

[12] "I desire any one to lay his hand upon his heart, and after serious consideration declare whether he thinks that the falsehood of such a book, supported by such testimony, would be more extraordinary and miraculous than all the miracles it relates."—Hume's *Essay on Miracles.*

Let it be borne in mind, that Hume (as I have above remarked) continually employs the term "miracle" and "prodigy" to signify anything that is highly *improbable* and *extraordinary.*

lieve *everything else,* however improbable, they will surely lay themselves open to the accusation brought against them of being unduly prejudiced against whatever relates to religion.

There is one more circumstance which I cannot forbear mentioning, because it so much adds to the air of fiction which pervades every part of this marvellous tale; and that is, the *nationality* of it.[18]

Buonaparte prevailed over all the hostile states in turn, *except England;* in the zenith of his power, his fleets were swept from the sea *by England;* his troops always defeat an equal, and frequently even a superior number of those of any other nation, *except the English;* and with them it is just the reverse; twice, and twice only, he is personally engaged against an *English commander,* and both times he is totally defeated—at Acre and at Waterloo; and to crown all, *England* finally crushes this tremendous power, which had so long kept the continent in subjection or in alarm, and to the *English* he surrenders himself prisoner! Thoroughly national, to be sure! It *may* be all very true; but I would only ask, *if* a story *had* been fabricated for the express purpose of amusing the English nation, could it have been contrived more ingeniously? It would do admirably for an epic poem; and, indeed, bears a considerable resemblance to the Iliad and the Æneid, in which Achilles and the Greeks, Æneas and the Trojans (the ancestors of the Romans), are so studiously held up to admiration. Buonaparte's exploits seem magnified in order to enhance the glory of his conquerors, just as Hector is allowed to triumph during the absence of Achilles, merely to give additional splendor to his overthrow by the arm of that invincible hero. Would not this circumstance alone render a history rather *suspicious* in the eyes of an acute critic, even if it were not filled with such gross improbabilities, and induce him to suspend his judgment till very satisfactory evi-

---

[18] "The wise lend a very academic faith to every report which favors the passion of the reporter, whether it magnifies his *country,* his family, or himself."—Hume's *Essay on Miracles.*

dence (far stronger than can be found in this case) should be produced?

Is it, then, too much to demand of the wary academic[14] a suspension of judgment as to the "life and adventures of Napoleon Buonaparte"? I do not pretend to *decide* positively that there is not, nor ever was, any such person, but merely to propose it as a *doubtful* point, and one the more deserving of careful investigation from the very circumstance of its having hitherto been admitted without inquiry. Far less would I undertake to decide what is, or has been, the real state of affairs. He who points out the improbability of the current story is not bound to suggest an hypothesis of his own;[15] though it may be safely affirmed that it would be hard to invent any one more improbable than the received one. One may surely be allowed to hesitate in admitting the stories which the ancient poets tell of earthquakes and volcanic eruptions being caused by imprisoned giants, without being called upon satisfactorily to account for those phenomena.

Amidst the defect of valid evidence under which, as I have already shown, we labor in the present instance, it is hardly possible to offer more than here and there a probable conjecture; or to pronounce how much may be true, and how much fictitious, in the accounts presented to us. For it is to be observed that this case is much *more* open to sceptical doubts even than some miraculous histories; for some of *them* are of such a nature that you cannot consistently admit a part and reject the rest, but are bound, if you are satisfied as to the reality of any one miracle, to embrace the whole system; so that it is necessary for the sceptic to impeach the evidence of *all* of them, separately and collectively; whereas *here* each single point requires to be *established* separately, since no one of them authenticates the rest. Supposing there be a

---

[14] "Nothing can be more contrary than such a philosophy" (the academic or sceptical) "to the supine indolence of the mind, its rash arrogance, its lofty pretensions, and its superstitious credulity."—*Fifth Essay.*

[15] See Hume's *Essay on Miracles.*

state prisoner, at St. Helena (which, by the way, it is acknowledged, many of the French disbelieve), how do we know who he is, or why he is confined there? There have been state prisoners, before now, who were never guilty of subjugating half Europe, and whose offences have been very imperfectly ascertained. Admitting that there have been bloody wars going on for several years past, which is highly probable, it does not follow that the events of those wars were such as we have been told; that Buonaparte was the author and conductor of them; or that such a person ever existed. What disturbances may have taken place in the government of the French people, we, and even nineteen twentieths of *them*, have no means of learning but from imperfect hearsay evidence; and how much credit they themselves attach to that evidence is very doubtful. This at least is certain—that a M. Berryer, a French advocate, has published memoirs, professing to record many of the recent events of the history of France, in which, among other things, he states his conviction that Buonaparte's escape from Elba was DESIGNED AND CONTRIVED BY THE ENGLISH GOVERNMENT.[16] And we are assured by many travellers that this was, and is, commonly reported in France.

Now, that the French should believe the whole story about Buonaparte, according to this version of it, does seem utterly incredible. Let any one suppose them seriously believing that we maintained for many years a desperate struggle against this formidable emperor of theirs, in the course of which we expended such an enormous amount of blood and treasure as is reported; that we finally, after encountering enormous risks, succeeded in subduing him, and secured him in a place of safe exile; and that, in less than a year after, we turned him out again, like a bag-fox, or rather a bag-lion, for the sake of amusing ourselves by again staking all that was dear to us on the event of a doubtful and bloody battle, in which defeat must be ruinous, and victory, if obtained at all, must cost us many thousands of our best soldiers. Let any one force him-

---

[16] See *Edinburgh Review* for October, 1842, p. 162.

self for a moment to conceive the French seriously believing
such a mass of absurdity; and the inference must be that
such a people must be prepared to believe anything. They
might fancy their own country to abound not only with Na-
poleons, but with dragons and centaurs, and "men whose
heads do grow beneath their shoulders," or anything else that
any lunatic ever dreamed of. If we could suppose the French
capable of such monstrous credulity as the above supposition
would imply, it is plain their testimony must be altogether
worthless.

But, on the other hand, suppose them to be aware that the
British Government have been all along imposing on us, and
it is quite natural that they should deride our credulity, and
try whether there is anything too extravagant for us to swallow. And, indeed, if Buonaparte was in fact altogether a
phantom conjured up by the British Ministers, then it is *true*
that his escape from Elba really *was*, as well as *the rest of his
exploits*, a contrivance of theirs.

But whatever may be believed by the French relative to
the recent occurrences in their own country, and whatever
may be the real character of these occurrences, of this, at
least, we are well assured, that there have been numerous
bloody wars with France under the dominion of the *Bour-
bons;* and we are now told that France is governed by a
Bourbon king, of the name of Lewis, who professes to be in
the twenty-third year of his reign. Let every one conjecture
for himself. I am far from pretending to decide who may have
been the governor or governors of the French nation, and the
leaders of their armies, for several years past. Certain it is,
that when men are indulging their inclination for the marvellous, they always show a strong propensity to accumulate
upon *one* individual (real or imaginary) the exploits of many;
besides multiplying and exaggerating these exploits a thou-
sand-fold. Thus, the expounders of the ancient mythology
tell us there were several persons of the name of Hercules
(either originally bearing that appellation, or having it applied to them as an honor), whose collective feats, after being

dressed up in a sufficiently marvellous garb, were attributed to a single hero. Is it not just possible, that during the rage for words of Greek derivation, the title of "Napoleon" (Ναπολέων), which signifies "lion of the forest," may have been conferred by the popular voice on more than one favorite general, distinguished for irresistible valor? Is it not also possible that "Buona parte" may have been originally a sort of cant term applied to the "good (that is, the bravest, or most patriotic) part" of the French army, collectively, and have been afterwards mistaken for the proper name of an individual?[17] I do not profess to support this conjecture; but it is certain that such mistakes may and do occur. Some critics have supposed that the Athenians imagined Anastis ("Resurrection") to be a new goddess, in whose cause Paul was preaching. Would it have been thought anything incredible if we had been told that the ancient Persians, who had no idea of any but a monarchical government, had supposed Aristocratia to be a queen of Sparta? But we need not confine ourselves to hypothetical cases: it is positively stated that the Hindoos at this day believe "the honorable East India Company" to be a venerable old lady of high dignity, residing in this country. The Germans, again, of the present day derive their name from a similar mistake. The first tribe of them who invaded Gaul assumed the honorable title of "*Ger-man*," which signifies "warriors" (the words "war" and "guerre," as well as "man," which remains in our language unaltered, are evidently derived from the Teutonic), and the Gauls applied this as a *name* to the whole *race*.

However, I merely throw out these conjectures, without by

---

[17] It is well known with how much learning and ingenuity the Rationalists of the German school have labored to throw discredit on the literal interpretation of the narratives, both of the Old and New Testaments; representing them as MYTHS, that is, fables allegorically describing some physical or moral phenomena—philosophical principles—systems, etc.—under the figure of actions performed by certain ideal personages; these allegories having been, afterwards, through the mistake of the vulgar, believed as history. Thus, the real historical existence of such a person as the supposed founder of the Christian religion, and the acts attributed to him, are denied in the literal sense, and the whole of the evangelical history is explained on the "mythical" theory.

Now it is a remarkable circumstance, in reference to the point at present before us, that an eminent authoress of this century has distinctly declared that Napoleon Buonaparte was NOT A MAN, but a SYSTEM.

any means contending that more plausible ones might not be suggested. But whatever supposition we adopt, or whether we adopt any, the objections to the commonly received accounts will remain in their full force, and imperiously demand the attention of the candid sceptic.

I call upon those, therefore, who profess themselves advocates of free inquiry—who disdain to be carried along with the stream of popular opinion, and who will listen to no testimony that runs counter to experience—to follow up their own principles fairly and consistently. Let the same mode of argument be adopted in all cases alike; and then it can no longer be attributed to hostile prejudice, but to enlarged and philosophical views. If they have already rejected some histories, on the ground of their being strange and marvellous —of their relating facts unprecedented and at variance with the established course of nature—let them not give credit to another history which lies open to the very same objections— the extraordinary and romantic tale we have been just considering. If they have discredited the testimony of witnesses, who are *said* at least to have been disinterested, and to have braved persecutions and death in support of their assertions, can these philosophers consistently listen to and believe the testimony of those who avowedly *get money* by the tales they publish, and who do not even pretend that they incur any serious risk in case of being detected in a falsehood? If, in other cases, they have refused to listen to an account which has passed through many intermediate hands before it reaches them, and which is defended by those who have an interest in maintaining it, let them consider through how many, and what very suspicious hands, *this* story has arrived to them, without the possibility, as I have shown, of tracing it back to any decidedly authentic source, after all—to any better authority, according to their own showing, than that of an *unnamed* and unknown foreign correspondent; and likewise how strong an interest, in every way, those who have hitherto imposed on them, have in keeping up the imposture. Let them, in short, show themselves as ready to detect the cheats and despise the fables of politicians as of priests.

But if they are still wedded to the popular belief in this point, let them be consistent enough to admit the same evidence in *other* cases which they yield to in *this*. If, after all that has been said, they cannot bring themselves to doubt of the existence of Napoleon Buonaparte, they must at least acknowledge that they do not apply to that question the same plan of reasoning which they have made use of in others; and they are consequently bound in reason and in honesty to renounce it altogether.

• • •

("Richard Whately, the future Archbishop of Dublin, wrote his *Historic Doubts Relative to Napoleon Buonaparte* when the world was still ringing with the crash of the French Empire. With singular penetration and cogency, he showed how the whole career of Napoleon strains honest belief. Between the alleged facts and the actual irrefutable evidence there is too great a discrepancy. A likely story, indeed, by all the canons of sound criticism! The little book is no mere 'jeu d'esprit,' for there is a reconstructive purpose behind the paradox. *Per se*, it is a good piece of critical literature, which may be read with profit by prospective students of Napoleonic lore; for it is surprisingly well done, even in its confidence-inspiring ponderosity."—Albert Leon Guérard, *Reflections on the Napoleonic Legend*, 1924)

(Whately "could justly claim, in the later editions of his *Logic*, that his work had done much to stimulate the notable revival of interest in logical studies."—John Passmore, *A Hundred Years of Philosophy*, 1957)

JOHN HENRY NEWMAN

[1801–1890]

A shy, earnest, ethereal youth of fifteen when he came to Oxford, Newman at twenty-seven was preaching before the university from the historic pulpit of St. Mary's. Deepened in his convictions through tireless study, and through illness and the death of his sisters, he soon began to react against the growing liberalism of the day and by 1832, the year of the Reform Bill, he and some of his friends were dedicated to a lifelong war against the prevailing tendencies of the time.

"It was the success of the Liberal cause which fretted me inwardly," he wrote years later (1864) in the *Apologia pro Vita Sua.* "I became fierce against its instruments and its manifestations. . . . I could not even look at the tricolor. My battle was with liberalism; by liberalism I mean the anti-dogmatic principle and its developments." In short, he distrusted and feared what he called "the wild living intellect of man" or "the immense energy of the aggressive, capricious, untrustworthy intellect." In order to meet this onset of Liberal principles he and a small group set out to breathe new life, thought, spirit, into the Church of England and so started the Oxford Movement, which Newman himself dated from John Keble's sermon on "National Apostasy" in the university pulpit on July 14, 1833.

"Tracts for the Times" were written; the early history of Christianity was studied with fresh eyes; sermons were preached; and around the magnetic personality of Newman gathered devoted young followers. It was a High Church movement, supposedly the "via media," avoiding evangelical emotionalism, lax latitudinarianism and Roman Catholicism.

Newman's series of sermons on Faith and Reason made a profound impression at the time and continued to do so as a volume, first published in 1843. Long afterward Newman considered it the best book he had ever written and to Maisie Ward today "it was the most philosophical and perhaps the most penetratingly psychological."

So we turn to the thirteenth of the Oxford University Sermons, originally delivered on Monday morning, St. Peter's Day, 1840.

. . .

IMPLICIT AND EXPLICIT REASON

1 Pet. iii. 15.

"Sanctify the Lord God in your hearts; and be ready always to give an answer to every man that asketh you a reason of the hope that is in you, with meekness and fear."

St. Peter's faith was one of his characteristic graces. It was ardent, keen, watchful, and prompt. It dispensed with argument, calculation, deliberation, and delay, whenever it heard the voice of its Lord and Saviour: and it heard that voice even when its accents were low, or when it was unaided by the testimony of the other senses. When Christ appeared walking on the sea, and said, "It is I," Peter answered Him, and said, "Lord, if it be Thou, bid me come unto Thee on the water." When Christ asked His disciples who He was, "Simon Peter answered and said," as we read in the Gospel for this day, "Thou art the Christ, the Son of the Living God," and obtained our Lord's blessing for such clear and ready Faith. At another time, when Christ asked the Twelve whether they would leave Him as others did, St. Peter said, "Lord, to whom shall we go? Thou hast the words of eternal life; and we believe and are sure that Thou art the Christ, the Son of the Living God." And after the Resurrection, when he heard from St. John that it was Christ who stood on the shore, he sprang out of the boat in which he was fishing, and cast himself into the sea, in his impatience to come near Him. Other instances of his faith might be mentioned. If ever Faith forgot self, and was occupied with its Great Object, it was the faith of Peter. If in any one Faith appears in contrast with what we commonly understand by Reason, and with Evidence, it so appears in the instance of Peter. When he reasoned, it was at times when Faith was lacking. "When he saw the wind boisterous, he was afraid"; and Christ in consequence called him, "Thou of little faith." When He asked, "Who touched Me?" Peter and others reasoned, "Master," said they, "the multitude throng Thee, and press Thee, and sayest Thou, Who touched Me?" And in like manner, when Christ said that he should one day follow Him in the way of suffering, "Peter said unto Him, Lord, *why* cannot I follow Thee now?"—and we know how his faith gave way soon afterwards.

2. Faith and Reason, then, stand in strong contrast in the history of Peter: yet it is Peter, and he not the fisherman of Galilee, but the inspired Apostle, who in the text gives us a precept which implies, in order to its due fulfilment, a careful exercise of our Reason, an exercise both upon Faith, considered as an act or habit of mind, and upon the Object of it. We are not only to "sanctify the Lord God in our hearts," not only to prepare a shrine within us in which our Saviour Christ may dwell, and where we may worship Him; but we are so to understand what we do, so to master our thoughts and feelings, so to recognize what we believe, and how we believe, so to trace out our ideas and impressions, and to contemplate the issue of them, that we may be "ready *always* to give an answer to *every* man that asketh us an account of the hope that is in us." In these words, I conceive, we have a clear warrant, or rather an injunction, to cast our religion into the form of Creed and Evidences.

3. It would seem, then, that though Faith is the characteristic of the Gospel, and Faith is the simple lifting of the mind to the Unseen God, without conscious reasoning or formal argument, still the mind may be allowably, nay, religiously engaged, in reflecting upon its own Faith; investigating the grounds and the Object of it, bringing it out into words, whether to defend, or recommend, or teach it to others. And St. Peter himself, in spite of his ardour and ear-

nestness, gives us in his own case some indications of such an exercise of mind. When he said, "Thou art the Christ, the Son of the Living God," he cast his faith, in a measure, into a dogmatic form: and when he said, "To whom shall we go? Thou hast the words of eternal life," he gave "an account of the hope that was in him," or grounded his faith upon Evidence.

4. Nothing would be more theoretical and unreal than to suppose that true Faith cannot exist except when moulded upon a Creed, and based upon Evidence; yet nothing would indicate a more shallow philosophy than to say that it ought carefully to be disjoined from dogmatic and argumentative statements. To assert the latter is to discard the science of theology from the service of Religion; to assert the former, is to maintain that every child, every peasant, must be a theologian. Faith cannot exist without grounds or without an object; but it does not follow that all who have faith should recognize, and be able to state what they believe, and why. Nor, on the other hand, because it is not identical with its grounds, and its object, does it therefore cease to be true Faith, on its recognizing them. In proportion as the mind reflects upon itself, it will be able "to give an account" of what it believes and hopes; as far as it has not thus reflected, it will not be able. Such knowledge cannot be wrong, yet cannot be necessary, as long as reflection is at once a natural faculty of our souls, yet not an initial faculty. Scripture gives instances of Faith in each of these states, when attended by a conscious exercise of Reason, and when not. When Nicodemus said, "No man can do these miracles that Thou doest, except God be with him," he investigated. When the Scribe said, "There is One God, and there is none other but He; and to love Him with all the heart . . . is more than all whole burnt offerings and sacrifices," his belief was dogmatical. On the other hand, when the cripple at Lystra believed, on St. Paul's preaching, or the man at the Beautiful gate believed in the Name of Christ, their faith was independent not of objects or grounds (for that is impossible) but of perceptible, recognized, producible objects and grounds: they believed, they could not

say what or why. True Faith, then, admits, but does not require, the exercise of what is commonly understood by Reason.

5. I hope it will not seem any want of reverence towards
a great Apostle, who reigns with Christ in heaven, if, instead of selecting one of the many lessons to which his history calls our attention, or of the points of doctrine in it which
might so profitably be enlarged upon, I employ his Day to
continue a subject to which I have already devoted such opportunities of speaking from this place, as have from time to
time occurred, though it be but incidentally connected with
him. Such a continuation of subject has some sanction in the
character of our first Lessons for Holy days, which, for the
most part, instead of being appropriate to the particular
Festivals on which they are appointed, are portions of a
course, and connected with those which are assigned to
others. And I will add that, if there is a question, the intrusion
of which may be excused in the present age, and to which
the mind is naturally led on the Days commemorative
of the first Founders of the Church, it is the relation of Faith
to Reason under the Gospel; and the means whereby, and
the grounds whereon, and the subjects wherein, the mind is
bound to believe and acquiesce, in matters of religion.

6. In the Epistle for this Day we have an account of St.
Peter, when awakened by the Angel, obeying him implicitly,
yet not understanding, while he obeyed. He girt himself, and
bound on his sandals, and cast his garments about him, and
"went out and followed him"; yet "wist not that it was true
which was done by the Angel, but thought he saw a vision."
Afterwards, when he "was come to himself, he said, Now I
know of a surety, that the Lord hath sent His Angel, and
hath delivered me." First he acted spontaneously, then he
contemplated his own acts. This may be taken as an illustration of the differences between the more simple faculties
and operations of the mind, and that process of analyzing
and describing them, which takes place upon reflection. We
not only feel, and think, and reason, but we know that we

feel, and think, and reason; not only know, but can inspect and ascertain our thoughts, feelings, and reasonings: not only ascertain, but describe. Children, for a time, do not realize even their material frames, or (as I may say) count their limbs; but, as the mind opens, and is cultivated, they turn their attention to soul as well as body; they contemplate all they are, and all they do; they are no longer beings of impulse, instinct, conscience, imagination, habit, or reason, merely; but they are able to reflect upon their own mind as if it were some external object; they reason upon their own reasonings. This is the point on which I shall now enlarge.

7. Reason, according to the simplest view of it, is the faculty of gaining knowledge without direct perception, or of ascertaining one thing by means of another. In this way it is able, from small beginnings, to create to itself a world of ideas, which do or do not correspond to the things themselves for which they stand, or are true or not, according as it is exercised soundly or otherwise. One fact may suffice for a whole theory; one principle may create and sustain a system; one minute token is a clue to a large discovery. The mind ranges to and fro, and spreads out, and advances forward with a quickness which has become a proverb, and a subtlety and versatility which baffle investigation. It passes on from point to point, gaining one by some indication; another on a probability; then availing itself of an association; then falling back on some received law; next seizing on testimony; then committing itself to some popular impression, or some inward instinct, or some obscure memory; and thus it makes progress not unlike a clamberer on a steep cliff, who, by quick eye, prompt hand, and firm foot, ascends how he knows not himself, by personal endowments and by practice, rather than by rule, leaving no track behind him, and unable to teach another. It is not too much to say that the stepping by which great geniuses scale the mountains of truth is as unsafe and precarious to men in general, as the ascent of a skilful mountaineer up a literal crag. It is a way which they alone can take; and its justification lies in their success. And such mainly

is the way in which all men, gifted or not gifted, commonly reason—not by rule, but by an inward faculty.

8. Reasoning, then, or the exercise of Reason, is a living spontaneous energy within us, not an art. But when the mind reflects upon itself, it begins to be dissatisfied with the absence of order and method in the exercise, and attempts to analyze the various processes which take place during it, to refer one to another, and to discover the main principles on which they are conducted, as it might contemplate and investigate its faculty of memory or imagination. The boldest, simplest, and most comprehensive theory which has been invented for the analysis of the reasoning process, is the well-known science for which we are indebted to Aristotle, and which is framed upon the principle that every act of reasoning is exercised upon neither more nor less than three terms. Short of this, we have many general words in familiar use to designate particular methods of thought, according to which the mind reasons (that is, proceeds from truth to truth), or to designate particular states of mind which influence its reasonings. Such methods are antecedent probability, analogy, parallel cases, testimony, and circumstantial evidence; and such states of mind are prejudice, deference to authority, party spirit, attachment to such and such principles, and the like. In like manner we distribute the Evidences of Religion into External and Internal; into *a priori* and *a posteriori;* into Evidences of Natural Religion and of Revealed; and so on. Again, we speak of proving doctrines either from the nature of the case, or from Scripture, or from history; and of teaching them in a dogmatic, or a polemical, or a hortatory way. In these and other ways we instance the reflective power of the human mind, contemplating and scrutinizing its own acts.

9. Here, then, are two processes, distinct from each other —the original process of reasoning, and next, the process of investigating our reasonings. All men reason, for to reason is nothing more than to gain truth from former truth, without the intervention of sense, to which brutes are limited; but all men do not reflect upon their own reasonings, much

less reflect truly and accurately, so as to do justice to their own meaning; but only in proportion to their abilities and attainments. In other words, all men have a reason, but not all men can give a reason. We may denote, then, these two exercises of mind as reasoning and arguing, or as conscious and unconscious reasoning, or as Implicit Reason and Explicit Reason. And to the latter belong the words, science, method, development, analysis, criticism, proof, system, principles, rules, laws, and others of a like nature.

10. That these two exercises are not to be confounded together would seem too plain for remark, except that they have been confounded. Clearness in argument certainly is not indispensable to reasoning well. Accuracy in stating doctrines or principles is not essential to feeling and acting upon them. The exercise of analysis is not necessary to the integrity of the process analyzed. The process of reasoning is complete in itself, and independent. The analysis is but an account of it; it does not make the conclusion correct; it does not make the inference rational. It does not cause a given individual to reason better. It does but give him a sustained consciousness, for good or for evil, that he is reasoning. How a man reasons is as much a mystery as how he remembers. He remembers better and worse on different subject-matters, and he reasons better and worse. Some men's reason becomes genius in particular subjects, and is less than ordinary in others. The gift or talent of reasoning may be distinct in different subjects, though the process of reasoning is the same. Now a good arguer or clear speaker is but one who excels in analyzing or expressing a process of reason, taken as his subject-matter. He traces out the connexion of facts, detects principles, applies them, supplies deficiencies, till he has reduced the whole into order. But his talent of reasoning, or the gift of reason as possessed by him, may be confined to such an exercise, and he may be as little expert in other exercises, as a mathematician need be an experimentalist; as little creative of the reasoning itself which he analyzes, as a critic need possess the gift of writing poems.

11. But if reasoning and arguing be thus distinct, what

is to be thought of assertions such as the following? Certainly, to say the least, they are very inaccurately worded, and may lead, as they have led, to great error.

12. Tillotson,[1] for instance, says: "Nothing ought to be received as a divine doctrine and revelation, *without good evidence* that it is so: that is, without some *argument* sufficient to *satisfy* a prudent and considerate man." Again: "Faith . . . is an assent of the mind to something as revealed by God: now all assent must be *grounded upon evidence;* that is, no man can believe anything, unless he have, or think he hath, some *reason* to do so. For to be confident of a thing without reason is not faith, but a presumptuous persuasion and obstinacy of mind." Such assertions either have an untrue meaning, or are unequal to the inferences which the writers proceed to draw from them.

13. In like manner Paley and others argue that miracles are not improbable unless a Revelation is improbable, on the ground that there is no other conceivable way of ascertaining a Revelation; that is, they would imply the necessity of a conscious investigation and verification of its claims, or the possession of grounds which are satisfactory in argument; whereas considerations which seem weak and insufficient in an explicit form may lead, and justly lead, us by an implicit process to a reception of Christianity; just as a peasant may from the look of the sky foretell tomorrow's weather, on grounds which, as far as they are producible, an exact logician would not scruple to pronounce inaccurate and inconsequent. "In what way," he asks, "can a Revelation be made," that is, as the context shows, be ascertained, "but by miracles? In none which we are able to conceive."

14. Again: another writer says, "There are but two ways by which God could reveal His will to mankind; either by an immediate influence on the mind of every individual of every age, or by selecting some particular persons to be His instruments . . . and for this purpose vested by Him with such powers as *might carry the strongest evidence* that they were

---

[1] Of course the statements of these various authors are true and important in their own place and from their own point of view.

really divine teachers." On the other hand, Bishop Butler
tells us that it is impossible to decide what evidence will be
afforded of a Revelation, supposing it made; and certainly
it might have been given without any supernatural display
at all, being left (as it is in a manner even now) to be received or rejected by each man according as his heart
sympathized in it, that is, on the influence of reasons, which,
though practically persuasive, are weak when set forth as the
argumentative grounds of conviction.

15. Faith, then, though in all cases a reasonable process,
is not necessarily founded on investigation, argument, or
proof; these processes being but the explicit form which the
reasoning takes in the case of particular minds. Nay, so far
from it, that the opposite opinion has, with much more
plausibility, been advanced, viz. that Faith is not even compatible with these processes. Such an opinion, indeed, cannot be maintained, particularly considering the light which
Scripture casts upon the subject, as in the text; but it may
easily take possession of serious minds. When they witness
the strife and division to which argument and controversy
minister, the proud self-confidence which is fostered by
strength of the reasoning powers, the laxity of opinion which
often accompanies the study of the Evidences, the coldness,
the formality, the secular and carnal spirit which is compatible with an exact adherence to dogmatic formularies;
and on the other hand, when they recollect that Scripture
represents religion as a divine life, seated in the affections and
manifested in spiritual graces, no wonder that they are
tempted to rescue Faith from all connexion with faculties
and habits which may exist in perfection without Faith, and
which too often usurp from Faith its own province, and profess to be a substitute for it. I repeat, such a persuasion is
extreme, and will not maintain itself, and cannot be acted on,
for any long time; it being as paradoxical to prohibit religious
inquiry and inference, as to make it imperative. Yet we
should not dismiss the notice of it, on many accounts, without doing justice to it; and therefore I propose now, before
considering some of the uses of our critical and analytical

powers, in the province of Religion, to state certain of the inconveniences and defects; an undertaking which will fully occupy what remains of our time this morning.

16. Inquiry and argument may be employed, first, in ascertaining the divine origin of Religion, Natural and Revealed; next, in interpreting Scripture; and thirdly, in determining points of Faith and Morals; that is, in the Evidences, Biblical Exposition, and Dogmatic Theology. In all three departments there is, first of all, an exercise of implicit reason, which is in its degree common to all men; for all men gain a certain impression, right or wrong, from what comes before them, for or against Christianity, for or against certain interpretations of Scripture, for or against certain doctrines. This impression, made upon their minds, whether by the claim itself of Revealed Religion, or by its documents, or by its teaching, it is the object of science to analyze, verify, methodize, and exhibit. We believe certain things, on certain grounds, through certain informants; and the analysis of these three, the why, the how, and the what, seems pretty nearly to constitute the science of divinity.

17. (1.) By the Evidences of Religion I mean the systematic analysis of all the grounds on which we believe Christianity to be true. I say "all," because the word Evidence is often restricted to denote only such arguments as arise out of the thing itself which is to be proved; or, to speak more definitely, facts and circumstances which presuppose the point under inquiry as a condition of their existence, and which are weaker or stronger arguments, according as that point approaches more or less closely to be a necessary condition of them. Thus blood on the clothes is an evidence of a murderer, just so far as a deed of violence is necessary to the fact of the stains, or alone accounts for them. Such are the Evidences as drawn out by Paley and other writers; and though only a secondary part, they are popularly considered the whole of the Evidences, because they can be exhibited and studied with far greater ease than antecedent considerations, presumptions, and analogies, which, vague and ab-

struse as they are, still are more truly the grounds on which religious men receive the Gospel; but on this subject something has been said on a former occasion.

18. (2.) Under the science of Interpretation is of course included all inquiry into its principles; the question of mystical interpretation, the theory of the double sense, the doctrine of types, the phraseology of prophecy, the drift and aim of the several books of Scripture; the dates when, the places where, and persons by and to whom they were written; the comparison and adjustment of book with book; the uses of the Old Testament; the relevancy of the Law to Christians and its relation to the Gospel; and the historical fulfilment of prophecy. And previous to such inquiries are others still more necessary, such as the study of the original languages in which the sacred Volume is written.

19. (3.) Under Dogmatic Theology must be included, not only doctrine, such as that of the Blessed Trinity, or the theory of Sacramental Influence, or the settlement of the Rule of Faith, but questions of morals and discipline also.

20. Now, in considering the imperfections and defects incident to such scientific exercises, we must carefully exempt from our remarks all instances of them which have been vouchsafed to us from above, and therefore have a divine sanction; and that such instances do exist, is the most direct and satisfactory answer to any doubts which religious persons may entertain, of the lawfulness of employing science in the province of Faith at all. Of such analyses and determinations as are certainly from man, we are at liberty to dispute both the truth and the utility: but what God has done is perfect, that is, perfect according to its subject-matter. Whether in the department of evidence, Scripture interpretation, or dogmatic teaching, what He has spoken must be received, not criticized; and in saying this, I have not to assign the limits or the channels of God's communications. Whether He speaks only by Scripture, or by private and personal suggestion, or by the first ages, or by Tradition, or by the Church collective, or by the Church in Council, or by the Chair of Saint Peter, are questions about which Christians may differ

without interfering with the principle itself, that what God
has given is true, and what He has not given may, if so be,
be not true. What He has not given by His appointed
methods, whatever they be, may be venerable for its antiquity, or authoritative as held by good men, or safer to
hold as held by many, or necessary to hold because it has
been subscribed, or persuasive from its probability, or expedient from its good effects; but after all, except that all
good things are from God, it is, as far as we know, a human
statement, and is open to criticism, because the work of
man. To such human inferences and propositions I confine
myself in the remarks that follow.

21. Now the great practical evil of method and form
in matters of religion—nay, in all moral matters—is obviously
this: their promising more than they can effect. At best the
science of divinity is very imperfect and inaccurate, yet the
very name of science is a profession of accuracy. Other and
more familiar objections readily occur; such as its leading to
familiarity with sacred things, and consequent irreverence;
its fostering formality; its substituting a sort of religious
philosophy and literature for worship and practice; its weakening the springs of action by inquiring into them; its stimulating to controversy and strife; its substituting, in matters
of duty, positive rules which need explanation for an instinctive feeling which commands the mind; its leading
the mind to mistake system for truth, and to suppose that an
hypothesis is real because it is consistent: but all such objections, though important, rather lead us to a cautious use of
science than to a distrust of it in religious matters. But its insufficiency in so high a province is an evil which attaches
to it from first to last, an inherent evil which there are no
means of remedying, and which, perhaps, lies at the root of
those other evils which I have just been enumerating. To
this evil I shall now direct my attention, having already
incidentally referred to it in some of the foregoing remarks.

22. No analysis is subtle and delicate enough to represent
adequately the state of mind under which we believe, or
the subjects of belief, as they are presented to our thoughts.

The end proposed is that of delineating, or, as it were, painting what the mind sees and feels: now let us consider what it is to portray duly in form and colour things material, and we shall surely understand the difficulty, or rather the impossibility, of representing the outline and character, the hues and shades, in which any intellectual view really exists in the mind, or of giving it that substance and that exactness in detail in which consists its likeness to the original, or of sufficiently marking those minute differences which attach to the same general state of mind or tone of thought as found in this or that individual respectively. It is probable that a given opinion, as held by several individuals, even when of the most congenial views, is as distinct from itself as are their faces. Now how minute is the defect in imitation which hinders the likeness of a portrait from being successful! how easy is it to recognize who is intended by it, without allowing that really he is represented! Is it not hopeless, then, to expect that the most diligent and anxious investigation can end in more than in giving some very rude description of the living mind, and its feelings, thoughts, and reasonings? And if it be difficult to analyze fully any state, or frame, or opinion of our own minds, is it a less difficulty to delineate, as Theology professes to do, the works, dealings, providences, attributes, or nature of Almighty God?

23. In this point of view we may, without irreverence, speak even of the words of inspired Scripture as imperfect and defective; and though they are not subjects for our judgment (God forbid), yet they will for that very reason serve to enforce and explain better what I would say, and how far the objection goes. Inspiration is defective, not in itself, but in consequence of the medium it uses and the beings it addresses. It uses human language, and it addresses man; and neither can man compass, nor can his hundred tongues utter, the mysteries of the spiritual world, and God's appointments in this. This vast and intricate scene of things cannot be generalized or represented through or to the mind of man; and inspiration, in undertaking to do so, necessarily lowers what is divine to raise what is human. What, for in-

stance, is the mention made in Scripture of the laws of God's government, of His providences, counsels, designs, anger, and repentance, but a gracious mode (the more gracious because necessarily imperfect) of making man contemplate what is far beyond him? Who shall give method to what is infinitely complex, and measure to the unfathomable? We are as worms in an abyss of divine works; myriads upon myriads of years would it take, were our hearts ever so religious, and our intellects ever so apprehensive, to receive from without the just impression of those works as they really are, and as experience would convey them to us: sooner, then, than we should know nothing, Almighty God has condescended to speak to us so far as human thought and language will admit, by approximations, in order to give us practical rules for our own conduct amid His infinite and eternal operations.

24. And herein consists one great blessing of the Gospel Covenant, that in Christ's death on the Cross, and in other parts of that all-gracious Economy, are concentrated, as it were, and so presented to us those attributes and works which fill eternity. And with a like graciousness we are also told, in human language, things concerning God Himself, concerning His Son and His Spirit, and concerning His Son's incarnation, and the union of two natures in His One Person—truths which even a peasant holds implicitly, but which Almighty God, whether by His Apostles, or by His Church after them, has vouchsafed to bring together and methodize, and to commit to the keeping of science.

25. Now all such statements are likely at first to strike coldly or harshly upon religious ears, when taken by themselves, for this reason if for no other—that they express heavenly things under earthly images, which are infinitely below the reality. This applies especially to the doctrine of the Eternal Sonship of our Lord and Saviour, as all know who have turned their minds to the controversies on the subject.

26. Again, it may so happen, that statements are only possible in the case of certain aspects of a doctrine, and that these seem inconsistent with each other, or mysteries,

when contrasted together, apart from what lies between them; just as if one were shown the picture of a little child and an old man, and were told that they represented the same person—a statement which would be incomprehensible to beings who were unacquainted with the natural changes which take place, in the course of years, in the human frame.

27. Or doctrinal statements may be introduced, not so much for their own sake, as because many consequences flow from them, and therefore a great variety of errors may, by means of them, be prevented. Such is the doctrine that our Saviour's personality is in His Godhead, not in His manhood; that He has taken the manhood into God. It is evident that such statements, being made for the sake of something beyond, when viewed apart from their end, or in themselves, are abrupt, and may offend hearers.

28. Again, so it is, however it be explained, that frequently we do not recognize our sensations and ideas, when put into words ever so carefully. The representation seems out of shape and strange, and startles us, even though we know not how to find fault with it. This applies, at least in the case of some persons, to portions of the received theological analysis of the impression made upon the mind by the Scripture notices concerning Christ and the Holy Spirit. In like manner, such phrases as "good works are a condition of eternal life," or "the salvation of the regenerate ultimately depends upon themselves," though unexceptionable, are of a nature to offend certain minds.

29. This difficulty of analyzing our more recondite feelings happily and convincingly, has a most important influence upon the science of the Evidences. Defenders of Christianity naturally select as reasons for belief, not the highest, the truest, the most sacred, the most intimately persuasive, but such as best admit of being exhibited in argument; and these are commonly not the real reasons in the case of religious men.

30. Nay, they are led for the same reason, to select such arguments as all will allow; that is, such as depend on principles which are a common measure for all minds. A science certainly is, in its very nature, public property; when,

then, the grounds of Faith take the shape of a book of Evidences, nothing properly can be assumed but what men in general will grant as true; that is, nothing but what is on a level with all minds, good and bad, rude and refined.

31. Again, as to the difficulty of detecting and expressing the real reasons on which we believe, let this be considered —how very differently an argument strikes the mind at one time and another, according to its particular state, or the accident of the moment. At one time it is weak and unmeaning, at another, it is nothing short of demonstration. We take up a book at one time, and see nothing in it; at another, it is full of weighty remarks and precious thoughts. Sometimes a statement is axiomatic, sometimes we are at a loss to see what can be said for it. Such, for instance, are the following, many like which are found in controversy: that true saints cannot but persevere to the end; or that the influences of the Spirit cannot but be effectual; or that there must be an infallible Head of the Church on earth; or that the Roman Church, extending into all lands, is the Catholic Church; or that a Church, which is Catholic abroad, cannot be schismatical in England; or that, if our Lord is the Son of God, He must be God; or that a Revelation is probable; or that, if God is All-powerful, He must be also All-good. Who shall analyze the assemblage of opinions in this or that mind, which occasions it almost instinctively to reject or to accept each of these and similar positions? Far be it from me to seem to insinuate that they are *but* opinions, neither true nor false, and approving themselves or not, according to the humour or prejudice of the individual: so far from it, that I would maintain that the recondite reasons which lead each person to take or décline them, are just the most important portion of the considerations on which his conviction depends; and I say so, by way of showing that the science of controversy, or again the science of Evidences, has done very little, since it cannot analyze and exhibit these momentous reasons; nay, so far has done worse than little, in that it professes to have done much, and leads the student to mistake what are but secondary points in debate, as if they were the most essential.

32. It often happens, for the same reason, that controversialists or philosophers are spoken of by this or that person as unequal, sometimes profound, sometimes weak. Such cases of inequality, of course, do occur; but we should be sure, when tempted so to speak, that the fault is not with ourselves, who have not entered into an author's meaning, or analyzed the implicit reasonings along which his mind proceeds in those parts of his writings which we not merely dissent from (for that we have a right to do), but criticize as inconsecutive.

33. These remarks apply especially to the proofs commonly brought, whether for the truth of Christianity, or for certain doctrines from texts of Scripture. Such alleged proofs are commonly strong or slight, not in themselves, but according to the circumstances under which the doctrine professes to come to us, which they are brought to prove; and they will have a great or small effect upon our minds, according as we admit those circumstances or not. Now, the admission of those circumstances involves a variety of antecedent views, presumptions, implications, associations, and the like, many of which it is very difficult to detect and analyze. One person, for instance, is convinced by Paley's argument from the Miracles, another is not; and why? Because the former admits that there is a God, that He governs the world, that He wishes the salvation of man, that the light of nature is not sufficient for man, that there is no other way of introducing a Revelation but miracles, and that men, who were neither enthusiasts nor impostors, could not have acted as the Apostles did, unless they had seen the miracles which they attested; the other denies some one, or more, of these statements, or does not feel the force of some other principle more recondite and latent still than any of these, which is nevertheless necessary to the validity of the argument.

34. Further, let it be considered, that, even as regards what are commonly called Evidences, that is, arguments *a posteriori*, conviction for the most part follows, not upon any one great and decisive proof or token of the point in debate, but upon a number of very minute circumstances

together, which the mind is quite unable to count up and methodize in an argumentative form. Let a person only call to mind the clear impression he has about matters of every day's occurrence, that this man is bent on a certain object, or that that man was displeased, or another suspicious; or that one is happy, and another unhappy; and how much depends in such impressions on manner, voice, accent, words uttered, silence instead of words, and all the many subtle symptoms which are felt by the mind, but cannot be contemplated; and let him consider how very poor an account he is able to give of his impression, if he avows it, and is called upon to justify it. This, indeed, is meant by what is called moral proof, in opposition to legal. We speak of an accused person being guilty without any doubt, even though the evidences of his guilt are none of them broad and definite enough in themselves to admit of being forced upon the notice of those who will not exert themselves to see them.

35. Now, should the proof of Christianity, or the Scripture proof of its doctrines, be of this subtle nature, of course it cannot be exhibited to advantage in argument: and even if it be not such, but contain strong and almost legal evidences, still there will always be a temptation in the case of writers on Evidence, or on the Scripture proof of doctrine, to overstate and exaggerate, or to systematize in excess; as if they were making a case in a court of law, rather than simply and severely analyzing, as far as is possible, certain existing reasons why the Gospel is true, or why it should be considered of a certain doctrinal character. It is hardly too much to say, that almost all reasons formally adduced in moral inquiries, are rather specimens and symbols of the real grounds, than those grounds themselves. They do but approximate to a representation of the general character of the proof which the writer wishes to convey to another's mind. They cannot, like mathematical proof, be passively followed with an attention confined to what is stated, and with the admission of nothing but what is urged. Rather, they are hints towards, and samples of, the true reasoning, and demand an active, ready, candid, and docile mind, which can throw itself into

what is said, neglect verbal difficulties, and pursue and carry out principles. This is the true office of a writer, to excite and direct trains of thought; and this, on the other hand, is the too common practice of readers, to expect every thing to be done for them—to refuse to think, to criticize the letter, instead of reaching forwards towards the sense, and to account every argument as unsound which is illogically worded.

36. Here is the fertile source of controversy, which may undoubtedly be prolonged without limit by those who desire it, while words are incomplete exponents of ideas, and complex reasons demand study, and involve prolixity. They, then, who wish to shorten the dispute, and to silence a captious opponent, look out for some strong and manifest argument which may be stated tersely, handled conveniently, and urged rhetorically; some one reason, which bears with it a show of vigour and plausibility, or a profession of clearness, simplicity, or originality, and may be easily reduced to mood and figure. Hence the stress often laid upon particular texts, as if decisive of the matter in hand: hence one disputant dismisses all parts of the Bible which relate to the Law, another finds the high doctrines of Christianity revealed in the Book of Genesis, another rejects certain portions of the inspired volume, as the Epistle of St. James, another gives up the Apocrypha, another rests the defence of Revelation on Miracles only, or the Internal Evidence only, another sweeps away all Christian teaching but Scripture—one and all from impatience at being allotted, in the particular case, an evidence which does little more than create an impression on the mind; from dislike of an evidence, varied, minute, complicated, and a desire of something producible, striking, and decisive.

37. Lastly, since a test is in its very nature of a negative character, and since argumentative forms are mainly a test of reasoning, so far they will be but critical, not creative. They will be useful in raising objections, and in ministering to scepticism; they will pull down, and will not be able to build up.

38. I have been engaged in proving the following points:

that the reasonings and opinions which are involved in the act of Faith are latent and implicit; that the mind reflecting on itself is able to bring them out into some definite and methodical form; that Faith, however, is complete without this reflective faculty, which, in matter of fact, often does interfere with it, and must be used cautiously.

39. I am quite aware that I have said nothing but what must have often passed through the minds of others; and it may be asked whether it is worth while so diligently to traverse old ground. Yet perhaps it is never without its use to bring together in one view, and steadily contemplate truths, which one by one may be familiar notwithstanding.

40. May we be in the number of those who, with the Blessed Apostle whom we this day commemorate, employ all the powers of their minds to the service of their Lord and Saviour, who are drawn heavenward by His wonder-working grace, whose hearts are filled with His love, who reason in His fear, who seek Him in the way of His commandments, and who thereby believe on Him to the saving of their souls!

•   •   •

In February, 1841, Newman continued his discussion of the "phenomenology of religious belief" in a series of public letters criticizing Sir Robert Peel's sweeping claims for a program of adult education. Nearly all of the sixth letter Newman quoted thirty years later in *The Grammar of Assent,* because it presented his position "with a freshness and force which I cannot now command" (1870). In his insistent contrast between religion and secular knowledge, Newman said: "The heart is commonly reached, not through the reason but through the imagination, by means of direct impressions, by the testimony of facts and events, by history, by description. Persons influence us, voices melt us, looks subdue us. Deeds inflame us. Many a person will live and die upon a dogma: no man will be a martyr for a conclusion. . . . I only say, that impressions lead to action, and that reasonings lead from it. Knowledge of premises, and inferences upon them—this is not to live."

February, 1841, also marked Newman's fortieth birthday and

the publication of *Tract 90* which everybody assumed—and quite rightly—was written by Newman. His main thesis was that "the [39] Articles of the Church of England do not oppose Catholic teaching; they but partially oppose Roman dogma; they for the most part oppose the dominant errors of Rome. And the problem was . . . to draw the line as to what they allowed and what they condemned."

Time was now running out. Early in 1843 Newman preached on "The Theory of Development in Religious Doctrine" in his last sermon in Oxford, and in the fall he preached on "The Parting of Friends" in his last sermon as an Anglican to a weeping congregation at nearby Littlemore.

During the first nine months of 1845 he was writing his *Essay on the Development of Christian Doctrine,* "in favor of the Roman Church and indirectly against the English," but not absolutely sure that he would publish it and not sure that he would not turn back from the journey that he had begun to take at least ten years before. He did not finish it and he did not turn back, but entered the Roman Catholic Church in October, 1845.

Nearly twenty years later, when his respect for truth was challenged by Charles Kingsley, who made no blanket withdrawal of his charges during the ensuing controversy, Newman wrote his *Apologia pro Vita Sua* in six weeks. The gist of that long and eloquent history of his spiritual pilgrimage appears in the following passage: "I had a great dislike of paper logic. For myself it was not logic that carried me on; as well might one say that the quicksilver in the barometer changes the weather. It is the concrete being that reasons; pass a number of years, and I find my mind in a new place; how? the whole man moves; paper logic is but the record of it."

This was the theme of his most elaborate technical work, *An Essay in Aid of A Grammar of Assent,* which develops his theory of the "illative" sense—"Newman's special term for the response of the whole man to truth." Leslie Paul, who suggests that Newman was "perhaps the outstanding philosopher-divine of the last century," finds that he "surprisingly anticipated the contemporary existentialist position, by teaching that assent is a total reaction of the whole being, beyond further analysis, and not an estimate of probabilities at an intellectual level."

KARL MARX

[1818–1883]

Early in 1888, Friedrich Engels found in an old notebook some comments which Marx had jotted down in Brussels forty years earlier; and he published them as "the first document in which is deposited the brilliant germ of the new world outlook." And it is reprinted here for the convenience of those who do not think that ignorance is bliss—especially with respect to a vast world power.

Marx was born into a comfortable Jewish family which had adopted Christianity. He entered the University of Berlin, to study jurisprudence and political economy, at his father's urgency; but he was drawn into philosophy by the enormous prestige of Hegel's system, almost irresistible in the decade after the master's death. Marx's doctoral dissertation, *The Difference between Democritean and Epicurean Philosophies of Nature,* was accepted by the University of Halle.

If forced under the threat of death to say something large about Hegel's thought in a single sentence, one might exclaim: "Reality is through and through rational; history is an orderly progressive spiral, however chaotic and terrible it may appear to the naïve observer; and the Prussian State is at least for the time being the ultimate embodiment of reason and justice." Some of those who were carried away by Hegel's limitless vision, by his apparent omniscience and by his profound grasp of historical events were given pause by his glorification of the *status quo.* For Prussia was a reactionary kingdom, with a pampered aristocracy, an impoverished peasantry and severe laws aimed at liberals and radicals of every hue. Censorship silenced criticism.

> The time is out of joint; O cursèd spite,
> That ever I was born to set it right!

But Hamlet's cry was not that of the "young Hegelians," for however much they might disagree with his politics and his system, they still possessed the weapon of the master, his famous dialectical method, which at its best is a kind of dynamic logic and at its worst a kind of pretentious magic. Irrational institutions had an air of unreality about them and deserved to be hurried into oblivion by criticism, reform or revolution. So the young Hegelians, Marx among them, plunged into further study of religion, philosophy, government, law, political economy, and they dashed off articles and books in spite of the police.

As a counterweight to Hegel, they found Ludwig Feuerbach who was "concerned with the whole reality (heart and stomach) of man." In *The Essence of Christianity* (1841), which was later translated by George Eliot, Feuerbach interpreted religion in psychological terms, as man's projection of himself into objectivity. In his *Preliminary Theses on the Reform of Philosophy,* Feuerbach attacked Hegel directly as a purveyor of old illusions under fancy names.

In the spring of 1845, Marx, a young exile in Brussels, got out his notebook and wrote as follows:

THESES ON FEUERBACH

I

The chief defect of all materialism up to now (including Feuerbach's) is, that the object, reality, what we apprehend through our senses, is understood only in the form of the *object* or *contemplation;* but not as *sensuous human activity*, as *practice;* not subjectively. Hence in opposition to materialism the *active* side was developed abstractly by idealism—which of course does not know real sensuous activity as such. Feuerbach wants sensuous objects, really distinguished from the objects of thought: but he does not understand human activity itself as *objective* activity. Hence, in *The Essence of Christianity*, he sees only the theoretical attitude as the true human attitude, while practice is understood and established only in its "dirty Jew" appearance. He therefore does not comprehend the significance of "revolutionary," of "practical-critical" activity.

II

The question whether objective truth is an attribute of human thought—is not a theoretical but a *practical* question. Man must prove the truth, i.e. the reality and power, the "this-sidedness" of his thinking in practice. The dispute over the reality or non-reality of thinking that is isolated from practice is a purely *scholastic* question.

III

The materialistic doctrine concerning the changing of circumstances and education forgets that circumstances are changed by men and that the educator himself must be educated. This doctrine has therefore to divide society into two parts, one of which is superior to society.

The coincidence of the changing of circumstances and of human activity or self-changing can only be comprehended and rationally understood as *revolutionary practice*.

IV

Feuerbach starts out from the fact of religious self-estrangement, of the duplication of the world into a religious and a secular one. His work consists in resolving the religious world into its secular basis. But that the secular basis raises itself above itself and establishes for itself an independent realm in the clouds can be explained only through the cleavage and self-contradictions within this secular basis. The latter must therefore in itself be both understood in its contradiction and revolutionized in practice. Therefore after, e.g., the earthly family is discovered to be the secret of the heavenly family, one must proceed to destroy the former both in theory and in practice.

V

Feuerbach, not satisfied with *abstract thought,* wants contemplation: but he does not understand our sensuous nature as *practical,* human-sensuous activity.

VI

Feuerbach resolves the essence of religion into the essence of *man.* But the essence of man is no abstraction inherent in each separate individual. In its reality it is the *ensemble* (aggregate) of social relations.

Feuerbach, who does not enter more deeply into the criticism of this real essence, is therefore forced:

1. To abstract from the process of history and to establish the religious temperament as something independent, and to postulate an abstract—*isolated*—human individual.
2. The essence of man can therefore be understood only as "genus," the inward, dumb generality which *naturally* unites the many individuals.

VII

Feuerbach therefore does not see that the "religious temperament" itself is a social product and that the abstract individual whom he analyses belongs to a particular form of society.

VIII

All social life is essentially *practical.* All the mysteries which urge theory into mysticism find their rational solution in human practice and in the comprehension of this practice.

IX

The highest point to which contemplative materialism can attain, i.e. that materialism which does not comprehend our sensuous nature as practical activity, is the contemplation of separate individuals and of civil society.

X

The standpoint of the old type of materialism is civil society, the standpoint of the new materialism is human society or social humanity.

XI

The philosophers have only *interpreted* the world differently, the point is, to *change* it.

•   •   •

(This is R. Pascal's translation of Marx's original *Theses*, not the slightly edited version published by Engels in 1888.)

JAMES McNEILL WHISTLER

[1834–1903]

Whistler is too easily remembered as an eccentric American expatriate who painted an all-too-famous picture of his mother and bested Oscar Wilde in duels of wit. It is too easily forgotten that he first exhibited the portrait of his mother as an "Arrangement in Grey and Black," and that he was a master in etching and lithography, in pastels and oils, one of the great protagonists of modern art.

He was born in Lowell, Massachusetts, although he sometimes suggested that he was born in St. Petersburg, for he lived there for several years in his boyhood while his father, a distinguished civil engineer, directed the building of the double-track railroad from St. Petersburg to Moscow. He also suggested at times that he might have been a major general if he had been correct in calling silicon a gas in a chemistry examination at West Point. But whatever the reason, he was flunked out of West Point and soon lost jobs with a locomotive works and with the Coast Survey. So he headed for the art battles of Paris with three hundred and fifty dollars annual allowance from his widowed mother, who could have hardly suspected that she was destined for immortality.

In Paris he at once plunged into a long career of hard, dedicated study, joined in the revolt against sentimental, anecdotal art, rejoiced in the newly discovered Japanese prints, and in 1863 achieved a considerable dash of fame with his "White Girl" in the Salon of the Rejected. But perhaps he realized that his painting as well as his posturing was far more needed in the smug atmosphere of Victorian London, for there he settled in the sixties, to carry on his love affair with the Thames at twilight. He was rewarded some years later when he exhibited eight of his finest works at the Grosvenor Gallery, for the aesthetic high priest, the first Slade Professor of Art at Oxford, John Ruskin, was particularly offended

199

by the beautiful nocturne "Black and Gold—The Falling Rocket." With his customary eloquence Ruskin solemnly announced: "I have seen and heard much of Cockney impudence before now, but never expected to hear a coxcomb ask two hundred guineas for flinging a pot of paint in the public's face."

Whistler brought suit for libel and a historic debate might have taken place but Ruskin suffered his long threatened breakdown in February, 1878, and did not recover in time to attend the trial which took place in the following November. So the result was a farce for the public and nearly all of the people in the courtroom, including the judge. Whistler had sued for a fortune and was awarded a ha'penny damage, so it was a kind of moral victory! But he was rendered bankrupt because he had to share the costs of the trial (Ruskin was a millionaire), lost his beautiful London house and withdrew for a year or two to Venice, where he found new themes for his magic.

But he came back! By 1885, he was so confident that he sent out invitations to a select audience to meet him on the evening of February 20 at ten o'clock at St. James's Hall. In immaculate dress and with perfect equanimity, he presented his aesthetic credo, during a war that was by no means won. You may be annoyed by some of his wit and rhetoric. You may not agree with all of his provocative assertions. But if you reject it entirely, you will be at odds with the great poet Mallarmé, who at the height of his fame took off time to make a careful translation of *The Ten O'Clock*.

·   ·   ·

THE TEN O'CLOCK

LADIES AND GENTLEMEN:

It is with great hesitation and much misgiving that I appear before you, in the character of The Preacher.

If timidity be at all allied to the virtue modesty, and can find favor in your eyes, I pray you, for the sake of that virtue, accord me your utmost indulgence.

I would plead for my want of habit, did it not seem preposterous, judging from precedent, that aught save the most efficient effrontery could be ever expected in connection with my subject—for I will not conceal from you that I mean to talk about Art. Yes, Art—that has of late become, as far as much discussion and writing can make it, a sort of common topic for the tea-table.

Art is upon the Town!—to be chucked under the chin by the passing gallant—to be enticed within the gates of the householder—to be coaxed into company, as a proof of culture and refinement.

If familiarity can breed contempt, certainly Art—or what is currently taken for it—has been brought to its lowest stage of intimacy.

The people have been harassed with Art in every guise, and vexed with many methods as to its endurance. They have been told how they shall love Art, and live with it. Their homes have been invaded, their walls covered with paper, their very dress taken to task—until, roused at last, bewildered and filled with the doubts and discomforts of senseless suggestion, they resent such intrusion, and cast forth the false prophets, who have brought the very name of the beautiful into disrepute, and derision upon themselves.

Alas! ladies and gentlemen, Art has been maligned. She has naught in common with such practices. She is a goddess of dainty thought—reticent of habit, abjuring all obtrusiveness, purposing in no way to better others.

She is, with all, selfishly occupied with her own perfection only—having no desire to teach—seeking and finding the beautiful in all conditions and in all times, as did her high priest, Rembrandt, when he saw picturesque grandeur and noble dignity in the Jews' quarter of Amsterdam, and lamented not that its inhabitants were not Greeks.

As did Tintoretto and Paul Veronese, among the Venetians, while not halting to change the brocaded silks for the classic draperies of Athens.

As did, at the Court of Philip, Velásquez, whose Infantas, clad in inaesthetic hoops, are, as works of Art, of the same quality as the Elgin marbles.

No reformers were these great men—no improvers of the way of others! Their productions alone were their occupation,

and filled with the poetry of their science, they required not
to alter their surroundings—for, as the laws of their Art
were revealed to them, they saw, in the development of their
work, that real beauty which, to them, was as much
a matter of certainty and triumph as is to the astronomer
the verification of the result, foreseen with the light given to
him alone. In all this, their world was completely severed
from that of their fellow-creatures, with whom sentiment is
mistaken for poetry; and for whom there is no perfect work
that shall not be explained by the benefit conferred upon
themselves.

Humanity takes the place of Art, and God's creations are
excused by their usefulness, beauty is confounded with
virtue, and, before a work of Art, it is asked: "What good
shall it do?"

Hence it is that nobility of action, in this life, is hopelessly
linked with the merit of the work that portrays it; and thus
the people have acquired the habit of looking, as who should
say, not *at* a picture but *through* it, at some human fact, that
shall, or shall not, from a social point of view, better their
mental or moral state. So we have come to hear of the painting that elevates, and of the duty of the painter—of the
picture that is full of thought, and of the panel that merely
decorates.

A favourite faith, dear to those who teach, is that certain
periods were especially artistic, and that nations, readily
named, were notably lovers of Art.

So we are told that the Greeks were, as a people, worship-
pers of the beautiful, and that in the fifteenth century Art
was engrained in the multitude.

That the great masters lived in common understanding
with their patrons—that the early Italians were artists—all—
and that the demand for the lovely thing produced it.

That we, of to-day, in gross contrast to this Arcadian
purity, call for the ungainly, and obtain the ugly.

That, could we but change our habits and climate—were
we willing to wander in groves—could we be roasted out of
broadcloth—were we to do without haste and journey with-

out speed, we should again *require* the spoon of Queen Anne, and pick at our peas with the fork of two prongs, and so, for the flock, little hamlets grow near Hammersmith, and the steam horse is scorned.

Useless! quite hopeless and false is the effort!—built upon fable, and all because "a wise man has uttered a vain thing and filled his belly with the East wind."

Listen! There never was an artistic period.

There never was an Art-loving nation.

In the beginning, man went forth each day—some to do battle, some to the chase; others, again, to dig and to delve in the field—all that they might gain and live, or lose and die. Until there was found among them one, differing from the rest, whose pursuits attracted him not, and so he stayed by the tents with the women, and traced strange devices with a burnt stick upon a gourd.

This man, who took no joy in the ways of his brethren—who cared not for conquest, and fretted in the field—this designer of quaint patterns, this deviser of the beautiful—who perceived in Nature about him curious curvings, as faces are seen in the fire—this dreamer apart, was the first artist.

And when, from the field and from afar, there came back the people, they took the gourd—and drank from out of it.

And presently there came to this man another—and, in time, others—of like nature, chosen by the Gods—and so they worked together; and soon they fashioned, from the moistened earth, forms resembling the gourd. And with the power of creation, the heirloom of the artist, presently they went beyond the slovenly suggestion of Nature, and the first vase was born in beautiful proportion.

And the toilers tilled, and were athirst; and the heroes returned from fresh victories, to rejoice and to feast; and all drank alike from the artists' goblets, fashioned cunningly, taking no note the while of the craftsman's pride, and understanding not his glory in his work; drinking at the cup, not from choice, not from a consciousness that it was beautiful, but because, forsooth, there was none other!

And time, with more state, brought more capacity for luxury, and it became well that men should dwell in large houses, and rest upon couches, and eat at tables; whereupon the artist, with his artificers, built palaces, and filled them with furniture, beautiful in proportion, and lovely to look upon.

And the people lived in marvels of art—and ate and drank out of masterpieces—for there was nothing else to eat and to drink out of, and no bad building to live in; no article of daily life, of luxury, or of necessity, that had not been handed down from the design of the master, and made by his workmen.

And the people questioned not, *and had nothing to say in the matter*.

So Greece was in its splendour, and Art reigned supreme —by force of fact, not by election—and there was no meddling from the outsider. The mighty warrior would no more have ventured to offer a design for the temple of Pallas Athene than would the sacred poet have proffered a plan for constructing the catapult.

And the Amateur was unknown—and the Dilettante undreamed of!

And history wrote on, and conquest accompanied civilisation, and Art spread, or rather its products were carried by the victors among the vanquished from one country to another. And the customs of cultivation covered the face of the earth so that all peoples continued to use what *the artist alone produced*.

And centuries passed in this using, and the world was flooded with all that was beautiful, until there arose a new class, who discovered the cheap, and foresaw fortune in the facture of the sham.

Then sprang into existence the tawdry, the common, the gewgaw.

The taste of the tradesman supplanted the science of the artist, and what was born of the million went back to them, and charmed them, for it was after their own heart; and the great and the small, the statesman and the slave, took to themselves the abomination that was tendered, and preferred it—and have lived with it ever since!

And the artist's occupation was gone, and the manufacturer and the huckster took his place.

And now the heroes filled from the jugs and drank from the bowls—with understanding—noting the glare of their new bravery, and taking pride in its worth.

And the people—this time—had much to say in the matter —and all were satisfied. And Birmingham and Manchester arose in their might—and Art was relegated to the curiosity shop.

Nature contains the elements, in colour and form, of all pictures, as the keyboard contains the notes of all music.

But the artist is born to pick, and choose, and group with science, these elements, that the result may be beautiful— as the musician gathers his notes, and forms his chords, until he brings forth from chaos glorious harmony.

To say to the painter, that Nature is to be taken as she is, is to say to the player, that he may sit on the piano.

That Nature is always right, is an assertion, artistically as untrue as it is one whose truth is universally taken for granted. Nature is very rarely right, to such an extent even, that it might almost be said that Nature is usually wrong; that is to say, the condition of things that shall bring about the perfection of harmony worthy a picture is rare, and not common at all.

This would seem, to even the most intelligent, a doctrine almost blasphemous. So incorporated with our education has the supposed aphorism become, that its belief is held to be part of our moral being, and the words themselves have, in our ear, the ring of religion. Still, seldom does Nature succeed in producing a picture.

The sun blares, the wind blows from the east, the sky is bereft of cloud, and without, all is of iron. The windows of the Crystal Palace are seen from all points of London. The holiday-maker rejoices in the glorious day, and the painter turns aside to shut his eyes.

How little this is understood, and how dutifully the casual

in Nature is accepted as sublime, may be gathered from the unlimited admiration daily produced by a very foolish sunset.

The dignity of the snow-capped mountain is lost in distinctness, but the joy of the tourist is to recognize the traveler on the top. The desire to see, for the sake of seeing, is, with the mass, alone the one to be gratified, hence the delight in detail.

And when the evening mist clothes the riverside with poetry, as with a veil, and the poor buildings lose themselves in the dim sky, and the tall chimneys become campanili, and the warehouses are palaces in the night, and the whole city hangs in the heavens, and fairy-land is before us—then the wayfarer hastens home; the working man and the cultured one, the wise man and the one of pleasure, cease to understand, as they have ceased to see, and Nature, who, for once, has sung in tune, sings her exquisite song to the artist alone, her son and her master—her son in that he loves her, her master in that he knows her.

To him her secrets are unfolded, to him her lessons have become gradually clear. He looks at her flower, not with the enlarging lens, that he may gather facts for the botanist, but with the light of the one who sees in her choice selection of brilliant tones and delicate tints, suggestions of future harmonies.

He does not confine himself to purposeless copying, without thought, each blade of grass, as commended by the inconsequent, but, in the long curve of the narrow leaf, corrected by the straight tall stem, he learns how grace is wedded to dignity, how strength enhances sweetness, that elegance shall be the result.

In the citron wing of the pale butterfly, with its dainty spots of orange, he sees before him the stately halls of fair gold, with their slender saffron pillars, and is taught how the delicate drawing high upon the walls shall be traced in tender tones of orpiment, and repeated by the base in notes of graver hue.

In all that is dainty and lovable he finds hints for his own combinations, and *thus* is Nature ever his resource and always at his service, and to him is naught refused.

Through his brain, as through the last alembic, is distilled the refined essence of that thought which began with the Gods, and which they left him to carry out.

Set apart by them to complete their works, he produces that wondrous thing called the masterpiece, which surpasses in perfection all that they have contrived in what is called Nature; and the Gods stand by and marvel, and perceive how far away more beautiful is the Venus of Melos than was their own Eve.

For some time past, the unattached writer has become the middleman in this matter of Art, and his influence, while it has widened the gulf between the people and the painter, has brought about the most complete misunderstanding as to the aim of the picture.

For him a picture is more or less a hieroglyph or symbol of story. Apart from a few technical terms, for the display of which he finds an occasion, the work is considered absolutely from a literary point of view; indeed, from what other can he consider it? And in his essays he deals with it as with a novel—a history—or an anecdote. He fails entirely and most naturally to see its excellences, or demerits—artistic—and so degrades Art, by supposing it a method of bringing about a literary climax.

It thus, in his hands, becomes merely a means of perpetrating something further, and its mission is made a secondary one, even as a means is second to an end.

The thoughts emphasised, noble or other, are inevitably attached to the incident, and become more or less noble, according to the eloquence or mental quality of the writer, who looks the while, with disdain, upon what he holds as "mere execution"—a matter belonging, he believes, to the training of the schools, and the reward of assiduity. So that, as he goes on with his translation from canvas to paper, the work becomes his own. He finds poetry where he would feel it were he himself transcribing the event, invention in the intricacy of the *mise en scène*, and noble philosophy in some detail of philanthropy, courage, modesty, or virtue, suggested to him by the occurrence.

All this might be brought before him, and his imagination be appealed to, by a very poor picture—indeed, I might safely say that it generally is.

Meanwhile, the *painter's* poetry is quite lost to him—the amazing invention that shall have put form and colour into such perfect harmony, that exquisiteness is the result, he is without understanding of—the nobility of thought that shall have given the artist's dignity to the whole, says to him absolutely nothing.

So that his praises are published, for virtues we would blush to possess—while the great qualities, that distinguish the one work from the thousand, that make of the masterpiece the thing of beauty that it is—have never been seen at all.

That this is so, we can make sure of, by looking back at old reviews upon past exhibitions, and reading the flatteries lavished upon men who have since been forgotten altogether—but, upon whose works, the language has been exhausted in rhapsodies—that left nothing for the National Gallery.

A curious matter, in its effect upon the judgment of these gentlemen, is the accepted vocabulary of poetic symbolism, that helps them, by habit, in dealing with Nature: a mountain, to them, is synonymous with height—a lake, with depth—the ocean, with vastness—the sun, with glory.

So that a picture with a mountain, a lake, and an ocean—however poor in paint—is inevitably "lofty," "vast," "infinite," and "glorious"—on paper.

There are those also, sombre of mien, and wise with the wisdom of books, who frequent museums and burrow in crypts; collecting—comparing—compiling—classifying—contradicting.

Experts these—for whom a date is an accomplishment—a hallmark, success!

Careful in scrutiny are they, and conscientious of judgment —establishing, with due weight, unimportant reputations—discovering the picture, by the stain on the back—testing the torso, by the leg that is missing—filling folios with doubts on the way of that limb—disputatious and dictatorial, concerning the birthplace of inferior persons—speculating, in much writing, upon the great worth of bad work.

True clerks of the collection, they mix memoranda with ambition, and, reducing Art to statistics, they "file" the fifteenth century, and "pigeon-hole" the antique!

Then the Preacher "appointed"!

He stands in high places—harangues and holds forth.

Sage of the Universities—learned in many matters, and of much experience in all, save his subject.

Exhorting—denouncing—directing.

Filled with wrath and earnestness.

Bringing powers of persuasion, and polish of language, to prove—nothing.

Torn with much teaching—having naught to impart.

Impressive—important—shallow.

Defiant—distressed—desperate.

Crying out, and cutting himself—while the gods hear not.

Gentle priest of the Philistine withal, again he ambles pleasantly from all point, and through many volumes, escaping scientific assertion—"babbles of green fields."

So Art has become foolishly confounded with education—that all should be equally qualified.

Whereas, while polish, refinement, culture, and breeding, are in no way arguments for artistic result, it is also no reproach to the most finished scholar or greatest gentleman in the land, that he be absolutely without eye for painting or ear for music—that in his heart he prefer the popular print to the scratch of Rembrandt's needle, or the songs of the hall to Beethoven's "C-Minor Symphony."

Let him have but the wit to say so, and not feel the admission a proof of inferiority.

Art happens—no hovel is safe from it, no Prince may depend upon it, the vastest intelligence cannot bring it about, and puny efforts to make it universal end in quaint comedy, and coarse farce.

This is as it should be—and all attempts to make it otherwise are due to the eloquence of the ignorant, the zeal of the conceited.

The boundary line is clear. Far from me to propose to bridge it over—that the pestered people be pushed across. No! I would save them from further fatigue. I would come to their relief, and would lift from their shoulders this incubus of Art.

Why, after centuries of freedom from it, and indifference to it, should it now be thrust upon them by the blind—until wearied and puzzled, they know no longer how they shall eat or drink—how they shall sit or stand—or wherewithal they shall clothe themselves—without afflicting Art.

But, lo! there is much talk without!

Triumphantly they cry, "Beware! This matter does indeed concern us. We also have our part in all true Art!—for, remember the 'one touch of Nature' that 'makes the whole world kin.'"

True, indeed. But let not the unwary jauntily suppose that Shakespeare herewith hands him his passport to Paradise, and thus permits him speech among the chosen. Rather, learn that, in this very sentence, he is condemned to remain without—to continue with the common.

This one chord that vibrates with all—this "one touch of Nature" that calls aloud to the response of each—that explains the popularity of the "Bull" of Paul Potter—that excuses the price of Murillo's "Conception"—this one unspoken sympathy that pervades humanity, is—Vulgarity!

Vulgarity—under whose fascinating influence "the many" have elbowed "the few," and the gentle circle of Art swarms with the intoxicated mob of mediocrity, whose leaders prate and counsel, and call aloud, where the Gods once spoke in whisper!

And now from their midst the Dilettante stalks abroad. The amateur is loosed. The voice of the aesthete is heard in the land, and catastrophe is upon us.

The meddler beckons the vengeance of the Gods, and ridicule threatens the fair daughters of the land.

And there are curious converts to a weird *culte*, in which

all instinct for attractiveness—all freshness and sparkle—all woman's winsomeness—is to give way to a strange vocation for the unlovely—and this desecration in the name of the Graces!

Shall this gaunt, ill-at-ease, distressed, abashed mixture of *mauvaise honte* and desperate assertion call itself artistic, and claim cousinship with the artist—who delights in the dainty, the sharp, bright gaiety of beauty?

No!—A thousand times no! Here are no connections of ours. We will have nothing to do with them.

Forced to seriousness, that emptiness may be hidden, they dare not smile—

While the artist, in fulness of heart and head, is glad, and laughs aloud, and is merry in his strength, and is merry at the pompous pretension—the solemn silliness that surrounds him.

For Art and Joy go together, with bold openness, and high head, and ready hand—fearing naught, and dreading no exposure.

Know, then, all beautiful women, that we are with you. Pay no heed, we pray you, to this outcry of the unbecoming—this last plea for the plain.

It concerns you not.

Your own instinct is near the truth—your own wit far surer guide than the untaught ventures of thick-heeled Apollos.

What! will you up and follow the first piper that leads you down Petticoat Lane, there, on a Sabbath, to gather, for the week, from the dull rags of ages wherewith to bedeck yourselves? that, beneath your travestied awkwardness, we have trouble to find your own dainty selves? Oh, fie! Is the world, then, exhausted? and must we go back because the thumb of the mountebank jerks the other way?

Costume is not dress.

And the wearers of wardrobes may not be doctors of taste!

For by what authority shall these be petty masters? Look well, and nothing have they invented—nothing put together for comeliness' sake.

Haphazard from their shoulders hang the garments of the

hawker—combining in their person the motley of many manners with the medley of the mummers' closet.

Set up as a warning, and a finger-post of danger, they point to the disastrous effect of Art upon the middle classes.

Why this lifting of the brow in deprecation of the present—this pathos in reference to the past?

If Art be rare to-day, it was seldom heretofore.

It is false, this teaching of decay.

The master stands in no relation to the moment at which he occurs—a monument of isolation—hinting of sadness—having no part in the progress of his fellow-men.

He is also no more the product of civilisation than is the scientific truth asserted dependent upon the wisdom of a period. The assertion itself requires the *man* to make it. The truth was from the beginning.

So Art is limited to the infinite, and beginning there cannot progress.

A silent indication of its wayward independence from all extraneous advance, is in the absolutely unchanged condition and form of implement since the beginning of things.

The painter has but the same pencil—the sculptor the chisel of centuries.

Colours are not more since the heavy hangings of night were first drawn aside, and the loveliness of light revealed.

Neither chemist nor engineer can offer new elements of the masterpiece.

False again, the fabled link between the grandeur of Art and the glories and virtues of the State, for Art feeds not upon nations, and peoples may be wiped from the face of the earth, but Art *is*.

It is indeed high time that we cast aside the weary weight of responsibility and co-partnership, and know that, in no way, do our virtues minister to its worth, in no way do our vices impede its triumph!

How irksome! how hopeless! how superhuman the self-imposed task of the nation! How sublimely vain the belief that it shall live nobly or Art perish.

Let us reassure ourselves, at our own option is our virtue. Art we in no way affect.

A whimsical goddess, and a capricious, her strong sense of joy tolerates no dulness, and, live we never so spotlessly, still may she turn her back upon us.

As, from time immemorial, she has done upon the Swiss in their mountains.

What more worthy people! Whose every Alpine gap yawns with tradition, and is stocked with noble story; yet, the perverse and scornful one will none of it, and the sons of patriots are left with the clock that turns the mill, and the sudden cuckoo, with difficulty restrained in its box!

For this was Tell a hero! For this did Gessler die!

Art, the cruel jade, cares not and hardens her heart, and hies her off to the East, to find, among the opium-eaters of Nankin, a favourite with whom she lingers fondly—caressing his blue porcelain, and painting his coy maidens, and marking his plates with her six marks of choice—indifferent in her companionship with him, to all save the virtue of his refinement!

He it is who calls her—he who holds her!

And again to the West, that her next lover may bring together the Gallery at Madrid, and show to the world how the Master towers above all; and in their intimacy they revel, he and she, in this knowledge; and he knows the happiness untasted by other mortal.

She is proud of her comrade, and promises that in after-years, others shall pass that way, and understand.

So in all time does this superb one cast about for the man worthy her love—and Art seeks the Artist alone.

Where he is, there she appears, and remains with him—loving and fruitful—turning never aside in moments of hope deferred—of insult—and of ribald misunderstanding; and when he dies she sadly takes her flight, though loitering yet in the land, from fond association, but refusing to be consoled. . . .

With the man, then, and not with the multitude, are her intimacies; and in the book of her life the names inscribed are few, scant, indeed, the list of those who have helped to write her story of love and beauty.

From the sunny morning, when, with her glorious Greek relenting, she yielded up the secret of repeated line, as, with his hand in hers, together they marked in marble, the measured rhyme of lovely limb and draperies flowing in unison, to the day when she dipped the Spaniard's brush in light and air, and made his people live within their frames, and *stand upon their legs,* that all nobility and sweetness, and tenderness, and magnificence should be theirs by right, ages had gone by, and few had been her choice.

. . . And so have we the ephemeral influence of the Master's memory—the after-glow, in which are warmed, for a while, the worker and disciple.

Countless, indeed, the horde of pretenders! But she knew them not.

A teeming, seething, busy mass, whose virtue was industry, and whose industry was vice!

Their names go to fill the catalogue of the collection at home, of the gallery abroad, for the delectation of the bagman and the critic.

Therefore have we cause to be merry!—and to cast away all care—resolved that all is well—as it ever was—and that it is not meet that we should be cried at, and urged to take measures!

Enough have we endured of dulness! Surely are we weary of weeping, and our tears have been cozened from us falsely, for they have called out woe! when there was no grief—and, alas! where all is fair!

We have then but to wait—until, with the mark of the Gods upon him—there comes among us again the chosen—who shall continue what has gone before. Satisfied that, even were he never to appear, the story of the beautiful is already complete—hewn in the marbles of the Parthenon—and broidered, with the birds, upon the fan of Hokusai—at the foot of Fusiyama.

FRIEDRICH NIETZSCHE

[1844–1900]

A philosopher, a prophet, a poet, a philosophical poet, Nietzsche has been many things to many people. He has even been turned into a militarist, a chauvinist and a blond beast by the heavy-handed manipulation of selected passages. When he said, "Be hard," he meant *be hard* on your own weakness, slackness, in-dolence—and he took his own advice heroically. When he said that "everyone lives under the sword of Damocles" or that "the great dancer comes from the stage with blood in her slippers," he no doubt assumed that metaphors, even the harshest, are to be taken with a grain of imagination. He was undoubtedly fascinated by such figures as Caesar, Cesare Borgia and Napoleon, as we all are, for what they had done for themselves; but his enduring heroes were Goethe and above all Socrates, the self-appointed gadfly of Athens. His final terrible testament, *Ecce Homo,* written on the edge of the abyss, was Nietzsche's Apology, as Walter A. Kaufmann makes clear in his admirable book.

Nietzsche loathed smugness, complacency, mass mediocrity. He feared the silent little man of resentment who is multiplying throughout the modern world. He feared material progress with the democratic emphasis on uniformity (not on liberty), which was leading straight toward the abyss of comfort—or universal conflagration.

In his desperate, neurotic way, he tried to be the gadfly of his time. He wanted to share that "genius of the heart" which he attributed to Socrates.

He cultivated with loving care the aphorism as his most awakening weapon, and he was in high form when he did the fourth section of *Beyond Good and Evil* (1886).

APHORISMS

63.

Whoever is fundamentally a teacher takes things—including himself—seriously only as they affect his students.

64.

"Insight for its own sake" is the ultimate snare that morality sets for us. We shall be completely entangled in it one day.

65.

The charm of insight would be small if there were not so much modesty to overcome on the way.

65a.

One is most dishonest toward one's God: he is not *permitted* to sin!

66.

The inclination to lower himself, to let himself be stolen from, lied to, and exploited, could be the modesty of a god who walks among men.

67.

Love for any one thing is barbaric, for it is exercised at the expense of everything else. This includes the love for God.

68.

"I did this," says my memory. "I cannot have done this," says my pride, remaining inexorable. Eventually, my memory yields.

69.

One has not watched life very observantly if one has never seen the hand that—kills tenderly.

70.

If one has character, one has also one's typical experience that recurs again and again.

71.

The wise man as astronomer: As long as you feel the stars to be "above" you, you do not gaze as one who has insight.

72.

Not the strength but the permanence of superior sensibilities is the mark of the superior man.

73.

Who reaches his ideal thereby surpasses it.

73a.

There is many a peacock who hides his tail from all eyes—and calls it his pride.

74.

A man of genius is unbearable if he does not have at least two other things: gratitude and cleanliness.

75.

The degree and the type of a man's sexuality reaches to the highest peaks of his spirit.

76.

When there is peace, the warlike man attacks himself.

77.

One uses one's principles to tyrannize or justify or honor or affront or conceal one's habits. Two men with similar principles may easily want totally different things with them.

78.

Whoever despises himself still esteems the despiser within himself.

79.

A soul who knows it is loved but does not love back reveals its sediment: it is turned completely bottom side up.

80.

A matter which has come to light ceases to matter to us. What did that god mean who advised man to "know thyself"? Did he mean "Cease to matter to yourself! Become objective!"? And what about Socrates? And the "scientist"?

81.

It is terrible to die of thirst at sea. Must you salt your truth so heavily that it cannot even any longer—quench thirst?

32.

"Compassion for all" would amount to rigor and tyranny for *you*, my dear neighbor!

83.

Instinct: When the house is on fire one forgets even the dinner.—Yes, but one goes to the ashes to eat it.

84.

A woman learns to hate in proportion as she unlearns how to enchant.

85.

The same passions in man and woman nonetheless differ in tempo; hence man and woman do not cease misunderstanding one another.

86.

Behind all their personal vanity, women still impersonally despise "woman."

87.

Heart in bond, spirit free. When one places one's heart in firm bonds and keeps it locked up, one can afford to give one's spirit many liberties. I already said this once. But people do not believe me—unless they know it already. . . .

88.

One begins to distrust very clever people when they become embarrassed. . . .

89.

Terrible experiences give one cause to speculate whether the one who experiences them may not be something terrible.

90.

Grave, melancholy men grow lighter and at times reach their surface through just those things which make others grave: through hatred and through love.

91.

So cold, so icy, that one burns one's fingers on him! Every hand that touches him receives a shock. This is why some think he is burning hot.

92.

Who has not at some time or other sacrificed himself, in order to save his reputation?

93.

There is no misanthropy in affability, but all the more contempt.

94.

Man's maturity: to have regained the seriousness that he had as a child at play.

95.

To be ashamed of one's un-morality is a rung of the ladder at whose end one is also ashamed of one's morality.

96.

One should part from life as Odysseus parted from Nausicaa: with a blessing rather than in love.

97.

A great man, did you say? All I ever see is the actor creating his own ideal image.

98.

When we coach our conscience, it kisses us as it bites.

99.

The disappointed one says: I hoped for a response and heard merely praise. . . .

100.

We all pretend to ourselves that we are more simple-minded than we are: that is how we get a rest from our fellowmen.

101.

A man of insight nowadays might easily feel that he was God incarnate in a beast.

102.

When love is returned, it should really disenchant the lover with the beloved creature. "What? She is so modest in her demands as to love even you? Or so dumb? Or, or. . . ."

103.

The danger in happiness: Now everything I touch turns out to be wonderful. Now I love any fate that comes along. Who feels like being my fate?

104.

Not their love, but the impotence of their love keeps today's Christians from—burning us at the stake.

105.

For the free thinker, for one who has "piety of insight," a pious fraud is even harder to swallow than an impious fraud. It runs counter to *his* piety. Hence his deep lack of understanding for the church. Insofar as he belongs to the type "free thinker," he takes the church to be *his* lack of freedom.

106.

The passions enjoy themselves in the form of music.

107.

When the mind is made up, the ear is deaf to even the best arguments. This is the sign of a strong character. In other words, an occasional will to stupidity.

108.

There are no moral phenomena, only a moral interpretation of phenomena. . . .

109.

Frequently the criminal is not the equal of his crime. He belittles it and slanders it.

110.

Criminal lawyers are rarely artists enough to turn the beautifully horrible aspect of a crime to the advantage of the criminal.

111

Our vanity is most difficult to wound when our pride has just been wounded.

112.

Whoever feels predestined for contemplation instead of faith finds all the faithful too noisy and obtrusive. He defends himself against them.

113.

You want him to be prejudiced in your favor? Then pretend you are embarrassed before him. . . .

114.

The enormous expectation that women have of sex, and the modesty involved in the expectation, spoils their perspective from the very beginning.

115.

Where love or hate have no share in the game, a woman's playing is mediocre.

116.

The great epochs of our lives come when we gain the courage to rebaptize our evil as our best.

117.

The will to overcome a passion is in the end merely the will of another or several other passions.

118.

There is an innocence in admiration. It is possessed by someone to whom it has not yet occurred that he, too, might be admired some day.

119.

Disgust at dirt can be so great that it keeps us from cleaning ourselves up—from "justifying" ourselves.

120.

Sensuality often grows too fast for love to keep up with. Then love's root remains weak and is easily torn up.

121.

There is a subtlety in the fact that God learned Greek when he wanted to become an author—and that he didn't learn it any better.

122.

The enjoyment of praise is in some people merely a courtesy of the heart—the very opposite of vanity of the intellect.

123.

Concubinage, too, has been corrupted—by marriage.

124.

Whoever is joyous when burning at the stake is not triumphant over pain, but over the fact that there is no pain where he expected it. A parable.

125.

When we must change our minds about someone, we charge the inconvenience he causes us heavily to his account.

126.

A people is nature's detour to six or seven great men. Yes, and then the means to get around even them.

127.

Science runs counter to the modesty of all genuine women. They feel as though it were being used to peek under their skins—worse yet, under their dress and make-up.

128.

The more abstract the truth you want to teach, the more thoroughly you must seduce the senses to accept it.

129.

The devil has the farthest perspectives for God—that is why he stays so far away from him. The devil, in other words, is the oldest friend of insight.

130.

What someone *is*, begins to be revealed when his talent abates, when he stops showing what he can *do*. Talent, too, is a form of cosmetics; cosmetics, too, are a hiding device.

131.

The sexes deceive themselves about one another. For fundamentally they honor and love only themselves (or their own ideal, to say it more pleasingly). Man, for example, wants woman to be peaceable, but women are unpeaceable *by their very nature*, like cats, however well they have trained themselves to appear peaceable.

132.

One is best punished for one's virtues.

133.

Who cannot find the way to his *own* ideal, lives more recklessly and impudently than a man without an ideal.

134.

Only from the senses comes all credibility, all clear conscience, all self-evidence of truth.

135.

Pharisaism is not a degeneracy of a good man; on the contrary, a large part of it is the necessary condition for being good.

136.

One person seeks a midwife for his thoughts; the other, someone he can assist. Here is the origin of a good conversation.

137.

When dealing with intellectuals and artists, one readily makes the opposite mistakes: beneath a remarkable intellectual there is often a mediocre man, but beneath a mediocre artist there is quite often a very remarkable man.

138.

What we do in our dreams we also do in our waking hours; we first invent and create the man with whom we are dealing and then—we forget immediately that we have done it.

139.

In revenge and in love, women are more barbaric than men.

140.

Advice in the form of a riddle: If you want the bond to hold, bite on it—free and bold.

141.

Man's belly is the reason why man does not easily take himself for a god.

142.

The chastest utterance I have heard: *"Dans le véritable amour c'est l'âme, qui enveloppe le corps."*[1]

143.

Our vanity would like to have it understood that what we do best comes hardest to us. A contribution toward the origin of many a morality.

144.

When a woman is intellectually inclined there is usually something wrong with her sex. Even barrenness disposes her to a certain masculinity of taste; for man—if I may say so—is the "barren animal."

145.

Comparing men and women as a whole, one may say that women would not have their genius for adornment if they did not have the instinct for playing a *secondary role.*

146.

Whoever battles with monsters had better see that it does not turn him into a monster. And if you gaze long into an abyss, the abyss will gaze back into you.

147.

This out of old Florentine *novellas,* and, incidentally, out of life: *buona femmina e mala femmina vuol bastone.* Sacchetti, *Nov.* 86.[2]

148.

To seduce their neighbor into thinking well of them, and then to believe implicitly in this opinion of their neighbor: who has greater skill in this than a woman?

---

[1] In true love it is the soul that envelops the body.

[2] Good women and bad women alike want to be beaten.

149.

What a given period feels to be evil is usually the unseasonable echo of something that used to be felt as good—the atavism of an older ideal.

150.

Around the hero, all things turn into tragedy; around the demigod, into a satyr-play; and around God all things turn into—did you say, "world"?

151.

To have a talent is not enough for you; one must also have your permission to have it, eh, my friends?

152.

"Wherever the tree of knowledge stands is Paradise," say the oldest and the youngest serpents.

153.

What is done out of love always happens beyond good and evil.

154.

Objections, non-sequiturs, cheerful distrust, joyous mockery —all are signs of health. Everything absolute belongs in the realm of pathology.

155.

The sense for tragedy increases and decreases with sensuality.

156.

Insanity is the exception in individuals. In groups, parties, peoples, and times, it is the rule.

157.

The thought of suicide is a strong consolation; one can get through many a bad night with it.

158.

Not only our reason but our conscience succumbs to our strongest drive, to the tyrant within us.

159.

We *must* repay both good and ill—but not necessarily to the person who did us the good or ill.

160.

One no longer loves one's insight enough when one communicates it.

161.

Poets behave shamelessly toward their experiences: they exploit them.

162.

The fellow next to us is not our neighbor; the one next to *him* is. So thinks every nation.

163.

Love brings out the high and hidden qualities of the lover —his rare, exceptional states. Hence it easily deceives us about his ordinary ways, his "rule."

164.

Jesus said to his Jews, "The Law was made for servants. Love God, as I do, love him as a son does. What do we sons of God care about morality!"

165.

Looking at any political party: Every shepherd needs a bell-wether to lead his flock—or else he must be one.

166.

We may lie with our lips, but we tell the truth with the face we make when we lie.

167.

In rigorous men, tenderness is a matter for modesty—and something precious.

168.

Christianity gave Eros poison to drink; he did not die of it but he degenerated into vice.

169.

Talking much about oneself may be a way of hiding oneself.

170.

There is more obtrusiveness in praise than in blame.

171.

Compassion works on a man of insight almost to make him laugh—like tender hands laid on a Cyclops.

172.

For sheer love of humanity one occasionally embraces some random person (because one cannot embrace everyone). But this is the one thing one must not let the random person know. . . .

173.

One does not hate as long as one has a low esteem of someone, but only when one esteems him as an equal or a superior.

174.

You Utilitarians! You too love utility only as a wagon-cart to transport your inclinations. You too really find the creaking of its wheels unbearable—do you?

175.

Ultimately one loves one's desire, not the desired object.

176.

The vanity of others runs counter to our taste only when it runs counter to our vanity.

177.

Perhaps no one yet has been sufficiently truthful about the nature of "truthfulness."

178.

One does not believe in the follies of clever men—this is unfair to human rights!

179.

The consequences of our actions grab us by the back of the neck, blithely disregarding the fact that we have meanwhile "reformed."

180.

There is a kind of innocence in a lie which is the sign of good faith in a cause.

181.

It is inhuman to bless where one is being cursed.

182.

The familiarity of one's superior makes one bitter because it cannot be reciprocated.

183.

"What has shaken me is not that you lied to me but that I no longer believe you now. . . ."

184.

There is an impetuosity of goodness that looks like malice.

185.

"I don't like it." "Why not?" "Because I am not up to handling it." Did ever a man answer thus?

CHARLES SANDERS PEIRCE
[1839–1914]

Writing from Paris in 1780 to his wife, John Adams grumbled hopefully: "I must study politics and war that my sons may have liberty to study mathematics and philosophy. My sons ought to study mathematics and philosophy, geography, natural history and naval architecture in order to give their children a right to study painting, poetry, music, architecture, statuary, tapestry, porcelain."

As a matter of fact, we Americans were quite fully occupied in forming a nation and conquering a continent, and then reforming a nation, without going in for philosophy in a technical way. We were long content to take over rewarmed or watered-down versions of European schools of thought such as Scotch realism and German idealism. Jonathan Edwards (1703–1758), the Calvinist divine of Colonial days, however, was a thinker of rare depth and rigor whose prestige was clouded by the coming of milder faiths. Benjamin Franklin and Thomas Jefferson lived their experimental philosophies in a revolutionary age, we may say with gratitude, whereas John Adams, James Madison, Alexander Hamilton and, later, John C. Calhoun brought fresh minds to political theory. Ralph Waldo Emerson made no pretense to system but he was certainly a sage in the best sense of the word. It is rumored that there is rich ore lying beneath the crabbed Swedenborgian prose of Henry James, Sr., the father of William James and Henry James.

Returning to John Adams' little sketch for the future, we find that his great-grandson, the philosophical historian and autobiographer Henry Adams, was the exact contemporary of Charles S. Peirce, "the most original and versatile of America's philosophers and America's greatest logician," according to Paul Weiss, in the *Dictionary of American Biography*. Yet Peirce was not respectable or "adaptable" enough to hold a regular academic post and his work has come down to us only in the form of scattered articles, supplemented by compilations from his manuscripts, published after his death—but still incomplete. As for his reputation, there was a scandal regarding his divorce from his genteel first wife; he was arrogant and difficult to work with, for he "did not suffer fools gladly"; and he drank! Consequently he made a meager living for thirty years doing scientific work for the U.S. Coast and Geodetic Survey, reviewing and a little lecturing—and spent the remaining twenty-five years living in lonely poverty with his second wife (French) in Milford, Pennsylvania.

James Mill, the liberal reformer, set out with ruthless severity to mold his helpless boy, John Stuart, into "the perfect Benthamite" —and almost succeeded. Benjamin Peirce, the distinguished mathematician and physicist, was thrilled by his son Charles's early promise and pushed him on with the excitement of a devoted friend and collaborator toward heights impossible to himself. Consequently, young Charles was solidly grounded in mathematics and logic (absorbing Whately's well-known text at thirteen) and steadily saturated in "the spirit of the physical sciences." He read deeply not only in ancient and modern philosophy but also, rare for his day, in medieval philosophy, particularly in the neglected work of Duns Scotus. Yet he became promptly concerned with the newer developments of statistics, formal logic and the implications of Darwinism. Incidentally, or rather not incidentally, he was a connoisseur of wines and throughout his career a coiner of new words, some of which have slipped permanently into the vocabulary of philosophy.

In 1868, the American *Journal of Speculative Philosophy* carried three long articles with strange titles: "Questions Concerning Faculties Claimed for Man," "Some Consequences of Four Incapacities," and "Grounds of Validity of the Laws of Logic: Further Consequences of Four Incapacities." Young William James found them "exceedingly bold, subtle and incomprehensible." Today they are considered difficult and cryptic, but landmarks in the history of thought and immediate evidence of courageous originality in Charles S. Peirce at the age of thirty. He was making a frontal attack on the never-sleeping tradition of Cartesianism dominant in the West since the seventeenth century. He denied to philosophers the privilege of universal doubt, the possibility of grandiosely sweeping away all prejudices and opinions and starting anew with a virginal mind. He denied the existence of an infallible faculty of intuition which grasps "clear and distinct ideas" unerringly, without the use of language or signs. He denied that any individual's claims to certainty in philosophy are compelling, for truth is a public matter to be achieved by the consensus of the competent community. Above all, Peirce from the very beginning stressed the importance of language and the nature of man as a symbol- or sign-using animal. "In fact, therefore, men and words reciprocally educate each other; each increase of a man's information involves, and is involved by, a corresponding increase of a word's information."

Ten years later Peirce brought out a series of six articles under the general title of *Illustrations of the Logic of Science*. The first two, "The Fixation of Belief" and "How to Make Our Ideas Clear," are now well known and often reprinted. The second one contains a highly condensed paragraph which is considered the germ of pragmatism and perhaps also of logical positivism and operationism: "It appears, then, that the rule for attaining the third grade of clearness of apprehension is as follows: Consider what effects, which might conceivably have practical bearings, we conceive the object of our conception to have. Then our conception of these effects is the whole of our conception of the object."

During his long years of retirement at Milford, Peirce worked away tirelessly on large and small projects and toward a master work, "A Guess at the Riddle," which, he noted, "if ever written, as it soon will be if I am in a situation to do it, will be one of the births of time." He was never in a situation to do it. But he did complete for publication in the early 1890's a series of brilliant, bold—some would say recklessly bold—essays pointing toward a whole overarching system:

1. The Architecture of Theories
2. The Doctrine of Necessity Examined
3. The Law of Mind
4. Man's Glassy Essence
5. Evolutionary Love

We have included the last one because Peirce came of age in the early years of the controversy *The Origin of Species* and because he was one of the first to appreciate the wider implications of that epoch-marking book whose centenary is being commemorated.

EVOLUTIONARY LOVE [1]

AT FIRST BLUSH. COUNTER-GOSPELS

Philosophy, when just escaping from its golden pupa-skin, mythology, proclaimed the great evolutionary agency of the universe to be Love. Or, since this pirate-lingo, English, is poor in such-like words, let us say Eros, the exuberance-love. Afterwards, Empedocles set up passionate-love and hate as the two co-ordinate powers of the universe. In some passages, kindness is the word. But certainly, in any sense in which it has an opposite, to be senior partner of that opposite, is the highest position that love can attain. Nevertheless, the onto-logical gospeller, in whose days those views were familiar topics, made the One Supreme Being, by whom all things have been made out of nothing, to be cherishing-love. What, then, can he say to hate? Never mind, at this time, what the scribe of the apocalypse, if he were John, stung at length by persecution into a rage unable to distinguish suggestions of evil from visions of heaven, and so become the Slanderer of God to men, may have dreamed. The question is rather what the sane John thought, or ought to have thought, in order to carry out his idea consistently. His statement that God is love seems aimed at that saying of Ecclesiastes that we cannot tell whether God bears us love or hatred. "Nay," says John, "we can tell, and very simply! We know and have trusted the love which God hath in us. God is love." There is no logic in this, unless it means that God loves all men. In the preceding para-graph, he had said, "God is light and in him is no darkness at all." We are to understand, then, that as darkness is merely the defect of light, so hatred and evil are mere imperfect stages of ἀγάπη and ἀγαθόν, love and loveliness. This con-

[1] *The Monist*, January, 1893.

cords with that utterance reported in John's Gospel: "God sent not the Son into the world to judge the world; but that the world should through him be saved. He that believeth on him is not judged: he that believeth not hath been judged already. . . . And this is the judgment, that the light is come into the world, and that men loved darkness rather than the light." That is to say, God visits no punishment on them; they punish themselves, by their natural affinity for the defective. Thus, the love that God is, is not a love of which hatred is the contrary; otherwise Satan would be a co-ordinate power; but it is a love which embraces hatred as an imperfect stage of it, an Anteros—yea, even needs hatred and hatefulness as its object. For self-love is no love; so if God's self is love, that which he loves must be defect of love; just as a luminary can light up only that which otherwise would be dark. Henry James, the Swedenborgian, says: "It is no doubt very tolerable finite or creaturely love to love one's own in another, to love another for his conformity to one's self: but nothing can be in more flagrant contrast with the creative Love, all whose tenderness *ex vi termini* must be reserved only for what intrinsically is most bitterly hostile and negative to itself." This is from *Substance and Shadow: an Essay on the Physics of Creation.* It is a pity he had not filled his pages with things like this, as he was able easily to do, instead of scolding at his reader and at people generally, until the physics of creation was well-nigh forgot. I must deduct, however, from what I just wrote: obviously no genius could make his every sentence as sublime as one which discloses for the problem of evil its everlasting solution.

The movement of love is circular, at one and the same impulse projecting creations into independency and drawing them into harmony. This seems complicated when stated so; but it is fully summed up in the simple formula we call the Golden Rule. This does not, of course, say, Do everything possible to gratify the egoistic impulses of others, but it says, Sacrifice your own perfection to the perfectionment of your neighbor. Nor must it for a moment be confounded with the

Benthamite, or Helvetian, or Beccarian motto, Act for the greatest good of the greatest number. Love is not directed to abstractions but to persons; not to persons we do not know, nor to numbers of people, but to our own dear ones, our family and neighbors. "Our neighbor," we remember, is one whom we live near, not locally perhaps, but in life and feeling.

Everybody can see that the statement of St. John is the formula of an evolutionary philosophy, which teaches that growth comes only from love, from—I will not say self-*sacrifice,* but from the ardent impulse to fulfil another's highest impulse. Suppose, for example, that I have an idea that interests me. It is my creation. It is my creature; for as shown in last July's *Monist,* it is a little person. I love it; and I will sink myself in perfecting it. It is not by dealing out cold justice to the circle of my ideas that I can make them grow, but by cherishing and tending them as I would the flowers in my garden. The philosophy we draw from John's gospel is that this is the way mind develops; and as for the cosmos, only so far as it yet is mind, and so has life, is it capable of further evolution. Love, recognizing germs of loveliness in the hateful, gradually warms it into life, and makes it lovely. That is the sort of evolution which every careful student of my essay *The Law of Mind* must see that *synechism* calls for.

The nineteenth century is now fast sinking into the grave, and we all begin to review its doings and to think what character it is destined to bear as compared with other centuries in the minds of future historians. It will be called, I guess, the Economical Century; for political economy has more direct relations with all the branches of its activity than has any other science. Well, political economy has its formula of redemption, too. It is this: Intelligence in the service of greed ensures the justest prices, the fairest contracts, the most enlightened conduct of all the dealings between men, and leads to the *summum bonum,* food in plenty and perfect comfort. Food for whom? Why, for the greedy master of intelligence. I do not mean to say that this is one of the legitimate conclusions of political economy, the scientific character of which I fully acknowledge. But the study of doctrines, themselves

true, will often temporarily encourage generalizations extremely false, as the study of physics has encouraged necessitarian-
ism. What I say, then, is that the great attention paid to economical questions during our century has induced an exaggeration of the beneficial effects of greed and of the unfortunate results of sentiment, until there has resulted a philosophy
which comes unwittingly to this, that greed is the great agent
in the elevation of the human race and in the evolution of the
universe.

I open a handbook of political economy—the most typical
and middling one I have at hand—and there find some remarks
of which I will here make a brief analysis. I omit qualifica-
tions, sops thrown to Cerberus, phrases to placate Christian
prejudice, trappings which serve to hide from author and
reader alike the ugly nakedness of the greed-god. But I have
surveyed my position. The author enumerates "three motives
to human action:

"The love of self;

"The love of a limited class having common interests and
feelings with one's self;

"The love of mankind at large."

Remark, at the outset, what obsequious title is bestowed
on greed—"the love of self." Love! The second motive *is* love.
In place of "a limited class" put "certain persons," and you
have a fair description. Taking "class" in the old-fashioned
sense, a weak kind of love is described. In the sequel, there
seems to be some haziness as to the delimitation of this motive. By the love of mankind at large, the author does not
mean that deep, subconscious passion that is properly so
called; but merely public-spirit, perhaps little more than a
fidget about pushing ideas. The author proceeds to a comparative estimate of the worth of these motives. Greed, says
he, but using, of course, another word, "is not so great an evil
as is commonly supposed. . . . Every man can promote his
own interests a great deal more effectively than he can promote any one else's, or than any one else can promote his."
Besides, as he remarks on another page, the more miserly a
man is, the more good he does. The second motive "is the

most dangerous one to which society is exposed." Love is all very pretty: "no higher or purer source of human happiness exists." (Ahem!) But it is a "source of enduring injury," and, in short, should be overruled by something wiser. What is this wiser motive? We shall see.

As for public-spirit, it is rendered nugatory by the "difficulties in the way of its effective operation." For example, it might suggest putting checks upon the fecundity of the poor and the vicious; and "no measure of repression would be too severe," in the case of criminals. The hint is broad. But unfortunately, you cannot induce legislatures to take such measures, owing to the pestiferous "tender sentiments of man towards man." It thus appears, that public-spirit, or Benthamism, is not strong enough to be the effective tutor of love (I am skipping to another page), which must, therefore, be handed over to "the motives which animate men in the pursuit of wealth," in which alone we can confide, and which "are in the highest degree beneficent." [2] Yes, in the "highest degree" without exception are they beneficent to the being upon whom all their blessings are poured out, namely, the Self, whose "sole object," says the writer, in accumulating wealth is his individual "sustenance and enjoyment." Plainly, the author holds the notion that some other motive might be in a higher degree beneficent even for the man's self to be a paradox wanting in good sense. He seeks to gloze and modify his doctrine; but he lets the perspicacious reader see what his animating principle is; and when, holding the opinions I have repeated, he at the same time acknowledges that society could not exist upon a basis of intelligent greed alone, he simply pigeon-holes himself as one of the eclectics of inharmonious opinions. He wants his mammon flavored with a *soupçon* of god.

The economists accuse those to whom the enunciation of their atrocious villainies communicates a thrill of horror of being *sentimentalists*. It may be so: I willingly confess to having

---

[2] How can a writer have any respect for science, as such, who is capable of confounding with the scientific propositions of political economy, which have nothing to say concerning what is "beneficent," such brummagem generalisations as this?

some tincture of sentimentalism in me, God be thanked! Ever
since the French Revolution brought this leaning of thought
into ill-repute—and not altogether undeservedly, I must admit,
true, beautiful, and good as that great movement was—it has
been the tradition to picture sentimentalists as persons incapable of logical thought and unwilling to look facts in the eyes.
This tradition may be classed with the French tradition that
an Englishman says *goddam* at every second sentence, the
English tradition that an American talks about "Britishers,"
and the American tradition that a Frenchman carries forms of
etiquette to an inconvenient extreme, in short with all those
traditions which survive simply because the men who use
their eyes and ears are few and far between. Doubtless some
excuse there was for all those opinions in days gone by; and
sentimentalism, when it was the fashionable amusement to
spend one's evenings in a flood of tears over a woeful performance on a candle-litten stage, sometimes made itself a
little ridiculous. But what after all is sentimentalism? It is an
ism, a doctrine, namely, the doctrine that great respect should
be paid to the natural judgments of the sensible heart. This is
what sentimentalism precisely is; and I entreat the reader to
consider whether to contemn it is not of all blasphemies the
most degrading. Yet the nineteenth century has steadily con-
temned it, because it brought about the Reign of Terror. That
it did so is true. Still, the whole question is one of *how much*.
The Reign of Terror was very bad; but now the Gradgrind
banner has been this century long flaunting in the face of
heaven, with an insolence to provoke the very skies to scowl
and rumble. Soon a flash and quick peal will shake economists
quite out of their complacency, too late. The twentieth century, in its latter half, shall surely see the deluge-tempest burst
upon the social order—to clear upon a world as deep in ruin
as that greed-philosophy has long plunged it into guilt. No
post-thermidorian high jinks then!

So a miser is a beneficent power in a community, is he?
With the same reason precisely, only in a much higher degree,
you might pronounce the Wall Street sharp to be a good angel,
who takes money from heedless persons not likely to guard it

properly, who wrecks feeble enterprises better stopped, and who administers wholesome lessons to unwary scientific men, by passing worthless checks upon them—as you did, the other day, to me, my millionaire Master in glomery, when you thought you saw your way to using my process without paying for it, and of so bequeathing to your children something to boast of their father about—and who by a thousand wiles puts money at the service of intelligent greed, in his own person. Bernard Mandeville, in his *Fable of the Bees,* maintains that private vices of all descriptions are public benefits, and proves it, too, quite as cogently as the economist proves his point concerning the miser. He even argues, with no slight force, that but for vice civilization would never have existed. In the same spirit, it has been strongly maintained and is to-day widely believed that all acts of charity and benevolence, private and public, go seriously to degrade the human race.

The *Origin of Species* of Darwin merely extends politico-economical views of progress to the entire realm of animal and vegetable life. The vast majority of our contemporary naturalists hold the opinion that the true cause of those exquisite and marvellous adaptations of nature for which, when I was a boy, men used to extol the divine wisdom is that creatures are so crowded together that those of them that happen to have the slightest advantage force those less pushing into situations unfavorable to multiplication or even kill them before they reach the age of reproduction. Among animals, the mere mechanical individualism is vastly re-enforced as a power making for good by the animal's ruthless greed. As Darwin puts it on his title-page, it is the struggle for existence; and he should have added for his motto: Every individual for himself, and the Devil take the hindmost! Jesus, in his sermon on the Mount, expressed a different opinion.

Here, then, is the issue. The gospel of Christ says that progress comes from every individual merging his individuality in sympathy with his neighbors. On the other side, the conviction of the nineteenth century is that progress takes place by virtue of every individual's striving for himself with all his might and trampling his neighbor under foot whenever he gets a chance to do so. This may accurately be called the Gospel of Greed.

Much is to be said on both sides. I have not concealed, I could not conceal, my own passionate predilection. Such a confession will probably shock my scientific brethren. Yet the strong feeling is in itself, I think, an argument of some weight in favor of the agapastic theory of evolution—so far as it may be presumed to bespeak the normal judgment of the Sensible Heart. Certainly, if it were possible to believe in agapasm without believing it warmly, that fact would be an argument against the truth of the doctrine. At any rate, since the warmth of feeling exists, it should on every account be candidly confessed; especially since it creates a liability to onesidedness on my part against which it behooves my readers and me to be severally on our guard.

SECOND THOUGHTS. IRENICA

Let us try to define the logical affinities of the different theories of evolution. Natural selection, as conceived by Darwin, is a mode of evolution in which the only positive agent of change in the whole passage from moner to man is fortuitous variation. To secure advance in a definite direction chance has to be seconded by some action that shall hinder the propagation of some varieties or stimulate that of others. In natural selection, strictly so called, it is the crowding out of the weak. In sexual selection, it is the attraction of beauty, mainly.

The *Origin of Species* was published toward the end of the year 1859. The preceding years since 1846 had been one of the most productive seasons, or if extended so as to cover the great book we are considering, *the* most productive period of equal length in the entire history of science from its beginnings until now. The idea that chance begets order, which is one of the corner-stones of modern physics (although Dr. Carus considers it "the weakest point in Mr. Peirce's system"), was at that time put into its clearest light. Quetelet had opened the discussion by his *Letters on the Application of*

Probabilities to the Moral and Political Sciences, a work which deeply impressed the best minds of that day, and to which Sir John Herschel had drawn general attention in Great Britain. In 1857, the first volume of Buckle's *History of Civilisation* had created a tremendous sensation, owing to the use he made of this same idea. Meantime, the "statistical method" had, under that very name, been applied with brilliant success to molecular physics. Dr. John Herapath, an English chemist, had in 1847 outlined the kinetical theory of gases in his *Mathematical Physics;* and the interest the theory excited had been refreshed in 1856 by notable memoirs by Clausius and Krönig. In the very summer preceding Darwin's publication, Maxwell had read before the British Association the first and most important of his researches on this subject. The consequence was that the idea that fortuitous events may result in a physical law, and further that this is the way in which those laws which appear to conflict with the principle of the conservation of energy are to be explained, had taken a strong hold upon the minds of all who were abreast of the leaders of thought. By such minds, it was inevitable that the *Origin of Species,* whose teaching was simply the application of the same principle to the explanation of another "non-conservative" action, that of organic development, should be hailed and welcomed. The sublime discovery of the conservation of energy by Helmholtz in 1847, and that of the mechanical theory of heat by Clausius and by Rankine, independently, in 1850, had decidedly overawed all those who might have been inclined to sneer at physical science. Thereafter a belated poet still harping upon "science peddling with the names of things" would fail of his effect. Mechanism was now known to be all, or very nearly so. All this time, utilitarianism—that improved substitute for the Gospel—was in its fullest feather; and was a natural ally of an individualistic theory. Dean Mansell's injudicious advocacy had led to mutiny among the bondsmen of Sir William Hamilton, and the nominalism of Mill had profited accordingly; and although the real science that Darwin was leading men to was sure some day to give a death-

blow to the sham-science of Mill, yet there were several elements of the Darwinian theory which were sure to charm the
followers of Mill. Another thing: anæsthetics had been in use
for thirteen years. Already, people's acquaintance with suffering had dropped off very much; and as a consequence, that
unlovely hardness by which our times are so contrasted with
those that immediately preceded them, had already set in, and
inclined people to relish a ruthless theory. The reader would
quite mistake the drift of what I am saying if he were to understand me as wishing to suggest that any of those things
(except perhaps Malthus) influenced Darwin himself. What I
mean is that his hypothesis, while without dispute one of the
most ingenious and pretty ever devised, and while argued
with a wealth of knowledge, a strength of logic, a charm of
rhetoric, and above all with a certain magnetic genuineness
that was almost irresistible, did not appear, at first, at all near
to being proved; and to a sober mind its case looks less hopeful now than it did twenty years ago; but the extraordinarily
favorable reception it met with was plainly owing, in large
measure, to its ideas being those toward which the age was
favorably disposed, especially, because of the encouragement
it gave to the greed-philosophy.

Diametrically opposed to evolution by chance, are those
theories which attribute all progress to an inward necessary
principle, or other form of necessity. Many naturalists have
thought that if an egg is destined to go through a certain
series of embryological transformations, from which it is perfectly certain not to deviate, and if in geological time almost
exactly the same forms appear successively, one replacing another in the same order, the strong presumption is that this latter succession was as predeterminate and certain to take place
as the former. So, Nägeli, for instance, conceives that it somehow follows from the first law of motion and the peculiar, but
unknown, molecular constitution of protoplasm, that forms
must complicate themselves more and more. Kölliker makes
one form generate another after a certain maturation has been
accomplished. Weismann, too, though he calls himself a Dar-

winian, holds that nothing is due to chance, but that all forms are simple mechanical resultants of the heredity from two parents.[3] It is very noticeable that all these different sectaries seek to import into their science a mechanical necessity to which the facts that come under their observation do not point. Those geologists who think that the variation of species is due to cataclysmic alterations of climate or of the chemical constitution of the air and water are also making mechanical necessity chief factor of evolution.

Evolution by sporting and evolution by mechanical necessity are conceptions warring against one another. A third method, which supersedes their strife, lies enwrapped in the theory of Lamarck. According to his view, all that distinguishes the highest organic forms from the most rudimentary has been brought about by little hypertrophies or atrophies which have affected individuals early in their lives, and have been transmitted to their offspring. Such a transmission of acquired characters is of the general nature of habit-taking, and this is the representative and derivative within the physiological domain of the law of mind. Its action is essentially dissimilar to that of a physical force; and that is the secret of the repugnance of such necessitarians as Weismann to admitting its existence. The Lamarckians further suppose that although some of the modifications of form so transmitted were originally due to mechanical causes, yet the chief factors of their first production were the straining of endeavor and the overgrowth superinduced by exercise, together with the opposite actions. Now, endeavor, since it is directed toward an end, is essentially psychical, even though it be sometimes unconscious; and the growth due to exercise, as I argued in my last paper, follows a law of a character quite contrary to that of mechanics.

Lamarckian evolution is thus evolution by the force of habit. —That sentence slipped off my pen while one of those neighbors whose function in the social cosmos seems to be that of an Interrupter, was asking me a question. Of course, it is non-

---

[3] I am happy to find that Dr. Carus, too, ranks Weismann among the opponents of Darwin, notwithstanding his flying that flag.

sense. Habit is mere inertia, a resting on one's oars, not a propulsion. Now it is energetic projaculation (lucky there is such a word, or this untried hand might have been put to inventing one) by which in the typical instances of Lamarckian evolution the new elements of form are first created. Habit, however, forces them to take practical shapes, compatible with the structures they affect, and in the form of heredity and otherwise, gradually replaces the spontaneous energy that sustains them. Thus, habit plays a double part; it serves to establish the new features, and also to bring them into harmony with the general morphology and function of the animals and plants to which they belong. But if the reader will now kindly give himself the trouble of turning back a page or two, he will see that this account of Lamarckian evolution coincides with the general description of the action of love, to which, I suppose, he yielded his assent.

Remembering that all matter is really mind, remembering, too, the continuity of mind, let us ask what aspect Lamarckian evolution takes on within the domain of consciousness. Direct endeavor can achieve almost nothing. It is as easy by taking thought to add a cubit to one's stature, as it is to produce an idea acceptable to any of the Muses by merely straining for it, before it is ready to come. We haunt in vain the sacred well and throne of Mnemosyne; the deeper workings of the spirit take place in their own slow way, without our connivance. Let but their bugle sound, and we may then make our effort, sure of an oblation for the altar of whatsoever divinity its savor gratifies. Besides this inward process, there is the operation of the environment, which goes to break up habits destined to be broken up and so to render the mind lively. Everybody knows that the long continuance of a routine of habit makes us lethargic, while a succession of surprises wonderfully brightens the ideas. Where there is a motion, where history is a-making, there is the focus of mental activity, and it has been said that the arts and sciences reside within the temple of Janus, waking when this is open, but slumbering when it is closed. Few psychologists have perceived how fundamental a fact this is. A portion of mind abundantly commissured to other portions works almost mechanically. It sinks to a condition of a railway junction. But a portion of mind almost isolated, a spiritual peninsula, or *cul-de-sac*, is like a railway terminus. Now mental commissures are habits. Where they abound, originality is not needed and is not found; but where they are in defect, spontaneity is set free. Thus, the first step in the Lamarckian evolution of mind is the putting of sundry thoughts into situations in which they are free to play. As to growth by exercise, I have already shown, in discussing *Man's Glassy Essence,* in last October's *Monist,* what its *modus operandi* must be conceived to be, at least, until a second equally definite hypothesis shall have been offered. Namely, it consists of the flying asunder of molecules, and the reparation of the parts by new matter. It is, thus, a sort of reproduction. It takes place only during exercise, because the activity of protoplasm consists in the molecular disturbance which is its necessary condition. Growth by exercise takes place also in the mind. Indeed, that is what it is to *learn.* But the most perfect illustration is the development of a philosophical idea by being put into practice. The conception which appeared, at first, as unitary, splits up into special cases; and into each of these new thought must enter to make a practicable idea. This new thought, however, follows pretty closely the model of the parent conception; and thus a homogeneous development takes place. The parallel between this and the course of molecular occurrences is apparent. Patient attention will be able to trace all these elements in the transaction called learning.

Three modes of evolution have thus been brought before us; evolution by fortuitous variation, evolution by mechanical necessity, and evolution by creative love. We may term them *tychastic* evolution, or *tychasm, anancastic* evolution, or *anancasm,* and *agapastic* evolution, or *agapasm.* The doctrines which represent these as severally of principal importance, we may term *tychasticism, anancasticism,* and *agapasticism.* On the other hand the mere propositions that absolute chance, mechanical necessity, and the law of love, are severally opera-

tive in the cosmos, may receive the names of *tychism,*
anancism, and *agapism.*

All three modes of evolution are composed of the same general elements. Agapasm exhibits them the most clearly. The
good result is here brought to pass, first, by the bestowal of
spontaneous energy by the parent upon the offspring, and,
second, by the disposition of the latter to catch the general
idea of those about it and thus to subserve the general purpose. In order to express the relation that tychasm and
anancasm bear to agapasm, let me borrow a word from geometry. An ellipse crossed by a straight line is a sort of cubic
curve, for a cubic is a curve which is cut thrice by a straight
line; now a straight line might cut the ellipse twice and its
associated straight line a third time. Still the ellipse with the
straight line across it would not have the characteristics of a
cubic. It would have, for instance, no contrary flexure, which
no true cubic wants; and it would have two nodes, which no
true cubic has. The geometers say that it is a *degenerate* cubic.
Just so, tychasm and anancasm are degenerate forms of
agapasm.

Men who seek to reconcile the Darwinian idea with Christianity will remark that tychastic evolution, like the agapastic,
depends upon a reproductive creation, the forms preserved
being those that use the spontaneity conferred upon them in
such wise as to be drawn into harmony with their original,
quite after the Christian scheme. Very good! This only shows
that just as love cannot have a contrary, but must embrace
what is most opposed to it, as a degenerate case of it, so
tychasm is a kind of agapasm. Only, in the tychastic evolution progress is solely owing to the distribution of the napkin-
hidden talent of the rejected servant among those not rejected,
just as ruined gamesters leave their money on the table to
make those not yet ruined so much the richer. It makes the
felicity of the lambs just the damnation of the goats, trans-
posed to the other side of the equation. In genuine agapasm,
on the other hand, advance takes place by virtue of a positive
sympathy among the created springing from continuity of

mind. This is the idea which tychasticism knows not how to manage.

The anancasticist might here interpose, claiming that the mode of evolution for which he contends agrees with agapasm at the point at which tychasm departs from it. For it makes development go through certain phases, having its inevitable ebbs and flows, yet tending on the whole to a foreordained perfection. Bare existence by this its destiny betrays an intrinsic affinity for the good. Herein, it must be admitted, anancasm shows itself to be in a broad acception a species of agapasm. Some forms of it might easily be mistaken for the genuine agapasm. The Hegelian philosophy is such an anancasticism. With its revelatory religion, with its synechism (however imperfectly set forth), with its "reflection," the whole idea of the theory is superb, almost sublime. Yet, after all, living freedom is practically omitted from its method. The whole movement is that of a vast engine, impelled by a *vis a tergo*, with a blind and mysterious fate of arriving at a lofty goal. I mean that such an engine it *would* be, if it really worked; but in point of fact, it is a Keely motor. Grant that it really acts as it professes to act, and there is nothing to do but accept the philosophy. But never was there seen such an example of a long chain of reasoning—shall I say with a flaw in every link?—no, with every link a handful of sand, squeezed into shape in a dream. Or say, it is a pasteboard model of a philosophy that in reality does not exist. If we use the one precious thing it contains, the idea of it, introducing the tychism which the arbitrariness of its every step suggests, and make that the support of a vital freedom which is the breath of the spirit of love, we may be able to produce that genuine agapasticism, at which Hegel was aiming.

A THIRD ASPECT. DISCRIMINATION

In the very nature of things, the line of demarcation between the three modes of evolution is not perfectly sharp. That does not prevent its being quite real; perhaps it is rather a mark of its reality. There is in the nature of things no sharp line of demarcation between the three fundamental colors, red, green, and violet. But for all that they are really different. The main question is whether three radically different evolutionary elements have been operative; and the second question is what are the most striking characteristics of whatever elements have been operative.

I propose to devote a few pages to a very slight examination of these questions in their relation to the historical development of human thought. I first formulate for the reader's convenience the briefest possible definitions of the three conceivable modes of development of thought, distinguishing also two varieties of anancasm and three of agapasm. The tychastic development of thought, then, will consist in slight departures from habitual ideas in different directions indifferently, quite purposeless and quite unconstrained whether by outward circumstances or by force of logic, these new departures being followed by unforeseen results which tend to fix some of them as habits more than others. The anancastic development of thought will consist of new ideas adopted without foreseeing whither they tend, but having a character determined by causes either external to the mind, such as changed circumstances of life, or internal to the mind as logical developments of ideas already accepted, such as generalizations. The agapastic development of thought is the adoption of certain mental tendencies, not altogether heedlessly, as in tychasm, nor quite blindly by the mere force of circumstances or of logic, as in anancasm, but by an immediate attraction for the idea itself, whose nature is divined before the mind possesses it, by the power of sympathy, that is, by virtue of the continuity of mind; and this mental tendency may be of three varieties, as follows: First, it may affect a whole people or community in its collective personality, and be thence communicated to such individuals as are in powerfully sympathetic connection with the collective people, although they may be intellectually incapable of attaining the idea by their private understandings or even perhaps of consciously apprehending it. Second, it may affect a private person directly, yet so that he is only enabled to apprehend the idea, or to appreciate its attractiveness, by virtue of his sympathy with his neighbors, under the influence of a striking experience or development of thought. The conversion of St. Paul may be taken as an example of what is meant. Third, it may affect an individual, independently of his human affections, by virtue of an attraction it exercises upon his mind, even before he has comprehended it. This is the phenomenon which has been well called the *divination* of genius; for it is due to the continuity between the man's mind and the Most High.

Let us next consider by means of what tests we can discriminate between these different categories of evolution. No absolute criterion is possible in the nature of things, since in the nature of things there is no sharp line of demarcation between the different classes. Nevertheless, quantitative symptoms may be found by which a sagacious and sympathetic judge of human nature may be able to estimate the approximate proportions in which the different kinds of influence are commingled.

So far as the historical evolution of human thought has been tychastic, it should have proceeded by insensible or minute steps; for such is the nature of chances when so multiplied as to show phenomena of regularity. For example, assume that of the native-born white adult males of the United States in 1880, one-fourth part were below 5 feet 4 inches in stature and one-fourth part above 5 feet 8 inches. Then by the principles of probability, among the whole population, we should expect

216 under 4 feet 6 inches,	216 above 6 feet 6 inches
48 " 4 " 5 "	48 " 6 " 7 "
9 " 4 " 4 "	9 " 6 " 8 "
less than 2 " 4 " 3 "	less than 2 " 6 " 9 "

I set down these figures to show how insignificantly few are the cases in which anything very far out of the common run presents itself by chance. Though the stature of only every second man is included within the four inches between 5 feet 4 inches and 5 feet 8 inches, yet if this interval be extended by thrice four inches above and below, it will embrace all our 8 millions odd of native-born adult white males (of 1880), except only 9 taller and 9 shorter.

The test of minute variation, if *not* satisfied, absolutely negatives tychasm. If it *is* satisfied, we shall find that it negatives anancasm but not agapasm. We want a positive test, satisfied by tychasm, only. Now wherever we find men's thought taking by imperceptible degrees a turn contrary to the purposes which animate them, in spite of their highest impulses, there, we may safely conclude, there has been a tychastic action.

Students of the history of mind there be of an erudition to fill an imperfect scholar like me with envy edulcorated by joyous admiration, who maintain that ideas when just started are and can be little more than freaks, since they cannot yet have been critically examined, and further that everywhere and at all times progress has been so gradual that it is difficult to make out distinctly what original step any given man has taken. It would follow that tychasm has been the sole method of intellectual development. I have to confess I cannot read history so; I cannot help thinking that while tychasm has sometimes been operative, at others great steps covering nearly the same ground and made by different men independently, have been mistaken for a succession of small steps, and further that students have been reluctant to admit a real entitative "spirit" of an age or of a people, under the mistaken and un-scrutinized impression that they should thus be opening the door to wild and unnatural hypotheses. I find, on the contrary, that, however it may be with the education of individual minds, the historical development of thought has seldom been of a tychastic nature, and exclusively in backward and barbarizing movements. I desire to speak with the extreme modesty which befits a student of logic who is required to survey so very wide a field of human thought that he can cover it only by a reconnaissance, to which only the greatest skill and most adroit methods can impart any value at all; but, after all, I can only express my own opinions and not those of anybody else; and in my humble judgment, the largest example of tychasm is afforded by the history of Christianity, from about its establishment by Constantine, to, say, the time of the Irish monasteries, an era or eon of about 500 years. Undoubtedly the external circumstance which more than all others at first inclined men to accept Christianity in its loveliness and tenderness, was the fearful extent to which society was broken up into units by the unmitigated greed and hardheartedness into which the Romans had seduced the world. And yet it was that very same fact, more than any other external circumstance, that fostered that bitterness against the wicked world of which the primitive gospel of Mark contains not a single trace. At least, I do not detect it in the remark about the blasphemy against the Holy Ghost, where nothing is said about vengeance, nor even in that speech where the closing lines of Isaiah are quoted, about the worm and the fire that feed upon the "carcasses of the men that have transgressed against me." But little by little the bitterness increases until in the last book of the New Testament, its poor distracted author represents that all the time Christ was talking about having come to save the world, the secret design was to catch the entire human race, with the exception of a paltry 144,000, and souse them all in a brimstone lake, and as the smoke of their torment went up forever and ever, to turn and remark, "There is no curse any more." Would it be an insensible smirk or a fiendish grin that should accompany such an utterance? I wish I could believe St. John did not write it; but it is his gospel which tells about the "resurrection unto condemnation" —that is of men's being resuscitated just for the sake of torturing them—and, at any rate, the Revelation is a very ancient composition. One can understand that the early Christians were like men trying with all their might to climb a steep declivity of smooth wet clay; the deepest and truest element of their life, animating both heart and head, was universal love; but they were continually, and against their wills, slipping into a party spirit, every slip serving as a precedent, in a fashion but too familiar to every man. This party feeling insensibly grew until by about A.D. 330 the luster of the pristine integrity that in St. Mark reflects the white spirit of light was so far tarnished that Eusebius (the Jared Sparks of that day), in the preface to his History, could announce his intention of exaggerating everything that tended to the glory of the church and of suppressing whatever might disgrace it. His Latin contemporary Lactantius is worse, still; and so the darkling went on increasing until before the end of the century the great library of Alexandria was destroyed by Theophilus,[4] until Gregory the Great, two centuries later, burnt the great library of Rome, proclaiming that "Ignorance is the mother of devotion" (which is true, just as oppression and injustice is the mother of spirituality), until a sober description of the state of the church would be a thing our not too nice newspapers would treat as "unfit for publication." All this movement is shown by the application of the test given above to have been tychastic. Another very much like it on a small scale, only a hundred times swifter, for the study of which there are documents by the library-full, is to be found in the history of the French Revolution.

Anancastic evolution advances by successive strides with pauses between. The reason is that in this process a habit of thought having been overthrown is supplanted by the next strongest. Now this next strongest is sure to be widely disparate from the first, and as often as not is its direct contrary. It reminds one of our old rule of making the second candidate vice-president. This character, therefore, clearly distinguishes anancasm from tychasm. The character which distinguishes it from agapasm is its purposelessness. But external and internal anancasm have to be examined separately. Development under the pressure of external circumstances, or cataclysmine evolution, is in most cases unmistakable enough. It has numberless degrees of intensity, from the brute force, the plain war, which has more than once turned the current of the world's thought, down to the hard fact of evidence, or what has been taken for it, which has been known to convince men by hordes. The only hesitation that can subsist in the presence of such a history is a quantitative one. Never are

---

[4] See *Draper's History of Intellectual Development,* Chap. x.

external influences the only ones which affect the mind, and therefore it must be a matter of judgment for which it would scarcely be worth while to attempt to set rules, whether a given movement is to be regarded as principally governed from without or not. In the rise of medieval thought, I mean scholasticism and the synchronistic art developments, undoubtedly the crusades and the discovery of the writings of Aristotle were powerful influences. The development of scholasticism from Roscellin to Albertus Magnus closely follows the successive steps in the knowledge of Aristotle. Prantl thinks that that is the whole story, and few men have thumbed more books than Carl Prantl. He has done good solid work, notwithstanding his slap-dash judgments. But we shall never make so much as a good beginning of comprehending scholasticism until the whole has been systematically explored and digested by a company of students regularly organized and held under rule for that purpose. But as for the period we are now specially considering, that which synchronised the Romanesque architecture, the literature is easily mastered. It does not quite justify Prantl's dicta as to the slavish dependence of these authors upon their authorities. Moreover, they kept a definite purpose steadily before their minds, throughout all their studies. I am, therefore, unable to offer this period of scholasticism as an example of pure external anancasm, which seems to be the fluorine of the intellectual elements. Perhaps the recent Japanese reception of western ideas is the purest instance of it in history. Yet in combination with other elements, nothing is commoner. If the development of ideas under the influence of the study of external facts be considered as external anancasm—it is on the border between the external and the internal forms—it is, of course, the principal thing in modern learning. But Whewell, whose masterly comprehension of the history of science critics have been too ignorant properly to appreciate, clearly shows that it is far from being the overwhelmingly preponderant influence, even there.

Internal anancasm, or logical groping, which advances upon a predestined line without being able to foresee whither it is to be carried nor to steer its course, this is the rule of development of philosophy. Hegel first made the world understand this; and he seeks to make logic not merely the subjective guide and monitor of thought, which was all it had been ambitioning before, but to be the very mainspring of thinking, and not merely of individual thinking but of discussion, of the history of the development of thought, of all history, of all development. This involves a positive, clearly demonstrable error. Let the logic in question be of whatever kind it may, a logic of necessary inference or a logic of probable inference (the theory might perhaps be shaped to fit either), in any case it supposes that logic is sufficient of itself to determine what conclusion follows from given premises; for unless it will do so much, it will not suffice to explain why an individual train of reasoning should take just the course it does take, to say nothing of other kinds of development. It thus supposes that from given premises, only one conclusion can logically be drawn, and that there is no scope at all for free choice. That from given premises only one conclusion can logically be drawn, is one of the false notions which have come from logicians' confining their attention to that Nantucket of thought, the logic of non-relative terms. In the logic of relatives, it does not hold good.

One remark occurs to me. If the evolution of history is in considerable part of the nature of internal anancasm, it resembles the development of individual men; and just as 33 years is a rough but natural unit of time for individuals, being the average age at which man has issue, so there should be an approximate period at the end of which one great historical movement ought to be likely to be supplanted by another. Let us see if we can make out anything of the kind. Take the governmental development of Rome as being sufficiently long and set down the principal dates.

B.C.   753, Foundation of Rome.
B.C.   510, Expulsion of the Tarquins.
B.C.   27, Octavius assumes title Augustus.
A.D.   476, End of Western Empire.

A.D. 962, Holy Roman Empire.
A.D. 1453, Fall of Constantinople.

The last event was one of the most significant in history, especially for Italy. The intervals are 243, 483, 502, 486, 491 years. All are rather curiously near equal, except the first which is half the others. Successive reigns of kings would not commonly be so near equal. Let us set down a few dates in the history of thought.

B.C. 585, Eclipse of Thales. Beginning of Greek philosophy.
A.D. 30, The crucifixion.
A.D. 529, Closing of Athenian schools. End of Greek philosophy.
A.D. 1125, (Approximate) Rise of the Universities of Bologna and Paris.
A.D. 1543, Publication of the "De Revolutionibus" of Copernicus. Beginning of Modern Science.

The intervals are 615, 499, 596, 418, years. In the history of metaphysics, we may take the following:

B.C. 322, Death of Aristotle.
A.D. 1274, Death of Aquinas.
A.D. 1804, Death of Kant.

The intervals are 1595 and 530 years. The former is about thrice the latter.

From these figures, no conclusion can fairly be drawn. At the same time, they suggest that perhaps there may be a rough natural era of about 500 years. Should there be any independent evidence of this, the intervals noticed may gain some significance.

The agapastic development of thought should, if it exists, be distinguished by its purposive character, this purpose being the development of an idea. We should have a direct agapic or sympathetic comprehension and recognition of it, by virtue of the continuity of thought. I here take it for granted that such continuity of thought has been sufficiently proved by the arguments used in my paper on "The Law of Mind" in *The Monist* of last July. Even if those arguments are not quite convincing in themselves, yet if they are re-enforced by an apparent agapasm in the history of thought, the two propositions will lend one another mutual aid. The reader will, I trust, be too well grounded in logic to mistake such mutual support for a vicious circle in reasoning. If it could be shown directly that there is such an entity as the "spirit of an age" or of a people, and that mere individual intelligence will not account for all the phenomena, this would be proof enough at once of agapasticism and of synechism. I must acknowledge that I am unable to produce a cogent demonstration of this; but I am, I believe, able to adduce such arguments as will serve to confirm those which have been drawn from other facts. I believe that all the greatest achievements of mind have been beyond the powers of unaided individuals; and I find, apart from the support this opinion receives from synechistic considerations, and from the purposive character of many great movements, direct reason for so thinking in the sublimity of the ideas and in their occurring simultaneously and independently to a number of individuals of no extraordinary general powers. The pointed Gothic architecture in several of its developments appears to me to be of such a character. All attempts to imitate it by modern architects of the greatest learning and genius appear flat and tame, and are felt by their authors to be so. Yet at the time the style was living, there was quite an abundance of men capable of producing works of this kind of gigantic sublimity and power. In more than one case, extant documents show that the cathedral chapters, in the selection of architects, treated high artistic genius as a secondary consideration, as if there were no lack of persons able to supply that; and the results justify their confidence. Were individuals in general, then, in those ages possessed of such lofty natures and high intellect? Such an opinion would break down under the first examination.

How many times have men now in middle life seen great discoveries made independently and almost simultaneously! The first instance I remember was the prediction of a planet exterior to Uranus by Leverrier and Adams. One hardly knows to whom the principle of the conservation of energy ought to be attributed, although it may reasonably be considered as the greatest discovery science has ever made. The mechanical theory of heat was set forth by Rankine and by Clausius during the same month of February, 1850; and there are eminent men who attribute this great step to Thomson.[5] The kinetical theory of gases, after being started by John Bernoulli and long buried in oblivion, was reinvented and applied to the explanation not merely of the laws of Boyle, Charles, and Avogadro, but also of diffusion and viscosity, by at least three modern physicists separately. It is well known that the doctrine of natural selection was presented by Wallace and by Darwin at the same meeting of the British Association; and Darwin in his "Historical Sketch" prefixed to the later editions of his book shows that both were anticipated by obscure forerunners. The method of spectrum analysis was claimed for Swan as well as for Kirchhoff, and there were others who perhaps had still better claims. The authorship of the Periodical Law of the Chemical Elements is disputed between a Russian, a German, and an Englishman; although there is no room for doubt that the principal merit belongs to the first. These are nearly all the greatest discoveries of our times. It is the same with the inventions. It may not be surprising that the telegraph should have been independently made by several inventors, because it was an easy corollary from scientific facts well made out before. But it was not so with the telephone and other inventions. Ether, the first anæsthetic, was introduced independently by three different New England physicians. Now ether had been a common article for a century. It had been in one of the pharmacopœias three centuries before. It is quite incredible that its anæsthetic property should not have been known; it was known. It had

---

[5] Thomson, himself, in his article *Heat* in the *Encyclopaedia Britannica*, never once mentions the name of Clausius.

probably passed from mouth to ear as a secret from the days of Basil Valentine; but for long it had been a secret of the Punchinello kind. In New England, for many years, boys had used it for amusement. Why then had it not been put to its serious use? No reason can be given, except that the motive to do so was not strong enough. The motives to doing so could only have been desire for gain and philanthropy. About 1846, the date of the introduction, philanthropy was undoubtedly in an unusually active condition. That sensibility, or sentimentalism, which had been introduced in the previous century, had undergone a ripening process, in consequence of which, though now less intense than it had previously been, it was more likely to influence unreflecting people than it had ever been. All three of the ether-claimants had probably been influenced by the desire for gain; but nevertheless they were certainly not insensible to the agapic influences.

I doubt if any of the great discoveries ought, properly, to be considered as altogether individual achievements; and I think many will share this doubt. Yet, if not, what an argument for the continuity of mind, and for agapasticism is here! I do not wish to be very strenuous. If thinkers will only be persuaded to lay aside their prejudices and apply themselves to studying the evidences of this doctrine, I shall be fully content to await the final decision.

•   •   •

While Peirce was still alive, William James and Josiah Royce paid him generous tribute. In 1918, C. I. Lewis sketched his contributions to symbolic logic; in 1923, Morris R. Cohen brought out a splendid collection of Peirce's philosophical essays under the title of *Chance, Love and Logic;* and between 1931 and 1935, Charles Hartshorne and Paul Weiss edited six monumental volumes of *Collected Papers,* published by the Harvard University Press—graceful amends from a university that more than once refused Peirce a job.[1] Now there is a Peirce Society and many younger men

---

[1] As we go to press, two final volumes have appeared, edited by Arthur W. Burks.

are pursuing hares—logical, epistemological and metaphysical—long since started by the lonely one.

Perhaps the most touching and characteristic fragment in the *Collected Papers* is one jotted down around 1897: "For years in the course of the ripening process, I used for myself to collect my ideas under the designation *fallibilism;* and indeed the first step toward *finding out* is to acknowledge you do not satisfactorily know already; so that no blight can so surely arrest all intellectual growth as intellectual cock-sureness; and ninety-nine of every hundred good heads are reduced to impotence by that malady—of whose inroads they are most strangely unaware!

"Indeed, out of a contrite fallibilism, combined with a high faith in the reality of knowledge, and an intense desire to find things out, all my philosophy has always seemed to me to grow. . . ."

WILLIAM JAMES
[1842–1910]

In 1793 an eighteen-year-old Irishman, one William James from County Cavan, settled in Albany, New York. He worked hard, prospered in business, invested wisely, supported the building of the Erie Canal, became a leading citizen of his adopted home, and died in 1832, leaving an estate valued at three million dollars.

His second son, Henry James, who injured a leg when putting out a stable fire at the age of thirteen and suffered for two years before seeing it amputated without benefit of anesthetic, allowed neither physical affliction nor independent means to interfere with his tireless religious Odyssey. After passing through a severe crisis, he began to develop a "spiritual universalism," based on Swedenborg, which some have considered profound and original, but it was far too obscure to win him more than a handful of readers in spite of his numerous books. He was capable of clear, vigorous writing, but he wasted himself, according to Peirce, in "scolding at his readers and at people generally, until the physics of creation was well-nigh forgot."

Whatever the merits of his work, Henry James was a devoted husband and father, the center of a family which included William James, Henry James, Jr., the novelist, the exceptionally sensitive Alice, who was to become a chronic invalid, and two other sons. He spent most of his time at home in vigorous conversation, study, and writing—or in moving the family back and forth across the Atlantic. In consequence of this dynamic domesticity, the future philosopher William had a rich but unsystematic education and had more trouble than his brother Henry in fixing on a career. At eighteen he was seriously studying painting in Newport, but a year later he entered the Lawrence Scientific School at Harvard and two years later entered the Harvard Medical School. He went on a scientific expedition to the Amazon with the great zoologist

Agassiz, studied medicine further in Germany, and returned to Harvard for his M.D. in 1868.

There followed a nervous breakdown and a period of despondency (much like his father's at about the same age) which may have been alleviated by a winter in Germany. Whatever the underlying causes, his release was marked by a passage in his notebook dated April 30, 1870: "I think that yesterday was a crisis in my life. I finished the first part of Renouvier's second 'Essais' and see no reason why his definition of Free Will—'the sustaining of a thought *because I choose to* when I might have other thoughts'— need be the definition of an illusion. My first act of free will shall be to believe in free will."[1] That faith, that assumption, he never abandoned. In 1909 he wrote to James Ward: "I think the center of my whole Anschauung, since years ago I read Renouvier, has been the belief that something is doing in the universe, and that novelty is real."[2] Finally, James requested that his unfinished manuscript, published after his death as *Some Problems of Philosophy*, be dedicated to "the great Renouvier's memory." "He was one of the greatest of philosophic characters, and but for the decisive impression made on me in the seventies by his masterly advocacy of pluralism, I might never have got free from the monistic superstition under which I had grown up."

At the invitation of Harvard's President Eliot, James began in 1873, at the age of thirty-one, to teach anatomy and physiology, moved partly into psychology and finally into philosophy. But a catalogue listing of his various courses is not always helpful, for, as G. S. Brett remarked: "James himself did not change, and he was so far indifferent to the formal distinctions as to be scarcely aware whether he was treating psychology philosophically or philosophy psychologically."[3]

In the summer of 1878, James entered upon a long and happy marriage and also signed an agreement with Henry Holt and Company to write a volume on psychology for their new American Science Series. He expected to finish the book "inside of two years," but what started out to be a more or less conventional survey turned into a monumental, epoch-making treatise, *The*

---

[1] *Letters*, I, 147.

[2] Ralph Barton Perry, *The Thought and Character of William James*, II, 656.

[3] R. S. Peters' edition of Brett's *History of Psychology*, 654.

Principles of Psychology, which required twelve years of sustained effort.

Those large events of the summer of 1878 obscure the fact that in the previous January, James's first original philosophical article, "Remarks on Spencer's Definition of Mind as Correspondence," appeared in the *Journal of Speculative Philosophy,* while Peirce's now famous paper "How to Make Our Ideas" appeared in the *Popular Scientific Monthly.* James's frontal attack on the reigning Spencer's passive, mechanical conception of mind ends with these characteristic words:

"I, for my part, cannot escape the consideration, forced upon me at every turn, that the knower is not simply a mirror floating with no foothold anywhere, and passively reflecting an order that he comes upon and finds simply existing. The knower is an actor, and co-efficient of the truth on one side, whilst on the other he registers the truth which he helps to create. Mental interests, hypotheses, postulates, so far as they are bases for human action—action which to a great extent transforms the world—help to make the truth which they declare. In other words, there belongs to mind from its birth upward, a spontaneity, a vote. It is in the game, and not a mere looker-on; and its judgments of the *should-be,* its ideals, cannot be peeled off from the body of the *cogitandum* as if they were excrescences, or meant, at most, survival. We know so little about the ultimate nature of things, or of ourselves, that it would be sheer folly dogmatically to say that an ideal rational order may not be real. The only objective criterion of reality is coerciveness, in the long run, over thought. Objective facts, Spencer's outer relations, are real only because they coerce sensation. Any interest which should be coercive on the same massive scale would be *eodem jure* real. By its very essence, the reality of a thought is proportionate to the way it grasps us. Its intensity, its seriousness—its interest, in a word—taking these qualities, not at any given instant, but as shown by the total upshot of experience. If judgments of the *should-be* are fated to grasp us in this way, they are what 'correspond.' The ancients placed the conception of Fate at the bottom of things—deeper than the gods themselves. 'The fate of thought,' utterly barren and indeterminate as such a formula is, is the only unimpeachable regulative Law of Mind."[4]

---

[4] *Collected Essays and Reviews,* 67-68.

This thesis, as against Spencer's, "that the central fact of mind is interest or preference . . . is the germinal idea of James's psychology, epistemology and philosophy of religion," the late Ralph Barton Perry pointed out in 1920 in his invaluable *Annotated Bibliography of the Writings of William James*. But other "germinal ideas" appeared between 1879 and 1884 in such characteristic essays as "The Sentiment of Rationality," "Great Men, Great Thoughts and Their Environment," "Reflex Action and Theism," "On Some Hegelisms," "Rationality, Activity and Faith," and "The Dilemma of Determinism," which were to form the bulk of his first explicitly philosophical volume, *The Will to Believe and Other Essays in Popular Philosophy* (1897). Here, for example, is another attack on that "immaculate perception" which Nietzsche, unknown to James, was even then writing about in *Thus Spake Zarathustra:*

"Pretend what we may, the whole man within us is at work when we form our philosophical opinions. Intellect, will, taste, and passion co-operate just as they do in practical affairs: and lucky it is if the passion be not something as petty as a love of personal conquest over the philosopher across the way. The absurd abstraction of an intellect verbally formulating all its evidence and carefully estimating the probability thereof by a vulgar fraction by the size of whose denominator and numerator alone it is swayed, is ideally as inept as it is actually impossible. It is almost incredible that men who are themselves working philosophers should pretend that any philosophy can be, or ever has been, constructed without the help of personal preference, belief or divination."

Already in the early eighties James was insisting that the deepest of all philosophic differences was that between monism and pluralism, and he rejected the specious consolation and aesthetic charm of the former for the real moral challenge of the latter. He admitted that his "pluralistic, restless universe, in which no single point of view can ever take in the whole scene" would have no appeal "to a mind possessed of the love of unity at any cost." "A friend with such a mind once told me that the thought of my universe made him sick, like the sight of the horrible motion of a mass of maggots in their carrion bed."[5]

---

[5] "The Dilemma of Determinism," *The Will to Believe and Other Essays in Popular Philosophy*, 177.

After the appearance of *The Principles of Psychology* (1890) and *Psychology—Briefer Course* (1892), James gave many lectures and addresses throughout the country, and to one of these he called special attention when it was first published in 1899 in *Talks to Teachers on Psychology and to Students on Some of Life's Ideals*. "I wish I were able," he said in the Preface, "to make 'On a Certain Blindness in Human Beings' more impressive. It is more than the mere piece of sentimentalism it may seem to some readers. It connects itself with a definite view of the world and of our relations to the same. Those who have done me the honor of reading my volume of philosophic essays will recognize that I mean the pluralistic or individualistic philosophy. According to that philosophy the truth is too great for any one actual mind, even though that mind be dubbed the Absolute, to know the whole of it. The facts and worths of life need many cognizers to take them in. There is no point of view absolutely public and universal. . . . The practical consequence of such a philosophy is the well-known democratic respect for the sacredness of individuality."

On sending a copy of this book to a friend, James wrote: "I send it to you merely that you might read the essay 'On a Certain Blindness,' which is really the perception on which my whole individualistic philosophy is based."

•   •   •

ON A CERTAIN BLINDNESS IN HUMAN BEINGS

Our judgments concerning the worth of things, big or little, depend on the *feelings* the things arouse in us. Where we judge a thing to be precious in consequence of the *idea* we frame of it, this is only because the idea is itself associated already with a feeling. If we were radically feelingless, and if ideas were the only things our mind could entertain, we should lose all our likes and dislikes at a stroke, and be unable to point to any one situation or experience in life more valuable or significant than any other.

Now the blindness in human beings, of which this discourse will treat, is the blindness with which we all are afflicted in regard to the feelings of creatures and people different from ourselves.

We are practical beings, each of us with limited functions and duties to perform. Each is bound to feel intensely the importance of his own duties and the significance of the situations that call these forth. But this feeling is in each of us a vital secret, for sympathy with which we vainly look to others. The others are too much absorbed in their own vital secrets to take an interest in ours. Hence the stupidity and injustice of our opinions, so far as they deal with the significance of alien lives. Hence the falsity of our judgments, so far as they presume to decide in an absolute way on the value of other persons' conditions or ideals.

Take our dogs and ourselves, connected as we are by a tie more intimate than most ties in this world; and yet, outside of that tie of friendly fondness, how insensible, each of us, to all that makes life significant for the other!—we to the rapture of bones under hedges, or smells of trees and lamp-posts, they to the delights of literature and art. As you sit reading the most moving romance you ever fell upon, what sort of a judge is your fox-terrier of your behaviour? With all his good will toward you, the nature of your conduct is absolutely excluded from his comprehension. To sit there like a senseless statue when you might be taking him to walk and throwing sticks for him to catch! What queer disease is this that comes over you every day, of holding things and staring at them like that for hours together, paralyzed of motion and vacant of all conscious life? The African savages came nearer the truth; but they, too, missed it when they gathered wonderingly round one of our American travellers who, in the interior, had just come into possession of a stray copy of the New York *Commercial Advertiser* and was devouring it column by column. When he got through, they offered him a high price for the mysterious object; and, being asked for what they wanted it, they said: "For an eye medicine"—that being the only reason they could conceive of for the protracted bath which he had given his eyes upon its surface.

The spectator's judgment is sure to miss the root of the

matter, and to possess no truth. The subject judged knows a part of the world of reality which the judging spectator fails to see, knows more while the spectator knows less; and, wherever there is conflict of opinion and difference of vision, we are bound to believe that the truer side is the side that feels the more, and not the side that feels the less.

Let me take a personal example of the kind that befalls each one of us daily:

Some years ago, while journeying in the mountains of North Carolina, I passed by a large number of "coves," as they call them there, or heads of small valleys between the hills, which had been newly cleared and planted. The impression on my mind was one of unmitigated squalor. The settler had in every case cut down the more manageable trees, and left their charred stumps standing. The larger trees he had girdled and killed, in order that their foliage should not cast a shade. He had then built a log cabin, plastering its chinks with clay, and had set up a tall zigzag rail fence around the scene of his havoc to keep the pigs and cattle out. Finally, he had irregularly planted the intervals between the stumps and trees with Indian corn, which grew among the chips; and there he dwelt with his wife and babes—an axe, a gun, a few utensils, and some pigs and chickens feeding in the woods, being the sum total of his possessions.

The forest had been destroyed; and what had "improved" it out of existence was hideous, a sort of ulcer, without a single element of artificial grace to make up for the loss of Nature's beauty. Ugly, indeed, seemed the life of the squatter, scudding, as the sailors say, under bare poles, beginning again away back where our first ancestors started, and by hardly a single item the better off for all the achievements of the intervening generations.

Talk about going back to nature! I said to myself, oppressed by the dreariness, as I drove by. Talk of a country life for one's old age and for one's children! Never thus, with nothing but the bare ground and one's bare hands to fight the battle! Never, without the best spoils of culture woven in! The beauties and commodities gained by the centuries are sacred.

They are our heritage and birthright. No modern person ought to be willing to live a day in such a state of rudimentariness and denudation.

Then I said to the mountaineer who was driving me, "What sort of people are they who have to make these new clearings?" "All of us," he replied. "Why, we ain't happy here unless we are getting one of these coves under cultivation." I instantly felt that I had been losing the whole inward significance of the situation. Because to me the clearings spoke of naught but denudation, I thought that to those whose sturdy arms and obedient axes had made them they could tell no other story. But, when *they* looked on the hideous stumps, what they thought of was personal victory. The chips, the girdled trees, and the vile split rails spoke of honest sweat, persistent toil and final reward. The cabin was a warrant of safety for self and wife and babes. In short, the clearing, which to me was a mere ugly picture on the retina, was to them a symbol redolent with moral memories and sang a very paean of duty, struggle, and success.

I had been as blind to the peculiar ideality of their conditions as they certainly would also have been to the ideality of mine, had they had a peep at my strange indoor academic ways of life at Cambridge.

Wherever a process of life communicates an eagerness to him who lives it, there the life becomes genuinely significant. Sometimes the eagerness is more knit up with the motor activities, sometimes with the perceptions, sometimes with the imagination, sometimes with reflective thought. But, wherever it is found, there is the zest, the tingle, the excitement of reality; and there *is* "importance" in the only real and positive sense in which importance ever anywhere can be.

Robert Louis Stevenson has illustrated this by a case, drawn from the sphere of the imagination, in an essay which I really think deserves to become immortal, both for the truth of its matter and the excellence of its form.

"Toward the end of September," Stevenson writes, "when school-time was drawing near, and the nights were already black, we would begin to sally from our respective villas, each equipped with a tin bull's-eye lantern. The thing was so well known that it had worn a rut in the commerce of Great Britain; and the grocers, about the due time, began to garnish their windows with our particular brand of luminary. We wore them buckled to the waist upon a cricket belt, and over them, such was the rigour of the game, a buttoned top-coat. They smelled noisomely of blistered tin. They never burned aright, though they would always burn our fingers. Their use was naught, the pleasure of them merely fanciful, and yet a boy with a bull's-eye under his top-coat asked for nothing more. The fishermen used lanterns about their boats, and it was from them, I suppose, that we had got the hint; but theirs were not bull's-eyes, nor did we ever play at being fishermen. The police carried them at their belts, and we had plainly copied them in that; yet we did not pretend to be policemen. Burglars, indeed, we may have had some haunting thought of; and we had certainly an eye to past ages when lanterns were more common, and to certain story-books in which we had found them to figure very largely. But take it for all in all, the pleasure of the thing was substantive; and to be a boy with a bull's-eye under his top-coat was good enough for us.

"When two of these asses met, there would be an anxious 'Have you got your lantern?' and a gratified 'Yes!' That was the shibboleth, and very needful, too; for, as it was the rule to keep our glory contained, none could recognize a lantern-bearer unless (like the polecat) by the smell. Four or five would sometimes climb into the belly of a ten-man lugger, with nothing but the thwarts above them—for the cabin was usually locked—or chose out some hollow of the links where the wind might whistle overhead. Then the coats would be unbuttoned, and the bull's-eyes discovered; and in the chequering glimmer, under the huge, windy hall of the night, and cheered by a rich steam of toasting tinware, these fortunate young gentlemen would crouch together in the cold sand of the links, or on the scaly bilges of the fishing-boat, and delight them with inappropriate talk. Woe is me that I cannot give some specimens! . . . But the talk was but a condiment, and these gatherings themselves only accidents in the career of the lantern-bearer. The essence of this bliss was to walk by yourself in the black night, the slide shut, the top-coat buttoned, not a ray escaping, whether to conduct your footsteps or to make your glory public—a mere pillar of darkness in the dark; and all the while, deep down in the privacy of your fool's heart, to know you had a bull's-eye at your belt, and to exult and sing over the knowledge.

"It is said that a poet has died young in the breast of the most stolid. It may be contended rather that a (somewhat minor) bard in almost every case survives, and is the spice of life to his possessor. Justice is not done to the versatility and the unplumbed childishness of man's imagination. His life from without may seem but a rude mound of mud: there will be some golden chamber at the heart of it in which he dwells delighted; and for as dark as his pathway seems to the observer, he will have some kind of bull's-eye at his belt.

". . . There is one fable that touches very near the quick of life—the fable of the monk who passed into the woods, heard a bird break into song, hearkened for a trill or two, and found himself at his return a stranger at his convent gates; for he had been absent fifty years, and of all his comrades there survived but one to recognize him. It is not only in the woods that this enchanter carols, though perhaps he is native there. He sings in the most doleful places. The miser hears him and chuckles, and his days are moments. With no more apparatus than an evil-smelling lantern, I have evoked him on the naked links. All life that is not merely mechanical is spun out of two strands—seeking for that bird and hearing him. And it is just this that makes life so hard to value, and the delight of each so incommunicable. And it is just a knowledge of this, and a remembrance of those fortunate hours in which the bird *has* sung to *us*, that fills us with such wonder when we turn to the pages of the realist. There, to be sure, we find a picture of life in so far as it consists of mud and of old iron, cheap desires and cheap fears, that which we are ashamed to remember and that which we are careless whether we forget; but of the note of that time-devouring nightingale we hear no news.

". . . Say that we came [in such a realistic romance] on some such business as that of my lantern-bearers on the links, and described the boys as very cold, spat upon by flurries of rain, and drearily surrounded, all of which they were; and their talk as silly and indecent, which it certainly was. To the eye of the observer they *are* wet and cold and drearily surrounded; but ask themselves, and they are in the heaven of a recondite pleasure, the ground of which is an ill-smelling lantern.

"For, to repeat, the ground of a man's joy is often hard to hit. It may hinge at times upon a mere accessory, like the lantern; it may reside in the mysterious inwards of psychology. . . . It has so little bond with externals . . . that it may even touch them not, and the man's true life, for which he consents to live, lies altogether in the field of fancy. . . . In such a case the poetry runs underground. The observer (poor soul, with his documents!) is all abroad. For to look at the man is but to court deception. We shall see the trunk from which he draws his nourishment; but he himself is above and abroad in the green dome of foliage, hummed through by winds and nested in by nightingales. And the true realism were that of the poets, to climb after him like a squirrel, and catch some glimpse of the heaven in which he lives. And the true realism, always and everywhere, is that of the poets: to find out where joy resides, and give it a voice far beyond singing.

"For to miss the joy is to miss all. In the joy of the actors lies the sense of any action. That is the explanation, that the excuse. To one who has not the secret of the lanterns the scene upon the links is meaningless. And hence the haunting and truly spectral unreality of realistic books. . . . In each we miss the personal poetry, the enchanted atmosphere, that rainbow work of fancy that clothes what is naked and seems to ennoble what is base; in each, life falls dead like dough instead of soaring away like a balloon into the colours of the sunset; each is true, each inconceivable; for no man lives in the external truth among salts and acids, but in the warm, phantasmagoric chamber of his brain, with the painted windows and the storied wall." [1]

These paragraphs are the best thing I know in all Stevenson. "To miss the joy is to miss all." Indeed, it is. Yet we are but finite, and each one of us has some single specialized vocation of his own. And it seems as if energy in the service of its particular duties might be got only by hardening the heart toward everything unlike them. Our deadness toward all but one particular kind of joy would thus be the price we inevitably have to pay for being practical creatures. Only in some pitiful dreamer, some philosopher, poet, or romancer, or when the common practical man becomes a lover, does the hard externality give way, and a gleam of insight into the ejective world, as Clifford called it, the vast world of inner life beyond us, so different from that of outer seeming, illuminate our mind. Then the whole scheme of our customary values gets confounded, then our self is riven and its narrow interests fly to pieces, then a new centre and a new perspective must be found.

The change is well described by my colleague, Josiah Royce:

"What, then, is our neighbour? Thou hast regarded his thought, his feeling, as somehow different from thine. Thou hast said, 'A pain in him is not like a pain in me, but something far easier to bear.' He seems to thee a little less living than thou; his life is dim, it is cold, it is a pale fire beside thy own burning desires. . . . So, dimly and by instinct hast thou lived with thy neighbour, and hast known him not, being blind. Thou hast made [of him] a thing, no Self at all. Have done with this illusion, and simply try to learn the truth. Pain is pain, joy is joy, everywhere, even as in thee. In all the songs of the forest birds; in all the cries of the wounded and dying, struggling in the captor's power; in the boundless sea where the myriads of water-creatures strive and die; amid all the countless hordes of savage men; in all sickness and sorrow; in

---

[1] "The Lantern-bearers," in the volume entitled *Across the Plains.* Abridged in the quotation. [It is reprinted in *Great Essays,* edited by Houston Peterson, published by Pocket Books, Inc.]

all exultation and hope, everywhere, from the lowest to the noblest, the same conscious, burning, wilful life is found, endlessly manifold as the forms of the living creatures, unquenchable as the fires of the sun, real as these impulses that even now throb in thine own little selfish heart. Lift up thy eyes, behold that life, and then turn away, and forget it as thou canst; but, if thou hast *known* that, thou hast begun to know thy duty." [2]

This higher vision of an inner significance in what, until then, we had realized only in the dead external way, often comes over a person suddenly; and, when it does so, it makes an epoch in his history. As Emerson says, there is a depth in those moments that constrains us to ascribe more reality to them than to all other experiences. The passion of love will shake one like an explosion, or some act will awaken a remorseful compunction that hangs like a cloud over all one's later day.

This mystic sense of hidden meaning starts upon us often from non-human natural things. I take this passage from *Obermann,* a French novel that had some vogue in its day: "Paris, March 7.—It was dark and rather cold. I was gloomy, and walked because I had nothing to do. I passed by some flowers placed breast-high upon a wall. A jonquil in bloom was there. It is the strongest expression of desire: it was the first perfume of the year. I felt all the happiness destined for man. This unutterable harmony of souls, the phantom of the ideal world, arose in me complete. I never felt anything so great or so instantaneous. I know not what shape, what analogy, what secret of relation it was that made me see in this flower a limitless beauty . . . I shall never enclose in a conception this power, this immensity that nothing will express; this form that nothing will contain; this ideal of a better world which one feels, but which it would seem that nature has not made." [3]

Wordsworth and Shelley are similarly full of this sense of a limitless significance in natural things. In Wordsworth it was

[2] *The Religious Aspect of Philosophy.*

[3] De Sénancour, *Obermann,* Lettre XXX.

a somewhat austere and moral significance—a "lonely cheer."

> "To every natural form, rock, fruit, or flower,
> Even the loose stones that cover the highway,
> I gave a moral life: I saw them feel,
> Or linked them to some feeling: the great mass
> Lay bedded in some quickening soul, and all
> That I beheld respired with inward meaning." [4]

"Authentic tidings of invisible things!" Just what this hidden presence in nature was, which Wordsworth so rapturously felt, and in the light of which he lived, tramping the hills for days together, the poet never could explain logically or in articulate conceptions. Yet to the reader who may himself have had gleaming moments of a similar sort, the verses in which Wordsworth simply proclaims the fact of them come with a heart-satisfying authority:

> "Magnificent
> The morning rose, in memorable pomp,
> Glorious as e'er I had beheld. In front
> The sea lay laughing at a distance; near,
> The solid mountains shone, bright as the clouds,
> Grain-tinctured, drenched in empyrean light;
> And in the meadows and the lower grounds
> Was all the sweetness of a common dawn—
> Dews, vapours, and the melody of birds,
> And labourers going forth to till the fields.
>
> "Ah! need I say, dear Friend, that to the brim
> My heart was full; I made no vows, but vows
> Were then made for me; bond unknown to me
> Was given, that I should be, else sinning greatly,
> A dedicated Spirit. On I walked
> In thankful blessedness, which yet survives." [5]

As Wordsworth walked, filled with his strange inner joy,

---

[4] *The Prelude*, Book III.
[5] *The Prelude*, Book IV.

responsive thus to the secret life of nature round about him, his rural neighbours, tightly and narrowly intent upon their own affairs, their crops and lambs and fences, must have thought him a very insignificant and foolish personage. It surely never occurred to any one of them to wonder what was going on inside of *him* or what it might be worth. And yet that inner life of his carried the burden of a significance that has fed the souls of others, and fills them to this day with inner joy.

Richard Jefferies has written a remarkable autobiographic document entitled *The Story of My Heart*. It tells in many pages of the rapture with which in youth the sense of the life of nature filled him. On a certain hill-top he says:

"I was utterly alone with the sun and the earth. Lying down on the grass, I spoke in my soul to the earth, the sun, the air, and the distant sea, far beyond sight. . . . With all the intensity of feeling which exalted me, all the intense communion I held with the earth, the sun and sky, the stars hidden by the light, with the ocean—in no manner can the thrilling depth of these feelings be written—with these I prayed as if they were the keys of an instrument. . . . The great sun, burning with light, the strong earth—dear earth—the warm sky, the pure air, the thought of ocean, the inexpressible beauty of all filled me with a rapture, an ecstasy, an inflatus. With this inflatus, too, I prayed. . . . The prayer, this soul-emotion, was in itself not for an object: it was a passion. I hid my face in the grass. I was wholly prostrated, I lost myself in the wrestle, I was rapt and carried away. . . . Had any shepherd accidentally seen me lying on the turf he would only have thought I was resting a few minutes. I made no outward show. Who could have imagined the whirlwind of passion that was going on in me as I reclined there!"

Surely, a worthless hour of life when measured by the usual standards of commercial value. Yet in what other *kind* of value can the preciousness of any hour, made precious by any standard, consist, if it consist not in feelings of excited significance like these, engendered in some one, by what the hour contains?

Yet so blind and dead does the clamour of our own practical interests make us to all other things, that it seems almost as if it were necessary to become worthless as a practical being, if one is to hope to attain to any breadth of insight into the impersonal world of worths as such, to have any perception of life's meaning on a large objective scale. Only your mystic, your dreamer, or your insolvent tramp or loafer can afford so sympathetic an occupation, an occupation which will change the usual standards of human value in the twinkling of an eye, giving to foolishness a place ahead of power, and laying low in a minute the distinctions which it takes a hard-working conventional man a lifetime to build up. You may be a prophet at this rate; but you cannot be a worldly success.

Walt Whitman, for instance, is accounted by many of us a contemporary prophet. He abolishes the usual human distinctions, brings all conventionalisms into solution, and loves and celebrates hardly any human attributes save those elementary ones common to all members of the race. For this he becomes a sort of ideal tramp, a rider on omnibus-tops and ferry-boats, and, considered either practically or academically, a worthless, unproductive being. His verses are but ejaculations—things mostly without subject or verb, a succession of interjections on an immense scale. He felt the human crowd as rapturously as Wordsworth felt the mountains, felt it as an overpoweringly significant presence, simply to absorb one's mind in which should be business sufficient and worthy to fill the days of a serious man. As he crosses Brooklyn ferry, this is what he feels:

"Flood-tide below me! I watch you, face to face;
    Clouds of the west! sun there half an hour high! I see you also face to face.
    Crowds of men and women attired in the usual costumes! how curious you are to me!
    On the ferry-boats, the hundreds and hundreds that cross, returning home, are more curious to me than you suppose;
    And you that shall cross from shore to shore years hence, are more to me, and more in my meditations, than you might suppose.
    Others will enter the gates of the ferry, and cross from shore to shore;

Others will watch the run of the flood-tide;

Others will see the shipping of Manhattan north and west, and
the heights of Brooklyn to the south and east;

Others will see the islands large and small;

Fifty years hence, others will see them as they cross, the sun half
an hour high.

A hundred years hence, or ever so many hundred years hence,
others will see them,

Will enjoy the sunset, the pouring in of the flood-tide, the falling
back to the sea of the ebb-tide.

It avails not, neither time nor place—distance avails not.

Just as you feel when you look on the river and sky, so I felt;

Just as any of you is one of a living crowd, I was one of a crowd;

Just as you are refresh'd by the gladness of the river and the bright
flow, I was refresh'd;

Just as you stand and lean on the rail, yet hurry with the swift
current, I stood, yet was hurried;

Just as you look on the numberless masts of ships, and the thick-
stemmed pipes of steamboats, I looked.

I too many and many a time cross'd the river, the sun half an hour
high;

I watched the Twelfth-month sea-gulls—I saw them high in the
air, with motionless wings, oscillating their bodies,

I saw how the glistening yellow lit up parts of their bodies, and
left the rest in strong shadow,

I saw the slow-wheeling circles, and the gradual edging toward
the south,

Saw the white sails of schooners and sloops, saw the ships at
anchor,

The sailors at work in the rigging, or out astride the spars;

The scallop-edged waves in the twilight, the ladled cups, the
frolicsome crests and glistening;

The stretch afar growing dimmer and dimmer, the grey walls of
the granite store-houses by the docks;

On the neighbouring shores, the fires from the foundry chimneys
burning high . . . into the night,

Casting their flicker of black . . . into the clefts of streets.

These, and all else, were to me the same as they are to you." [6]

---

[6] *Crossing Brooklyn Ferry.*

And so on, through the rest of a divinely beautiful poem. And, if you wish to see what this hoary loafer considered the most worthy way of profiting by life's heaven-sent opportunities, read the delicious volume of his letters to a young car-conductor who had become his friend:

"NEW YORK, *Oct.* 9, 1868.

"DEAR PETE—It is splendid here this forenoon—bright and cool. I was out early taking a short walk by the river only two squares from where I live. . . . Shall I tell you about [my life] just to fill up? I generally spend the forenoon in my room writing, etc., then take a bath, fix up, and go out about twelve and loaf somewhere or call on some one down town or on business, or perhaps, if it is very pleasant and I feel like it, ride a trip with some driver friend on Broadway, from 23rd Street to Bowling Green, three miles each way. (Every day I find I have plenty to do, every hour is occupied with something.) You know it is a never-ending amusement and study and recreation for me to ride a couple of hours on a pleasant afternoon on a Broadway stage in this way. You see everything as you pass, a sort of living, endless panorama—shops and splendid buildings and great windows: on the broad sidewalks crowds of women richly dressed continually passing, altogether different, superior in style and looks from any to be seen anywhere else—in fact a perfect stream of people—men, too, dressed in high style, and plenty of foreigners—and then in the streets the thick crowd of carriages, stages, carts, hotel and private coaches, and in fact all sorts of vehicles and many first-class teams, mile after mile, and the splendour of such a great street and so many tall, ornamental, noble buildings, many of them of white marble, and the gaiety and motion on every side: you will not wonder how much attraction all this is on a fine day to a great loafer like me, who enjoys so much seeing the busy world move by him and exhibiting itself for his amusement while he takes it easy and just looks on and observes." [7]

---

[7] *Calamus.*

Truly a futile way of passing the time, some of you may say, and not altogether creditable to a grown-up man. And yet, from the deepest point of view, who knows the more of truth and who knows the less—Whitman on his omnibus-top, full of the inner joy with which the spectacle inspires him, or you, full of the disdain which the futility of his occupation excites?

When your ordinary Brooklynite or New Yorker, leading a life replete with too much luxury, or tired and careworn about his personal affairs, crosses the ferry or goes up Broadway, *his* fancy does not thus "soar away into the colours of the sunset," as did Whitman's, nor does he inwardly realize at all the indisputable fact that this world never did anywhere or at any time contain more of essential divinity, or of eternal meaning, than is embodied in the fields of vision over which his eyes so carelessly pass. There is life; and there, a step away, is death. There is the only kind of beauty there ever was. There is the old human struggle and its fruits together. There is the text and the sermon, the real and the ideal in one. But to the jaded and unquickened eye it is all dead and common, pure vulgarism, flatness, and disgust. "Hech! it is a sad sight!" says Carlyle, walking at night with some one who appeals to him to note the splendour of the stars. And that very repetition of the scene to new generations of men in *secula seculorum,* that eternal recurrence of the common order, which so fills a Whitman with mystic satisfaction, is to a Schopenhauer, with the emotional anaesthesia, the feeling of "awful inner emptiness" from out of which he views it all, the chief ingredient of the tedium it instils. What is life on the largest scale, he asks, but the same recurrent inanities, the same dog barking, the same fly buzzing for evermore? Yet of the kind of fibre of which such inanities consist is the material woven of all the excitements, joys, and meanings that ever were, or ever shall be, in this world.

To be rapt with satisfied attention, like Whitman, to the mere spectacle of the world's presence is one way, and the most fundamental way, of confessing one's sense of its unfathomable significance and importance. But how can one attain to the feeling of the vital significance of an experience if one have it not to begin with? There is no receipt which one can follow. Being a secret and a mystery, it often comes in mysteriously unexpected ways. It blossoms sometimes from out of the very grave wherein we imagined that our happiness was buried. Benvenuto Cellini, after a life all in the outer sunshine, made of adventures and artistic excitements, suddenly finds himself cast into a dungeon in the Castle of San Angelo. The place is horrible. Rats and wet and mould possess it. His leg is broken and his teeth fall out, apparently with scurvy. But his thoughts turn to God as they have never turned before. He gets a Bible, which he reads during the one hour in the twenty-four in which a wandering ray of daylight penetrates his cavern. He has religious visions. He sings psalms to himself and composes hymns. And thinking, on the last day of July, of the festivities customary on the morrow in Rome, he says to himself: "All these past years I celebrated this holiday with the vanities of the world: from this year henceforward I will do it with the divinity of God. And then I said to myself, 'Oh, how much more happy I am for this present life of mine than for all those things remembered!' " [8]

But the great understander of these mysterious ebbs and flows is Tolstoi. They throb all through his novels. In his *War and Peace*, the hero, Peter, is supposed to be the richest man in the Russian empire. During the French invasion he is taken prisoner and dragged through much of the retreat. Cold, vermin, hunger, and every form of misery assail him, the result being a revelation to him of the real scale of life's values. "Here only, and for the first time, he appreciated, because he was deprived of it, the happiness of eating when he was hungry, of drinking when he was thirsty, of sleeping when he was sleepy, and of talking when he felt the desire to exchange some words. . . . Later in life he always recurred with joy to this month of captivity, and never failed to speak with enthusiasm of the powerful and ineffaceable sensations, and espe-

[8] *Vita*, Lib. II, Chap. IV.

cially of the moral calm which he had experienced at this epoch. When at daybreak, on the morrow of his imprisonment, he saw [I abridge here Tolstoi's description] the mountains with their wooded slopes disappearing in the greyish mist; when he felt the cool breeze caress him; when he saw the light drive away the vapours, and the sun rise majestically behind the clouds and cupolas, and the crosses, the dew, the distance, the river, sparkle in the splendid, cheerful rays—his heart overflowed with emotion. This emotion kept continually with him and increased a hundred-fold as the difficulties of his situation grew graver. . . . He learnt that man is meant for happiness and that this happiness is in him, in the satisfaction of the daily needs of existence, and that unhappiness is the fatal result, not of our need but of our abundance. . . . When calm reigned in the camp, and the embers paled and little by little went out, the full moon had reached the zenith. The woods and the fields round about lay clearly visible; and, beyond the inundation of light which filled them, the view plunged into the limitless horizon. Then Peter cast his eyes upon the firmament, filled at that hour with myriads of stars. 'All that is mine,' he thought. 'All that is in me, is me! And that is what they think they have taken prisoner! That is what they have shut up in a cabin!' So he smiled and turned in to sleep among his comrades."

The occasion and the experience, then, are nothing. It all depends on the capacity of the soul to be grasped, to have its life-currents absorbed by what is given. "Crossing a bare common," says Emerson, "in snow puddles, at twilight, under a clouded sky, without having in my thoughts any occurrence of special good fortune, I have enjoyed a perfect exhilaration. I am glad to the brink of fear."

Life is always worth living, if one have such responsive sensibilities. But we of the highly educated classes (so called) have most of us got far, far away from Nature. We are trained to seek the choice, the rare, the exquisite exclusively, and to overlook the common. We are stuffed with abstract conceptions and glib with verbalities and verbosities; and in the culture of these higher functions the peculiar sources of joy connected with our simpler functions often dry up, and we grow stone-blind and insensible to life's more elementary and general goods and joys.

The remedy under such conditions is to descend to a more profound and primitive level. To be imprisoned or shipwrecked or forced into the army would permanently show the good of life to many an over-educated pessimist. Living in the open air and on the ground, the lop-sided beam of the balance slowly rises to the level line; and the oversensibilities and insensibilities even themselves out. The good of all the artificial schemes and fevers fades and pales; and that of seeing, smelling, tasting, sleeping, and daring and doing with one's body, grows and grows. The savages and children of nature, to whom we deem ourselves so much superior, certainly are alive where we are often dead, along these lines; and, could they write as glibly as we do, they would read us impressive lectures on our impatience for improvement and on our blindness to the fundamental static goods of life. "Ah! my brother," said a chieftain to his white guest, "thou wilt never know the happiness of both thinking of nothing and doing nothing. This, next to sleep, is the most enchanting of all things. Thus we were before our birth, and thus we shall be after death. Thy people . . . when they have finished reaping one field, they begin to plough another; and, if the day were not enough, I have seen them plough by moonlight. What is their life to ours—the life that is as naught to them? Blind that they are, they lose it all! But we live in the present." [9]

The intense interest that life can assume when brought down to the non-thinking level, the level of pure sensorial perception, has been beautifully described by a man who can write, Mr. W. H. Hudson, in his volume *Idle Days in Patagonia.*

"I spent the greater part of one winter," says this admirable author, "at a point on the Rio Negro seventy or eighty miles from the sea.

". . . It was my custom to go out every morning on horse-

---

[9] Quoted by Lotze, *Microcosmus.*

back with my gun and, followed by one dog, to ride away
from the valley; and no sooner would I climb the terrace and
plunge into the gray, universal thicket than I would find myself as completely alone as if five hundred instead of only five
miles separated me from the valley and river. So wild and
solitary and remote seemed that gray waste, stretching away
into infinitude, a waste untrodden by man, and where the
wild animals are so few that they have made no discoverable
path in the wilderness of thorns. . . . Not once nor twice nor
thrice, but day after day I returned to this solitude, going to it
in the morning as if to attend a festival, and leaving it only
when hunger and thirst and the westering sun compelled me.
And yet I had no object in going—no motive which could be
put into words; for, although I carried a gun, there was nothing to shoot—the shooting was all left behind in the valley.
. . . Sometimes I would pass a whole day without seeing one
mammal, and perhaps not more than a dozen birds of any size.
The weather at that time was cheerless, generally with a gray
film of cloud spread over the sky, and a bleak wind, often
cold enough to make my bridle-hand quite numb. . . . At a
slow pace, which would have seemed intolerable under other
circumstances, I would ride about for hours together at a
stretch. On arriving at a hill, I would slowly ride to its summit, and stand there to survey the prospect. On every side it
stretched away in great undulations, wild and irregular. How
gray it all was! Hardly less so near at hand than on the haze-
wrapped horizon where the hills were dim and the outline
obscured by distance. Descending from my outlook, I would
take up my aimless wanderings again, and visit other eleva-
tions to gaze on the same landscape from another point; and
so on for hours. And at noon I would dismount, and sit or lie
on my folded poncho for an hour or longer. One day in these
rambles I discovered a small grove composed of twenty or
thirty trees, growing at a convenient distance apart, that had
evidently been resorted to by a herd of deer or other wild animals. This grove was on a hill differing in shape from other
hills in its neighbourhood; and, after a time, I made a point
of finding and using it as a resting-place every day at noon. I

did not ask myself why I made choice of that one spot, sometimes going out of my way to sit there, instead of sitting down
under any one of the millions of trees and bushes on any other
hillside. I thought nothing about it, but acted unconsciously.
Only afterwards it seemed to me that, after having rested
there once, each time I wished to rest again, the wish came
associated with the image of that particular clump of trees,
with polished stems and clean bed of sand beneath; and in a
short time I formed a habit of returning, animal like, to repose
at that same spot.

"It was, perhaps, a mistake to say that I would sit down
and rest, since I was never tired; and yet, without being tired,
that noon-day pause, during which I sat for an hour without
moving, was strangely grateful. All day there would be no
sound, not even the rustling of a leaf. One day, while *listening*
to the silence, it occurred to my mind to wonder what the
effect would be if I were to shout aloud. This seemed at the
time a horrible suggestion which almost made me shudder.
But during those solitary days it was a rare thing for any
thought to cross my mind. In the state of mind I was in,
thought had become impossible. My state was one of *suspense
and watchfulness;* yet I had no expectation of meeting an adventure, and felt as free from apprehension as I feel now while
sitting in a room in London. The state seemed familiar rather
than strange, and accompanied by a strong feeling of elation;
and I did not know that some thing had come between me
and my intellect until I returned to my former self—to thinking and the old insipid existence [again].

"I had undoubtedly *gone back;* and that state of intense
watchfulness or alertness, rather, with suspension of the higher
intellectual faculties, represented the mental state of the pure
savage. He thinks little, reasons little, having a surer guide in
his [mere sensory perceptions]. He is in perfect harmony with
nature, and is nearly on a level, mentally, with the wild animals he preys on, and which in their turn sometimes prey on
him."

For the spectator, such hours as Mr. Hudson writes of form
a mere tale of emptiness, in which nothing happens, nothing

is gained, and there is nothing to describe. They are meaningless and vacant tracts of time. To him who feels their inner secret, they tingle with an importance that unutterably vouches for itself. I am sorry for the boy or girl, or man or woman, who has never been touched by the spell of this mysterious sensorial life, with its irrationality, if so you like to call it, but its vigilance and its supreme felicity. The holidays of life are its most vitally significant portions, because they are, or at least should be, covered with just this kind of magically irresponsible spell.

And now what is the result of all these considerations and quotations? It is negative in one sense, but positive in another. It absolutely forbids us to be forward in pronouncing on the meaninglessness of forms of existence other than our own; and it commands us to tolerate, respect, and indulge those whom we see harmlessly interested and happy in their own ways, however unintelligible these may be to us. Hands off: neither the whole of truth nor the whole of good is revealed to any single observer, although each observer gains a partial superiority of insight from the peculiar position in which he stands. Even prisons and sick-rooms have their special revelations. It is enough to ask of each of us that he should be faithful to his own opportunities and make the most of his own blessings, without presuming to regulate the rest of the vast field.

•   •   •

In his final decade of increasing popularity and uncertain health, James gave his best energies to three notable series of public lectures while vainly hoping to round out his life with a systematic presentation of his views. *The Varieties of Religious Experience*, *Pragmatism*, and *A Pluralistic Universe* are widely known and have had their full share of praise and blame. But at the end James was probably more interested in a series of technical articles written around 1904-1905 but published only after his death in a volume of *Essays in Radical Empiricism*.

To the French philosopher, François Pillon, James wrote in 1904: "My philosophy is what I call a radical empiricism, a pluralism, a 'tychism,' which represents order as being gradually won and always in the making. It is theistic, but not *essentially* so. It rejects all doctrines of the Absolute. It is finitist; but it does not attribute to the question of the Infinite the great methodological importance which you and Renouvier attribute to it. I fear that you may find my system too bottomless and romantic. I am sure that, be it in the end true or false, it is essential to the evolution of clearness in philosophic thought that someone should defend a pluralistic empiricism radically."

Two months later, in a letter to L. T. Hobhouse, James discussed the misunderstandings of his famous essay "The Will to Believe" (which, he admitted, should have been called "The Right to Believe"); and suggested that every philosopher is influenced by a "bogey" at the back of his mind. "Your bogey is superstition; my bogey is desiccation, and each, for his contrast-effect, clutches at any text that can be used to represent the enemy, regardless of exegetical proprieties.

"In my essay the evil shape was a vision of 'Science' in the form of abstraction, priggishness and sawdust, lording it over all."

Fifty years later the brilliant Gilbert Ryle suspected that "James's biggest influence will turn out to be this. He restored to philosophy, what had been missing since Hume, that sense of the ridiculous which saves one from taking seriously everything that is said solemnly. James brought back the pinch of salt."

BERTRAND RUSSELL

[1872–1970]

Three compact little books published between 1956 and 1958—
*Philosophical Analysis: Its Development Between the Two World
Wars*, by J. O. Urmson, *The Revolution in Philosophy*, by Ayer,
Ryle and others, and *English Philosophy Since 1900*, by G. J. War-
nock—tell much the same story, in three overlapping parts. (1)
The revolt of two young Cambridge philosophers, G. E. Moore and
Bertrand Russell, against the absolute idealism of the Oxford
giant, F. H. Bradley, and their diverging careers. (2) Ludwig
Wittgenstein's stay in Cambridge in 1912-1913, to study under
Russell, with his immediate influence on Russell's logical atomism
and, after the war, his effect on the logical positivism of the
Vienna Circle. (3) The return of Wittgenstein to Cambridge in
1929 and his transition to a new position, "ordinary language
philosophy," or a new version of analytic philosophy, which now
pervades the English-speaking world.

As for the feared and revered figure of G. E. Moore, "with an
intellect as deeply passionate as Spinoza's" (Russell), with "the
courage to seem naïve" (G. A. Paul), with a life devoted to
"the steady pursuit of methodical questioning" (L. Susan Stebbing), he has been identified with no schools or *isms* except the
truisms of common sense which he has defended without apology.
How many a statement has been stifled at birth by the mere
thought of Moore's pained expression and painful question, "Do
you *really* believe that?" or "What in the world do you mean
by that?"

As for Bertrand Russell, what can one say briefly of the amazing
man who wrote his own obituary in 1937 and suggested that
it "will (or will not) be published in *The Times* for June 1, 1962,
on the occasion of my lamented but belated death," at the age
of ninety? His technical works are so difficult that only experts

can follow them and his untechnical works are so lucid that some experts appear to disdain them. But here are a few facts to keep the calendar straight.

Bertrand Russell was a grandson of Lord John Russell, who was most famous for his support of the first Reform Bill (1832) and his lifelong advocacy of civil liberties; he was a son of two dashing radical young aristocrats who selected John Stuart Mill for his godfather before their early deaths in Russell's childhood. He was privately tutored until the age of eighteen, when he went to Cambridge, where he found himself in "a new world of infinite delight." But he was not delighted by the puerile instruction in mathematics, for he had been pondering over the *foundations* of mathematics since the age of eleven—so to escape from boredom he turned to philosophy for his remaining year at Cambridge, and became a follower of Hegel and Bradley!

In 1894, Russell married and the following year made two trips to Germany, for he was not yet sure of his ability to do mathematics or philosophy and at times cast his eyes toward political economy. With that "sense for important impending developments" which his lamented friend and biographer Alan Wood stressed, Russell went to Berlin and "investigated the two forces destined to shape the world's history for the next fifty years and more: German militarism and Marxian Communism." In his first book, now quite forgotten, *German Social Democracy* (1896), Russell urged German and English Socialist parties to cooperate with Liberal parties in pressing their reforms. "If his advice had been followed," concluded Wood, "there might not have been a First World War."

"The most important year in my intellectual life was the year 1900, and the most important event in that year was my visit to the International Congress of Philosophy in Paris," wrote Russell in an autobiographical essay (1944), for on that occasion he heard Peano and his pupils talk fluently and profoundly about the foundations of mathematics. Now learning Peano's symbolism and using it for the first time, Russell wrote a paper on "The Logic of Relations," which was perhaps the first clear indication, according to R. C. Marsh, that he was "a creative mind of the first order."

Early in 1901, Russell had an experience which he himself has compared to a religious conversion. Under the influence of the Webbs he had become something of an imperialist and a supporter of the Boer War. But then he "became suddenly and vividly aware of the loneliness in which most people live, and passionately desirous of finding ways of diminishing this tragic isolation. In the course of a few minutes I changed my mind about the Boer War, about harshness in education and in the criminal law, and about combativeness in private relations. I expressed the outcome of this experience in *A Free Man's Worship*." But he could not yield to this mood at the time, for he was too absorbed in vast abstractions.

First he had to complete and see through the press his first major book, *The Principles of Mathematics* (1903), which contained in an appendix "a rough sketch" of his now classic *theory of types*. He also had to complete a paper, "On Denoting," which contained a preliminary statement of his "greatest philosophical discovery" (G. E. Moore), the *theory of descriptions*. But the really overwhelming, the Herculean task, was the completion with Alfred North Whitehead of the *Principia Mathematica*, which absorbed their best energies for a full decade. They had largely succeeded in reducing mathematics to logic and in "taking the mystery out of mathematics," and so placed themselves among the greatest thinkers of all time. The three volumes of the *Principia* were published between 1910 and 1913.

With that tremendous burden off his shoulders, Russell was able to write a popular little masterpiece, *The Problems of Philosophy* (1912) for the Home University Library, in which he described the eternal world of Platonic universals with an eloquent reverence which he was soon to abandon. For Santayana successfully shook his belief in the objectivity of moral judgments, and Wittgenstein arrived in Cambridge to further sharpen Russell's already sharp analytic tools.

The result was *Our Knowledge of the External World*, perhaps Russell's most important and influential work outside of pure logic and mathematics. It was first tried out as a series of lectures in Cambridge, England, before being presented as the Lowell Lectures in Boston, in March and April, 1914. Where Russell's work is discussed, emphasis is invariably placed on the second lecture in this series as a milestone in twentieth-century philosophy. The first lecture was a general discussion of "Current Tendencies," namely, the classical tendency stemming from Kant and Hegel; evolutionism, as stemming from Darwin and Spencer but best represented later by James and Bergson; and "logical atomism," which Russell himself then proposed to advocate.

. . .

LOGIC AS THE ESSENCE OF PHILOSOPHY

The topics we discussed in our first lecture, and the topics we shall discuss later, all reduce themselves, in so far as they are genuinely philosophical, to problems of logic. This is not due to any accident, but to the fact that every philosophical problem, when it is subjected to the necessary analysis and purification, is found either to be not really philosophical at all, or else to be, in the sense in which we are using the word, logical. But as the word "logic" is never used in the same sense by two different philosophers, some explanation of what I mean by the word is indispensable at the outset.

Logic, in the Middle Ages, and down to the present day in teaching, meant no more than a scholastic collection of technical terms and rules of syllogistic inference. Aristotle had spoken, and it was the part of humbler men merely to repeat the lesson after him. The trivial nonsense embodied in this tradition is still set in examinations, and defended by eminent authorities as an excellent "propædeutic," *i.e.*, a training in those habits of solemn humbug which are so great a help in later life. But it is not this that I mean to praise in saying that all philosophy is logic. Ever since the beginning of the seventeenth century, all vigorous minds that have concerned themselves with inference have abandoned the mediæval tradition, and in one way or other have widened the scope of logic.

The first extension was the introduction of the inductive method by Bacon and Galileo—by the former in a theoretical and largely mistaken form, by the latter in actual use in establishing the foundations of modern physics and astronomy. This is probably the only extension of the old logic which has become familiar to the general educated public. But induction, important as it is when regarded as a method of investigation, does not seem to remain when its work is done: in the final form of a perfected science, it would seem that everything ought to be deductive. If induction remains at all, which is a difficult question, it will remain merely as one of the principles according to which deductions are effected. Thus the ultimate result of the introduction of the inductive method seems not the creation of a new kind of non-deductive reasoning, but rather the widening of the scope of deduction by pointing out a way of deducing which is certainly not syllogistic, and does not fit into the mediæval scheme.

The question of the scope and validity of induction is of great difficulty, and of great importance to our knowledge. Take such a question as, "Will the sun rise tomorrow?" Our first instinctive feeling is that we have abundant reason for saying that it will, because it has risen on so many previous mornings. Now, I do not myself know whether this does afford a ground or not, but I am willing to suppose that it does. The question which then arises is: What is the principle of inference by which we pass from past sunrises to future ones? The answer given by Mill is that the inference depends upon the law of causation. Let us suppose this to be true; then what is the reason for believing in the law of causation? There are broadly three possible answers: (1) that it is itself known *a priori;* (2) that it is a postulate; (3) that it is an empirical generalisation from past instances in which it has been found to hold. The theory that causation is known *a priori* cannot be definitely refuted, but it can be rendered very unplausible by the mere process of formulating the law exactly, and thereby showing that it is immensely more complicated and less obvious than is generally supposed. The theory that causation is a postulate, *i.e.*, that it is something which we choose to assert although we know that it is very likely false, is also incapable of refutation; but it is plainly also incapable of justifying any use of the law in inference. We are thus brought to the theory that the law is an empirical generalisation, which is the view held by Mill.

But if so, how are empirical generalisations to be justified? The evidence in their favour cannot be empirical, since we wish to argue from what has been observed to what has not been observed, which can only be done by means of some known relation of the observed and the unobserved; but the unobserved, by definition, is not known empirically, and therefore its relation to the observed, if known at all, must be known independently of empirical evidence. Let us see what Mill says on this subject.

According to Mill, the law of causation is proved by an admittedly fallible process called "induction by simple enumeration." This process, he says, "consists in ascribing the nature of general truths to all propositions which are true in every instance that we happen to know of."[1] As regards its fallibility, he asserts that "the precariousness of the method of simple enumeration is in an inverse ratio to the largeness of the generalisation. The process is delusive and insufficient, exactly in proportion as the subject-matter of the observation is special and limited in extent. As the sphere widens, this unscientific method becomes less and less liable to mislead; and the most universal class of truths, the law of causation for instance, and the principles of number and of geometry, are duly and satisfactorily proved by that method alone, nor are they susceptible of any other proof."[2]

In the above statement, there are two obvious lacunæ: (1) How is the method of simple enumeration itself justified? (2) What logical principle, if any, covers the same ground as this method, without being liable to its failures? Let us take the second question first.

A method of proof which, when used as directed, gives

---

[1] *Logic*, Book III, Chapter III, § 2.
[2] *Ibid.*, Book III, Chapter XXI, § 3.

sometimes truth and sometimes falsehood—as the method of simple enumeration does—is obviously not a valid method, for validity demands invariable truth. Thus, if simple enumeration is to be rendered valid, it must not be stated as Mill states it. We shall have to say, at most, that the data render the result *probable*. Causation holds, we shall say, in every instance we have been able to test; therefore it *probably* holds in untested instances. There are terrible difficulties in the notion of probability, but we may ignore them at present. We thus have what at least *may* be a logical principle, since it is without exception. If a proposition is true in every instance that we happen to know of, and if the instances are very numerous, then, we shall say, it becomes very probable, on the data, that it will be true in any further instance. This is not refuted by the fact that what we declare to be probable does not always happen, for an event may be probable on the data and yet not occur. It is, however, obviously capable of further analysis, and of more exact statement. We shall have to say something like this: that every instance of a proposition[3] being true increases the probability of its being true in a fresh instance, and that a sufficient number of favourable instances will, in the absence of instances to the contrary, make the probability of the truth of a fresh instance approach indefinitely near to certainty. Some such principle as this is required if the method of simple enumeration is to be valid.

But this brings us to our other question, namely, how is our principle known to be true? Obviously, since it is required to justify induction, it cannot be proved by induction; since it goes beyond the empirical data, it cannot be proved by them alone; since it is required to justify all inferences from empirical data to what goes beyond them, it cannot itself be even rendered in any degree probable by such data. Hence, *if* it is known, it is not known by experience, but independently of experience. I do not say that any such principle is known: I only say that it is required to justify

---

[3] Or rather a propositional function.

the inferences from experience which empiricists allow, and that it cannot itself be justified empirically.

A similar conclusion can be proved by similar arguments concerning any other logical principle. Thus logical knowledge is not derivable from experience alone, and the empiricist's philosophy can therefore not be accepted in its entirety, in spite of its excellence in many matters which lie outside logic.

Hegel and his followers widened the scope of logic in quite a different way—a way which I believe to be fallacious, but which requires discussion if only to show how their conception of logic differs from the conception which I wish to advocate. In their writings, logic is practically identical with metaphysics. In broad outline, the way this came about is as follows. Hegel believed that, by means of *a priori* reasoning, it could be shown that the world *must* have various important and interesting characteristics, since any world without these characteristics would be impossible and self-contradictory. Thus what he calls "logic" is an investigation of the nature of the universe, in so far as this can be inferred merely from the principle that the universe must be logically self-consistent. I do not myself believe that from this principle alone anything of importance can be inferred as regards the existing universe. But, however that may be, I should not regard Hegel's reasoning, even if it were valid, as properly belonging to logic: it would rather be an application of logic to the actual world. Logic itself would be concerned rather with such questions as what self-consistency is, which Hegel, so far as I know, does not discuss. And though he criticises the traditional logic, and professes to replace it by an improved logic of his own, there is some sense in which the traditional logic, with all its faults, is uncritically and unconsciously assumed throughout his reasoning. It is not in the direction advocated by him, it seems to me, that the reform of logic is to be sought, but by a more fundamental, more patient, and less ambitious investigation into the presuppositions which his system shares with those of most other philosophers.

The way in which, as it seems to me, Hegel's system assumes the ordinary logic which it subsequently criticises, is exemplified by the general conception of "categories" with which he operates throughout. This conception is, I think, essentially a product of logical confusion, but it seems in some way to stand for the conception of "qualities of Reality as a whole." Mr. Bradley has worked out a theory according to which, in all judgment, we are ascribing a predicate to Reality as a whole; and this theory is derived from Hegel. Now the traditional logic holds that every proposition ascribes a predicate to a subject, and from this it easily follows that there can be only one subject, the Absolute, for if there were two, the proposition that there were two would not ascribe a predicate to either. Thus Hegel's doctrine, that philosophical propositions must be of the form, "the Absolute is such-and-such," depends upon the traditional belief in the universality of the subject-predicate form. This belief, being traditional, scarcely self-conscious, and not supposed to be important, operates underground, and is assumed in arguments which, like the refutation of relations, appear at first sight such as to establish its truth. This is the most important respect in which Hegel uncritically assumes the traditional logic. Other less important respects—though important enough to be the source of such essentially Hegelian conceptions as the "concrete universal" and the "union of identity in difference"—will be found where he explicitly deals with formal logic.[4]

There is quite another direction in which a large technical

---

[4] See the translation by H. S. Macran, *Hegel's Doctrine of Formal Logic,* Oxford, 1912. Hegel's argument in this portion of his "Logic" depends throughout upon confusing the "is" of predication, as in "Socrates is mortal," with the "is" of identity, as in "Socrates is the philosopher who drank the hemlock." Owing to this confusion, he thinks that "Socrates" and "mortal" must be identical. Seeing that they are different, he does not infer, as others would, that there is a mistake somewhere, but that they exhibit "identity in difference." Again, Socrates is particular, "mortal" is universal. Therefore, he says, since Socrates is mortal, it follows that the particular is the universal—taking the "is" to be throughout expressive of identity. But to say "the particular is the universal" is self-contradictory. Again Hegel does not suspect a mistake, but proceeds to synthesise particular and universal in the individual, or concrete universal. This is an example of how, for want of care at the start, vast and imposing systems of philosophy are built upon stupid and trivial confusions, which, but for the almost incredible fact that they are unintentional, one would be tempted to characterise as puns.

development of logic has taken place: I mean the direction of what is called logistic or mathematical logic. This kind of logic is mathematical in two different senses: it is itself a branch of mathematics, and it is the logic which is specially applicable to other more traditional branches of mathematics. Historically, it began as *merely* a branch of mathematics: its special applicability to other branches is a more recent development. In both respects, it is the fulfilment of a hope which Leibniz cherished throughout his life, and pursued with all the ardour of his amazing intellectual energy. Much of his work on this subject has been published recently, after his discoveries had been remade by others; but none was published by him, because his results persisted in contradicting certain points in the traditional doctrine of the syllogism. We now know that on these points the traditional doctrine is wrong, but respect for Aristotle prevented Leibniz from realising that this was possible.[5]

The modern development of mathematical logic dates from Boole's *Laws of Thought* (1854). But in him and his successors, before Peano and Frege, the only thing really achieved, apart from certain details, was the invention of a mathematical symbolism for deducing consequences from the premisses which the newer methods shared with those of Aristotle. This subject has considerable interest as an independent branch of mathematics, but it has very little to do with real logic. The first serious advance in real logic since the time of the Greeks was made independently by Peano and Frege—both mathematicians. They both arrived at their logical results by an analysis of mathematics. Traditional logic regarded the two propositions, "Socrates is mortal" and "All men are mortal," as being of the same form;[6] Peano and Frege showed that they are utterly different in form. The philosophical importance of logic may be illustrated by the fact that this confusion—which is still committed by most writers—obscured not only the whole study of the forms of

---

[5] *Cf.* Couturat, *La Logique de Leibniz,* pp. 361, 386.

[6] It was often recognised that there was *some* difference between them, but it was not recognised that the difference is fundamental, and of very great importance.

judgment and inference, but also the relations of things to their qualities, of concrete existence to abstract concepts, and of the world of sense to the world of Platonic ideas. Peano and Frege, who pointed out the error, did so for technical reasons, and applied their logic mainly to technical developments; but the philosophical importance of the advance which they made is impossible to exaggerate.

Mathematical logic, even in its most modern form, is not *directly* of philosophical importance except in its beginnings. After the beginnings, it belongs rather to mathematics than to philosophy. Of its beginnings, which are the only part of it that can properly be called *philosophical* logic, I shall speak shortly. But even the later developments, though not directly philosophical, will be found of great indirect use in philosophising. They enable us to deal easily with more abstract conceptions than merely verbal reasoning can enumerate; they suggest fruitful hypotheses which otherwise could hardly be thought of; and they enable us to see quickly what is the smallest store of materials with which a given logical or scientific edifice can be constructed. Not only Frege's theory of number, which we shall deal with in Lecture VII, but the whole theory of physical concepts which will be outlined in our next two lectures, is inspired by mathematical logic, and could never have been imagined without it.

In both these cases, and in many others, we shall appeal to a certain principle called "the principle of abstraction." This principle, which might equally well be called "the principle which dispenses with abstraction," and is one which clears away incredible accumulations of metaphysical lumber, was directly suggested by mathematical logic, and could hardly have been proved or practically used without its help. The principle will be explained in our fourth lecture, but its use may be briefly indicated in advance. When a group of objects have that kind of similarity which we are inclined to attribute to possession of a common quality, the principle in question shows that membership of the group will serve all the purposes of the supposed common quality, and that therefore, unless some common quality is actually known, the group or class of similar objects may be used to replace the common quality, which need not be assumed to exist. In this and other ways, the indirect uses of even the later parts of mathematical logic are very great; but it is now time to turn our attention to its philosophical foundations.

In every proposition and in every inference there is, besides the particular subject-matter concerned, a certain *form*, a way in which the constituents of the proposition or inference are put together. If I say, "Socrates is mortal," "Jones is angry," "The sun is hot," there is something in common in these three cases, something indicated by the word "is." What is in common is the *form* of the proposition, not an actual constituent. If I say a number of things about Socrates —that he was an Athenian, that he married Xantippe, that he drank the hemlock—there is a common constituent, namely Socrates, in all the propositions I enunciate, but they have diverse forms. If, on the other hand, I take any one of these propositions and replace its constituents, one at a time, by other constituents, the form remains constant, but no constituent remains. Take (say) the series of propositions, "Socrates drank the hemlock," "Coleridge drank the hemlock," "Coleridge drank opium," "Coleridge ate opium." The form remains unchanged throughout this series, but all the constituents are altered. Thus form is not another constituent, but is the way the constituents are put together. It is forms, in this sense, that are the proper object of philosophical logic.

It is obvious that the knowledge of logical forms is something quite different from knowledge of existing things. The form of "Socrates drank the hemlock" is not an existing thing like Socrates or the hemlock, nor does it even have that close relation to existing things that drinking has. It is something altogether more abstract and remote. We might understand all the separate words of a sentence without understanding the sentence: if a sentence is long and complicated, this is apt to happen. In such a case we have knowledge of the constituents, but not of the form. We may also have

knowledge of the form without having knowledge of the
constituents. If I say, "Rorarius drank the hemlock," those
among you who have never heard of Rorarius (supposing
there are any) will understand the form, without having
knowledge of all the constituents. In order to understand a
sentence, it is necessary to have knowledge both of the constituents and of the particular instance of the form. It is in
this way that a sentence conveys information, since it tells us
that certain known objects are related according to a certain
known form. Thus some kind of knowledge of logical forms,
though with most people it is not explicit, is involved in all
understanding of discourse. It is the business of philosophical
logic to extract this knowledge from its concrete integuments,
and to render it explicit and pure.

In all inference, form alone is essential: the particular
subject-matter is irrelevant except as securing the truth of
the premisses. This is one reason for the great importance
of logical form. When I say, "Socrates was a man, all men
are mortal, therefore Socrates was mortal," the connection of
premisses and conclusion does not in any way depend upon
its being Socrates and man and mortality that I am mentioning. The general form of the inference may be expressed
in some such words as, "If a thing has a certain property,
and whatever has this property has a certain other property,
then the thing in question also has that other property."
Here no particular things or properties are mentioned: the
proposition is absolutely general. All inferences, when stated
fully, are instances of propositions having this kind of generality. If they seem to depend upon the subject-matter
otherwise than as regards the truth of the premisses, that is
because the premisses have not been all explicitly stated. In
logic, it is a waste of time to deal with inferences concerning particular cases: we deal throughout with completely
general and purely formal implications, leaving it to other
sciences to discover when the hypotheses are verified and
when they are not.

But the forms of propositions giving rise to inferences are
not the simplest forms: they are always hypothetical, stating

that if one proposition is true, then so is another. Before considering inference, therefore, logic must consider those simpler forms which inference presupposes. Here the traditional logic failed completely: it believed that there was only one form of simple proposition (*i.e.*, of proposition not stating a relation between two or more other propositions), namely, the form which ascribes a predicate to a subject. This is the appropriate form in assigning the qualities of a given thing—we may say "this thing is round, and red, and so on." Grammar favours this form, but philosophically it is so far from universal that it is not even very common. If we say "this thing is bigger than that," we are not assigning a mere quality of "this," but a relation of "this" and "that." We might express the same fact by saying "that thing is smaller than this," where grammatically the subject is changed. Thus propositions stating that two things have a certain relation have a different form from subject-predicate propositions, and the failure to perceive this difference or to allow for it has been the source of many errors in traditional metaphysics.

The belief or unconscious conviction that all propositions are of the subject-predicate form—in other words, that every fact consists in some thing having some quality—has rendered most philosophers incapable of giving any account of the world of science and daily life. If they had been honestly anxious to give such an account, they would probably have discovered their error very quickly; but most of them were less anxious to understand the world of science and daily life, than to convict it of unreality in the interests of a super-sensible "real" world. Belief in the unreality of the world of sense arises with irresistible force in certain moods—moods which, I imagine, have some simple physiological basis, but are none the less powerfully persuasive. The conviction born of these moods is the source of most mysticism and of most metaphysics. When the emotional intensity of such a mood subsides, a man who is in the habit of reasoning will search for logical reasons in favour of the belief which he finds in himself. But since the belief already exists, he will be very hospitable to any reason that suggests itself. The paradoxes apparently proved by his logic are really the paradoxes of mysticism, and are the goal which he feels his logic must reach if it is to be in accordance with insight. It is in this way that logic has been pursued by those of the great philosophers who were mystics—notably Plato, Spinoza, and Hegel. But since they usually took for granted the supposed insight of the mystic emotion, their logical doctrines were presented with a certain dryness, and were believed by their disciples to be quite independent of the sudden illumination from which they sprang. Nevertheless their origin clung to them, and they remained—to borrow a useful word from Mr. Santayana—"malicious" in regard to the world of science and common sense. It is only so that we can account for the complacency with which philosophers have accepted the inconsistency of their doctrines with all the common and scientific facts which seem best established and most worthy of belief.

The logic of mysticism shows, as is natural, the defects which are inherent in anything malicious. While the mystic mood is dominant, the need of logic is not felt; as the mood fades, the impulse to logic reasserts itself, but with a desire to retain the vanishing insight, or at least to prove that it *was* insight, and that what seems to contradict it is illusion. The logic which thus arises is not quite disinterested or candid, and is inspired by a certain hatred of the daily world to which it is to be applied. Such an attitude naturally does not tend to the best results. Everyone knows that to read an author's books simply in order to refute him is not the way to understand him; and to read the book of Nature with a conviction that it is all illusion is just as unlikely to lead to understanding. If our logic is to find the common world intelligible, it must not be hostile, but must be inspired by a genuine acceptance such as is not usually to be found among metaphysicians.

Traditional logic, since it holds that all propositions have the subject-predicate form, is unable to admit the reality of relations: all relations, it maintains, must be reduced to properties of the apparently related terms. There are many ways of refuting this opinion; one of the easiest is derived from the consideration of what are called "asymmetrical" relations. In order to explain this, I will first explain two independent ways of classifying relations.

Some relations when they hold between A and B, also hold between B and A. Such, for example, is the relation "brother or sister." If A is a brother or sister of B, then B is a brother or sister of A. Such again is any kind of similarity, say similarity of colour. Any kind of dissimilarity is also of this kind: if the colour of A is unlike the colour of B, then the colour of B is unlike the colour of A. Relations of this sort are called *symmetrical*. Thus a relation is symmetrical if, whenever it holds between A and B, it also holds between B and A.

All relations that are not symmetrical are called *non-symmetrical*. Thus "brother" is non-symmetrical, because, if A is a brother of B, it may happen that B is a *sister* of A.

A relation is called *asymmetrical* when, if it holds between A and B, it *never* holds between B and A. Thus husband, father, grandfather, etc., are asymmetrical relations. So are *before, after, greater, above, to the right of,* etc. All the relations that give rise to series are of this kind.

Classification into symmetrical, asymmetrical, and merely non-symmetrical relations is the first of the two classifications we had to consider. The second is into transitive, intransitive, and merely non-transitive relations, which are defined as follows.

A relation is said to be *transitive*, if, whenever it holds between A and B and also between B and C, it holds between A and C. Thus *before, after, greater, above* are transitive. All relations giving rise to series are transitive, but so are many others. The transitive relations just mentioned were asymmetrical, but many transitive relations are symmetrical—for instance, equality in any respect, exact identity of colour, being equally numerous (as applied to collections), and so on.

A relation is said to be *non-transitive* whenever it is not transitive. Thus "brother" is non-transitive, because a brother of one's brother may be oneself. All kinds of dissimilarity are non-transitive.

A relation is said to be *intransitive* when, if A has the relation to B, and B to C, A never has it to C. Thus "father" is intransitive. So is such a relation as "one inch taller" or "one year later."

Let us now, in the light of this classification, return to the question whether all relations can be reduced to predications.

In the case of symmetrical relations—*i.e.*, relations which, if they hold between A and B, also hold between B and A— some kind of plausibility can be given to this doctrine. A symmetrical relation which is transitive, such as equality, can be regarded as expressing possession of some common property, while one which is not transitive, such as inequality, can be regarded as expressing possession of different properties. But when we come to asymmetrical relations, such as before and after, greater and less, etc., the attempt to reduce them to properties becomes obviously impossible. When for example, two things are merely known to be unequal, without our knowing which is greater, we may say that the inequality results from their having different magnitudes, because inequality is a symmetrical relation; but to say that when one thing is *greater* than another, and not merely unequal to it, that means that they have different magnitudes, is formally incapable of explaining the facts. For if the other thing had been greater than the one, the magnitudes would also have been different, though the fact to be explained would not have been the same. Thus mere *difference* of magnitude is not *all* that is involved, since if it were, there would be no difference between one thing being greater than another, and the other being greater than the one. We shall have to say that the one magnitude is *greater* than the other, and thus we shall have failed to get rid of the relation "greater." In short, both possession of the same property and possession of different properties are *symmetrical* relations, and therefore cannot account for the existence of *asymmetrical* relations.

Asymmetrical relations are involved in all series—in space and time, greater and less, whole and part, and many others of the most important characteristics of the actual world. All these aspects, therefore, the logic which reduces everything to subjects and predicates is compelled to condemn as error and mere appearance. To those whose logic is not malicious, such a wholesale condemnation appears impossible. And in fact there is no reason except prejudice, so far as I can discover, for denying the reality of relations. When once their reality is admitted, all *logical* grounds for supposing the world of sense to be illusory disappear. If this is to be supposed, it must be frankly and simply on the ground of mystic insight unsupported by argument. It is impossible to argue against what professes to be insight, so long as it does not argue in its own favour. As logicians, therefore, we may admit the possibility of the mystic's world, while yet, so long as we do not have his insight, we must continue to study the everyday world with which we are familiar. But when he contends that our world is impossible, then our logic is ready to repel his attack. And the first step in creating the logic which is to perform this service is the recognition of the reality of relations.

Relations which have two terms are only one kind of relations. A relation may have three terms, or four, or any number. Relations of two terms, being the simplest, have received more attention than the others, and have generally been alone considered by philosophers, both those who accepted and those who denied the reality of relations. But other relations have their importance, and are indispensable in the solution of certain problems. Jealousy, for example, is a relation between three people. Professor Royce mentions the relation "giving": when A gives B to C, that is a relation of three terms.[7] When a man says to his wife: "My dear, I wish you could induce Angelina to accept Edwin," his wish con-

---

[7] *Encyclopædia of the Philosophical Sciences*, Vol. I, p. 97.

stitutes a relation between four people, himself, his wife, Angelina, and Edwin. Thus such relations are by no means recondite or rare. But in order to explain exactly how they differ from relations of two terms, we must embark upon a classification of the logical forms of facts, which is the first business of logic, and the business in which the traditional logic has been most deficient.

The existing world consists of many things with many qualities and relations. A complete description of the existing world would require not only a catalogue of the things, but also a mention of all their qualities and relations. We should have to know not only this, that, and the other thing, but also which was red, which yellow, which was earlier than which, which was between which two others, and so on. When I speak of a "fact," I do not mean one of the simple things in the world; I mean that a certain thing has a certain quality, or that certain things have a certain relation. Thus, for example, I should not call Napoleon a fact, but I should call it a fact that he was ambitious, or that he married Josephine. Now a fact, in this sense, is never simple, but always has two or more constituents. When it simply assigns a quality to a thing, it has only two constituents, the thing and the quality. When it consists of a relation between two things, it has three constituents, the things and the rela- tion. When it consists of a relation between three things, it has four constituents, and so on. The constituents of facts, in the sense in which we are using the word "fact," are not other facts, but are things and qualities or relations. When we say that there are relations of more than two terms, we mean that there are single facts consisting of a single relation and more than two things. I do not mean that one relation of two terms may hold between A and B, and also between A and C, as, for example, a man is the son of his father and also the son of his mother. This constitutes two distinct facts: if we choose to treat it as one fact, it is a fact which has facts for its constituents. But the facts I am speaking of have no facts among their constituents, but only things and relations. For example, when A is jealous of B on account of C, there is only one fact, involving three people; there are not two instances of jealousy, but only one. It is in such cases that I speak of a relation of three terms, where the simplest possible fact in which the relation occurs is one involving three things in addition to the relation. And the same applies to relations of four terms or five or any other number. All such relations must be admitted in our inventory of the logical forms of facts: two facts involving the same number of things have the same form, and two which involve different numbers of things have different forms.

Given any fact, there is an assertion which expresses the fact. The fact itself is objective, and independent of our thought or opinion about it; but the assertion is something which involves thought, and may be either true or false. An assertion may be positive or negative: we may assert that Charles I was executed, or that he did *not* die in his bed. A negative assertion may be said to be a *denial*. Given a form of words which must be either true or false, such as "Charles I died in his bed," we may either assert or deny this form of words: in the one case we have a positive assertion, in the other a negative one. A form of words which must be either true or false I shall call a *proposition*. Thus a proposition is the same as what may be significantly asserted or denied. A proposition which expresses what we have called a fact, *i.e.*, which, when asserted, asserts that a certain thing has a certain quality, or that certain things have a certain relation, will be called an atomic proposition, because, as we shall see immediately, there are other propositions into which atomic propositions enter in a way analogous to that in which atoms enter into molecules. Atomic propositions, although, like facts, they may have any one of an infinite number of forms, are only one kind of propositions. All other kinds are more complicated. In order to preserve the parallelism in language as regards facts and propositions, we shall give the name "atomic facts" to the facts we have hitherto been considering. Thus atomic facts are what determine whether atomic propositions are to be asserted or denied.

Whether an atomic proposition, such as "this is red," or "this is before that," is to be asserted or denied can only be known empirically. Perhaps one atomic fact may sometimes be capable of being inferred from another, though I do not believe this to be the case; but in any case it cannot be inferred from premisses no one of which is an atomic fact. It follows that, if atomic facts are to be known at all, some at least must be known without inference. The atomic facts which we come to know in this way are the facts of sense-perception; at any rate, the facts of sense-perception are those which we most obviously and certainly come to know in this way. If we knew all atomic facts, and also knew that there were none except those we knew, we should, theoretically, be able to infer all truths of whatever form.[8] Thus logic would then supply us with the whole of the apparatus required. But in the first acquisition of knowledge concerning atomic facts, logic is useless. In pure logic, no atomic fact is ever mentioned: we confine ourselves wholly to forms, without asking ourselves what objects can fill the forms. Thus pure logic is independent of atomic facts; but conversely, they are, in a sense, independent of logic. Pure logic and atomic facts are the two poles, the wholly *a priori* and the wholly empirical. But between the two lies a vast intermediate region, which we must now briefly explore.

"Molecular" propositions are such as contain conjunctions —*if, or, and, unless,* etc.—and such words are the marks of a molecular proposition. Consider such an assertion as, "If it rains, I shall bring my umbrella." This assertion is just as capable of truth or falsehood as the assertion of an atomic proposition, but it is obvious that either the corresponding fact, or the nature of the correspondence with fact, must be quite different from what it is in the case of an atomic proposition. Whether it rains, and whether I bring my um-

---

[8] This perhaps requires modification in order to include such facts as beliefs and wishes, since such facts apparently contain propositions as components. Such facts, though not strictly atomic, must be supposed included if the statement in the text is to be true.

brella, are each severally matters of atomic fact, ascertainable by observation. But the connection of the two involved in saying that *if* the one happens, *then* the other will happen, is something radically different from either of the two separately. It does not require for its truth that it should actually rain, or that I should actually bring my umbrella; even if the weather is cloudless, it may still be true that I should have brought my umbrella if the weather had been different. Thus we have here a connection of two propositions, which does not depend upon whether they are to be asserted or denied, but only upon the second being inferable from the first. Such propositions, therefore, have a form which is different from that of any atomic proposition.

Such propositions are important to logic, because all inference depends upon them. If I have told you that if it rains I shall bring my umbrella, and if you see that there is a steady downpour, you can infer that I shall bring my umbrella. There can be no inference except where propositions are connected in some such way, so that from the truth or falsehood of the one something follows as to the truth or falsehood of the other. It seems to be the case that we can sometimes know molecular propositions, as in the above instance of the umbrella, when we do not know whether the component atomic propositions are true or false. The *practical* utility of inference rests upon this fact.

The next kind of propositions we have to consider are *general* propositions, such as "all men are mortal," "all equilateral triangles are equiangular." And with these belong propositions in which the word "some" occurs, such as "some men are philosophers" or "some philosophers are not wise." These are the denials of general propositions, namely (in the above instances), of "all men are non-philosophers" and "all philosophers are wise." We will call propositions containing the word "some" *negative* general propositions, and those containing the word "all" *positive* general propositions. These propositions, it will be seen, begin to have the appearance of the propositions in logical text-books. But their peculiarity and complexity are not known to the text-books,

and the problems which they raise are only discussed in the
most superficial manner.

When we were discussing atomic facts, we saw that we
should be able, theoretically, to infer all other truths by
logic if we knew all atomic facts and also knew that there
were no other atomic facts besides those we knew. The
knowledge that there are no other atomic facts is positive
general knowledge; it is the knowledge that "all atomic
facts are known to me," or at least "all atomic facts are
in this collection"—however the collection may be given.
It is easy to see that general propositions, such as "all men
are mortal," cannot be known by inference from atomic
facts alone. If we could know each individual man, and
know that he was mortal, that would not enable us to know
that all men are mortal, unless we *knew* that those were all
the men there are, which is a general proposition. If we
knew every other existing thing throughout the universe,
and knew that each separate thing was not an immortal
man, that would not give us our result unless we *knew* that
we had explored the whole universe, *i.e.*, unless we knew
"all things belong to this collection of things I have examined." Thus general truths cannot be inferred from particular truths alone, but must, if they are to be known, be
either self-evident, or inferred from premisses of which at
least one is a general truth. But all *empirical* evidence is of
particular truths. Hence, if there is any knowledge of general truths at all, there must be *some* knowledge of general
truths which is independent of empirical evidence, *i.e.*,
does not depend upon the data of sense.

The above conclusion, of which we had an instance in
the case of the inductive principle, is important, since it
affords a refutation of the older empiricists. They believed
that all our knowledge is derived from the senses and dependent upon them. We see that, if this view is to be maintained, we must refuse to admit that we know any general
propositions. It is perfectly possible logically that this should
be the case, but it does not appear to be so in fact, and
indeed no one would dream of maintaining such a view

except a theorist at the last extremity. We must therefore admit that there is general knowledge not derived from sense, and that some of this knowledge is not obtained by inference but is primitive.

Such general knowledge is to be found in logic. Whether there is any such knowledge not derived from logic, I do not know; but in logic, at any rate, we have such knowledge. It will be remembered that we excluded from pure logic such propositions as, "Socrates is a man, all men are mortal, therefore Socrates is mortal," because *Socrates* and *man* and *mortal* are empirical terms, only to be understood through particular experience. The corresponding proposition in pure logic is: "If anything has a certain property, and whatever has this property has a certain other property, then the thing in question has the other property." This proposition is absolutely general: it applies to all things and all properties. And it is quite self-evident. Thus in such propositions of pure logic we have the self-evident general propositions of which we were in search.

A proposition such as "If Socrates is a man, and all men are mortal, then Socrates is mortal," is true in virtue of its *form* alone. Its truth, in this hypothetical form, does not depend upon whether Socrates actually is a man, nor upon whether in fact all men are mortal; thus it is equally true when we substitute other terms for *Socrates* and *man* and *mortal.* The general truth of which it is an instance is purely formal, and belongs to logic. Since it does not mention any particular thing, or even any particular quality or relation, it is wholly independent of the accidental facts of the existent world, and can be known, theoretically, without any experience of particular things or their qualities and relations.

Logic, we may say, consists of two parts. The first part investigates what propositions are and what forms they may have; this part enumerates the different kinds of atomic propositions, of molecular propositions, of general propositions, and so on. The second part consists of certain supremely general propositions, which assert the truth of all propositions of certain forms. This second part merges into pure mathematics, whose propositions all turn out, on analysis, to be such general formal truths. The first part, which merely enumerates forms, is the more difficult, and philosophically the more important; and it is the recent progress in this first part, more than anything else, that has rendered a truly scientific discussion of many philosophical problems possible.

The problem of the nature of judgment or belief may be taken as an example of a problem whose solution depends upon an adequate inventory of logical forms. We have already seen how the supposed universality of the subject-predicate form made it impossible to give a right analysis of serial order, and therefore made space and time unintelligible. But in this case it was only necessary to admit relations of two terms. The case of judgment demands the admission of more complicated forms. If all judgments were true, we might suppose that a judgment consisted in apprehension of a *fact*, and that the apprehension was a relation of a mind to the fact. From poverty in the logical inventory, this view has often been held. But it leads to absolutely insoluble difficulties in the case of error. Suppose I believe that Charles I died in his bed. There is no objective fact "Charles I's death in his bed" to which I can have a relation of apprehension. Charles I and death and his bed are objective, but they are not, except in my thought, put together as my false belief supposes. It is therefore necessary, in analysing a belief, to look for some other logical form than a two-term relation. Failure to realise this necessity has, in my opinion, vitiated almost everything that has hitherto been written on the theory of knowledge, making the problem of error insoluble and the difference between belief and perception inexplicable.

Modern logic, as I hope is now evident, has the effect of enlarging our abstract imagination, and providing an infinite number of possible hypotheses to be applied in the analysis of any complex fact. In this respect it is the exact opposite of the logic practised by the classical tradition. In that logic, hypotheses which seem *prima facie* possible are professedly proved impossible, and it is decreed in advance that reality must have a certain special character. In modern logic, on the contrary, while the *prima facie* hypotheses as a rule remain admissible, others, which only logic would have suggested, are added to our stock, and are very often found to be indispensable if a right analysis of the facts is to be obtained. The old logic put thought in fetters, while the new logic gives it wings. It has, in my opinion, introduced the same kind of advance into philosophy as Galileo introduced into physics, making it possible at last to see what kinds of problems may be capable of solution, and what kinds must be abandoned as beyond human powers. And where a solution appears possible, the new logic provides a method which enables us to obtain results that do not merely embody personal idiosyncrasies, but must command the assent of all who are competent to form an opinion.

*   *   *

Russell returned to England, which was soon an England at war. A militant pacifist "tortured by patriotism," he felt as if he heard the voice of God directing him to do everything possible to bring an end to the conflict. He collaborated with individuals and groups; he wrote and spoke on street corners; he even carried on for about a year a hectic and impossible friendship with D. H. Lawrence because they held one view in common. Having lived in Germany, Russell favored an early German victory with an England still strong rather than a general holocaust, with a shattered England and the Continent in chaos. He still thinks he was right, pointing to Fascism, Nazism and Communism growing out of the prolonged war. He admits that Russia would have had a revolution in any case, but not one so earth-shaking, if she had not already been undermined by disaster.

Whatever Russell's wisdom or unwisdom at the time, he was prosecuted in 1918 and sent to prison for four and a half months. Through the solicitations of powerful friends, he was permitted to read and write as much as he liked, provided that he did not write anti-war propaganda.

The result was the *Introduction to Mathematical Philosophy,* containing the famous chapter on "Descriptions" and preparation for another important book, *The Analysis of Mind,* which contained his theory of *neutral monism,* largely inspired by William James.

WILLIAM PEPPERELL MONTAGUE
[1873–1953]

In the Harvard Department of Philosophy at the turn of the century, there was not only a world-famous galaxy of professors—William James, Josiah Royce, Hugo Munsterberg, George Herbert Palmer, George Santayana; and off the campus, as an occasional visitor, the tragic, jobless Charles S. Peirce—there was also a corresponding galaxy of remarkable graduate students—John E. Boodin, William E. Savery, Arthur O. Lovejoy, Wilmon H. Sheldon, William Pepperell Montague and Ralph Barton Perry. "Of us all," says Professor Sheldon, the surviving member of the group, "Montague was considered by the department the most brilliant and original," and Peirce agreed with them.

Those to whom Montague is only a name will find a sketch of his adventurous philosophy and something of his delightfully disarming personality in "Confessions of an Animistic Materialist," included in *The Ways of Things;* and in the Montague memorial issue of *The Journal of Philosophy* (October 14, 1954), the stranger will find beautifully affectionate tributes by colleagues who had known him for years. He taught philosophy at Columbia University for nearly half a century and was head of the department at Barnard College.

While recalling these Harvard years and expressing gratitude to his distinguished teachers, especially Royce, Montague wrote: "For Peirce himself I had a kind of worship. While his intellect was cold and clear, his metaphysical imagination was capricious, scintillating, and unbridled, and his whole personality was so rich and mysterious that he seemed a being apart, a superman. I would rather have been like him than like anyone else I ever met."

As a matter of fact, Montague was a good deal like Peirce in those respects—but with no suggestion of the arrogance and omniscience begotten by loneliness. On the contrary, he had an in-

313

imitable way of presenting a bold hypothesis, a fantastic insight, or even a bit of conventional optimism, as if he were shyly confessing a crime. This semi-playful sense of guilt is perhaps not so surprising, after all, for his lifelong interest was the mind-body problem—from his first paper, "A Plea for Soul Substance" (1899), to the epilogue of his last book, *Great Visions of Philosophy*, and he repeatedly put forward ingenious arguments for the independence of consciousness and its possible survival of bodily death, by conceiving consciousness as a form of potential energy! He thus managed to bewilder or antagonize both the spiritualists, who were suspicious of physical categories, and the materialists, who were jealous of such free use of their sacred terminology. But let the reader actually turn to *The Chances of Surviving Death* and then turn back to Plato's *Phaedo*.

Montague's ethical theory was illustrated by his bookplate with the figure of Prometheus suggesting liberty; St. Francis, love; and Dionysus, enthusiasm; and elaborated in his brilliant volume of Terry Lectures, *Belief Unbound: A Promethean Religion for the Modern World*. He insists on an autonomous ethics, "a sanctionless morality," for as might can never make right, divinity itself, however benign, cannot alter the eternal forms of the good. Yet he was deeply interested in theology, an unorthodox theology, and on the basis of two postulates, "(1) The Problem of Good is insoluble in terms of the traditional Atheism. (2) The Problem of Evil is insoluble in the terms of the traditional Theism," he argued for a God unlimited in goodness but limited in power.

Underlying all of these discussions was Montague's general conception of philosophy, which he presented in the first of his Carus lectures (1933), and published as the first chapter of his magnificent swan song, *Great Visions of Philosophy*.

* * *

PHILOSOPHY AS VISION

There are many kinds of philosophers and many definitions of philosophy. Implicit in all of these definitions is the conception of a domain of inquiry broader and vaguer, deeper and more subtle than the domain of ordinary knowledge. As I see it, there are three main types of question which philosophy asks. They are questions of methodology, of metaphysics, and of axiology.

First: What are the ways in which we should attain and verify our knowledge, and how should we interpret truth when we have attained it—as subjective and dependent upon our minds, or as objective and identical with reality? These are the questions comprising methodology with its two branches, logic and epistemology.

Second: What is the general structure of our cosmos and what are the fundamental forms and principles which under-lie that structure and which are presupposed by the sciences that investigate its parts? These are the questions of meta-physics—of synthetic metaphysics or cosmology, and of analytic metaphysics or ontology.

Third: What are the kinds of thing which, whether actually existent or merely ideal, arouse in us the specific attitude of "approval" and to which in token of that attitude we apply the name "values"—be they exemplified in the beauty of sensory combinations such as those of tone and color, or in the righteousness or moral goodness of character and conduct? These are the questions of axiology, including ethics and esthetics.

The three groups of questions, when considered in themselves and in their relations to one another, cover pretty completely the entire field of philosophy.

If the foregoing is an approximately correct account of the meaning of philosophy and of its main departments, the nature of its relations to its nearest neighbors, science and religion, is easy to see. Philosophy differs from science in that its questions are more comprehensive and more fundamental, with the natural result that its answers have none of the definitely verifiable character that scientists demand for their answers. Philosophy resembles science not in the success of its inquiry but in the spirit in which the inquiry is made. The philosopher, like the scientist, is engaged in an intellectual enterprise. They both seek to attain the truth irrespective of whether that truth shall turn out to be glad or sad, edifying or demoralizing. Dispassionate concern for objective truth governs or ought to govern every intellectual quest, whether broadly philosophic or narrowly scientific.

The relation in which philosophy stands to religion is the opposite of that in which it stands to science. Religion and philosophy resemble each other in content but are contrasted in spirit. Both seek answers to ultimate rather than proximate problems concerning the universe and man's place in it; but the way of religion is not the way of philosophy. Instead of the audacious individualistic attempt of the philosopher to plumb the mysteries of nature with his own little mind, the religionist, with humility, piety, and faith joins up with bands of his fellows in the acceptance and practice of beliefs which he feels to be not his own discovery but a divine revelation to men greater than himself, the saints and prophets of his church. Even when the religiously minded person consents to describe his creed as the one true philosophy, he will stress the fact that it is not his philosophy but God's. And conversely, when the philosopher arrives by free speculative inquiry at a result identical with the creed of his ancestors, he will stress the fact that his conclusions are vindicated by reason rather than accepted on faith.

Up to this point I hope and believe that I have said nothing very new and nothing that is not in accord with the traditional and conventional conception of philosophy and its affiliations. I wish now to offer for your consideration some ideas that I have deeply at heart as to what might be and ought to be the aim and function of the philosopher. These ideas, though not in contradiction to the conventional account already given, involve a reversal of what, if I am not mistaken, has been the main emphasis in the traditional procedure of philosophy.

Knowledge or truth is like a magnitude of two dimensions. We wish it to be as broad as possible and we wish it to have as high an approximation to certainty as possible. Breadth and richness of content constitute its extensive dimension, degree of validity its intensive dimension. A system of perfect knowledge would cover the entire range of being and each of its propositions would possess complete certainty. Now, in the search for knowledge as in most other human undertakings, we are forced to recognize not only that perfection in any respect is unattainable, but that even the approach to perfection in some one direction is often incompatible with the approach to perfection in some other direction. He who would master a single trade must resign himself to ignorance of others; a Jack-of-all-trades can be master of none. To be deep is to be narrow, and to be broad is to be shallow. This tragic incompatibility of the extensive and the intensive coefficients of success is, to be sure, not always present. In some types of enterprise there is the blessing of a positive rather than a negative correlation between depth and breadth; but usually we must choose the one or the other as the object of our principal emphasis.

Assuredly in philosophy such a choice is forced upon us, however loath we may be to recognize it. If in a moment of detachment from our private preoccupations with this or that phase of philosophy we gaze upon the panorama of mighty systems from Democritus and Plato to Hegel and Bergson, we shall I think be struck by two facts significant in themselves and still more significant in their relation to each other. First, the value of the great philosophers consists far more in breadth and richness of vision than in cogency or rigor of demonstration. Second, in each of the famous systems there is implicitly or explicitly manifested a pathetic pride on the part of its author in the degree of certainty with which his far-flung theories have been proved.

Now it is common enough to find people who are proud of characteristics in which they are really weak, and correspondingly humble in their appraisal of the virtues which they do possess. But in the case of the great philosophers this familiar and engaging human blindness is not only pathetic and comical but most unfortunate in its effects upon the prosperity of the enterprise to which both they and we are committed. Is it not too obvious to mention that the differing pictures of the cosmos cannot all be true, if only because of their contradictoriness to one another? And is it not almost as obvious that no one of them even if it were true in fact, could be proved to be so for reason? The abysmal gap between a metaphysician's conclusions and the meager data on which they are founded is not to be bridged by any logic of demonstration. If the worth of philosophy were to be measured by its certainty, philosophy would be in a very poor way. Despite this, the claim to cogency is always present. Are we not ourselves, as teachers, obsessed by this claim when we strive to disprove this or that doctrine opposed to our own? And do we not in our courses produce in the minds of many of our own students the conviction that philosophy is something of a fraud and a bluff—pretending to have scientific validity while completely lacking in that consensus of agreement that science exhibits? If this were all, we could probably bear it; for the disillusionment of students should not be allowed to spoil the games played by their teachers. But unfortunately this is by no means all. Disillusionment and a mood of defeatism is making itself felt throughout our entire guild. How can we go on with speculative theories about the constitution of reality when the winds of scientific knowledge in physics, chemistry, biology, and psychology are sweeping around us and covering the once fertile fields of fancy with the arid sands of fact? The ancient Ionians were not plagued with quantum mechanics, benzene rings, reflex arcs, and "learning curves," and there were few known facts to cramp their style. But for us it is different.

When something of the same fate that impends for us overtook our cousins, the theologians, we looked on condescendingly and observed with amusement the growth of unemployment among demons and deities, as one group after another of supernatural powers was replaced and their work more efficiently performed by the machinery of natural law. But now, perhaps, we shall find that Comte was right, and that metaphysical conceptions are quite as useless and far less exciting than the gods and ghosts of our fathers.

The growth of science and the spread of the scientific spirit, with its stress upon the concrete and the particular, the practically useful and the empirically verifiable, have lent a vast momentum to the quest for certainty. And, in the light of this quest, the grandiose creations of the metaphysical imagination appear thin and insubstantial. For at their very best they are terribly uncertain; and if certainty is to be the single goal of the mind's activity it would seem as though the knell of philosophy had struck. Despite the somberness of the prospect there are several plans that are being hopefully advanced for meeting the present emergency.

There is in the first place the old plan that has been employed by the devotees of various subjects, and particularly by philosophers during periods of depression—the plan of substituting the history of a subject for the subject itself. Even though our primary function as philosophers be out-moded we can fall back upon the past and preserve our lives by feeding like cannibal ghouls upon our glorious dead. There are, however, two objections to this most obvious of the schemes for coping with the present predicament. As the bones are increasingly picked, the pickings grow thinner. It is more and more difficult to discover new and worth-while facts about Berkeley, for example, when so many facts have already been discovered by those who preceded us. A second and more serious objection to restricting philosophy to the history of philosophy is that for all except professional historians an interest in the history of a subject depends largely upon an interest in the subject. If philosophy itself is to cease it will not be long before its history will be relegated to some rather unimportant footnotes to history as such.

The second of the current policies proposed for philosophers is to beat a final retreat from the field of metaphysics and con-centrate their forces on the problems of human nature and conduct. "Natural philosophy," it is urged, should pass in fact as it has already passed in name, and the sciences of the physical world should be left alone to do in theory what they will do anyhow in practice: viz., settle their own difficulties without the aid of well-meaning but futile and meddlesome philosophical amateurs. There is, we are told, no longer any need—if, indeed, there ever was any need—for a metaphysical superstate to arbitrate the disputes and organize and unify the relations between the several groups of natural scientists.

Now to this proposal for a wholesale retreat of the

philosophers from the field of nature to the field of human nature, there is the grave objection that it is likely at best to afford only a temporary respite. For in the course of another generation or so the social scientists may become regular scientists and we shall then be driven from our new trenches by the same attacks as those which are now driving us from the ones we have traditionally occupied. Psychology has already seceded from our sovereignty. The newer subjects of anthropology, sociology, economics, and political science betray no sign of interest in our existence. I see nothing whatever to justify the hope that the type of speculative inquiry constituting philosophy will be permitted to arrogate to itself the study of human habits and human values. In this field no less than in the field of matter, empirical observation and experiment, more or less supplemented by mathematical calculation and deduction, will replace philosophical argumentation as the means for ascertaining the facts of existence.

A third and last plan of retreat remains—the plan of those who may, perhaps, be called the Cambridge School. One thinks here of Moore and Russell, Whitehead in his pre-cosmological period, Susan Stebbing and other members of the Aristotelian Society, and of Wittgenstein. If I am not mistaken, what is explicitly or implicitly advocated by this group is the policy of restricting philosophy neither to history nor to social problems, but to a determinedly rigorous analysis of experience and its categories.

To this attempt to save philosophy from the advance of science I find two objections. In the first place the field of refuge is very narrow and pretty dry. If metaphysical analysis is to attain the absolute rigor of mathematical demonstration it will be necessary to limit its subject matter to such bits and forms of experience as can be identified and defined with complete absence of ambiguity. Even the rather unexciting tables and chairs upon which the philosopher has relied in the past for undisputed illustrations of this or that will have to be abandoned as being far too rich and juicy, and as fairly reeking with vague conflicting meanings. Patches of color would be better. Have their hue and brightness accurately determined by the methods of physics and then take them as they would appear to a human observer whose precise degree of visual acuity had been measured by the methods of psychology. Even with such rather meager material there would be the danger that the cognitive and emotional preoccupations of the observer would creep in to corrupt the purity of the sensory datum. The stuff of concrete experience is like quicksand and far too oozy and transitory to be crystallized into forms freed from all indefiniteness. There would be a tendency for the new analytic philosophy to follow the evolution of modern mathematics and withdraw more and more from the domain of intuitable stuff to the domain of forms artificially conventionalized and therefore perfectly controllable. These forms, if they were not to coincide with those already preempted by mathematics, would have to be, or at any rate would tend to be, not forms of experience but forms of discourse about experience—in short, forms of grammar. The leading member of the group of philosophers that we are discussing declares to us that metaphysics (old style) is nothing but "bad grammar." And apropos of this famous jibe a colleague of mine has remarked that, while the new metaphysics may be good grammar, it appears to be nothing much else. Now of course grammar is all right, yet it is surely a far small cry from the philosophy that most of us love.

But, in the second place, be the new stuff what it may and as good and great as you please, I doubt that even here philosophy will find permanent sanctuary. Despite the valiant attempt of Professor Stebbing in her recent paper before the Aristotelian Society to differentiate metaphysical analysis from the type of mathematical analysis investigated by modern logic, I fear for the reasons that I have stated that an increasing demand for increasing rigor will inevitably result in a complete symbolic formalization. And, if that result does come about, the only proper people to handle the new metaphysical grammar will be our colleagues the mathematical logicians or logisticians. And as to them I venture the prediction that at no distant day their already noticeable restlessness at the meetings of old-time philosophers will culminate in a

definite secession from our body. They will go the way of the
psychologists and set up shop for themselves. And when they
go they will take with them what is alleged to be our last
remaining function of distinctive and legitimate inquiry.

In short, as philosophers we appear to be doomed. Province
after province of our once mighty empire is being invaded.
Natural scientists and social scientists, historians, grammarians
and mathematicians hem us in and perform our one-time
business better than we can ourselves perform it.

Where can we go and what can we do?

The quest for certainty—happily so christened by John
Dewey but by him also happily not too meticulously pursued—
that is the real source of our trouble. We should rid ourselves
once for all of our preoccupation with *proving* our theories
and engage upon a quite different enterprise. Does this mean
that we should give up that search for knowledge without
which the love of wisdom is but sentimentality? I think not.

Knowledge possesses two quite different levels. There is
knowledge of the *what* and there is knowledge of the *which*.
The former usually precedes the latter. Before we can know
which of two possibilities is realized in fact we must know
at least to some extent what the possibilities are between
which a choice is to be made. In any pursuit of truth imaginative anticipation precedes logical proof. The proof may
be of the concrete empirical kind established by observation
and experiment; or it may be of the abstract, mathematical
kind established by formal demonstration. Proof of this second
kind gives that superior sort of actuality that is called "necessity" to distinguish it from "contingent" or "brute" fact—
fact merely as such. The necessary facts confirmed by mathematical deduction are thicker and richer than the ordinary
kind established by sensory observation, but the realm in
which they are found is poorer and thinner, comprising as it
does only the domain of abstract forms. But whether the
verification be inductive or deductive, a knowledge of what
is to be proved must come before the proof itself. Logic can
never create or discover, and its function, however important,

is secondary rather than primary. It is the censor and arbiter of our fancies, not their maker. In short, it is imagination that proposes and reason that disposes. Each quite obviously needs the other, and neither is ever found without something of the other. Scientists like Faraday or Einstein may be blessed with glorious imaginations and their fame may rest as much upon the hypotheses that they have constructed as upon the proofs that they have carried out or inspired others to carry out. But for these aristocrats no less than for their humbler brethren who grub for facts with pick and shovel, microscope or camera, the ultimate concern of science as such, whether directed to the concrete field of perceptual events or to the abstract field of conceptual forms, is to find out which are and which are not the actual facts. The quest for certainty is the quest of science, and no domain of actuality whatever can be permanently shut off from those who pursue that quest. In very truth the scientists want the earth; and I suggest that we give it to them, while the giving is good. And for us in philosophy what then will remain? Why, of course, the sea will remain, the ocean of possibilities to be discovered by imagination and vision and enjoyed without limit or surcease by us and by all who love beauty and wonder.

But if this proposal be accepted, it should not be accepted sulkily and with a feeling of *faute de mieux*. In leaving behind us forever the dry land of fact we are leaving the scene of a series of battles in which we have been increasingly beaten by the ever increasing armies of science. And in abandoning the place of our defeats we should abandon also that mood of defeatism which has been steadily growing upon us, weakening our courage, withering our spirit, and shamefully narrowing the field of our activities and ambitions. If philosophers will consent gladly and with right good will to embark on this voyage and sail forever the blue waters where possible rather than proven truths are to be found, I believe that philosophy herself will suffer a sea change into something which, if not rich and strange, will at least be more like her ancient self and refreshingly different from the

rather doleful and bedraggled creature which, during recent
years, she seems to have become.

To the proposal that philosophy abandon the domain of the
actual for the domain of the possible and substitute inquiry
as to the *what* for inquiry as to the *which*, I shall receive from
some of my colleagues a rough response. "Thank you for
nothing," they will say. "Is it not bad enough that science
has taken all our possessions and left us holding the bag—
a bag that once contained all time and existence but which
now holds but empty air? Are we to add irony to tragedy and
continue as ghosts of our former selves, mere play-boys of
the intellectual world, blowing vain bubbles of fancy? Nor
because the scientists will have none of us is there reason
for supposing that the artists will make much of us. The thin
and grandiose abstractions of the metaphysician are even
poorer for poetry than for science. Far better that we surrender completely, in the knowledge that we have outlasted
our time and are needed no longer. We live in a world of
science and are ruled by a dictatorship of fact. Under that
iron rule there is no place for the free activity of philosophical
imagination."

To escape being utterly crushed by such rejoinders to my
plan for preserving philosophy by offering to it a new function
and a new domain, I beg leave to return for a moment to the
shelter of the metaphor that I have been playing with, and to
point out that when I urge that philosophers should cruise
the seas of possibility, it is a quite special cruise that I have
in mind. Not the cruise to distant havens, still less the jolly
week-end cruise to Nowhere with which Prohibition made
us familiar—rather would I urge a sober and conservative
cruise along the shores of fact, keeping within easy distance
of the great land-marks of established knowledge and directing our imaginative vision only upon those possibilities
which are severely pertinent to the truths already discovered
and to the truths that are still to come. In short, philosophy
should be concerned not with bare possibilities but with real
possibilities—not the golden mountain and the moon calf or

any idle fancy, but the real alternatives between which a later knowledge will or may decide.

Plato was eternally and completely right in holding that the actualities of existence no less than the certainties of knowledge do incarnate and exemplify and therefore presuppose the prior and primordial realm of ideal possibility. But Aristotle, too, was right, though only partly and pragmatically, in holding that the already actual selectively determines the possible, and that knowledge of the actual is most practically helpful in revealing to our vision the possibilities still open to existence.

In abandoning to science the quest for certainty and taking for herself the field of vision, philosophy is by no means to abandon science. Each new certainty of reason opens up new possibilities for imagination to envisage; and the more a philosopher can learn of science the richer will be his field of vision. Having laid down the increasingly heavy and increasingly inappropriate burden of proving this or that possibility to be the actual truth, he will have more time and more energy to enjoy the possibilities themselves and to exploit their rival meanings and values. And in this exercise of imaginative vision it will not always be that philosophy is debtor to science. Sometimes it will be the other way around. We have often said and may still say that the physics of today is the metaphysics of yesterday. And from this it is but a short and tempting step to the boast that what is metaphysics today will be science tomorrow. Were not the present-day scientific certitudes of a world of atoms and a world of evolution envisioned as possibilities by the creative imagination of the ancient philosophers? And why may not we be as lucky as they in prophetic anticipations? Is it not still true that in the seas of possibility there are just as good fish as ever were caught?

Tempting as such talk may be to us in philosophy, we must go a bit easy. For we shall be reminded that the modern theories of atoms and evolution, as held by science, owe their strength to empirical discovery rather than to ancient prophecy. Their ancestry, so far as it is relevant, is to be traced to such scientists as Dalton and Prout, Darwin and Lamarck, rather than to the Ionian philosophers. And as for our chance of anticipating future science by happy guesses, we must not be over-optimistic. We may, to be sure, have luck and strike it right, but even so the scientists will pay small attention until by their own empirical methods they supplement our imagination with their demonstration. Taken more broadly, however, the debt of science to philosophy may be greater than the foregoing statements would make it appear. The philosopher will follow up the envisioning of possibilities with clarifying analyses of their implications. And these may be helpful even for the business of observation and experiment.

It would be, however, not merely a misunderstanding of the position I am defending but a vast pity in itself if a philosophy of vision were to rest its main justification on the occasional chance of its being useful to science. Existence at best can constitute only a very small and frequently a very sordid fraction of the mighty realm of Being lying open before us. Demos of Harvard knows this; so, of course, does Santayana. And in two essays to which my own indebtedness is obvious, "More Things in Heaven and Earth" and "Unwritten Philosophies," my colleague, Helen Huss Parkhurst, has sketched the far horizons on which imagination can descry the outlines of ideas and systems of ideas which might have come and still may come but which as yet have not.

To confine one's attention to the actual is to narrow one's spirit to brutish dimensions. The distinctive glory of the human mind is its power to detach itself not only from the here and now but from the there and then of existence and bathe its tired memories in ideal waters. So it is that the great visions of philosophy, even if considered merely as visions, are precious and imperishable possessions of our culture. Even when their content has been proved false to the world of fact they lend to that world depth and richness of meaning, and norms for appraising its values which otherwise could never come. The pride of philosophy is in its disclosure of significant possibility. This ought to be so in the future and it has been so in the past. We should interpret our subject in this way, not only because there is nothing else that we can do in an age of science, but also because, as we have already said, the best work of our predecessors has exemplified this ideal and no other. Great in vision, poor in proof, philosophy at its highest has ever been.

Take, for example, the philosophy of Spinoza and consider his argument for the proposition that the universe as a whole is the one and only substance. Descartes, the forerunner of Spinoza as well as other philosophers, had applied the term "substance" to that which could exist independently and in its own right and not as an adjective of some other thing or as a mere idea in the mind. Spinoza would have us conceive of the kind of independence that would entitle a thing to be called "substance" as consisting in its lack of relation to any other thing external to itself. Now, if we agree to mean by the word "substance" something so internally independent that there is nothing outside of it to be related to it, then Spinoza can triumphantly prove to us that the universe itself is the one and only substance, because *only that which has everything inside of it will be that which has nothing outside of it.* How incredibly paltry! And what a pathetic caricature of the great deductions of Euclid, whose mere form was slavishly imitated in this and other similar proofs. Yet, when we turn from the proofs of Spinoza to the philosophy they were designed to substantiate, the vision disclosed to us is anything but paltry. It is sublime and majestic to a degree hardly equaled in history. A universe infinite in each of its infinity of generic aspects or "attributes," of which mind and matter are the only two that we can know. A universe in which each seemingly substantive thing or individual is but a dependent and transitory "mode," a cog in a vast machine in which every happening occurs with an absolute necessity that is at once mechanical and logico-mathematical. A universe in which human personality and all its fears and hopes are concomitants of the perishable body and lacking in significance or value for the impersonal whole of which they are fragments. Here is a world not proved but possible, a world that is to

some a thing of awful beauty, to others a nightmare of immeasurable gloom, but to all who once behold it a thing to
pierce the spirit unforgettably. Who, moreover, can remain
unmoved at the spectacle of its author, the outcast Jew of
quiet courage, the lonely man without a country, who wrought
the vision and then with all the ardor of a Christian saint took
the bleak thing to his own bleak heart, called it *God,* and in
its cold embrace found peace.

Surely in such a matter all talk of proof, scientific proof or
any higher fancy proof such as philosophers are sometimes
wont to boast of, is quite absurdly out of place. And as with
Spinoza, so too with Kant and all the rest, not in their proofs
but in their visions lie their greatness.

But while lacking the value of their primary intent, the
arguments of philosophy often possess a real though secondary
importance. They may clarify the meaning of the vision though
failing utterly to substantiate its truth. For this reason the
study of a philosopher's vision should sometimes include the
study of the proofs advanced in its support. And, for the same
reason, a consideration of the biography of a philosopher
and of the age and social setting in which he lived may be
pertinent to an appreciation of his *aperçu.* To that extent
and to that extent alone should the facts of philosophic history
and the circumstances under which a philosophic vision was
produced be of concern to students of philosophy. For the
rest, they should be left to the professional historians who, because they are comparatively undistracted by the duties of
interpreting and evaluating the meaning of past performances,
will be the better able to describe to us accurately the times
and places of their occurrence.

How is philosophy as vision related to art which is also
vision? That the two are not identical we can be certain.
Neither of them is science, and both are concerned with
possibilities envisioned by imagination. But there the resemblance ends. We have already seen that the fact that the
scientists do not want us in their field is no reason for supposing that the artists will welcome us to theirs. Art, and especially poetry, may be philosophic, philosophy may be poetic,

and the same person may be both philosopher and poet. Moreover, many of the great systems of philosophy conform in their unities and harmonies and symmetries to the canons of art. But there is, I take it, a fundamental difference of intent between the two forms of imaginative enterprise. The aim of the artist is to satisfy the feelings, while the aim of the philosopher is to satisfy the mind. That the two satisfactions are by no means incompatible, and are, indeed, often combined, in no way obliterates their essential difference. The artist who makes himself primarily an expositor of truth or an exhorter to duty is apt to be tiresome. His art becomes edifying or tendentious or pedantic. While the philosopher who forgets that his aim should be knowledge, albeit knowledge of the what rather than knowledge of the which, and seeks merely beauty, is disloyal to his own ideal, and will incidentally be most apt to fail in attaining that of the artist.

But now a fear comes to me that in spite of my efforts, first to restrict the aim of philosophy to vision of the possible, and then to justify the importance of our subject when thus restricted, you may still feel that the philosopher's imaginative knowledge of the what is a poor thin thing when compared with the scientist's proven knowledge of the which. May I, then, strengthen my case by reminding you that knowledge of the what is supplemented by a knowledge of the *if—then*. The possibilities discovered by imagination are not, like the essences of Santayana, logically isolated from one another. They are connected and interconnected by the silvery stepping stones of implication by means of which the nimble feet of dialectic can pass from possible to possible. And these internal relations of connective meaning which are usually *de trop* in the realm of fact are precious to the realm of essence. For Dialectic is the handmaid of Imagination, and the joy of discovering a cosmic possibility always can and always should be followed by the pleasure of reasoning out its implications for thought and action. "*If* this, *then* that" or "*If not* that, *then not* this." Such deductions, always available to the philosopher, lend not only fun and zest to his professional activity but help to make his visions of consequence to life. Visions are never inconsequential except when through logical laziness their ultimate implications are left undrawn.

But knowledge of the what is not only supplemented by the hypothetical knowledge of *if—then*. It is supplemented also by the disjunctive knowledge of *either—or*. However it may be with the space of existence, the space which possibilities inhabit is the space of Riemann, not the space of Euclid. That is to say, it is not infinite but rather is it curved round into itself. And the horizons toward which we sail in imagination, though like ordinary horizons they recede, yet unlike ordinary horizons they grow more narrow as we approach. And as the possibles in any one direction decrease in number and become more definite and more definitely exhaustive of the domain in which they lie, possibility becomes probability. What was at first a mere series of *this* and *this* and *this*, without visible end or limit, is now a closed circuit of *either* this *or* that *or* the other, *and nothing else*. This is a great step forward. Knowledge of what may be has developed into a knowledge of what must be, though *which* of the *whats* will prove to be the fact is something we cannot yet tell.

At this advanced stage of philosophic insight the situation is analogous to one in which we know that our friend is one of the people in a hall, and we can see all the people in the hall and consequently we can see our friend, but which of the people our friend is, that we cannot see. We know each of the two sides of a penny, or of the six sides of a die that is to be tossed. We know that these are all and hence that one of them must come face up on the toss. But *which?* That we do not know. This, then, is probability, a strange hybrid, begotten by Ignorance on the body of Knowledge and sharing the natures of both parents. It is disjunctive knowledge of *either* this or that, and categorical ignorance of *whether* this or that. Probability may vary in luminosity from the faint and formal light in which is disclosed the necessity that a proposition or else its contradictory is true, up to that relatively bright light in which each of all possible alternatives is known positively and precisely as to its content. What proof is to science, and what faith is to religion, probability is to philosophy. An elusive, glimmering, dancing light, it nevertheless gives to imagination a sense of proportion, and to the visions of imagination it gives a perspective whereby their greatly varying values can be discovered and appraised. And though probability for the philosopher never rises to certainty, it suffices to keep him in wholesome proximity to the land of fact. That land he has abandoned to science, but he need never lose sight of its snug and sheltering harbors to which upon occasion he may retreat.

Having now to the best of my ability set forth the general reasons for making philosophy an enterprise of imagination whose primary function is to be the attainment of vision— vision of the possible and probable rather than proof of the actual and certain—I shall conclude with a statement or confession of a quite special and private reason that in my own thinking reinforces the case as already presented.

I hold with Douglas Fawcett that the works of Nature herself bear all the earmarks of creative imagination, and that a philosopher, in using his imagination to evolve knowledge, is using the same sort of power that Nature has used and still uses to evolve reality.

Much has been said or sung of a world as Will and a world as Idea, a world that is a senseless flux of sensory experience and one that is an objectification of absolute reason, a world that is the fortuitous effect of stone-blind atoms and a world that is omnipotently created by a benevolent and all-seeing God. No one of these worlds nor any simple compound of them seems to me quite right. The universe, and the life that colors and stains it, is not too good and not too bad. Whatever its whole may be, it is in its constituent parts a great and terrible welter.

The biological sky is more thickly studded with stabs of pain, of agony, and of defeat of every kind than the sky we know with stars. And on life itself has been put the curse, worthy of a primordial demon's genius, of having to feed upon itself, and carry on by murder and betrayal of its very own. We happy and successful members of the conquering human race bask in the sunlight of the high peaks on which the evolution of our species has put us. We forget that this mountain on which we live is a mountain of skulls, and that the failures, deaths, and miseries of our humbler brethren make up the purchase price of our estate. We look with fatuous dislike at the pessimists who have heard life's cries and would echo them unpleasantly to us. We charge them with being failures, nursing a grouch, saddling nature with their own short-comings, and hysterically exaggerating the ills of things. But pessimists as yet have hardly scratched the surface of life's woe. I venture to believe that, should one ever come with the ability to give us in his writing a vivid first-hand sense of even a tithe of those agonies actually existing at a single moment, his words would burn our eyes blind, and melt the foulest hearts with pity.

And yet in this same world some loveliness is everywhere. Great joys are had, and great ideals are successfully fulfilled. All life is shot with meanings, and probably non-life too, could we but see them—meanings that are often abortive and repulsive or grotesque, yet rich and challenging on the whole. And, as offset to pain and the black shadow of fear which forewarns of its coming, there are the saints and the heroes in every land who have kept their rendezvous with death and with every sort of hellish terror. We may not dare to play their game, but all too clearly from our safe distance we can see not only that they played and won but that the high stakes they wagered were not a bit too high for what they won.

All this, of course, is immensely to the good. It is not, however, the pains of the conquering strong that call for our pity, but rather the pains of the utterly vanquished and crushed. Pains, for example, of small rabbits delivered as playthings to young eagles or fox pups by their mothers to be nibbled, gnawed, or pecked at slowly; toads beneath the harrow, cats beneath the wheels of our cars, or captured mice in the claws of those same cats. For such pains there is no compensating heroism, no high religion or philosophy to snatch victory from defeat—nothing but writhing and screaming, trembling, terror and despair.

There is an old, mean piety that would justify the ways of God at any price, even at the price of conscience, pity and sincerity. Contemptuously disregardful of all animal suffering, such piety concentrates on those few cases in which human pain can cancel human sin or hang a moral to a tale. There are such cases, but they make so small an islet in the seas of nature's agony that one needs must have the mind of a fool and a heart much worse to treat them as "solving the problem of evil" and freeing from blame a supposedly omnipotent creator. The puzzled, mounting wretchedness of a single dog lost on the streets of a city would be enough to damn with shame any God who ever lived in heaven if, with omnipotence to draw upon, he had ordained it so.

If we are to follow the ancient custom and make God in our own image—or, to put the thought with less of hackneyed flippancy and more of modesty—if we are to conceive of natural powers on the analogy of our own natures, what phase of our make-up should we select? Where do we find in ourselves anything resembling the mêlée of multiform and conflicting tendencies, purposes, and meanings that is offered by life and by the world as a whole? Where but in Imagination? Yet that domain of mind is all but unexplored. Psychologists have been most busy with our conative and affective activities and with sensation and reason. They have told us how we select from our ideas and ideals to make judgments of fact and value, how we carry out with conscious teleology a telos once envisioned, or how such a telos is carried out mechanically by the atoms of our brains with no meddling interaction of our free wills and struggling motives. On such matters there is no lack of information, or at least of conversation. But what I should like to know is how come the ideas and ideals themselves. Before a telos can be carried out in action, or a meaning be affirmed in judgment, the telos and the meaning must be born into conscious existence. Before the useful variations of an organism can be preserved by

natural selection they must have been originated in the germ
from which that organism grew. And before potentialities of
any kind are finally actualized in nature they must be born
into material existence or somehow attain a status of material
efficacy.

Now imagination is the pre-teleological and pre-conscious
womb within which are formed the ideas and ideals which,
after a longer or a shorter gestation, are born into overt, conscious life, there to be dealt with by the decidedly secondary
activities of reasoning and will. Spending of money or energy
presupposes a process of saving or accumulating. Before
katabolism there must be anabolism—and it is in imagination
that the pure anabolism of our stuff takes place. It is a vast,
disorderly progeny that imagination bears, grotesques and
monsters, horrible, trivial, and beautiful mingled indifferently
with the mere memories from whose ribs they have been
fashioned. There is here not much of birth control, but once
born, the mortality of our fancies is terrific; and only a wee
minority survive the mere preliminary ordeal of selection by
attention.

Now the whole realm of nature, taken both individually and
collectively, organically and even inorganically, appears to me
unmistakably like the fruit of a World-imagination. Existence
is not a tale told by an idiot nor by a theologian; it is a tale
told in many languages and not overly censored in any, such
a tale as we might hear if all the eternal possibles of Being
gave tongue at once in space and time, and raced together
in pursuit of actuality. I called the tale not overly censored,
but it must more or less censor itself as it goes along, to make
its parts agree. This coming to terms of the parts with one
another is more than merely mechanical and gives intimations
of increasing purpose running through it all. We see this
working like a little leaven in a mighty dough and call it evolution.

This dim vision haunts my fancy. It makes me feel that
between creative evolution and creative imagination there is
more than a rhetorical analogy, and so makes me urge again

that there is nothing poor or shameful in treating philosophy as imaginative vision rather than as rational demonstration. For the ways of imagination and vision are, I think, man's nearest approach to the ways of primordial Being.

SIGMUND FREUD

[1856–1939]

'Tis strange, but true; for Truth is always strange;
   Stranger than fiction: if it could be told,
How much would novels gain by the exchange!
   How differently the world would men behold!
How oft would Vice and Virtue places change!
   The new world would be nothing to the old,
If some Columbus of the moral seas
Would show mankind their Souls' antipodes.

Not a bad prophecy of Freud and his influence, considering the
fact that it was made by Lord Byron in March, 1823, for the fourteenth canto of *Don Juan*.

The third and final volume of the monumental *The Life and
Work of Sigmund Freud* was completed by Dr. Ernest Jones only
a year before his own death at the age of seventy-nine. He was
the last survivor of the "Committee" of seven which gathered
around the master in 1913, after the defections of Adler and Jung.
When Dr. Jones asked Freud one day what were the favorites
among his writings, he took from his shelves *The Interpretation of
Dreams* (1900) and *Three Essays on the Theory of Sexuality*
(1905), commenting: "It seems to be my fate to discover only the
obvious: that children have sexual feelings, which every nursemaid
knows; and that night dreams are just as much wish-fulfillment as
day dreams." But Freud used much more formidable and imperious language in his *History of the Psychoanalytic Movement*
(1914), an indispensable document in which he summed up his
contributions to that date.

The early stages of the First World War released new energies
in Freud's mind, and during six amazing weeks in the spring of
1915, he wrote five of his most remarkable papers: "Instincts and

336

Their Vicissitudes," "Repression," "The Unconscious," "The Meta-psychological Supplement to the Theory of Dreams," and "Mourning and Melancholia." During the winter of 1915–1917 he gave three courses of public lectures at the University of Vienna, which became his basic book for laymen, *A General Introduction to Psychoanalysis*. But his lingering sympathy for Germany had now disappeared and he was beginning to find the world "repellently loathsome."

However, in 1919, Freud entered into a third period of extraordinary fruitfulness with the writing of *Beyond the Pleasure Principle* and further books in metapsychology which developed his new conceptions of the Death instinct, the super-ego, the id, and a revised theory of anxiety. But in April, 1923, in the midst of this renaissance, he underwent the first of thirty-three operations for cancer of the jaw—thirty-three operations during the ensuing sixteen years—but he continued at work almost to the end, whether in Nazi threatened, and finally infested, Vienna or in hospitable London.

In order to help his periodicals, he decided in 1932 to embody his later ideas in a new series of *Introductory Lectures*, in spite of five recent operations. He even decided to number the eight new lectures in continuation with the first series, beginning with XXIX, although fully realizing that he would never again address an audience. So as we read Lecture XXXV, we might glance up from time to time at the tortured old warrior writing away, with his golden chow, Jo-fi, beside him. There he sits alone—majestic in all his truculence.

* * *

A PHILOSOPHY OF LIFE

Ladies and Gentlemen—In the last lecture we were occupied with trivial everyday affairs, with putting, as it were, our modest house in order. We will now take a bold step, and risk an answer to a question which has repeatedly been raised in non-analytic quarters, namely, the question whether

psychoanalysis leads to any particular *Weltanschauung*, and if
so, to what.

'*Weltanschauung*' is, I am afraid, a specifically German
notion, which it would be difficult to translate into a foreign
language. If I attempt to give you a definition of the word,
it can hardly fail to strike you as inept. By *Weltanschauung*,
then, I mean an intellectual construction, which gives a
unified solution of all the problems of our existence in virtue
of a comprehensive hypothesis, a construction, therefore, in
which no question is left open and in which everything in
which we are interested finds a place. It is easy to see that
the possession of such a *Weltanschauung* is one of the ideal
wishes of mankind. When one believes in such a thing, one
feels secure in life, one knows what one ought to strive after,
and how one ought to organise one's emotions and interests
to the best purpose.

If that is what is meant by a *Weltanschauung*, then the
question is an easy one for psychoanalysis to answer. As a
specialised science, a branch of psychology—'depth-psycholo-
gy' or psychology of the unconscious—it is quite unsuited to
form a *Weltanschauung* of its own; it must accept that of
science in general. The scientific *Weltanschauung* is, however, markedly at variance with our definition. The *unified*
nature of the explanation of the universe is, it is true, accepted by science, but only as a programme whose fulfilment is postponed to the future. Otherwise it is distinguished
by negative characteristics, by a limitation to what is, at
any given time, knowable, and a categorical rejection of certain elements which are alien to it. It asserts that there is
no other source of knowledge of the universe, but the intellectual manipulation of carefully verified observations, in
fact, what is called research, and that no knowledge can be
obtained from revelation, intuition or inspiration. It appears
that this way of looking at things came very near to receiving
general acceptance during the last century or two. It has
been reserved for the present century to raise the objection
that such a *Weltanschauung* is both empty and unsatisfying,

that it overlooks all the spiritual demands of man, and all the needs of the human mind.

This objection cannot be too strongly repudiated. It cannot be supported for a moment, for the spirit and the mind are the subject of scientific investigation in exactly the same way as any non-human entities. Psychoanalysis has a peculiar right to speak on behalf of the scientific *Weltanschauung* in this connection, because it cannot be accused of neglecting the part occupied by the mind in the universe. The contribution of psychoanalysis to science consists precisely in having extended research to the region of the mind. Certainly without such a psychology, science would be very incomplete. But if we add to science the investigation of the intellectual and emotional functions of men (and animals), we find that nothing has been altered as regards the general position of science, that there are no new sources of knowledge or methods of research. Intuition and inspiration would be such, if they existed; but they can safely be counted as illusions, as fulfilments of wishes. It is easy to see, moreover, that the qualities which, as we have shown, are expected of a *Weltanschauung* have a purely emotional basis. Science takes account of the fact that the mind of man creates such demands and is ready to trace their source, but it has not the slightest ground for thinking them justified. On the contrary, it does well to distinguish carefully between illusion (the results of emotional demands of that kind) and knowledge.

This does not at all imply that we need push these wishes contemptuously aside, or underestimate their value in the lives of human beings. We are prepared to take notice of the fulfilments they have achieved for themselves in the creations of art and in the systems of religion and philosophy; but we cannot overlook the fact, that it would be wrong and highly inexpedient to allow such things to be carried over into the domain of knowledge. For in that way one would open the door which gives access to the region of the psychoses, whether individual or group psychoses, and one would drain off from these tendencies valuable energy which is directed towards reality and which seeks by means of reality to satisfy wishes and needs as far as this is possible.

From the point of view of science we must necessarily make use of our critical powers in this direction, and not be afraid to reject and deny. It is inadmissible to declare that science is one field of human intellectual activity, and that religion and philosophy are others, at least as valuable, and that science has no business to interfere with the other two, that they all have an equal claim to truth, and that every one is free to choose whence he shall draw his convictions and in what he shall place his belief. Such an attitude is considered particularly respectable, tolerant, broad-minded, and free from narrow prejudices. Unfortunately it is not tenable; it shares all the pernicious qualities of an entirely unscientific *Weltanschauung* and in practice comes to much the same thing. The bare fact is that truth cannot be tolerant and cannot admit compromise or limitations, that scientific research looks on the whole field of human activity as its own, and must adopt an uncompromisingly critical attitude towards any other power that seeks to usurp any part of its province.

Of the three forces which can dispute the position of science, religion alone is a really serious enemy. Art is almost always harmless and beneficent, it does not seek to be anything else but an illusion. Save in the case of a few people who are, one might say, obsessed by Art, it never dares to make any attacks on the realm of reality. Philosophy is not opposed to science, it behaves itself as if it were a science, and to a certain extent it makes use of the same methods; but it parts company with science, in that it clings to the illusion that it can produce a complete and coherent picture of the universe, though in fact that picture must needs fall to pieces with every new advance in our knowledge. Its methodological error lies in the fact that it overestimates the epistemological value of our logical operations, and to a certain extent admits the validity of other sources of knowledge, such as intuition. And often enough one feels that the poet Heine is not unjustified when he says of the philosopher:

With his night-cap and his night-shirt tatters,
He botches up the loop-holes in the structure of the
   world.

But philosophy has no immediate influence on the great majority of mankind; it interests only a small number even of the thin upper stratum of intellectuals, while all the rest find it beyond them. In contradistinction to philosophy, religion is a tremendous force, which exerts its power over the strongest emotions of human beings. As we know, at one time it included everything that played any part in the mental life of mankind, that it took the place of science, when as yet science hardly existed, and that it built up a *Weltanschauung* of incomparable consistency and coherence, although it has been severely shaken, which has lasted to this day.

If one wishes to form a true estimate of the full grandeur of religion, one must keep in mind what it undertakes to do for men. It gives them information about the source and origin of the universe, it assures them of protection and final happiness amid the changing vicissitudes of life, and it guides their thoughts and actions by means of precepts which are backed by the whole force of its authority. It fulfils, therefore, three functions. In the first place, it satisfies man's desire for knowledge; it is here doing the same thing that science attempts to accomplish by its own methods, and here, therefore, enters into rivalry with it. It is to the second function that it performs, that religion no doubt owes the greater part of its influence. In so far as religion brushes away men's fear of the dangers and vicissitudes of life, in so far as it assures them of a happy ending, and comforts them in their misfortunes, science cannot compete with it. Science, it is true, teaches how one can avoid certain dangers and how one can combat many sufferings with success; it would be quite untrue to deny that science is a powerful aid to human beings, but in many cases it has to leave them to their suffering, and can only advise them to submit to the inevitable. In the performance of its third function, the provision of precepts, prohibitions, and restrictions, religion is furthest removed from science. For science is content with discovering and stating the facts. It is true that from the applications of science, rules and recommendations for behaviour may be deduced. In certain circumstances they may be the same as those which are laid down by religion, but even so the reasons for them will be different.

It is not quite clear why religion should combine these three functions. What has the explanation of the origin of the universe to do with the inculcation of certain ethical precepts? Its assurances of protection and happiness are more closely connected with these precepts. They are the reward for the fulfilment of the commands; only he who obeys them can count on receiving these benefits, while punishment awaits the disobedient. For the matter of that something of the same kind applies to science; for it declares that any one who disregards its inferences is liable to suffer for it.

One can only understand this remarkable combination of teaching, consolation and precept in religion, if one subjects it to genetic analysis. We may begin with the most remarkable item of the three, the teaching about the origin of the universe—for why should a cosmogony be a regular element of religious systems? The doctrine is that the universe was created by a being similar to man, but greater in every respect, in power, wisdom, and strength of passion, in fact by an idealized superman. Where you have animals as creators of the universe, you have indications of the influence of Totemism, which I shall touch on later, at any rate with a brief remark. It is interesting to notice that this creator of the universe is always a single god, even when many gods are believed in. Equally interesting is the fact that the creator is nearly always a male, although there is no lack of indication of the existence of female deities and many mythologies make the creation of the world begin precisely with a male god triumphing over a female goddess, who is degraded into a monster. This raises the most fascinating minor problems, but we must hurry on. The rest of our enquiry is made easy because this God-Creator is openly called Father. Psychoanalysis concludes that he really is the father, clothed in the grandeur in which he once appeared to the small child. The religious man's picture of the creation of the universe is the same as his picture of his own creation.

If this is so, then it is easy to understand how it is that the comforting promises of protection and the severe ethical commands are found together with the cosmogony. For the same individual, to whom the child owes its own existence, the father (or, more correctly, the parental function which is composed of the father and the mother), has protected and watched over the weak and helpless child, exposed as it is to all the dangers which threaten in the external world; in its father's care it has felt itself safe. Even the grown man, though he may know that he possesses greater strength, and though he has greater insight into the dangers of life, rightly feels that fundamentally he is just as helpless and unprotected as he was in childhood and that in relation to the external world he is still a child. Even now, therefore, he cannot give up the protection which he has enjoyed as a child. But he has long ago realised that his father is a being with strictly limited powers and by no means endowed with every desirable attribute. He therefore looks back to the memory-image of the overrated father of his childhood, exalts it into a Deity, and brings it into the present and into reality. The emotional strength of this memory-image and the lasting nature of his need for protection are the two supports of his belief in God.

The third main point of the religious programme, its ethical precepts, can also be related without any difficulty to the situation of childhood. In a famous passage, which I have already quoted in an earlier lecture, the philosopher Kant speaks of the starry heaven above us and the moral law within us as the strongest evidence for the greatness of God. However odd it may sound to put these two side by side—for what can the heavenly bodies have to do with the question whether one man loves another or kills him? nevertheless it touches on a great psychological truth. The same father (the parental function) who gave the child his life and preserved it from the dangers which that life involves, also taught it what it may or may not do, made it accept certain limitations of its instinctual wishes, and told it what consideration it would be expected to show towards its parents and brothers and sisters, if it wanted to be tolerated and liked as a member of the family circle, and later on of more extensive groups. The child is brought up to know its social duties by means of a system of love-rewards and punishments, and in this way it is taught that its security in life depends on its parents (and, subsequently, other people) loving it and being able to believe in its love for them. This whole state of affairs is carried over by the grown man unaltered into his religion. The prohibitions and commands of his parents live on in his breast as his moral conscience; God rules the world of men with the help of the same system of rewards and punishments, and the degree of protection and happiness which each individual enjoys, depends on his fulfilment of the demands of morality; the feeling of security, with which he fortifies himself against the dangers both of the external world and of his human environment, is founded on his love of God and the consciousness of God's love for him. Finally, he has in prayer a direct influence on the divine will, and in that way insures for himself a share in the divine omnipotence.

I am sure that while you have been listening to me, a whole host of questions must have come into your minds which you would like to have answered. I cannot undertake to do so here and now, but I am perfectly certain that none of these questions of detail would shake our thesis that the religious *Weltanschauung* is determined by the situation that subsisted in our childhood. It is therefore all the more remarkable that, in spite of its infantile character, it nevertheless has a forerunner. There was, without doubt, a time when there were no religions and no gods. It is known as the age of animism. Even at that time the world was full of spirits in the semblance of men (demons, as we call them), and all the objects in the external world were their dwelling-place or perhaps identical with them, but there was no supreme power which had created them all, which controlled them, and to which it was possible to turn for protection and aid. The demons of animism were usually hostile to man, but it seems as though man had more confidence in himself in those days than later on. He was no doubt in constant terror of these evil spirits, but he defended himself against them by means of certain actions to which he ascribed the power to drive them away. Nor did he think himself entirely powerless in other ways. If he wanted something from nature—rain, for instance—he did not direct a prayer to the Weather-god, but used a spell, by means of which he expected to exert a direct influence over nature; he himself made something which resembled rain. In his fight against the powers of the surrounding world his first weapon was magic, the first forerunner of our modern technology. We suppose that this confidence in magic is derived from the overestimation of the individual's own intellectual operations, from the belief in the "omnipotence of thoughts," which, incidentally, we come across again in our obsessional neurotics. We may imagine that the men of that time were particularly proud of their acquisition of speech, which must have been accompanied by a great facilitation of thought. They attributed magic power to the spoken word. This feature was later on taken over by religion. "And God said: Let there be light, and there was light." But the fact of magic actions shows that animistic man did not rely entirely on the force of his own wishes. On the contrary, he depended for success upon the performance of an action, which would cause Nature to imitate it. If he wanted it to rain, he himself poured out water; if he wanted to stimulate the soil to fertility, he offered it a performance of sexual intercourse in the fields.

You know how tenaciously anything that has once found psychological expression persists. You will therefore not be surprised to hear that a great many manifestations of animism have lasted up to the present day, mostly as what are called superstitions, side by side with and behind religion. But

more than that, you can hardly avoid coming to the conclusion that our philosophy has preserved essential traits
of animistic modes of thought such as the overestimation of
the magic of words and the belief that real processes in the
external world follow the lines laid down by our thoughts.
It is, to be sure, an animism without magical practices. On
the other hand we should expect to find that in the age of
animism there must already have been some kind of morality,
some rules governing the intercourse of men with one another.
But there is no evidence that they were closely bound up with
animistic beliefs. Probably they were the immediate expression of the distribution of power and of practical necessities.

It would be very interesting to know what determined
the transition from animism to religion; but you may imagine
in what darkness this earliest epoch in the evolution of the
human mind is still shrouded. It seems to be a fact that
the earliest form in which religion appeared was the remarkable one of totemism, the worship of animals, in the
train of which followed the first ethical commands, the
taboos. In a book called *Totem und Tabu,* I once worked out
a suggestion, in accordance with which this change is to be
traced back to an upheaval in the relationships in the human
family. The main achievement of religion, as compared with
animism, lies in the psychic binding of the fear of demons.
Nevertheless, the evil spirit still has a place in the religious
system as a relic of the previous age.

So much for the pre-history of the religious *Weltanschauung.* Let us now turn to consider what has happened
since, and what is still going on under our own eyes. The
scientific spirit, strengthened by the observation of natural
processes, began in the course of time to treat religion as a
human matter, and to subject it to a critical examination.
This test it failed to pass. In the first place, the accounts of
miracles roused a feeling of surprise and disbelief, since
they contradicted everything that sober observation had
taught, and betrayed all too clearly the influence of human
imagination. In the next place, its account of the nature
of the universe had to be rejected, because it showed evi-

dence of a lack of knowledge which bore the stamp of earlier days, and because, owing to increasing familiarity with the laws of nature, it had lost its authority. The idea that the universe came into being through an act of generation or creation, analogous to that which produces an individual human being, no longer seemed to be the most obvious and self-evident hypothesis; for the distinction between living and sentient beings and inanimate nature had become apparent to the human mind, and had made it impossible to retain the original animistic theory. Besides this, one must not overlook the influence of the comparative study of different religious systems, and the impression they give of mutual exclusiveness and intolerance.

Fortified by these preliminary efforts, the scientific spirit at last summoned up courage to put to the test the most important and the most emotionally significant elements of the religious *Weltanschauung*. The truth could have been seen at any time, but it was long before any one dared to say it aloud: the assertions made by religion that it could give protection and happiness to men, if they would only fulfil certain ethical obligations, were unworthy of belief. It seems not to be true that there is a power in the universe, which watches over the well-being of every individual with parental care and brings all his concerns to a happy ending. On the contrary the destinies of man are incompatible with a universal principle of benevolence or with—what is to some degree contradictory—a universal principle of justice. Earthquakes, floods and fires do not differentiate between the good and devout man, and the sinner and unbeliever. And, even if we leave inanimate nature out of account and consider the destinies of individual men in so far as they depend on their relations with others of their own kind, it is by no means the rule that virtue is rewarded and wickedness punished, but it happens often enough that the violent, the crafty and the unprincipled seize the desirable goods of the earth for themselves, while the pious go empty away. Dark, unfeeling and unloving powers determine human destiny; the system of rewards and punishments, which, according to religion, governs the world, seems to have no existence. This is another occasion for abandoning a portion of the animism which has found refuge in religion.

The last contribution to the criticism of the religious *Weltanschauung* has been made by psychoanalysis, which has traced the origin of religion to the helplessness of childhood, and its content to the persistence of the wishes and needs of childhood into maturity. This does not precisely imply a refutation of religion, but it is a necessary rounding off of our knowledge about it, and, at least on one point, it actually contradicts it, for religion lays claim to a divine origin. This claim, to be sure, is not false if our interpretation of God is accepted.

The final judgment of science on the religious *Weltanschauung*, then, runs as follows. While the different religions wrangle with one another as to which of them is in possession of the truth, in our view the truth of religion may be altogether disregarded. Religion is an attempt to get control over the sensory world, in which we are placed, by means of the wish-world, which we have developed inside us as a result of biological and psychological necessities. But it cannot achieve its end. Its doctrines carry with them the stamp of the times in which they originated, the ignorant childhood days of the human race. Its consolations deserve no trust. Experience teaches us that the world is not a nursery. The ethical commands, to which religion seeks to lend its weight, require some other foundations instead, for human society cannot do without them, and it is dangerous to link up obedience to them with religious belief. If one attempts to assign to religion its place in man's evolution, it seems not so much to be a lasting acquisition, as a parallel to the neurosis which the civilised individual must pass through on his way from childhood to maturity.

You are, of course, perfectly free to criticise this account of mine, and I am prepared to meet you half way What I have said about the gradual crumbling of the religious *Weltanschauung* was no doubt an incomplete abridgment of the whole story; the order of the separate events was not quite correctly given, and the cooperation of various forces towards the awakening of the scientific spirit was not traced. I have also left out of account the alterations which occurred in the religious *Weltanschauung* itself, both during the period of its unchallenged authority and afterwards under the influence of awakening criticism. Finally I have, strictly speaking, limited my remarks to one single form of religion, that of the Western peoples. I have, as it were, constructed a lay-figure for the purposes of a demonstration which I desired to be as rapid and as impressive as possible. Let us leave on one side the question of whether my knowledge would in any case have been sufficient to enable me to do it better or more completely. I am aware that you can find all that I have said elsewhere, and find it better said; none of it is new. But I am firmly convinced that the most careful elaboration of the material upon which the problems of religion are based would not shake these conclusions.

As you know, the struggle between the scientific spirit and the religious *Weltanschauung* is not yet at an end; it is still going on under our very eyes to-day. However little psychoanalysis may make use as a rule of polemical weapons, we will not deny ourselves the pleasure of looking into this conflict. Incidentally, we may perhaps arrive at a clearer understanding of our attitude towards the *Weltanschauung*. You will see how easily some of the arguments which are brought forward by the supporters of religion can be disproved; though others may succeed in escaping refutation.

The first objection that one hears is to the effect that it is an impertinence on the part of science to take religion as a subject for its investigations, since religion is something supreme, something superior to the capacities of the human understanding, something which must not be approached with the sophistries of criticism. In other words, science is not competent to sit in judgment on religion. No doubt it is quite useful and valuable, so long as it is restricted to its own province; but religion does not lie in that province, and with religion it can have nothing to do. If we are not deterred by this brusque dismissal, but enquire on what grounds religion bases its claim to an exceptional position among human concerns, the answer we receive, if indeed we are honoured with an answer at all, is that religion cannot be measured by human standards, since it is of divine origin, and has been revealed to us by a spirit which the human mind cannot grasp. It might surely be thought that nothing could be more easily refuted than this argument; it is an obvious *petitio principii,* a "begging of the question." The point which is being called in question is whether there is a divine spirit and a revelation; and it surely cannot be a conclusive reply to say that the question cannot be asked, because the Deity cannot be called in question. What is happening here is the same kind of thing as we meet with occasionally in our analytic work. If an otherwise intelligent patient denies a suggestion on particularly stupid grounds, his imperfect logic is evidence for the existence of a particularly strong motive for his making the denial, a motive which can only be of an affective nature and serve to bind an emotion.

Another sort of answer may be given, in which a motive of this kind is openly admitted. Religion must not be critically examined, because it is the highest, most precious and noblest thing that the mind of man has brought forth, because it gives expression to the deepest feelings, and is the only thing that makes the world bearable and life worthy of humanity. To this we need not reply by disputing this estimate of religion, but rather by drawing attention to another aspect of the matter. We should point out that it is not a question of the scientific spirit encroaching upon the sphere of religion, but of religion encroaching upon the sphere of scientific thought. Whatever value and importance religion may have, it has no right to set any limits to thought, and therefore has no right to except itself from the application of thought.

Scientific thought is, in its essence, no different from the normal process of thinking, which we all, believers and unbelievers alike, make use of when we are going about our business in everyday life. It has merely taken a special form in certain respects: it extends its interest to things which have no immediate obvious utility, it endeavours to eliminate personal factors and emotional influences, it carefully examines the trustworthiness of the sense perceptions on which it bases its conclusions, it provides itself with new perceptions which are not obtainable by everyday means, and isolates the determinants of these new experiences by purposely varied experimentation. Its aim is to arrive at correspondence with reality, that is to say with what exists outside us and independently of us, and, as experience has taught us, is decisive for the fulfilment or frustration of our desires. This correspondence with the real external world we call truth. It is the aim of scientific work, even when the practical value of that work does not interest us. When, therefore, religion claims that it can take the place of science and that, because it is beneficent and ennobling, it must therefore be true, that claim is, in fact, an encroachment, which, in the interests of every one, should be resisted. It is asking a great deal of a man, who has learnt to regulate his everyday affairs in accordance with the rules of experience and with due regard to reality, that he should entrust precisely what affects him most nearly to the care of an authority which claims as its prerogative freedom from all the rules of rational thought. And, as for the protection that religion promises its believers, I hardly think that any of us would be willing even to enter a motor-car, if the driver informed us that he drove without allowing himself to be distracted by traffic regulations, but in accordance with the impulses of an exalted imagination.

And indeed the ban which religion has imposed upon thought in the interests of its own preservation is by no means without danger both for the individual and for society. Analytic experience has taught us that such prohibitions, even though they were originally confined to some particular field, have a tendency to spread, and then become the cause of severe inhibitions in people's lives. In women a process of this sort can be observed to follow from the prohibition against their occupying themselves, even in thought, with the sexual side of their nature. The biographies of almost all the eminent people of past times show the disastrous results of the inhibition of thought by religion. Intellect, on the other hand—or rather, to call it by a more familiar name, reason—is among the forces which may be expected to exert a unifying influence upon men—creatures who can be held together only with the greatest difficulty, and whom it is therefore scarcely possible to control. Think how impossible human society would be if every one had his own particular multiplication table and his own private units of weight and length. Our best hope for the future is that the intellect— the scientific spirit, reason—should in time establish a dictatorship over the human mind. The very nature of reason is a guarantee that it would not fail to concede to human emotions and to all that is determined by them, the position to which they are entitled. But the common pressure exercised by such a domination of reason would prove to be the strongest unifying force among men, and would prepare the way for further unifications. Whatever, like the ban laid upon thought by religion, opposes such a development is a danger for the future of mankind.

The question may now be asked why religion does not put an end to this losing fight by openly declaring: "It is a fact that I cannot give you what men commonly call truth; to obtain that, you must go to science. But what I have to give you is incomparably more beautiful, more comforting and more ennobling than anything that you could ever get from science. And I therefore say to you that it is true in a different and higher sense." The answer is easy to find. Religion cannot make this admission, because if it did it would lose all influence over the mass of mankind. The ordinary man knows only one "truth"—truth in the ordinary sense of the word. What may be meant by a higher, or a highest, truth, he cannot imagine. Truth seems to him as little capable of having degrees as death, and the necessary leap from the beautiful to the true is one that he cannot make. Perhaps you will agree with me in thinking that he is right in this.

The struggle, therefore, is not yet at an end. The followers of the religious *Weltanschauung* act in accordance with the old maxim: the best defence is attack. "What," they ask, "is this science that presumes to depreciate our religion, which has brought salvation and comfort to millions of men for many thousands of years? What has science for its part so far accomplished? What more can be expected of it? On its own admission, it is incapable of comforting or ennobling us. We will leave that on one side, therefore, though it is by no means easy to give up such benefits. But what of its teaching? Can it tell us how the world began, and what fate is in store for it? Can it even paint for us a coherent picture of the universe, and show us where the unexplained phenomena of life fit in, and how spiritual forces are able to operate on inert matter? If it could do that we should not refuse it our respect. But it has done nothing of the sort, not one single problem of this kind has it solved. It gives us fragments of alleged knowledge, which it cannot harmonize with one another, it collects observations of uniformities from the totality of events, and dignifies them with the name of laws and subjects them to its hazardous interpretations. And with what a small degree of certitude does it establish its conclusions! All that it teaches is only provisionally true; what is prized to-day as the highest wisdom is overthrown to-morrow and experimentally replaced by something else. The latest error is then given the name of truth. And to this truth we are asked to sacrifice our highest good!"

Ladies and Gentlemen—in so far as you yourselves are supporters of the scientific *Weltanschauung* I do not think you will be very profoundly shaken by this critic's attack. In Imperial Austria an anecdote was once current which I should like to call to mind in this connection. On one occasion the old Emperor was receiving a deputation from a political party which he disliked: "This is no longer ordinary opposition," he burst out, "this is factious opposition." In just the same way you will find that the reproaches made against science for not having solved the riddle of the universe are unfairly and spitefully exaggerated. Science has had too little time for such a tremendous achievement. It is still very young, a recently developed human activity. Let us bear in mind, to mention only a few dates, that only about three hundred years have passed since Kepler discovered the laws of planetary movement; the life of Newton, who split up light into the colours of the spectrum, and put forward the theory of gravitation, came to end in 1727, that is to say a little more than two hundred years ago; and Lavoisier discovered oxygen shortly before the French Revolution. I may be a very old man to-day, but the life of an individual man is very short in comparison with the duration of human development, and it is a fact that I was alive when Charles Darwin published his work on the origin of species. In the same year, 1859, Pierre Curie, the discoverer of radium, was born. And if you go back to the beginnings of exact natural science among the Greeks, to Archimedes, or to Aristarchus of Samos (*circa* 250 B.C.), the forerunner of Copernicus, or even to the tentative origins of astronomy among the Babylonians, you will only be covering a very small portion of the period which anthropology requires for the evolution of man from his original ape-like form, a period which certainly embraces more than a hundred thousand years. And it must not be forgotten that the last century has brought with it such a quantity of new discoveries and such a great acceleration of scientific progress that we have every reason to look forward with confidence to the future of science.

It has to be admitted that the other objections are valid within certain limits. Thus it is true that the path of science is slow, tentative and laborious. That cannot be denied or altered. No wonder that the gentlemen of the opposition are dissatisfied; they are spoilt, they have had an easier time of it with their revelation. Progress in scientific work is made in just the same way as in analysis. The analyst brings expectations with him to his work, but he must keep them in the background. He discovers something new by observation, now here and now there, and at first the bits do not fit together. He puts forward suppositions, he brings constructions to one's aid, and gives them up if they are not confirmed, he must have a great deal of patience, must be prepared for all possibilities, and must not jump at conclusions for fear of their leading him to overlook new and unexpected factors.

And in the end the whole expenditure of effort is rewarded, the scattered discoveries fall into place and he obtains an understanding of a whole chain of mental events; he has finished one piece of work and is ready for the next. But the analyst is unlike other scientific workers in this one respect that he has to do without the help which experiment can bring to research.

But the criticism of science which I have quoted also contains a great deal of exaggeration. It is not true to say that it swings blindly from one attempt to another, and exchanges one error for the next. As a rule the man of science works like a sculptor with a clay model, who persistently alters the first rough sketch, adds to it and takes away from it, until he has obtained a satisfactory degree of similarity to some object, whether seen or imagined. And, moreover, at least in the older and more mature sciences, there is already a solid foundation of knowledge, which is now only modified and elaborated and no longer demolished. The outlook, in fact, is not so bad in the world of science.

And finally, what is the purpose of all these passionate disparagements of science? In spite of its present incompleteness and its inherent difficulties, we could not do without it and could not put anything else in its place. There is no limit to the improvement of which it is capable, and this can certainly not be said of the religious *Weltanschauung*. The latter is complete in its essentials; if it is an error, it must remain one for ever. No attempt to minimise the importance of science can alter the fact that it attempts to take into account our dependence on the real external world, while religion is illusion, and it derives its strength from the fact that it falls in with our instinctual desires.

I must now go on to mention some other types of *Weltanschauung*, which are in opposition to the scientific one; I do so, however, unwillingly, because I know that I am not competent to form a judgment upon them. I hope, therefore, that you will bear this confession in mind in listening to what I have to say, and that if your interest is aroused you will go elsewhere for more trustworthy information.

In the first place I ought at this point to name the various philosophical systems which have ventured to draw a picture of the world, as it is reflected in the minds of thinkers whose eyes are as a rule turned away from it. But I have already attempted to give a general characterisation of philosophy and its methods, and I believe I am more unfitted than almost any one to pass the individual systems under review. I shall ask you, therefore, instead to turn your attention to two other phenomena which, particularly in these days, cannot be ignored.

The *Weltanschauung* to which I shall first refer is, as it were, a counterpart of political anarchism, and may perhaps have emanated from it. No doubt there have been intellectual nihilists of this kind before, but at the present day the theory of relativity of modern physics seems to have gone to their heads. It is true that they start out from science, but they succeed in forcing it to cut the ground from under its own feet, to commit suicide, as it were; they make it dispose of itself by getting it to refute its own premises. One often has an impression that this nihilism is only a temporary attitude, which will only be kept up until this task has been completed. When once science has been got rid of, some kind of mysticism, or, indeed, the old religious *Weltanschauung*, can spring up in the space that has been left vacant. According to this anarchistic doctrine, there is no such thing as truth, no assured knowledge of the external world. What we give out as scientific truth is only the product of our own needs and desires, as they are formulated under varying external conditions; that is to say, it is illusion once more. Ultimately we find only what we need to find, and see only what we desire to see. We can do nothing else. And since the criterion of truth, correspondence with an external world, disappears, it is absolutely immaterial what views we accept. All of them are equally true and false. And no one has a right to accuse any one else of error.

For a mind which is interested in epistemology, it would be tempting to enquire into the contrivances and sophistries by means of which the anarchists manage to elicit a final product of this kind from science. One would no doubt be brought up against situations like the one involved in the familiar example of the Cretan who says that all Cretans are liars. But I am not desirous, nor am I capable, of going deeper into this. I will merely remark that the anarchistic theory only retains its remarkable air of superiority so long as it is concerned with opinions about abstract things; it breaks down the moment it comes in contact with practical life. Now the behaviour of men is guided by their opinions and knowledge, and the same scientific spirit which speculates about the structure of the atom or the origin of man is concerned in the building of a bridge that will bear its load. If it were really a matter of indifference what we believed, if there were no knowledge which was distinguished from among our opinions by the fact that it corresponds with reality, then we might just as well build our bridges of cardboard as of stone, or inject a tenth of a gramme of morphia into a patient instead of a hundredth, or take tear-gas as a narcotic instead of ether. But the intellectual anarchists themselves would strongly repudiate such practical applications of their theory.

The other opposing *Weltanschauung* is to be taken far more seriously, and in this case I very deeply regret the insufficiency of my knowledge. I dare say that you know more about this subject than I do and that you have long ago taken up your position for or against Marxism. The investigations of Karl Marx into the economic structure of society and into the influence of various forms of economic organisation upon all departments of human life have in our day acquired an authority that cannot be denied. How far they are right or wrong in detail, I naturally do not know. I gather that it is not easy even for better informed people to decide. Some of the propositions in Marx's theory seem strange to me, such as that the evolution of forms of society is a process of natural history, or that the changes in social stratification proceed from one another in the manner of a dialectical process. I am by no means certain that I understand these statements rightly; moreover, they do not sound "materialistic" but like traces of the obscure Hegelian philosophy under the influence of which Marx at one time passed. I do not know how I can throw off the view which I share with other laymen, who are inclined to trace back the formation of classes in society to the struggles which went on from the beginning of history between various human hordes. These hordes differed to a slight degree from one another; and it is my view that social differences go back to these original differences of tribe or race. Psychological factors, such as the amount of constitutional aggressiveness and also the degree of cohesion within the horde, and material factors, such as the possession of better weapons, decided the victory. When they came to live together in the same territory, the victors became the masters and conquered the slaves. There is no sign in all this of natural laws or conceptual modifications; on the other hand, we cannot fail to recognise the influence which the progressive control over natural forces exerts on the social relationships between men, since men always place their newly won powers at the service of their aggressiveness, and use them against one another. The introduction of metals, of bronze and iron, put an end to whole cultural epochs and their social institutions. I really believe that gun-powder and fire-arms overthrew chivalry and the domination of the aristocracy, and that the Russian despotism was already doomed before the war was lost, since no amount of in-breeding among the ruling families of Europe could have produced a race of Tsars capable of withstanding the explosive force of dynamite.

It may be, indeed, that with the present economic crisis which followed upon the Great War, we are merely paying the price of our latest triumph over nature, the conquest of the air. This does not sound very convincing, but at least the first links in the chain of argument are clearly recognisable. The policy of England was based on the security guaranteed by the seas which encircle her coasts. The moment Blériot flew over the Channel in his aeroplane, this protective isolation was broken through; and on the night on which, in a time of peace, a German Zeppelin made an experimental cruise over London, war against Germany became a certainty.[1] Nor must the threat of submarines be forgotten in this connection.

I am almost ashamed of treating a theme of such importance and complexity in such a slight and inadequate manner, and I am also aware that I have not said anything that is new to you. I only wanted to call your attention to the fact that the factor of man's control over nature, from which he obtains his weapons for his struggle with his fellowmen, must of necessity also affect his economic arrangements. We seem to have travelled a long way from the problems of a *Weltanschauung*, but we shall soon come back to the point. The strength of Marxism obviously does not lie in its view of history or in the prophecies about the future which it bases upon that view, but in its clear insight into the determining influence which is exerted by the economic conditions of man upon his intellectual, ethical and artistic reactions. A whole collection of correlations and causal sequences were thus discovered, which had hitherto been almost completely disregarded. But it cannot be assumed that economic motives are the only ones which determine the behaviour of men in society. The unquestionable fact that different individuals, races and nations behave differently under the same economic conditions, in itself proves that the economic factor cannot be the sole determinant. It is quite impossible to understand how psychological factors can be overlooked where the reactions of living human beings are involved; for not only were such factors already concerned in the establishment of these economic conditions, but, even in obeying these conditions, men can do no more than set their original instinctual impulses in motion—their self-preservative instinct, their love of aggression, their need for love, and their impulse to attain pleasure and avoid pain. In an earlier lecture we have emphasised the importance of the part played by the super-ego, which represents tradition and the ideals of the past, and which will resist for some time the pressure exerted by new economic situations. And, finally, we must

---

[1] I was informed of this in the first year of the war on trustworthy authority.

not forget that the mass of mankind, subjected though they are to economic necessities, are borne on by a process of cultural development—some call it civilisation—which is no doubt influenced by all the other factors, but is equally certainly independent of them in its origin; it is comparable to an organic process, and is quite capable of itself having an effect upon the other factors. It displaces the aims of the instincts, and causes men to rebel against what has hitherto been tolerable; and, moreover, the progressive strengthening of the scientific spirit seems to be an essential part of it. If any one were in a position to show in detail how these different factors—the general human instinctual disposition, its racial variations, and its cultural modifications—behave under the influence of varying social organisations, professional activities and methods of subsistence, how these factors inhibit or aid one another—if, I say, any one could show this, then he would not only have improved Marxism but would have made it into a true social science. For sociology, which deals with the behaviour of man in society, can be nothing other than applied psychology. Strictly speaking, indeed, there are only two sciences—psychology, pure and applied, and natural science.

When at last the far-reaching importance of economic conditions began to be realised, the temptation arose to bring about an alteration in them by means of revolutionary interference, instead of leaving the change to the course of historical development. Theoretical Marxism, as put into effect in Russian Bolshevism, has acquired the energy, the comprehensiveness and the exclusiveness of a *Weltanschauung*, but at the same time it has acquired an almost uncanny resemblance to what it is opposing. Originally it was itself a part of science, and, in its realisation, was built up on science and technology, but it has nevertheless established a ban upon thought, which is as inexorable as was formerly that of religion. All critical examination of the Marxist theory is forbidden; doubts of its validity are as vindictively punished as heresy once was by the Catholic Church. The works of Marx, as the source of revelation, have taken the place of the Bible and the Koran, although they are no freer from contradictions and obscurities than these earlier holy books.

And although practical Marxism has remorselessly swept away all idealistic systems and illusions, it has nevertheless developed illusions itself, which are no less dubious and unverifiable than their predecessors. It hopes, in the course of a few generations, so to alter men that they will be able to live together in the new order of society almost without friction, and that they will do their work voluntarily. In the meantime it moves elsewhere the instinctual barriers which are essential in any society, it directs outwards the aggressive tendencies, which threaten every human community, and finds its support in the hostility of the poor against the rich, and of the hitherto powerless against the former holders of power. But such an alteration in human nature is very improbable. The enthusiasm with which the mob follow the Bolshevist lead at present, so long as the new order is incomplete and threatened from outside, gives no guarantee for the future, when it will be fully established and no longer in danger. In exactly the same way as religion, Bolshevism is obliged to compensate its believers for the sufferings and deprivations of the present life, by promising them a better life hereafter, in which there will be no unsatisfied needs. It is true that this paradise is to be in this world; it will be established on earth, and will be inaugurated within a measurable time. But let us remember that the Jews, whose religion knows nothing of a life beyond the grave, also expected the coming of the Messiah here on earth, and that the Christian Middle Ages constantly believed that the Kingdom of God was at hand.

There is no doubt what the answer of Bolshevism to these criticisms will be. "Until men have changed their nature," it will say, "one must employ the methods which are effective with them to-day. One cannot do without compulsion in their education or a ban upon thinking or the application of force even to the spilling of blood; and if one did not awake in them the illusions you speak of, one would not be able to bring them to submit to this compulsion." And it might politely ask us to say how else it could be done. At this point we should be defeated. I should know of no advice to give. I should admit that the conditions of this experiment would have restrained me, and people like me, from undertaking it; but we are not the only ones concerned. There are also men of action, unshakable in their convictions, impervious to doubt, and insensitive to the sufferings of any one who stands between them and their goal It is owing to such men that the tremendous attempt to institute a new order of society of this kind is actually being carried out in Russia now. At a time when great nations are declaring that they expect to find their salvation solely from a steadfast adherence to Christian piety, the upheaval in Russia—in spite of all its distressing features—seems to bring a promise of a better future. Unfortunately, neither our own misgivings nor the fanatical belief of the other side gives us any hint of how the experiment will turn out. The future will teach us. Perhaps it will show that the attempt has been made prematurely and that a fundamental alteration of the social order will have little hope of success until new discoveries are made that will increase our control over the forces of nature, and so make easier the satisfaction of our needs. It may be that only then will it be possible for a new order of society to emerge which will not only banish the material want of the masses, but at the same time meet the cultural requirements of individual men. But even so we shall still have to struggle for an indefinite length of time with the difficulties which the intractable nature of man puts in the way of every kind of social community.

Ladies and Gentlemen—Let me in conclusion sum up what I had to say about the relation of psychoanalysis to the question of a *Weltanschauung*. Psychoanalysis is not, in my opinion, in a position to create a *Weltanschauung* of its own. It has no need to do so, for it is a branch of science, and can subscribe to the scientific *Weltanschauung*. The latter, however, hardly merits such a high-sounding name, for it does not take everything into its scope, it is incomplete, and it makes no claim to being comprehensive or to constituting a system. Scientific thought is still in its infancy; there are very many of the great problems with which it has as yet been unable to cope. A *Weltanschauung* based upon science has, apart from the emphasis it lays upon the real world, essentially negative characteristics, such as that it limits itself to truth, and rejects illusions. Those of our fellow men who are dissatisfied with this state of things and who desire something more for their momentary peace of mind may look for it where they can find it. We shall not blame them for doing so; but we cannot help them and cannot change our own way of thinking on their account.

ALFRED NORTH WHITEHEAD
[1861–1947]

Those young students of philosophy who suddenly came upon *Science and the Modern World* soon after publication some thirty years ago had a sense of momentous discovery. Here was a book indeed! Perhaps they did not read it through. Certainly they could not understand it entirely. But they felt sure almost from the first page that it was bold, original, comprehensive, epoch-making. Here were logic and learning, wit and wisdom. Here was a mathematician steeped in science but not overwhelmed. Here was a mathematician telling us that "the intolerant use of abstractions is the major vice of the intellect" and finding his key insights in the romantic poets. Here was high praise of the great scientists of "the age of genius" and the Newtonian synthesis, "the greatest single intellectual success that mankind has achieved"—yet an achievement with such a bleak picture of nature that it has enfeebled or depressed the Western mind. "Nature is a dull affair, soundless, scentless, colorless; merely the hurrying of material, endlessly, meaninglessly." But an alternative view is possible, announced the redoubtable sage. "The only way of mitigating mechanism is by the discovery that it is not mechanism."

We were struck by the contention that modern science is an anti-intellectualistic movement in revolt against the rationalism of the Middle Ages. We were moved by his illustrations, such as his comparison of a meeting of the Royal Society in London hearing that photographs of an eclipse of the sun had confirmed certain predictions of Einstein, with an audience attending a tragedy in ancient Athens. Of course, we were immediately impressed by that still relevant final chapter on "Requisites for Social Progress," in which Whitehead accounted for the indifference to ugliness in our environment and deplored the lack of concrete aesthetic experience in our education, as distinguished from the overemphasis on intellectual analysis. As for that monstrous novelty in our educational development, the method of training professionals, the production of "minds in a groove" brings about "the restraint of serious thought within the groove." Hence, Whitehead said, in perhaps the gravest of all his warnings: "The directive force of reason is weakened. The leading intellects lack balance. They see this set of circumstances or that set; but not both sets together. The task of coordination is left to those who lack either the force or the character to succeed in some definite career." If more balanced intellects are now appearing in America, it may well be because he not only wrote but taught at Harvard between 1924 and 1937.

It is easily and often said that Whitehead's career falls into three periods. Child of a long line of parsons and school masters, Whitehead completed his formal education at Cambridge University and taught mathematics there for a quarter of a century, 1885-1910, meanwhile writing his classic *Treatise on Universal Algebra* (1898) and collaborating for ten years with Bertrand Russell on the monumental *Principia Mathematica* (3 volumes, 1910-1913). But in 1910, he and his family "deliberately pulled up stakes and moved to London," where he held various positions, both as teacher and administrator, in the great sprawling University of London. During this period he wrote three books in the philosophy of science, *An Enquiry Concerning the Principles of Natural Knowledge* (1919), *The Concept of Nature* (1920) and *The Principle of Relativity* (1922), and delivered those brilliant lectures which later were to make up most of *The Aims of Education and Other Essays.*

Then occurred one of the happiest events in the history of thought, of education, of philosophy. Whitehead. sixty-three and approaching retirement, entitled to rest on his oars at the end of a noble career, received a letter from President Lowell of Harvard, inviting him to become a member of the Department of Philosophy. The idea originated with Lawrence Henderson, the physiologist, and the funds of the professorship were provided by Henry Osborn Taylor, facts not known to the Whiteheads until many years later, we are told by Lucien Price in his fascinating *Dialogues of Alfred North Whitehead.* When Mrs. Whitehead asked him what he thought about the invitation, he replied, to her astonishment, "I would rather do that than anything in the world," and thereupon became a professor of philosophy for the first time in his life! As their ship entered Boston harbor in August, 1924, "We felt very small and very wee, wondering what was going to happen to us," he later confessed; but they soon discovered that just about everything good was to happen to them in the way of hospitality, friendship, thoughtfulness—and the faculty and students of Harvard soon found that they had a witty, radiant sage in their midst, to whom they could not give too much affectionate admiration.

Within six months of his arrival, he gave a series of eight Lowell Lectures, written at the rate of one a week as wanted for delivery, and "at white heat," according to Mrs. Whitehead. They were soon to form three-fourths of that startling, seminal and dramatic book, *Science and the Modern World*. There followed from his Gifford Lectures at Edinburgh in 1927-1928 the book he "most wanted to write," *Process and Reality*, which presents his philosophy of organism, "more profound and mysterious than anything else in contemporary metaphysics," according to Leslie Paul, and perhaps not to be fully appreciated for generations. The least sympathetic readers of *Process and Reality* have intimated roughly that the book is a succession of huge cloudy thoughts pierced from time to time by unforgettable flashes of aphoristic lightning. But we may ask, Could there be *so much* cloud where there is *so much* lightning?

But have no fear, dear reader, our selection will not be taken from *Process and Reality* but from the third and most personal volume of this loosely connected trilogy, *Adventures of Ideas*.

"Foresight," Chapter VI of Part I, was originally given as an address at the Harvard Business School in the depths of the Depression and published as the preface to Dean Donham's book all too aptly entitled *Business Adrift*.

We reprint it here, for although business may not be adrift at the moment, most of the world seems to be.

·   ·   ·

FORESIGHT

SECTION I. By the phrase Historical Foresight, I mean something quite different from the accurate exercise of Scientific Induction. Science is concerned with generalities. The generalities apply, but they do not determine the course of history apart from some anchorage in fact. There might have been many alternative courses of history conditioned by the same laws. Perhaps, if we knew enough of the laws, then we should understand that the development of the future from the past is completely determined by the details of the past and by these scientific laws which condition all generation. Unfortunately our knowledge of scientific laws is woefully defective, and our knowledge of the relevant facts of the present and the past is scanty in the extreme. Thus as the result of all our science, we are ignorant of that remote epoch when there will be a second collision between the sun and a passing star, we are ignorant of the future of life on the earth, we are ignorant of the future of mankind, we are ignorant of the course of history a year hence, we are ignorant of most of the domestic details of our lives tomorrow, we are even ignorant of the term that has been set to our own existence.

This catalogue of ignorances at once reminds us that our state is not that of blank absence of knowledge. Our ignorance is suffused with Foresight. Also the basis of our defect in Foresight is our scant knowledge of the relevant detailed facts in past and present which are required for the application of the scientific laws. Where the circumstances are comparatively simple, as in Astronomy, we know that the facts and the astronomical laws provide an apparatus of great accuracy in forecast. The main difficulty in Historical Foresight is the power of collecting and selecting the facts relevant to the particular type of forecast which we wish to make. Discussions on the method of science wander off onto the topic of experiment. But experiment is nothing else than a mode of cooking the facts for the sake of exemplifying the law. Unfortunately the facts of history, even those of private individual history, are on too large a scale. They surge forward beyond control.

It is thus evident that this topic of Historical Foresight is not to be exhausted by a neat description of some definite methods. It is faced with two sources of difficulty, where science has only one. Science seeks the laws only, but Foresight requires in addition due emphasis on the

relevant facts from which the future is to emerge. Of the
two tasks required for Foresight, this selection amid the welter
is the more difficult. Probably a neat doctrine of Foresight
is impossible. But what can be done is to confine attention
to one field of human activity, and to describe the type of
mentality which seems requisite for the attainment of Foresight within that field. The present state of the world, and
the course of the discussions in this book, suggest the field of
Commercial relations. This field will therefore be chosen to
illustrate the function of ideas in the provision of anticipation
and purpose.

To avoid misunderstanding I must disclaim the foolish
notion that it is possible for anyone, devoid of personal
experience of commerce, to provide useful suggestions for
its detailed conduct. There is no substitute for first-hand
practice. Also the word "commerce" is here used in the
largest sense of that term, in which it includes a variety of
activities. Any useful theory, capable of immediate application
to specific instances, must depend on a direct knowledge of
the relevant reactions of men and women composing that
society, or perhaps group of nations, within which the specific
business in question is to flourish. In this discussion there is
no pretence of such detailed knowledge.

There remains, however, the question of the general type
of mentality which in the present condition of the world will
promote the general success of a commercial community.
Such a type is, of course, very complex. But we are considering one unquestioned element in it, namely Foresight, and
will discuss the conditions for its development and its successful exercise.

Some people are born with astounding knacks of the mind.
For example, there are calculating boys who can perform
intricate operations of mental arithmetic in a flash, there are
also other sorts of peculiar faculties of divination; in particular
there are men with a knack of shrewdness in judging circumstances within the narrow range of their immediate observation. But after all, bankers prefer that their clerks should
learn arithmetic, and trained geologists are preferred to men

with divining rods. In the same way, there are general conditions of training which promote the development of a wider type of Foresight.

It is a great mistake to divide people into sharp classes, namely, people with such-and-such a knack and people without it. These trenchant divisions are simply foolish. Most humans are born with certain aptitudes. But these aptitudes can easily remain latent unless they are elicited into activity by fortunate circumstances. If anyone has no aptitude of a certain type, no training can elicit it. But, granted the aptitude, we can discuss the ways of training it. Foresight depends upon understanding. In practical affairs it is a habit. But the habit of foreseeing is elicited by the habit of understanding. To a large extent, understanding can be acquired by a conscious effort and it can be taught. Thus the training of Foresight is by the medium of Understanding. Foresight is the product of Insight.

SECTION II. The general topic to be understood is the entire internal functioning of human society, including its technologies, the biological and physical laws on which these technologies depend, and including the sociological reactions of humans depending on fundamental psychological principles. In fact, the general topic is sociology in the broadest sense of the term, including its auxiliary sciences. Such a width of understanding is, of course, beyond the grasp of any single human. But no part of it is entirely foreign to the provision of Foresight in business. Such a complete understanding is a cooperative enterprise; and a business community maintains its success for long periods so far as its average Foresight is dominated by some approach to such general understanding.

We shall comprehend better the varieties of individual understanding which go to complete this general equipment of an ideal business community, if we commence by considering the contrast between understanding and routine.

Routine is the god of every social system; it is the seventh heaven of business, the essential component in the success of every factory, the ideal of every statesman. The social machine should run like clockwork. Every crime should be followed by an arrest, every arrest by a judicial trial, every trial by a conviction, every conviction by a punishment, every punishment by a reformed character. Or, you can conceive an analogous routine concerning the making of a motor car, starting with the iron in the ore, and the coal in the mine, and ending with the car driving out of the factory and with the President of the Corporation signing the dividend warrants, and renewing his contracts with the mining Corporations. In such a routine everyone from the humblest miner to the august president is exactly trained for his special job. Every action of miner or president is the product of conditioned reflexes, according to current physiological phraseology. When the routine is perfect, understanding can be eliminated, except such minor flashes of intelligence as are required to deal with familiar accidents, such as a flooded mine, a prolonged drought, or an epidemic of influenza. A system will be the product of intelligence. But when the adequate routine is established, intelligence vanishes, and the system is maintained by a coordination of conditioned reflexes. What is then required from the humans is receptivity of special training. No one, from president to miner, need understand the system as a whole. There will be no Foresight, but there will be complete success in the maintenance of the routine.

Now it is the beginning of wisdom to understand that social life is founded upon routine. Unless society is permeated, through and through, with routine, civilization vanishes. So many sociological doctrines, the products of acute intellects, are wrecked by obliviousness to this fundamental sociological truth. Society requires stability, Foresight itself presupposes stability, and stability is the product of routine. But there are limits to routine, and it is for the discernment of these limits, and for the provision of the consequent action, that Foresight is required.

The two extremes of complete understanding and of complete routine are never realized in human society. But of the two, routine is more fundamental than understanding, that is to say, routine modified by minor flashes of short range intelligence. Indeed the notion of complete understanding controlling action is an ideal in the clouds, grotesquely at variance with practical life. But we have under our eyes countless examples of societies entirely dominated by routine. The elaborate social organizations of insects appear to be thoroughgoing examples of routine. Such organizations achieve far-reaching, complex purposes: they involve a differentiation of classes, from cows to serfs, from serfs to workers, from workers to warriors, from warriors to janitors, and from janitors to queens. Such organizations have regard to needs in a distant future, especially if the comparatively short space of life of the individual insects is taken into account as the unit of measurement.

These insect societies have been astoundingly successful, so far as concerns survival power. They seem to have a past extending over tens of thousands of years, perhaps of millions of years. It is the greatest of mistakes to believe that it has required the high-grade intelligence of mankind to construct an elaborate social organization. A particular instance of this error is the prevalent assumption that any social routine whose purposes are not obvious to our analysis is thereby to be condemned as foolish. We can observe insects performing elaborate routine actions whose purposes they cannot possibly understand, which yet are essential either for their own individual survival or for race-survival.

But these insect societies have one great characteristic in common. They are not progressive. It is exactly this characteristic that discriminates communities of mankind from communities of insects. Further, this great fact of progressiveness, be it from worse to better, or from better to worse, has become of greater and greater importance in Western civilization as we come to modern times. The rate of change has increased even in my life-time. It is possible that in future ages mankind may relapse into the stage of stable societies. But such a relapse is extremely unlikely within any span of time which we need take into account.

SECTION III. The recent shortening of the time-span between notable changes in social customs is very obvious, if we examine history. Originally it depended upon some slow

development of physical causes. For example, a gradual
change of physical configuration such as the elevation of
mountains: the time-span for such a change is of the order of
a million years. Again, a gradual change of climate: the time-
span for such a change is of the order of five-thousand years.
Again a gradual over-population of the region occupied by
some community with its consequent swarming into new
territories: having regard to the huge death-rate of pre-
scientific ages, the time-span for such a change was of the
order of five-hundred years. Again, the sporadic inventions of
new technologies, such as the chipping of flints, the invention
of fire, the taming of animals, the invention of metallurgy: in
the pre-scientific ages, the average time-span for such changes
was, at least, of the order of five-hundred years. If we compare the technologies of civilizations west of Mesopotamia at
the epochs 100 A.D., the culmination of the Roman Empire,
and 1400 A.D., the close of the Middle Ages, we find practically no advance in technology. There was some gain in
metallurgy, some elaboration of clockwork, the recent invention of gunpowder with its influence all in the future, some
advance in the art of navigation, also with its influence in the
future. If we compare 1400 A.D. with 1700 A.D., there is a
great advance; gunpowder, and printing, and navigation, and
the technique of commerce, had produced their effect. But
even then, the analogy between life in the eighteenth century
and life in the great period of ancient Rome was singularly
close, so that the peculiar relevance of Latin literature was
felt vividly. In the fifty years between 1780 and 1830, a number of inventions came with a rush into effective operation.
The age of steam power and of machinery was introduced.
But for two generations, from 1830 to 1890, there was a
singular uniformity in the principles of technology which
were regulating the structure of society and the usages of
business.

The conclusion to be drawn from this survey is a momentous one. Our sociological theories, our political philosophy, our practical maxims of business, our political economy,
and our doctrines of education, are derived from an unbroken

tradition of great thinkers and of practical examples, from the age of Plato in the fifth century before Christ to the end of the last century. The whole of this tradition is warped by the vicious assumption that each generation will substantially live amid the conditions governing the lives of its fathers and will transmit those conditions to mould with equal force the lives of its children. We are living in the first period of human history for which this assumption is false.

Of course in the past, there were great catastrophes: for example, plagues, floods, barbarian invasions. But, if such catastrophes were warded off, there was a stable, well-known condition of civilized life. This assumption subtly pervades the premises of political economy, and has permitted it to confine attention to a simplified edition of human nature. It is at the basis of our conception of the reliable business man, who has mastered a technique and never looks beyond his contracted horizon. It colours our political philosophy and our educational theory, with their overwhelming emphasis on past experience. The note of recurrence dominates the wisdom of the past, and still persists in many forms even where explicitly the fallacy of its modern application is admitted. The point is that in the past the time-span of important change was considerably longer than that of a single human life. Thus mankind was trained to adapt itself to fixed conditions.

Today this time-span is considerably shorter than that of human life, and accordingly our training must prepare individuals to face a novelty of conditions. But there can be no preparation for the unknown. It is at this point that we recur to the immediate topic, Foresight. We require such an understanding of the present conditions, as may give us some grasp of the novelty which is about to produce a measurable influence on the immediate future. Yet the doctrine, that routine is dominant in any society that is not collapsing, must never be lost sight of. Thus the grounds, in human nature and in the successful satisfaction of purpose, these grounds for the current routine must be understood; and at the same time the sorts of novelty just entering into social effectiveness have got to be weighed against the

old routine. In this way the type of modification and the
type of persistence exhibited in the immediate future may
be foreseen.

SECTION IV. It is now time to give some illustrations of
assertions already made. Consider our main conclusions that
our traditional doctrines of sociology, of political philosophy,
of the practical conduct of large business, and of political
economy are largely warped and vitiated by the implicit assumption of a stable unchanging social system. With this
assumption it is comparatively safe to base reasoning upon a
simplified edition of human nature. For well-known stimuli
working under well-known conditions produce well-known
reactions. It is safe then to assume that human nature, for the
purpose in hand, is adequately described in terms of some of
the major reactions to some of the major stimuli. For example,
we can all remember our old friend, the economic man.

The beauty of the economic man was that we knew exactly
what he was after. Whatever his wants were, he knew them
and his neighbours knew them. His wants were those developed in a well-defined social system. His father and grandfather had the same wants, and satisfied them in the same
way. So whenever there was a shortage, everyone—including
the economic man himself—knew what was short, and knew
the way to satisfy the consumer. In fact, the consumer knew
what he wanted to consume. This was the demand. The
producer knew how to produce the required articles, hence
the supply. The men who got the goods onto the spot first,
at the cheapest price, made their fortunes; the other producers
were eliminated. This was healthy competition. This is
beautifully simple and with proper elaboration is obviously
true. It expresses the dominant truth exactly so far as there
are stable well-tried conditions. But when we are concerned
with a social system which in important ways is changing,
this simplified conception of human relations requires severe
qualification.

It is, of course, common knowledge that the whole trend
of political economy during the last thirty or forty years
has been away from these artificial simplifications. Such sharp-

cut notions as "the economic man," "supply and demand," "competition," are now in process of dilution by a close study of the actual reactions of various populations to the stimuli which are relevant to modern commerce. This exactly illustrates the main thesis. The older political economy reigned supreme for about a hundred years from the time of Adam Smith, because in its main assumptions it did apply to the general circumstances of life as led, then and for innumerable centuries in the past. These circumstances were then already passing away. But it still remained a dominant truth that in commercial relations men were dominated by well-conditioned reactions to completely familiar stimuli.

In the present age, the element of novelty which life affords is too prominent to be omitted from our calculations. A deeper knowledge of the varieties of human nature is required to determine the reaction, in its character and its strength, to those elements of novelty which each decade of years introduces into social life. The possibility of this deeper knowledge constitutes the Foresight under discussion.

Another example which concerns sociological habits, and thence business relations and the shifting values of property, is to be seen in the history of cities. Throughout the whole span of civilization up to the present moment, the growth of condensed aggregates of humans, which we call cities, has been an inseparable accompaniment of the growth of civilization. There are many obvious reasons, the defence of accumulated wealth behind city walls, the concentration of materials requisite for manufacture, the concentration of power in the form of human muscles and, later, in the form of available heat energy, the ease of mutual intercourse required for business relations, the pleasure arising from a concentration of aesthetic and cultural opportunities, the advantages of a concentration of governmental and other directing agencies, administrative, legal, and military.

But there are disadvantages in cities. As yet no civilization has been self-supporting. Each civilization is born, it culminates, and it decays. There is a widespread testimony that this ominous fact is due to inherent biological defects in the crowded life of cities. Now, slowly and at first faintly, an opposite tendency is showing itself. Better roads and better vehicles at first induced the wealthier classes to live on the outskirts of the cities. The urgent need for defence had also vanished. This tendency is now spreading rapidly downwards. But a new set of conditions is just showing itself. Up to the present time, throughout the eighteenth and nineteenth centuries, this new tendency placed the homes in the immediate suburbs, but concentrated manufacturing activity, business relations, government, and pleasure, in the centres of the cities. Apart from the care of children, and periods of sheer rest, the active lives were spent in the cities. In some ways, the concentration of such activities was even more emphasized, and the homes were pushed outwards even at the cost of the discomfort of commuting. But, if we examine the trend of technology during the past generation, the reasons for this concentration are largely disappearing. Still more, the reasons for the choice of sites for cities are also altering. Mechanical power can be transmitted for hundreds of miles, men can communicate almost instantaneously by telephone, the chiefs of great organizations can be transported by airplanes, the cinemas can produce plays in every village, music, speeches, and sermons can be broadcast. Almost every reason for the growth of cities, concurrently with the growth of civilization, has been profoundly modified.

What then is to be the future of cities, three hundred years hence, a hundred years hence, or even thirty years hence? I do not know. But I venture a guess: that those who are reasonably fortunate in this Foresight will make their fortunes, and that others will be ruined by mistakes in calculation.

My second point that the reasons for the choice of sites for cities have also been modified is illustrated by recent changes in my own country, England. The first effect of the new industrial age of the eighteenth and nineteenth centuries was to concentrate population round the coalfields. Thus the central portion of England on its northern edge has become one huge city, disguised under different names for its various regional parts. But the novel conditions are shifting population and manufactures to the south of England, near to the great southern ports which look towards the Mediterranean, the South Atlantic Ocean, and the Panama Canal. They are the best ports, with the easiest navigation, and with uncrowded land around them. At present the transmission of electric power is one of the major preoccupations of the government of England.

The effect of new technologies on the sites of cities, and on the transformation of cities, is one of the fundamental problems which must enter into all sociological theories, including the forecasting of business relations. We must not exaggerate the importance of these particular examples. They are just two examples selected from a whole situation which can be analysed into innumerable examples with the same moral. I mean nothing so absurd as that all industrialists should meditate on the future of cities. The topic may be quite irrelevant to the future activities of most of them. Also I am ignorant as to how much Political Economy they should study.

But we are faced with a fluid, shifting situation in the immediate future. Rigid maxims, a rule-of-thumb routine, and cast-iron particular doctrines will spell ruin. The business of the future must be controlled by a somewhat different type of men to that of previous centuries. The type is already changing, and has already changed so far as the leaders are concerned. The Business Schools of Universities are concerned with spreading this newer type throughout the nations by aiming at the production of the requisite mentality.

SECTION V. I will conclude this chapter by a sketch of the Business Mind of the future. In the first place it is fundamental that there be a power of conforming to routine, of supervising routine, of constructing routine, and of understanding routine both as to its internal structure and as to its external purposes. Such a power is the bedrock of all practical efficiency. But for the production of the requisite Foresight, something more is wanted. This extra endowment can only be described as a philosophic power of understanding the complex flux of the varieties of human societies: for instance, the habit of noting varieties of demands on life, of serious pur-

poses, of frivolous amusements. Such instinctive grasp of the
relevant features of social currents is of supreme importance.
For example, the time-span of various types of social behaviour is of the essence of their effect on policy. A widespread
type of religious interest, with its consequent modes of behaviour, has a dominant life of about a hundred years, while a
fashion of dress survives any time between three months and
three years. Methods of agriculture change slowly. But the scientific world seems to be on the verge of far-reaching biological discoveries. The assumption of slow changes in agriculture
must therefore be scanned vigilantly. This example of time-
spans can be generalized. The quantitative aspect of social
changes is of the essence of business relations. Thus the habit
of transforming observation of qualitative changes into quantitative estimates should be a characteristic of business mentality.

I have said enough to show that the modern commercial
mentality requires many elements of discipline, scientific and
sociological. But the great fact remains that details of relevant
knowledge cannot be foreseen. Thus even for mere success,
and apart from any question of intrinsic quality of life, an
unspecialized aptitude for eliciting generalizations from particulars and for seeing the divergent illustration of generalities
in diverse circumstances is required. Such a reflective power
is essentially a philosophic habit: it is the survey of society
from the standpoint of generality. This habit of general
thought, undaunted by novelty, is the gift of philosophy, in
the widest sense of that term.

SECTION VI. But the motive of success is not enough. It
produces a short-sighted world which destroys the sources
of its own prosperity. The cycles of trade depression which
afflict the world warn us that business relations are infected
through and through with the disease of short-sighted motives. The robber barons did not conduce to the prosperity of Europe in the Middle Ages, though some of them
died prosperously in their beds. Their example is a warning to our civilization. Also we must not fall into the fallacy
of thinking of the business world in abstraction from the rest

of the community. The business world is one main part of the very community which is the subject-matter of our study. The behaviour of the community is largely dominated by the business mind. A great society is a society in which its men of business think greatly of their functions. Low thoughts mean low behaviour, and after a brief orgy of exploitation low behaviour means a descending standard of life. The general greatness of the community, qualitatively as well as quantitatively, is the first condition for steady prosperity, buoyant, self-sustained, and commanding credit. The Greek philosopher who laid the foundation of all our finer thoughts ended his most marvellous dialogue with the reflection that the ideal state could never arrive till philosophers are kings. Today, in an age of democracy, the kings are the plain citizens pursuing their various avocations. There can be no successful democratic society till general education conveys a philosophic outlook.

Philosophy is not a mere collection of noble sentiments. A deluge of such sentiments does more harm than good. Philosophy is at once general and concrete, critical and appreciative of direct intuition. It is not—or, at least, should not be—a ferocious debate between irritable professors. It is a survey of possibilities and their comparison with actualities. In philosophy, the fact, the theory, the alternatives, and the ideal, are weighed together Its gifts are Insight and Foresight, and a sense of the worth of life, in short, that sense of importance which nerves all civilized effort. Mankind can flourish in the lower stages of life with merely barbaric flashes of thought. But when civilization culminates, the absence of a coordinating philosophy of life, spread throughout the community, spells decadence, boredom, and the slackening of effort.

Every epoch has its character determined by the way its populations react to the material events which they encounter. This reaction is determined by their basic beliefs—by their hopes, their fears, their judgments of what is worth while. They may rise to the greatness of an opportunity, seizing its drama, perfecting its art, exploiting its adventure, mastering

intellectually and physically the network of relations that
constitutes the very being of the epoch. On the other hand,
they may collapse before the perplexities confronting them.
How they act depends partly on their courage, partly on
their intellectual grasp. Philosophy is an attempt to clarify
those fundamental beliefs which finally determine the
emphasis of attention that lies at the base of character.

Mankind is now in one of its rare moods of shifting its
outlook. The mere compulsion of tradition has lost its force.
It is our business—philosophers, students, and practical men—
to re-create and re-enact a vision of the world, including those
elements of reverence and order without which society lapses
into riot, and penetrated through and through with unflinch-
ing rationality. Such a vision is the knowledge which Plato
identified with virtue. Epochs for which, within the limits
of their development, this vision has been widespread are the
epochs unfading in the memory of mankind.

Our discussion has insensibly generalized itself. It has
passed beyond the topic of Commercial Relations to the
function of a properly concrete philosophy in guiding the
purposes of mankind.

•   •   •

As a mathematician and logician, Whitehead had had some experience in rigor and precision, but in the realm of speculative
philosophy he refused to be bullied by excessive or premature
claims for precision, exactitude, perfect clarity. To those who have
such faith in the adequacy of existent language, he attributed "the
Fallacy of the Perfect Dictionary."[1] Again and again he declared or
implied that "Philosophy in its advance must involve obscurity of
expression and novel phrases."[2] His very last piece of writing, the
essay on Immortality, concludes (as he pointed out to Lucien
Price) with these words: "My point is that the final outlook of
philosophic thought cannot be based upon the exact statements
which form the basis of the special sciences.

"The exactness is a fake."[3]

[1] Radcliffe College, October 25, 1935.
[2] Cambridge Symposium, December 29, 1936.
[3] Ingersoll Lecture, April 22, 1941.

JOHN DEWEY
[1859–1952]

The direct approach to John Dewey and his work is often obstructed by his competing admirers and irascible adversaries. The common objection to his style—which is certainly not classic or felicitous—tends to ignore the fact that he was struggling, as did Whitehead, to think out fresh ideas and not restate old ones. In any case, he is a giant figure not to be dismissed lightly because someone's retarded daughter did not get along well in a progressive school.

"He was the first decadent, he once jokingly put it, in seven generations of Vermont farmers," according to the late Irwin Edman. In his third year at the University of Vermont, the study of T. H. Huxley's *Elementary Physiology* seems to have first awakened his philosophic interest, not because of the subject of the book, but because it gave him "a sense of interdependence and interrelated unity," a model for his later reflections. In the fourth year the seniors were permitted to roam rather widely in a course covering the social sciences and various branches of philosophy, with emphasis on the philosophy of religion, taught by the sensitive, though "constitutionally timid," Professor H. A. P. Torrey. After graduating, Dewey taught high school for three years—a crucial period never sufficiently emphasized. He then studied philosophy privately for a year under Professor Torrey, who "let his mind go more freely than in the classroom," and continued to receive favorable comment on the articles he had been sending from time to time to Dr. W. T. Harris, the editor of the only philosophic journal in America, *The Journal of Speculative Philosophy.* Torrey and Harris together were no doubt the chief influences on Dewey's decision to go to Johns Hopkins for graduate work in philosophy.

It was at Johns Hopkins that Dewey came under the spell of the neo-Hegelian idealism which dominated British and American philosophy in the last two or three decades of the nineteenth century; but it was a moderated Hegelianism, thanks to the interpretation of the scholarly Professor George Sylvester Morris, who "retained something of his early Scotch philosophical training in a common-sense belief in the existence of the external world." Although Dewey drifted steadily away from Hegelianism during the next fifteen years, he never ceased to be grateful to Professor Morris and to Hegel for his numberless rich insights, for his passion for unity and interrelatedness—apart from his too systematic system.

Practically all of these details are taken from an invaluable autobiographical essay, "From Absolutism to Experimentalism," which Dewey wrote at the age of seventy for *Contemporary American Philosophy* (1930), edited by G. P. Adams and W. P. Montague. He there stressed four special points in his life which he did not pretend to place in a developmental order:

(1) "The practice and theory of education, especially the education of the young," for he had little confidence in so-called "higher" education which was not based on sound foundations. Hence his experimental school at Chicago, his early book, *The School and Society* (1899) and his many other writings, culminating in *Democracy and Education* (1916). That was the book in which for many years his philosophy was most fully expounded, but he noted wryly it was rarely consulted by his philosophical critics—as if education were not a proper theme for a serious philosopher! "This handle is offered," he added, "to any subsequent critic who may wish to lay hold of it."

(2) ". . . the intellectual scandal . . . involved in the current (and traditional) *dualism* in logical standpoint and method between something called 'science' on the one hand and something called 'morals' on the other"—as if the vast stores of carefully, patiently organized knowledge could have no bearing on the means and ends of conduct. It was largely this intellectual "scandal," Dewey himself asserted, which forced him to develop his "instrumentalism," a more rigorous pragmatism, in which ideas are guides and tools to a richer life, not merely passive mirrors of an unchangeable "reality."

(3) Although Dewey believed that people and situations rather than books were the chief influences in his life, there was the out-

standing exception of James's *Principles of Psychology,* "which was much the greatest single influence in changing the direction of his philosophical thinking." The biological, dynamic, and objective elements in the *Principles,* with such illuminating chapters as those on Conception, Discrimination and Comparison, and Reasoning, gave Dewey an authentic sense of "life in terms of life as action" which he had not found in the more aloof tradition of classical philosophy. Along these lines he would now proceed—for more than sixty years!

(4) Finally, Dewey maintained in 1930 that "the Jamesian psychology led straight to the perception of the importance of distinctive social categories, especially communication and participation," categories that the cloistered intellectual tends to neglect. In his discussion of "how we think," in his emphasis on "learning by doing" and "interest and effort," in his tireless argument for "the new individualism" and "social action," Dewey was certainly making his own contributions to the *social categories.* At ninety he published a series of highly technical articles written with Arthur F. Bentley, *Knowing and the Known,* dealing with vagueness in logic and chaos in semantics. So much for the category of communication.

But what if *Democracy and Education,* published before Dewey was sixty, had remained the fullest statement of his philosophy? It would have meant that his supreme work, *Experience and Nature,* the most nearly systematic presentation of his "empirical naturalism" or "naturalistic humanism," would have gone unwritten. Yet that was precisely the work to which Justice Holmes paid the supreme tribute in a letter to Sir Frederick Pollock: ". . . although Dewey's book is incredibly ill-written, it seemed to me after several rereadings to have a feeling of intimacy with the inside of the cosmos that I found unequaled. So methought God would have spoken had He been inarticulate but keenly desirous to tell you how it was." In a friend's copy of *Experience and Nature,* Holmes wrote that "it came nearest to expressing 'the cosmic wiggle' of any book he knew."[1] Many share this judgment with the great Justice although they may express it in more technical language.

If Dewey had died before he was seventy, he would not have delivered the Gifford Lectures, which compose a second major

---

[1] *The Practical Cogitator,* edited by Charles P. Curtis, Jr., and Ferris Greenslet, 527.

work, *The Quest for Certainty: A Study of the Relation of Knowledge and Action,* his most elaborate attempt to bridge the gap between theory and practice, between the remote abstractions of science and the common things of everyday life. Among Deweyans the chapters on "The Supremacy of Method" and "The Construction of Good" are particular favorites. But except for his most sympathetic and careful readers, the immense surprise came in 1934 with the publication of *Art As Experience.* Was this not a foreign realm to Dewey? Was his style not sufficient proof that he would always be insensitive to the arts? It was not generally known that he had for many years read on the subject in English, French and German and since 1915 had been the teacher, the pupil and the warm friend of Albert C. Barnes. That prodigious eccentric, with his fortune made from the invention of Argyrol and Ovoferrin, had built up at Merion, Pennsylvania, perhaps the finest collection in the world of modern French painting—not to mention masterpieces of earlier artists. But Dr. Barnes was not only a shrewd collector, he was a dedicated student of art, an educator, an author— and he shared all he knew with Dewey. But whatever its inspiration, *Art As Experience,* with its sheer delight in consummatory values, with its emphasis on art as "communication in its pure and undefiled form," with the declaration that art is "incomparable for the adventure of philosophic thought," became the veritable crown of Dewey's work, whereas the huge *Logic: The Theory of Inquiry,* published in his seventy-ninth year, rounded out and solidified the foundation.

In closing this too brief or too lengthy note, we turn back to Dewey's 1929 preface to the second edition of *Experience and Nature* and quote a passage in which he comments on the revised opening chapter: "It points to faith in experience when intelligently used as a means of disclosing the realities of nature. It finds that nature and experience are not enemies or alien. Experience is not a veil that shuts man off from nature; it is a means of penetrating continually further into the heart of nature. There is in the character of human experience no index-hand pointing to agnostic conclusions, but rather a growing progressive self-disclosure of nature herself. The failures of philosophy have come from lack of confidence in the directive powers that inhere in human experience, if men have but the wit and courage to follow them."

Our selection here was made by Dewey himself for Whit Burnett's huge anthology *The World's Best,* to which one hundred and five living authors contributed their own favorites. It was first read as a lecture to a congress of physicians in St. Louis in the fall of 1937.

* * *

THE UNITY OF THE HUMAN BEING

We have no words that are prepared in advance to be fit for framing and expressing sound and tested ideas about the unity of the human being, the wholeness of the self. If we ask an economist "What is money?" the proper official reply is that it is a medium of exchange. The answer does not stand in the way of a great deal of money being accumulated by using it to obstruct the processes of exchange. Similarly, we say that words are a means of communicating ideas. But upon some subjects—and the present one falls in this class—the words at our disposal are largely such as to *prevent* the communication of ideas. The words are so loaded with associations derived from a long past that instead of being tools for thought, our thoughts become subservient tools of words.

The meanings of such words as soul, mind, self, unity, even body, are hardly more than condensed epitomes of mankind's agelong efforts at interpretation of its experience. These efforts began when man first emerged from the state of the anthropoid ape. The interpretations which are embodied in the words that have come down to us are the products of desire and hope, of chance circumstance and ignorance, of the authority exercised by medicine men and priests as well as of acute observation and sound judgment.

Physicists had in the beginning a like problem. They are solving it by the invention of technical terms and a technical language. Symbols have, in principle, only the meanings that are put upon them because of special inquiries engaged in. It will be a long time before anything of this sort will be accomplished for human beings. To expel traditional meanings and replace them by ideas that are products of controlled inquiries is a slow and painful process.

Doubtless advance is possible, and will be made, by invention of words that are not charged with the debris of man's past experience. But it is also possible that this process cannot be carried with safety as far as it can be with physical things. Our technical terms might easily represent such artificial constructions that they would fail to help us in dealings with human beings—with the John Smiths and Susan Joneses with whom we rub elbows in daily life.

The words in which I try to communicate ideas to you are, then, at best, but means of stimulating personal observation and reflection. This statement holds even of the phrase "the unity of the human being." At first, the words have only a meaning derived from a contrasting effect. The idea of man as an integral whole is projected against a background of beliefs about man which are chiefly of emotional origin and force; against belief in a dualism that was the expression of religious and moral institutions and traditions.

The phrase "unity of man" has at first, accordingly, a negative meaning. It expresses a way of *not* talking about soul *and* body, body *and* mind. The word "unity" is a protest against the canonized dualism expressed in the presence of the word "and." Nevertheless, the split expressed in this word is so engrained in our emotional and intellectual habits that no sooner have we consciously rejected it in one form than it recurs in another. The dualism is found today even among those who have abandoned its earlier manifestations. It is shown in separations made between the structural and the functional; between the brain and the rest of the body; between the central nervous system and the vegetative nervous system and viscera; and most fundamentally, between the organism and the environment. For the first of each of these pairs of terms—structure, brain, organism—retains something of the isolation and alleged independence that used to belong to the "soul" and the "mind" and later to "consciousness."

While it is necessary to advance from the negative meaning of the phrase "the unity of man" the idea of unity also has its perils. For it has taken on associations during centuries of philosophic discussion that make it a dangerous word. It has become almost an invitation to set an abstraction in place of concrete phenomena. You and I can easily think of comprehensive systems—psychiatric, therapeutic, philosophical and psychological—suggested in the first place by undoubted facts, which under the protecting shield of the idea of unity, have been built up so as to force the facts, disguising and distorting them. At the present time there is a revulsion against the endless splitting up of human beings into bits. It is going on with respect to cells, structures and organs, sensations, ideas, reflexes; and with respect to atoms and electrons. The phrase "unity of man" is a protest against analysis of man into separate ultimate elements, as well as against the traditional split into body and soul. But it is easier, much easier, to set up the idea of unity in a vague way, than it is to translate it into definite facts.

"Unity of the human being" only indicates, at best, a point of view, and the point of view has no meaning save as it is used as a vantage point from which to observe and interpret actual phenomena.

We often hear such phrases as the unity of a family, the unity of a nation. These phrases stand for something. Yet in the history of social and political speculation, men have allowed the words to take the bit in their teeth and run away from inquiry into the actual facts to which they refer. These instances of the use of "unity" may, however, provide a suggestion from which it is safe to set out. Whatever else the unity is or is not, it at least means the way in which a number of different persons and things work together toward a common end. This *working together* exists in action, operation, not as a static object or collection of objects. It is the kind of unity that seems to me to give the clew to understanding the unity of the human being.

We can recognize and identify a man as a single object, a numerical unit, by observation which marks out boundaries, as we note that the bounded object moves as a whole. In that way you recognize me as a single object standing here on the

stage before you. That is the way in which we recognize a
rock, tree or house as a single object, as a unity and whole.
But that which makes a rock a single whole is the interaction
of swarms of molecules, atoms, and electrons; its unity is an
affair of the way elements work together. The boundaries by
which we mark off a human being as a unit are very different
from the energies and organization of energies that make
him a unified human being. We can observe the boundaries
at a single moment. We can grasp the unity only, so to speak,
longitudinally—only as something that goes on in a stretch of
time. It is not found in any number of cross-sectional views.

Nevertheless, if we could look into the minds of our neighbors, I think we should not be much surprised to find in them
quite frequently the notion that a man exists within the
boundaries which are visible, tangible, and observable. In a
word, the man is identified with what is underneath his skin.
We incline to suppose that we would know all about him if
we could find out everything that is happening in his brain
and other parts of his nervous system: in his glands, muscles,
viscera, heart and lungs and so on.

Now up to a certain point we are on the right track, provided we emphasize sufficiently the interaction, the working
together, of all these diverse processes. We can get a better
idea of the unity of the human being as we know more about
all these processes and the way they work together, as they
check, and stimulate one another and bring about a balance.
But the one positive point I wish to present is that while this
is necessary it is not enough. We must observe and understand
these internal processes and their interactions from the standpoint of their interaction with what is going on outside the
skin—with that which is called the *environment*—if we are to
obtain a genuine conception of the unity of the human being.

Our attitude with respect to this matter is a strange mixture. In special points we take for granted the inclusion of the
conditions and energies that are outside the boundaries set by
the skin. No one supposes for a moment that there can be
respiration without the surrounding air; or that the lungs are
anything more than organs of interaction with what is outside

the body. No one thinks of separating the processes of digestion from connection with foodstuffs derived by means of other organs from the environment. We know that eye, ear and hand, and somatic musculature, are concerned with objects and events outside the boundaries of the body. These things we take for granted so regularly and unconsciously that it seems foolish to mention them. Physiologists at least recognize that what is true of breathing and digestion holds also of the circulation of fluids that goes on entirely within the body, although the connection of these processes with environing conditions is a stage more indirect. The structure and processes of the central nervous system do not have that immediate connection with the outside world that the peripheral neural structures have.

Yet an authority upon the anatomy and physiology of the nervous system recently used these words: "Every movement is the result of the messages which pass from the central mass of nerve cells to the muscles, and the outgoing messages are varied according to the reports submitted by the sense organs. These show what is happening in the world outside, and the nervous system must evolve a plan of action appropriate to the occasion." [1]

That movements affected by the muscles have to do, directly and indirectly, with activities of seeking, defense, and taking possession of energies of the outside world is obvious. The central nervous system has the function of evolving the plans and procedures that take effect in dealing with outside conditions as they are reported through sense organs—and I suppose it would be admitted that these reports vary, depending upon what the body was doing previously in connection with outside conditions.

In other words, with respect to every special set of organic structures and processes, we take it for granted that things beyond the body are involved in interaction with those inside the body, and that we cannot understand the latter in isolation. This states a fact so generally recognized as to be a

---

[1] N. Adrian, *Harvard Tercentenary Publications*, Vol. I, p. 4.

commonplace. The strangeness of the mixture of which I
spoke consists in the fact that while we recognize the involve-
ment of conditions external to the body in all organic
processes, when they are taken one by one, we often fail to
recognize and act upon the idea as an inclusive principle
by which to understand the unity of man and the disorders
which result from disruption of this unity.

Whole philosophical systems have been built up, for example, by treating thinking, especially in so-called abstract
ideas, as having no connection with the activities the body
executes in the environment in use and enjoyment of the
conditions it presents. There is many a mathematician who
would be shocked if he were told that his constructions had
anything to do with activities carried on in the environment.
Yet we know that neural structures and processes developed in
control and use of the environment are the organs of all thinking. Even some who call themselves behaviorists, who pride
themselves on their strictly scientific attitude, have identified
the behavior about which they talk with the behavior of the
nervous system in and by itself. Having, for example, identified thought with language—a position for which much may
be said—they go on to locate language in the vocal cords,
ignoring the transaction of communication in which, directly
and indirectly, other human beings take part. It may even
be that on occasion physicians think of diseases, and even
psychical disorders, as something that goes on wholly inside
the body, so that they treat what goes on outside as, at most,
an external cause rather than a constituent and interacting
factor in the disease.

At all events, there is a good deal of description and interpretation in many fields in which the structural and static
lord it over the active and functioning. Whenever we find this
to be the case we may be sure that some structure of the body
has been described and interpreted in isolation from its connection with an activity in which an environment plays an
integral part.

On the other hand, when physicians proceed to regulate
the diet, sleep and exercise of patients, when they inquire

into and give advice about their habits, they are dealing with the "use of the self" in its active functional connection with the outside world. What, then, I am urging is simply the systematic and constant projection of what is here involved into all our observations, judgments and generalizations about the unity and the breakdowns of unity of human beings. For its implications are that all beliefs and practices which gratuitously split up the unity of man have their final root in the separation of what goes on inside the body from integrated interaction with what goes on outside.

This abstract principle becomes concrete as soon as one thinks not of environment in general, but of the human environment—that which is formed by contacts and relations with our human fellows. Psychiatrists have made us familiar with disturbances labeled "withdrawal from reality." They have pointed out the role of this withdrawal in many pathological occurrences. What are these withdrawals but cases of the interruption or cessation of "the active operative presence of environing conditions in the activities of a human being"? What are the resulting pathological phenomena but evidences that the self loses its integrity *within itself* when it loses integration with the medium in which it lives?

It is only necessary to think of those mild instances of withdrawal, forming ordinary day-dreaming and fantasy building, to appreciate that the environment which is involved is human or social. When a person builds up not only a systematized delusion of wealth but engages in a daydream in which he has come into possession of a large sum of money, it is not the physical money he is thinking of, but the prestige and power it gives him over his fellows. If a fantasy becomes habitual and controlling, it brings about, sooner or later, retraction from even the physical environment. But these withdrawals from physical surroundings originate in disturbances of relationship with the human environment. They go back to such things as pettings and coddlings, personal rejections, failure to win recognition and approvals, fear of those in authority, frustration of hope and desire by social conditions.

We may then anticipate a time when our entire traditional psychology will be looked upon as extraordinarily one-sided in its exclusive concern with actions and reactions of human beings with their physical surroundings to the neglect of interpersonal relationships. We have, to be sure, reached a point where we have chapters and books entitled "social psychology." But we are far from having reached the point in which it is seen that the whole difference between animal and human psychology is constituted by the transforming effect exercised upon the former by intercourse and association with other persons and groups of persons. For, apart from unconditioned reflexes, like the knee-jerk, it may be questioned whether there is a single human activity or experience which is not profoundly affected by the social and cultural environment. Would we have any intellectual operations without the language which is a social product? As for our emotional life, permit me to cite two passages written by a physician: "Contact with human beings is the stimulus that elicits emotional and visceral reactions. It is not the clatter of railways and motors, this 'fast hurrying age in which we live' so often spoken of; it is rather the pride, the envy, the ambition, the rage, the disappointment, the defeat that develop in purely human relations that stir the viscera"; and again: "There is an immense amount of hokum uttered about the psychological tensions caused by our swiftly moving era, as though the telephone, the radio, and the electric refrigerator were instruments that could swerve the viscera. The emotional life does not actually hinge on machinery but on the type of response to living situations, situations that for the most part are created by human contacts."[2]

I do not believe I am going beyond the implications of these passages when I say that the operation of "living situations created by human contacts" is the only intelligible ground upon which we can distinguish between what we call the *higher* and the *lower* (the physical on one side and the ideal and "spiritual" on the other) in human experience.

---

[2] Houston, *The Art of Treatment*, pp. 348-349; p. 450.

The occurrence of a sensation, for example, may be described as an interaction between certain neural processes and certain vibrations. The principle involved here is the same in animals and in man. But the *significance* of a quality of red depends upon the part it plays in the customary uses and enjoyments of the social group of which a person is a member. To a bull, its presence is a purely physiological stimulus. For a child, it may be that a dress, worn perhaps only on a festal occasion or a ribbon worn for adornment in the presence of others, is that which fixes the significance of red. When we wait in an automobile for a traffic light to turn, red is still a physiological stimulus. But it has its *significance* in terms of adaptation of the behavior of individuals to one another. The emotional importance of red in a red, white and blue flag to a patriotic American citizen is surely not native in physiological structure.

Examples do not *prove* the principle laid down. But I do believe that reflection upon these and similar cases will show that the only verifiable basis we have for marking off the experiences that have practical, emotional and intellectual significance from those which do not is the influence of cultural and social forces upon internal physiological processes.

At least, what I have said is a challenge to produce any instance of an experience having so-called ideal or even "spiritual" meaning that cannot be accounted for on this ground. Otherwise we must have recourse to the old division between soul and body. Take the case of those who revolt against the old dualism, and who because of their revolt imagine they must throw away and deny the existence of all phenomena that go by the names of "higher," intellectual and moral. Such persons exist. They suppose they are not scientific unless they reduce everything to the exclusively somatic and physiological. This procedure is a conspicuous instance of what must happen when observation, description and interpretation of human events are confined to what goes on under the skin to the exclusion of their integrated interaction with environmental conditions, particularly the environment formed by other human beings. Knowledge of

strictly somatic organs and processes is certainly necessary
for scientific understanding of "higher" phenomena. But only
half-way science neglects and rules out the other factor.

We may reject the traditional dualism. In my conviction
we should reject it. We cannot be scientific save as we seek
for the physiological, the physical factor in every emotional,
intellectual and volitional experience. As more is known
of this factor, more intellectual capital and more resources
of control are at our command. In the case of the physician
especially is it so true as to be a truism, that the more
anatomical, chemical and immunological information he has,
the better prepared is he for his work. And it is also true that
our knowledge of social relations and their effects upon
native and original physiological processes is scanty and un-
organized in comparison with the physical knowledge at our
command.

But in view of the role played by human contacts and relations in developing and sustaining the emotional and intellectual quality of human experience on one side, and in
bringing disturbance and disorder into it on the other, this
fact is all the more reason for devoting constant attention
to the as yet relatively unknown factor in the case of every
human being who comes under observation. This need cannot be met by knowledge of even the most up-to-date scientific psychology which now exists. For, unfortunately, this
psychology suffers for the most part from exactly the one-
sided concern in question: the failure to take into account
the operations and effects of relationships between human
beings.

To me, a layman, it appears that physicians have a unique
opportunity for building up just the kind of knowledge that
is now so largely lacking. Physicians are the persons who
have the most direct, intimate and continued contact with
the living situations in which the problem is most acutely
present. Since the decline of the influence of priest and
pastor, no other professional body is in a position to make
such a contribution and render such a service—though it
should be acknowledged that the group of teachers also has

an opportunity of which it fails to take adequate advantage. I am impressed, as every one else naturally is, with the now oft-made statement that at least one-half of those who consult physicians are suffering from ailments having a strictly neural basis and that show psychopathological traits. Indeed, this statement seems to me to be actually a great under-statement of the seriousness of the situation.

For the conception of good health is so vague that most persons do not go to see a physician until their ailments have become rather extreme. No one knows how many who do not come suffer loss of energy, efficiency and happiness because of difficulties that have a psychic aspect. A fair guess would be, I take it, that this group includes in some degree, everybody. If the factor of human relationships is as fundamental in production of these disorders, slight and intense, as we now have reason to believe is the case, it is impossible to over-state the extent or the importance of the concrete body of knowledge physicians can build up.

At this point, I must invite your attention again to the dubious and controversial state in which the whole matter of so-called higher mental state finds itself, and the disastrous consequences that ensue. In saying this, I am not referring to controversies between philosophers and psychologists about the relations of the mental and physical—controversies that pass under the names of interactionism, parallelism, materialism, etc. I think these are of no great practical importance save as they reflect certain divisions of a more practical kind that are rife. There are some who are so impressed with the influence of mind upon body, and with opportunities for exploiting those whose troubles have a marked psychic phase, that they form special cults, while there are others who react to the opposite extreme. They will have as little to do with anything that cannot be located and described in some specific lesion or specific somatic process. The respective views and practices of the two groups supply ammunition the one to the other. It is this situation which gives practical point to the search for the unity of the human being, and that justifies presentation of the view that unity and its breakdowns must be sought for in the interactions between individual organisms and their environment, especially that of human associations.

In this connection may be cited some rather simple facts which indicate that there is nothing mystical or metaphysical in acknowledgment of the "higher" functions when they are interpreted by the view that has been set forth. When one of us steps on the toes of his neighbor in a crowded place, we offer regrets—since otherwise we are likely to subject ourselves to sour looks, irritation and resentment. A strictly physical event has taken place, but even from an ordinary common-sense point of view, the physical is not the whole of the matter. The presence of a personal relation introduces a qualifying factor.

If I stub my toe on an object left lying on a public street my response is quite different from that which happens if I stub it on the root of a tree in climbing a mountain. In the first case, I feel the object has no business there, that somebody has been careless, that something ought to be done about such things. A personal element has modified an otherwise purely physical reaction. In the second case, I may suffer equal or greater pain, but if the pain should be partly that of irritation, the irritation is directed at my own awkwardness. Again, I can hardly imagine anyone thinking that the pain a child suffers from colic is of the same quality as the agony of torture a sensitive child suffers from an act of injustice or unkindness at the hands of some one from whom he expects different treatment.

Sentimentalists put the pain a dog suffers in undergoing an act of vivisection on the same level with what a parent suffers who has lost a child. To other people, this attitude seems to display rather extraordinary callousness towards distinctively human pain—a pain that is what it is because the processes of the human organism have been profoundly affected by relations with another human being.

The point illustrated by these simple instances is that the whole ground for the difference between a sensation and an emotion seems to lie in the absence or presence of a response coming from another human being. Persons acquire likes and dislikes for physical objects and physical scenes. But upon the strictly physical level—meaning by that, one in which a human relation plays no part—a dislike is expressed by simple rejection, as, say, one "doesn't like olives or castor oil." When the rejection is accompanied by emotion, even a layman suspects there is something back of it. When such cases are studied it is found, practically without exception, that the object rejected is of a kind that has been socially "conditioned," as the term goes. The strong stirring of emotional interest that most people experience when revisiting, after a lapse of years, the scenes of their childhood is called out by the fact that these scenes were not merely the theatrical stage and properties of early activities, but have entered so intimately into personal relations with father and mother, brothers and sisters and playmates, that it is impossible to draw a line and say the influence of the physical ends *here* and that of the social begins *there*.

It may be assumed, I suppose, that all students of biology and physiology now take it for granted that there is no recollection apart from a modification of neural structure undergone in consequence of an earlier experience. But would any one attempt to read off from even the most minute and thorough study of the structure of the modified neural cells and the chemical processes going on in them, what the nature of the earlier experience was? I imagine not; I also imagine that there are few indeed who think any possible future development of knowledge will enable this result to come to pass, making it possible to reconstitute a past experience on the basis of what can be observed about an organic structure. What is relied upon is personal contact and communication; while personal attitudes, going deeper than the mere asking of questions, are needed in order to establish the confidence which is a condition for the patient's telling the story of his past. The organic modification is there—it is indispensable. Without it the patient would not be able to recall past incidents. But this is not enough. The physical fact has to be taken up into the context of personal

relations between human being and human being before it
becomes a fact of the living present.

Intellectual operations are discriminative. They bring
things to a focus, to a point, down, as we say, to brass tacks.
But when we are angry or depressed, we are mad or sad
all over. A *physical* pain may be more or less definitely and
accurately localized. But while we may feel severe local
burnings and constrictions in the case of severe grief, there
is also a *total* experienced response which occurs. It operates
through organic structures, especially the viscera. But if it
were referred exclusively to them, to the exclusion of a relation to another human being, it would not *be* grief.

I remember as a child trying to reinstate on a hot summer's day the experience of a day in winter—not just to
recall intellectually that it was cold, but to recover the
actual feeling. Naturally, I never succeeded, and I was not
aware that if I had succeeded it would have been an hal-
lucination. What I was attempting, was, however, hardly
more difficult than it is, when we are experiencing an intense
emotion, to procure or permit the introduction of ideas associated with another mood. Elation and strong hope take
such possession of us that we cannot entertain ideas that
suggest the possibility of failure as long as the emotions last.
The person depressed with melancholy has no room for any
idea connected with success or vital hope.

Now it may be doubted whether there is any idea, no
matter how intellectual and abstract, that is not tinged, if not
dyed, with the emotion that arises from the total response of
the whole organism to its surroundings. The cases, then, of
the influence of emotions upon somatic conditions, even to
the extent of producing neuroses in some cases and creating
astonishing recoveries in other cases, have nothing mystical
or metaphysical about them. They are expressions of the
regulative force exercised over partial organic processes by
the whole of which they are part.

I have given a number of illustrations which by themselves are commonplace rather than weighty. The principle
they are intended to illustrate is, however, of the utmost

importance. For, as I have suggested, disruption of the unity of the self is not limited to the cases that come to physicians and institutions for treatment. They accompany every disturbance of normal relations of husband and wife, parent and child, group and group, class and class, nation and nation. Emotional responses are so total as compared with the partial nature of intellectual responses, of ideas and abstract conceptions, that their consequences are more pervasive and more enduring. I can, accordingly, think of nothing of greater practical importance than that the psychic effects of human relationships, normal and abnormal, should be the object of continued study, including among the consequences the indirect somatic effects.

We cannot understand the conditions that produce unity in the human being and conditions that generate disruptions of this unity until the study of the relations of human beings to one another is as alert, as unremitting and as systematic as the study of strictly physiological and anatomical processes and structures has been in the past. The plea is not for any remission on the side of the latter. But we need to recover from the impression, now widespread, that the essential problem is solved when chemical, immunological, physiological and anatomical knowledge is sufficiently obtained. We cannot understand and employ this knowledge until it is placed integrally in the context of what human beings do to one another in the vast variety of their contacts and associations. Until the study is undertaken in this spirit, neglect will continue to breed and so support belief in the soul, and in mental processes supposed to be wholly independent of the organism and of somatic conditions. The consequences produced by this belief will not be confined to errors of theory. The practical outcome is division and conflict in action where unity and cooperation of social effort are urgently required.

I may rephrase what I have said by saying that the fine old saying "A sound mind in a sound body" can and should be extended to read "A sound human being in a sound human environment." The mere change in wording is nothing.

A change in aims and methods of working in that direction
would mean more than any of us can estimate. Is there anything in the whole business of politics, economics, morals,
education—indeed in any profession—save the construction
of a proper human environment that will serve, by its very
existence, to produce sound and whole human beings, who
in turn will maintain a sound and healthy human environment?

This is the universal and all-embracing human task. Its
first phase cannot be turned over to politicians alone, and the
second phase cannot be turned over to parents, preachers
and teachers alone. It is not the peculiar business of any
special calling. Yet perhaps there is none who is more intimately concerned with aiding production of sound individual human beings than the physician. There is none who
has as much opportunity as he has to observe the effects of
disturbed and disordered human relations in production of
warped and divided personalities. The situations with which
physicians deal are not artificially produced in laboratories.
They are nevertheless sufficiently extensive and varied to
provide conditions of control like those of the laboratory.

I cannot help thinking that the idea of preventive medicine
and of public health policies has bearing and application
upon the point made. Because of the unity of the human
being, because of the inextricable intertwining of the physical
and psychical in his makeup, the work of preventing disease
and disorders is not completely done when the physical conditions of sanitation, pure water, and milk supply, sewage
disposal, and healthy homes have been attended to. The
social conditions that make for the production of unified,
effective, reasonably happy human beings and their opposites,
come into the picture also. We may solve the problems of
dualism and monism satisfactorily in theory, and yet not have
touched the sore spots in society and in individuals, and this
is the place where they have to be resolved practically.

ERICH FROMM

[1900–   ]

Dr. Fromm is a practicing psychoanalyst and one of the best-known writers and lecturers in his field. He is a leader in the so-called neo-Freudian revisionist group, which included the late Karen Horney and Harry Stack Sullivan. The revisionists maintain that they have a more adequate conception of man than did Freud himself because they take social factors more fully into consideration as well as the latest findings in anthropology and sociology. They deplore Freud's overemphasis on sexual satisfaction and reject his theory of a death instinct. In short, they consider the Freudian view of human nature too dark and defeatist, whereas the Freudians in their turn consider the revisionists superficial and painfully optimistic!

Born and educated in Germany, Dr. Fromm came here to lecture in 1933 and settled permanently the following year. His first book in the language of his new country, *Escape from Freedom*, made an especially deep impression because it was an explanation of why people submit to totalitarianism, and it appeared not long before we entered a war against totalitarianism. "It is the thesis of this book that modern man, freed from the bonds of pre-individualistic society, which simultaneously gave him security and limited him, has not gained freedom in the positive sense of the realization of his individual self; that is the expression of his intellectual, emotional and sensuous potentialities. Freedom, though it has brought him independence and rationality, has made him isolated and, thereby, anxious and powerless. This isolation is unbearable and the alternatives which he is confronted with are either to escape from the burden of this freedom into new dependencies and submission, or to advance to the full realization of positive freedom which is based upon the uniqueness and individuality of man."

Escape from Freedom is an analysis or a diagnosis of people accepting the first alternative; his own version of the second alternative he has recently painted with utopian colors in *The Sane Society*.

An article by Dr. Fromm on an age-old problem had acquired a kind of secret fame before it appeared in revised form in *Man for Himself* (1947).

* * *

SELFISHNESS, SELF-LOVE, AND SELF-INTEREST[1]

Thou shalt love thy neighbour as thyself.
—Bible

Modern culture is pervaded by a tabu on selfishness. We are taught that to be selfish is sinful and that to love others is virtuous. To be sure, this doctrine is in flagrant contradiction to the practice of modern society, which holds the doctrine that the most powerful and legitimate drive in man is selfishness and that by following this imperative drive the individual makes his best contribution to the common good. But the doctrine which declares selfishness to be the arch evil and love for others to be the greatest virtue is still powerful. Selfishness is used here almost synonymously with self-love. The alternative is to love others, which is a virtue, or to love oneself, which is a sin.

This principle has found its classic expression in Calvin's theology, according to which man is essentially evil and powerless. Man can achieve absolutely nothing that is good on the basis of his own strength or merit. "We are not our own," says Calvin. "Therefore neither our reason nor our will should predominate in our deliberations and actions. We are not our own; therefore let us not propose it as our end to seek what may be expedient for us according to the flesh. We are not our own; therefore, let us, as far as possible, forget ourselves and all things that are ours. On the con-

---

[1] Cf. Erich Fromm, "Selfishness and Self-Love," *Psychiatry* (November, 1939). The following discussion of selfishness and self-love is a partial repetition of the earlier paper.

trary, we are God's; for Him, therefore, let us live and die.
For, as it is the most devastating pestilence which ruins
people if they obey themselves, it is the only haven of salvation not to know or to want anything by oneself but to be
guided by God Who walks before us."[2] Man should have
not only the conviction of his absolute nothingness but he
should do everything to humiliate himself. "For I do not
call it humility if you suppose that we have anything left . . .
we cannot think of ourselves as we ought to think without
utterly despising everything that may be supposed an excellence in us. This humility is unfeigned submission of a
mind overwhelmed with a weighty sense of its own misery
and poverty; for such is the uniform description of it in the
word of God."[3]

This emphasis on the nothingness and wickedness of the
individual implies that there is nothing he should like and
respect about himself. The doctrine is rooted in self-contempt
and self-hatred. Calvin makes this point very clear: he speaks
of self-love as "a pest."[4] If the individual finds something
"on the strength of which he finds pleasure in himself," he
betrays this sinful self-love. This fondness for himself will
make him sit in judgment over others and despise them.
Therefore, to be fond of oneself or to like anything in oneself is one of the greatest sins. It is supposed to exclude love
for others[5] and to be identical with selfishness.[6]

The view of man held by Calvin and Luther has been of
tremendous influence on the development of modern West-

---

[2] Johannes Calvin, *Institutes of the Christian Religion,* trans. by John Allen
(Philadelphia: Presbyterian Board of Christian Education, 1928), in particular
Book III, Chap. 7, p. 619. From "For, as it is . . . ." the translation is mine
from the Latin original (Johannes Calvini. *Institutio Christianae Religionis.
Editionem curavit,* A. Tholuk, Berolini, 1935, par. 1. p. 445).

[3] *Ibid.,* Chap. 12, par. 6, p. 681.

[4] *Ibid.,* Chap. 7, par. 4, p. 622.

[5] It should be noted, however, that even love for one's neighbor, while it is
one of the fundamental doctrines of the New Testament, has not been given a
corresponding weight by Calvin. In blatant contradiction to the New Testament, Calvin says: "For what the schoolmen advance concerning the priority
of charity to faith and hope, is a mere reverie of a distempered imagination
. . . ."—Chap. 24, par. 1, p. 531.

[6] Despite Luther's emphasis on the spiritual freedom of the individual, his
theology, different as it is in many ways from Calvin's, is pervaded by the
same conviction of man's basic powerlessness and nothingness.

ern society. They laid the foundations for an attitude in which man's own happiness was not considered to be the aim of life but where he became a means, an adjunct, to ends beyond him, of an all-powerful God, or of the not less powerful secularized authorities and norms, the state, business, success. Kant, who, with regard to the idea that man should be an end in himself and never a means only, was perhaps the most influential ethical thinker of the Enlightenment period, nevertheless had the same condemnation for self-love. According to him, it is a virtue to want happiness for others, but to want one's own happiness is ethically indifferent, since it is something for which the nature of man is striving, and since a natural striving cannot have a positive ethical value.[7] Kant admits that one must not give up one's claims to happiness; under certain circumstances it may even be a duty to be concerned with it, partly because health, wealth, and the like may be means necessary for the fulfillment of one's duty, partly because the lack of happiness —poverty—can prevent one from fulfilling his duty.[8] But love for oneself, striving for one's own happiness, can never be a *virtue*. As an ethical principle, the striving for one's own happiness "is the most objectionable one, not merely because it is false . . . but because the springs it provides for morality are such as rather to undermine it and destroy its sublimity. . . ."[9]

Kant differentiates egotism, self-love, *philautia*—a benevolence for oneself—and arrogance, the pleasure in oneself. But even "rational self-love" must be restricted by ethical principles, the pleasure in oneself must be battered down, and the individual must come to feel humiliated in comparing himself with the sanctity of moral laws.[10] The individual

---

[7] Compare Immanuel Kant, *Kant's Critique of Practical Reason and Other Works on the Theory of Ethics,* trans. by Thomas Kingsmill Abbott (New York: Longmans, Green & Co., 1909), Part I, Book I, Chap. I, par. VIII, Remark II, p. 126.

[8] *Ibid.,* in particular Part I, Book I, Ch. III, p. 186.

[9] *Loc. cit., Fundamental Principles of the Metaphysics of Morals;* second section, p. 61.

[10] *Loc. cit.,* Part I, Book I, Ch. III, p. 165.

should find supreme happiness in the fulfillment of his duty. The realization of the moral principle—and, therefore, of the individual's happiness—is only possible in the general whole, the nation, the state. But "the welfare of the state"—and *salus rei publicae suprema lex est*—is not identical with the welfare of the citizens and their happiness."

In spite of the fact that Kant shows a greater respect for the integrity of the individual than did Calvin or Luther, he denies the individual's right to rebel even under the most tyrannical government; the rebel must be punished with no less than death if he threatens the sovereign.[12] Kant emphasizes the native propensity for evil in the nature of man,[13] for the suppression of which the moral law, the categorical imperative, is essential lest man should become a beast and human society end in wild anarchy.

In the philosophy of the Enlightenment period the individual's claims to happiness have been emphasized much more strongly by others than by Kant, for instance, by Helvetius. This trend in modern philosophy has found its most radical expression in Stirner and Nietzsche.[14] But while they take the opposite position to that of Calvin and Kant with regard to the value of selfishness, they agree with them in the assumption that love for others and love for oneself are alternatives. They denounce love for others as weakness and self-sacrifice and postulate egotism, selfishness, and self-love —they too confuse the issue by not clearly differentiating between these last—as virtue. Thus Stirner says: "Here, egoism, selfishness must decide, not the principle of love, not love motives like mercy, gentleness, good-nature, or even

[11] Immanuel Kant, *Immanuel Kants Werke* (Berlin: Cassierer), in particular "Der Rechtslehre Zweiter Teil" I. Abschnitt, par. 49, p. 124. I translate from the German text, since this part is omitted in the English translation of *The Metaphysics of Ethics* by I. W. Semple (Edinburgh: 1871).

[12] *Ibid.*, p. 126.

[13] Compare Immanuel Kant, *Religion Within the Limits of Reason Alone*, trans. by T. M. Greene and H. H. Hudson (Chicago: Open Court, 1934), Book I.

[14] In order not to make this chapter too long I discuss only the modern philosophical development. The student of philosophy will know that Aristotle's and Spinoza's ethics consider self-love a virtue, not a vice, in striking contrast to Calvin's standpoint.

justice and equity—for *iustitia* too is a phenomenon of love, a product of love; love knows only sacrifice and demands self-sacrifice."[15]

The kind of love denounced by Stirner is the masochistic dependence by which the individual makes himself a means for achieving the purposes of somebody or something outside himself. Opposing this concept of love, he did not avoid a formulation, which, highly polemical, overstates the point. The positive principle with which Stirner was concerned[16] was opposed to an attitude which had been that of Christian theology for centuries—and which was vivid in the German idealism prevalent in his time; namely, to bend the individual so that he submits to, and finds his center in, a power and a principle outside himself. Stirner was not a philosopher of the stature of Kant or Hegel, but he had the courage to rebel radically against that side of idealistic philosophy which negated the concrete individual and thus helped the absolute state to retain its oppressive power over him.

In spite of many differences between Nietzsche and Stirner, their ideas in this respect are very much the same. Nietzsche too denounces love and altruism as expressions of weakness and self-negation. For Nietzsche, the quest for love is typical of slaves unable to fight for what they want and who therefore try to get it through love. Altruism and love for mankind thus have become a sign of degeneration.[17] For Nietzsche it is the essence of a good and healthy aristocracy that it is ready to sacrifice countless people for its

---

[15] Max Stirner, *The Ego and His Own*, trans. by S. T. Byington (London: A. C. Fifield, 1912), p. 339.

[16] One of his positive formulations, for example, is: "But how does one use life? In using it up like the candle one burns. . . . Enjoyment of life is using life up." F. Engels has clearly seen the one-sidedness of Stirner's formulations and has attempted to overcome the false alternative between love for oneself and love for others. In a letter to Marx in which he discusses Stirner's book, Engels writes: "If, however, the concrete and real individual is the true basis for our 'human' man, it is self-evident that egotism—of course not only Stirner's egotism of reason, but also the egotism of the heart—is the basis for our love of man."—*Marx-Engels Gesamtausgabe* (Berlin: Marx-Engels Verlag, 1929), p. 6.

[17] Friedrich Nietzsche, *The Will to Power*, trans. by Anthony M. Ludovici (Edinburgh and London: T. N. Foulis, 1910), stanzas 246, 326, 369, 373, and 728.

interests without having a guilty conscience. Society should be a "foundation and scaffolding by means of which a select class of beings may be able to elevate themselves to their higher duties, and in general to a higher existence."[18] Many quotations could be added to document this spirit of contempt and egotism. These ideas have often been understood as *the* philosophy of Nietzsche. However, they do not represent the true core of his philosophy.[19]

There are various reasons why Nietzsche expressed himself in the sense noted above. First of all, as with Stirner, his philosophy is a reaction—a rebellion—against the philosophical tradition of subordinating the empirical individual to powers and principles outside himself. His tendency to overstatement shows this reactive quality. Second, there were, in Nietzsche's personality, feelings of insecurity and anxiety that made him emphasize the "strong man" as a reaction formation. Finally, Nietzsche was impressed by the theory of evolution and its emphasis on the "survival of the fittest." This interpretation does not alter the fact that Nietzsche believed that there is a contradiction between love for others and love for oneself; yet his views contain the nucleus from which this false dichotomy can be overcome. The "love" which he attacks is rooted not in one's own strength, but in one's own weakness. "Your neighborlove is your bad love of yourselves. Ye flee unto your neighbor from yourselves and would fain make a virtue thereof! But I fathom your 'unselfishness.'" He states explicitly, "You cannot stand yourselves and you do not love yourselves sufficiently."[20] For Nietzsche the individual has "an enormously great significance."[21] The "strong" individual is the one who has "true kindness, nobility, greatness of soul, which

---

[18] Friedrich Nietzsche, *Beyond Good and Evil*, trans. by Helen Zimmer (New York: The Macmillan Company, 1907), stanza 258.

[19] Cf. G. A. Morgan, *What Nietzsche Means* (Cambridge: Harvard University Press, 1943).

[20] Friedrich Nietzsche, *Thus Spake Zarathustra*, trans. by Thomas Common (New York: Modern Library), p. 75.

[21] *The Will to Power*, stanza 785.

does not give in order to take, which does not want to excel
by being kind;—'waste' as type of true kindness, wealth of
the person as a premise."[22] He expresses the same thought
also in *Thus Spake Zarathustra:* "The one goeth to his neighbor because he seeketh himself, and the other because he
would fain lose himself."[23]

The essence of this view is this: Love is a phenomenon
of abundance; its premise is the strength of the individual
who can give. Love is affirmation and productiveness. "It
seeketh to create what is loved!"[24] To love another person
is only a virtue if it springs from this inner strength, but it
is a vice if it is the expression of the basic inability to be
oneself.[25] However, the fact remains that Nietzsche left the
problem of the relationship between self-love and love for
others as an unsolved antinomy.

The doctrine that selfishness is the arch-evil and that to
love oneself excludes loving others is by no means restricted
to theology and philosophy, but it became one of the stock
ideas promulgated in home, school, motion pictures, books;
indeed in all instruments of social suggestion as well. "Don't
be selfish" is a sentence which has been impressed upon
millions of children, generation after generation. Its meaning is somewhat vague. Most people would say that it means
not to be egotistical, inconsiderate, without any concern for
others. Actually, it generally means more than that. Not
to be selfish implies not to do what one wishes, to give up
one's own wishes for the sake of those in authority. "Don't
be selfish," in the last analysis, has the same ambiguity that
it has in Calvinism. Aside from its obvious implication, it
means, "don't love yourself," "don't be yourself," but submit yourself to something more important than yourself,
to an outside power or its internalization, "duty." "Don't

[22] *Ibid.*, stanza 935.

[23] *Thus Spake Zarathustra*, p. 76.

[24] *Ibid.*, p. 102.

[25] See Friedrich Nietzsche, *The Twilight of Idols,* trans. by A. M. Ludovici
(Edinburgh: T. N. Foulis, 1911), stanza 35; *Ecce Homo,* trans. by A. M.
Ludovici (New York: The Macmillan Company, 1911), stanza 2; *Nachlass,
Nietzsches Werke* (Leipzig: A. Kroener), pp. 63-64.

be selfish" becomes one of the most powerful ideological tools in suppressing spontaneity and the free development of personality. Under the pressure of this slogan one is asked for every sacrifice and for complete submission: only those acts are "unselfish" which do not serve the individual but somebody or something outside himself.

This picture, we must repeat, is in a certain sense one-sided. For besides the doctrine that one should not be selfish, the opposite is also propagandized in modern society: keep your own advantage in mind, act according to what is best for you; by so doing you will also be acting for the greatest advantage of all others. As a matter of fact, the idea that egotism is the basis of the general welfare is the principle on which competitive society has been built. It is puzzling that two such seemingly contradictory principles could be taught side by side in one culture; of the fact, however, there is no doubt. One result of this contradiction is confusion in the individual. Torn between the two doctrines, he is seriously blocked in the process of integrating his personality. This confusion is one of the most significant sources of the bewilderment and helplessness of modern man.[26]

The doctrine that love for oneself is identical with "selfishness" and an alternative to love for others has pervaded theology, philosophy, and popular thought; the same doctrine has been rationalized in scientific language in Freud's theory of narcissism. Freud's concept presupposes a fixed amount of libido. In the infant, all of the libido has the child's own person as its objective, the stage of "primary narcissism," as Freud calls it. During the individual's development, the libido is shifted from one's own person toward other objects. If a person is blocked in his "object-relationships," the libido is withdrawn from the objects and returned to his own person; this is called "secondary narcissism." According to Freud, the more love I turn toward the outside world the less love is left for myself, and vice versa.

---

[26] This point has been emphasized by Karen Horney, *The Neurotic Personality of Our Time* (New York: W. W. Norton & Company, 1937), and by Robert S. Lynd, *Knowledge for What?* (Princeton: Princeton University Press, 1939).

He thus describes the phenomenon of love as an impoverishment of one's self-love because all libido is turned to an
object outside oneself.

These questions arise: Does psychological observation
support the thesis that there is a basic contradiction and a
state of alternation between love for oneself and love for
others? Is love for oneself the same phenomenon as selfishness, or are they opposite? Furthermore, is the selfishness
of modern man really a *concern for himself* as an individual,
with all his intellectual, emotional, and sensual potentialities? Has "he" not become an appendage of his socioeconomic role? *Is his selfishness identical with self-love or is it
not caused by the very lack of it?*

Before we start the discussion of the psychological aspect
of selfishness and self-love, the logical fallacy in the notion
that love for others and love for oneself are mutually exclusive should be stressed. If it is a virtue to love my neighbor as a human being, it must be a virtue—and not a vice—
to love myself since I am a human being too. There is
no concept of man in which I myself am not included. A
doctrine which proclaims such an exclusion proves itself to
be intrinsically contradictory. The idea expressed in the
Biblical "Love thy neighbor as thyself!" implies that respect
for one's own integrity and uniqueness, love for and understanding of one's own self, can not be separated from respect for and love and understanding of another individual.
The love for my own self is inseparably connected with the
love for any other self.

We have come now to the basic psychological premises
on which the conclusions of our argument are built. Generally, these premises are as follows: not only others, but we
ourselves are the "object" of our feelings and attitudes; the
attitudes toward others and toward ourselves, far from being
contradictory, are basically *conjunctive*. With regard to the
problem under discussion this means: Love of others and
love of ourselves are not alternatives. On the contrary, an
attitude of love toward themselves will be found in all those
who are capable of loving others. *Love*, in principle, *is in-*

divisible as far as the connection between "objects" and one's own self is concerned. Genuine love is an expression of productiveness and implies care, respect, responsibility, and knowledge. It is not an "affect" in the sense of being affected by somebody, but an active striving for the growth and happiness of the loved person, rooted in one's own capacity to love.

To love is an expression of one's power to love, and to love somebody is the actualization and concentration of this power with regard to one person. It is not true, as the idea of romantic love would have it, that there is only *the* one person in the world whom one could love and that it is the great chance of one's life to find that one person. Nor is it true, if that person be found that love for him (or her) results in a withdrawal of love from others. Love which can only be experienced with regard to one person demonstrates by this very fact that it is not love, but a symbiotic attachment. The basic affirmation contained in love is directed toward the beloved person as an incarnation of essentially human qualities. Love of one person implies love of man as such. The kind of "division of labor" as William James calls it, by which one loves one's family but is without feeling for the "stranger," is a sign of basic inability to love. Love of man is not, as is frequently supposed, an abstraction coming after the love for a specific person, but it is its premise, although, genetically, it is acquired in loving specific individuals.

From this it follows that my own self, in principle, must be as much an object of my love as another person. *The affirmation of one's own life, happiness, growth, freedom, is rooted in one's capacity to love,* i.e., in care, respect, responsibility, and knowledge. If an individual is able to love productively, he loves himself too; if he can love *only* others, he can not love at all.

Granted that love for oneself and for others in principle is conjunctive, how do we explain selfishness, which obviously excludes any genuine concern for others? The selfish person is interested only in himself, wants everything for himself, feels no pleasure in giving, but only in taking. The world outside is looked at only from the standpoint of what he can get out of it; he lacks interest in the needs of others, and respect for their dignity and integrity. He can see nothing but himself; he judges everyone and everything from its usefulness to him; he is basically unable to love. Does not this prove that concern for others and concern for oneself are unavoidable alternatives? This would be so if selfishness and self-love were identical. But that assumption is the very fallacy which has led to so many mistaken conclusions concerning our problem. *Selfishness and self-love, far from being identical, are actually opposites.* The selfish person does not love himself too much but too little; in fact he hates himself. This lack of fondness and care for himself, which is only one expression of his lack of productiveness, leaves him empty and frustrated. He is necessarily unhappy and anxiously concerned to snatch from life the satisfactions which he blocks himself from attaining. He seems to care too much for himself but actually he only makes an unsuccessful attempt to cover up and compensate for his failure to care for his real self. Freud holds that the selfish person is narcissistic, as if he had withdrawn his love from others and turned it toward his own person. *It is true that selfish persons are incapable of loving others, but they are not capable of loving themselves either.*

It is easier to understand selfishness by comparing it with greedy concern for others, as we find it, for instance, in an oversolicitous, dominating mother. While she consciously believes that she is particularly fond of her child, she has actually a deeply repressed hostility toward the object of her concern. She is overconcerned not because she loves the child too much, but because she has to compensate for her lack of capacity to love him at all.

This theory of the nature of selfishness is borne out by psychoanalytic experience with neurotic "unselfishness," a symptom of neurosis observed in not a few people who usually are troubled not by this symptom but by others connected with it, like depression, tiredness, inability to work, failure in love relationships, and so on. Not only is unselfishness not felt as a "symptom"; it is often the one redeeming character trait on which such people pride themselves. The "unselfish" person "does not want anything for himself"; he "lives only for others," is proud that he does not consider himself important. He is puzzled to find that in spite of his unselfishness he is unhappy, and that his relationships to those closest to him are unsatisfactory. He wants to have what he considers are his symptoms removed—but not his unselfishness. Analytic work shows that his unselfishness is not something apart from his other symptoms but one of them; in fact often the most important one; that he is paralyzed in his capacity to love or to enjoy anything; that he is pervaded by hostility against life and that behind the façade of unselfishness a subtle but not less intense self-centeredness is hidden. This person can be cured only if his unselfishness too is interpreted as a symptom along with the others so that his lack of productiveness, which is at the root of both his unselfishness *and* his other troubles, can be corrected.

The nature of unselfishness becomes particularly apparent in its effect on others and most frequently, in our culture, in the effect the "unselfish" mother has on her children. She believes that by her unselfishness her children will experience what it means to be loved and to learn, in turn, what it means to love. The effect of her unselfishness, however, does not at all correspond to her expectations. The children do not show the happiness of persons who are convinced that they are loved; they are anxious, tense, afraid of the mother's disapproval and anxious to live up to her expectations. Usually, they are affected by their mother's hidden hostility against life, which they sense rather than recognize, and eventually become imbued with it themselves. Altogether, the effect of the "unselfish" mother is not too different from that of the selfish one; indeed, it is often worse because the mother's unselfishness prevents the children from criticizing her. They are put under the obligation not to disappoint her; they are taught, under the mask of virtue, dislike for life. If one has a chance to study the effect of a mother with genuine self-love, one can see that there is nothing more conducive to giving a child the experience of what love, joy, and happiness are than being loved by a mother who loves herself.

Having analyzed selfishness and self-love we can now proceed to discuss the concept of *self-interest,* which has become one of the key symbols in modern society. It is even more ambiguous than selfishness or self-love, and this ambiguity can be fully understood only by taking into account the historical development of the concept of self-interest. The problem is what is considered to constitute self-interest and how it can be determined.

There are two fundamentally different approaches to this problem. One is the objectivistic approach most clearly formulated by Spinoza. To him self-interest or the interest "to seek one's profit" is identical with virtue. "The more," he says, "each person strives and is able to *seek his profit,* that is to say, to preserve his being, the more virtue does he possess; on the other hand, in so far as each person neglects his own profit he is impotent."[27] According to this view, the interest of man is to preserve his existence, which is the same as realizing his inherent potentialities. This concept of self-interest is objectivistic inasmuch as "interest" is not conceived in terms of the subjective feeling of what one's interest is but in terms of what the nature of man is, objectively. Man has only one real interest and that is the full development of his potentialities, of himself as a human being. Just as one has to know another person and his real needs in order to love him, one has to know one's own self in order to understand what the interests of this self are and how they can be served. It follows that man can deceive himself about his real self-interest if he is ignorant of his self and its real needs and that the science of man is the basis for determining what constitutes man's self-interest.

In the last three hundred years the concept of self-interest

---

[27] Spinoza, *Ethics,* IV, Prop. 20.

has increasingly been narrowed until it has assumed almost the opposite meaning which it has in Spinoza's thinking. It has become identical with selfishness, with interest in material gains, power, and success; and instead of its being synonymous with virtue, its conquest has become an ethical commandment.

This deterioration was made possible by the change from the objectivistic into the erroneously subjectivistic approach to self-interest. Self-interest was no longer to be determined by the nature of man and his needs; correspondingly, the notion that one could be mistaken about it was relinquished and replaced by the idea that what a person *felt* represented the interest of his self was necessarily his true self-interest.

The modern concept of self-interest is a strange blend of two contradictory concepts: that of Calvin and Luther on the one hand, and on the other, that of the progressive thinkers since Spinoza. Calvin and Luther had taught that man must suppress his self-interest and consider himself only an instrument for God's purposes. Progressive thinkers, on the contrary, have taught that man ought to be only an end for himself and not a means for any purpose transcending him. What happened was that man has accepted the contents of the Calvinistic doctrine while rejecting its religious formulation. He has made himself an instrument, not of God's will but of the economic machine or the state. He has accepted the role of a tool, not for God but for industrial progress; he has worked and amassed money but essentially not for the pleasure of spending it and of enjoying life but in order to save, to invest, to be successful. Monastic asceticism has been, as Max Weber has pointed out, replaced by an *inner-worldly asceticism* where personal happiness and enjoyment are no longer the real aims of life. But this attitude was increasingly divorced from the one expressed in Calvin's concept and blended with that expressed in the progressive concept of self-interest, which taught that man had the right—and the obligation—to make the pursuit of his self-interest the supreme norm of life. The result is that modern man *lives* according to the prin-

ciples of self-denial and *thinks* in terms of self-interest. He
believes that he is acting in behalf of *his* interest when actually his paramount concern is money and success; he deceives himself about the fact that his most important human potentialities remain unfulfilled and that he loses himself in the process of seeking what is supposed to be best for
him.

The deterioration of the meaning of the concept of self-
interest is closely related to the change in the concept of
self. In the Middle Ages man felt himself to be an intrinsic
part of the social and religious community in reference to
which he conceived his own self when he as an individual
had not yet fully emerged from his group. Since the beginning of the modern era, when man as an individual was
faced with the task of experiencing himself as an independent entity, his own identity became a problem. In the eighteenth and nineteenth centuries the concept of self was narrowed down increasingly; the self was felt to be constituted
by the property one had. The formula for this concept of
self was no longer "I am what I think" but "I am what I
have," "what I possess."[28]

In the last few generations, under the growing influence
of the market, the concept of self has shifted from meaning
"I am what I possess" to meaning "I am as you desire

---

[28] William James expressed this concept very clearly. "To have," he says,
"a self that I can care for, Nature must first present me with some object
interesting enough to make me instinctively wish to appropriate it for its own
sake. . . . My own body and what ministers to its needs are thus the primitive
object, instinctively determined, of my egoistic interests. Other objects may
become interesting derivatively, through association with any of these things,
either as means or as habitual concomitants; and so, in a thousand ways,
the primitive sphere of the egoistic emotions may enlarge and change its
boundaries. This sort of interest is really the meaning of the word *mine*.
Whatever has it, is, *eo ipso*, a part of me!"—*Principles of Psychology* (New
York: Henry Holt and Company, 2 vols., 1896), I, 319, 324. Elsewhere James
writes: "It is clear that between what a man calls *me* and what he simply
calls *mine,* the line is difficult to draw. We feel and act about certain things
that are ours very much as we feel and act about ourselves. Our fame, our
children, the work of our hands, may be as dear to us as our bodies are, and
arouse the same feelings and the same acts of reprisal if attacked. . . . In its
widest possible sense, however, a man's Self *is* the sum-total of all that he
can call his, not only his body, and his psychic powers, but his clothes and
his house, his wife and children, his ancestors and friends, his reputation and
works, his land and horses and yacht and bank account. All these things give
him the same emotions. If they wax or prosper, he feels triumphant, if they
dwindle and die away, he feels cast down—not necessarily in the same degree
for each thing, but in much the same way for all."—*Ibid.,* I, 291-292.

me."[29] Man, living in a market economy, feels himself to be a commodity. He is divorced from himself, as the seller of a commodity is divorced from what he wants to sell. To be sure, he is interested in himself, immensely interested in his success on the market, but "he" is the manager, the employer, the seller—and the commodity. His self-interest turns out to be the interest of "him" as the subject who employs "himself," as the commodity which should obtain the optimal price on the personality market.

The "fallacy of self-interest" in modern man has never been described better than by Ibsen in *Peer Gynt*. Peer Gynt believes that his whole life is devoted to the attainment of the interests of his *self*. He describes this self as:

> "The Gyntian Self!
> —An army, that, of wishes, appetites, desires!
> The Gyntian Self!
> It is a sea of fancies, claims and aspirations;
> In fact, it's all that swells within my breast
> And makes it come about that I am I and live as such."[30]

At the end of his life he recognizes that he had deceived himself; that while following the principle of "self-interest" he had failed to recognize what the interests of his real self were, and had lost the very self he sought to preserve. He is told that he never had been himself and that therefore he is to be thrown back into the melting pot to be dealt with as raw material. He discovers that he has lived according to the Troll principle: "To thyself be enough"—which is the opposite of the human principle: "To thyself be true." He is seized by the horror of nothingness to which he, who has no self, can not help succumbing when the props of pseudo self, success, and possessions are taken away or seriously questioned. He is forced to recognize that in trying to gain

---

[29] Pirandello in his plays has expressed this concept of self and the self-doubt resulting from it.

[30] *Loc. cit.*, Act V, Scene I.

all the wealth of the world, in relentlessly pursuing what seemed to be his interest, he had lost his soul—or, as I would rather say, his self.

The deteriorated meaning of the concept of self-interest which pervades modern society has given rise to attacks on democracy from the various types of totalitarian ideologies. These claim that capitalism is *morally* wrong because it is governed by the principle of selfishness, and commend the moral superiority of their own systems by pointing to their principle of the unselfish subordination of the individual to the "higher" purposes of the state, the "race," or the "socialist fatherland." They impress not a few with this criticism because many people feel that there is no happiness in the pursuit of selfish interest, and are imbued with a striving, vague though it may be, for a greater solidarity and mutual responsibility among men.

We need not waste much time arguing against the totalitarian claims. In the first place, they are insincere since they only disguise the extreme selfishness of an "elite" that wishes to conquer and retain power over the majority of the population. Their ideology of unselfishness has the purpose of deceiving those subject to the control of the elite and of facilitating their exploitation and manipulation. Furthermore, the totalitarian ideologies confuse the issue by making it appear that they represent the principle of unselfishness when they apply to the state as a whole the principle of ruthless pursuit of selfishness. Each citizen ought to be devoted to the common welfare, but the state is permitted to pursue its own interest without regard to the welfare of other nations. But quite aside from the fact that the doctrines of totalitarianism are disguises for the most extreme selfishness, they are a revival—in secular language—of the religious idea of intrinsic human powerlessness and impotence and the resulting need for submission, to overcome which was the essence of modern spiritual and political progress. Not only do the authoritarian ideologies threaten the most precious achievement of Western culture, the respect for the uniqueness and dignity of the individual; they also tend to block the way to constructive criticism of modern society, and thereby to necessary changes. The failure of modern culture lies not in its principle of individualism, not in the idea that moral virtue is the same as the pursuit of self-interest, but in the deterioration of the meaning of self-interest; not in the fact that people are *too much concerned with their self-interest*, but that they are *not concerned enough with the interest of their real self; not in the fact that they are too selfish, but that they do not love themselves*.

If the causes for persevering in the pursuit of a fictitious idea of self-interest are as deeply rooted in the contemporary social structure as indicated above, the chances for a change in the meaning of self-interest would seem to be remote indeed, unless one can point to specific factors operating in the direction of change.

Perhaps the most important factor is the inner dissatisfaction of modern man with the results of his pursuit of "self-interest." The religion of success is crumbling and becoming a façade itself. The social "open spaces" grow narrower; the failure of the hopes for a better world after the First World War, the depression at the end of the twenties, the threat of a new and immensely destructive war so shortly after the Second World War, and the boundless insecurity resulting from this threat, shake the faith in the pursuit of this form of self-interest. Aside from these factors, the worship of success itself has failed to satisfy man's ineradicable striving to be himself. Like so many fantasies and daydreams, this one too fulfilled its function only for a time, as long as it was new, as long as the excitement connected with it was strong enough to keep man from considering it soberly. There is an increasing number of people to whom everything they are doing seems futile. They are still under the spell of the slogans which preach faith in the secular paradise of success and glamour. But doubt, the fertile condition of all progress, has begun to beset them and has made them ready to ask what their real self-interest as human beings is.

This inner disillusionment and the readiness for a revaluation of self-interest could hardly become effective unless the economic conditions of our culture permitted it. I have pointed out that while the canalizing of all human energy into work and the striving for success was one of the indispensable conditions of the enormous achievement of modern capitalism, a stage has been reached where the problem of *production* has been virtually solved and where the problem of the *organization* of social life has become the paramount task of mankind. Man has created such sources of mechanical energy that he has freed himself from the task of putting all his human energy into work in order to produce the material conditions for living. He could spend a considerable part of his energy on the task of living itself.

Only if these two conditions, the subjective dissatisfaction with a culturally patterned aim and the socioeconomic basis for a change, are present, can an indispensable third factor, rational insight, become effective. This holds true as a principle of social and psychological change in general and of the change in the meaning of self-interest in particular. The time has come when the anesthetized striving for the pursuit of man's real interest is coming to life again. Once man knows what his self-interest is, the first, and the most difficult, step to its realization has been taken.

LUDWIG WITTGENSTEIN

[1889–1951]

Since nothing by Wittgenstein is suitable for our purposes, we turn to an acknowledged master of language who is a distinguished philosopher in his own right, Gilbert Ryle, Waynflete Professor of Metaphysical Philosophy in the University of Oxford and editor of *Mind.* Although he scorns labels and maintains that philosophers should not take sides, he is on the side of "analysis" and argued in a classic paper some twenty-five years ago that the chief function of philosophy is to detect "systematically misleading expressions." In *The Concept of Mind,* Ryle at once declared that "the philosophical arguments which constitute this book are intended not to increase what we know about minds, but to rectify the logical geography of the knowledge which we already possess."

*   *   *

LUDWIG WITTGENSTEIN [1]

BY GILBERT RYLE [1900–   ]

An original and powerful philosopher, Ludwig Wittgenstein, an Austrian who finally became a naturalized British subject, came to England shortly before the First World War to study engineering. In 1912, bitten by logical and philosophical problems about the nature of mathematics, he migrated to Cambridge to work with Bertrand Russell. During that war, he was in the Austrian army and ended up a prisoner of war. In this period he wrote his one book, the famous *Tractatus Logico-Philosophicus,* of which a not quite reliable English translation was published in 1922. He

---

[1] First delivered as a B.B.C. Third Programme talk, May 26, 1951, and later printed in *Analysis,* XII (1951).

taught in an Austrian village school for some time, during which he came into close philosophical touch with a few of the leading members of the Vienna Circle. In 1929 he came to Cambridge, where the importance of his ideas had been quickly recognized. In 1939 he became Professor. For part of the last war he was a hospital orderly at Guy's Hospital. In 1947 he resigned his Chair. Besides the *Tractatus,* he published only one article.

In the last twenty years, so far as I know, he published nothing; attended no philosophical conferences; gave no lectures outside Cambridge; corresponded on philosophical subjects with nobody and discouraged the circulation even of notes of his Cambridge lectures and discussions. But with his serious students and a few colleagues, economists, mathematicians, physicists and philosophers, he would discuss philosophical matters unwearyingly. Yet from his jealously preserved little pond, there have spread waves over the philosophical thinking of much of the English speaking world. Philosophers who never met him—and few of us did meet him—can be heard talking philosophy in his tones of voice; and students who can barely spell his name now wrinkle up their noses at things which had a bad smell for him. So what is the difference that he has made to philosophy?

It is vain to try to forecast the verdict of history upon a contemporary. I have to try to do this for one who has for about thirty years avoided any publication of his ideas. So what I offer is a set of impressions, interpretations, partly, of mere echoes of echoes.

From the time of Locke to that of Bradley philosophers had debated their issues as if they were psychological issues. Certainly their problems were, often, genuine philosophical problems, but they discussed them in psychological terms. And if they asked themselves, as they seldom did ask, what they were investigating, they tended to say that they were investigating the workings of the mind, just as physical scientists investigate the workings of bodies. The sorts of "Mental Science" that they talked were sometimes positivistic, sometimes idealistic, according, roughly, as they were more impressed by chemistry than by theology or *vice versa*.

However, fifty years ago philosophers were getting their feet out of these psychological boots. For psychology had now begun to be done in laboratories and clinics, so arm-chair psychology became suspect. But even more influential was the fact that logical quandaries had recently been exposed at the very roots of pure mathematics. The mathematicians needed lifelines, which they could not provide for themselves. Logicians had to work out the logic of mathematics, and they could not base this logic on the findings of any empirical science, especially of so hazy a science as psychology. If logic and philosophy were not psychological enquiries, what were they?

During the first twenty years of this century, many philosophers gave another answer to this question, a Platonic answer. Philosophy studies not the workings of minds or, of course, of bodies either; it studies the denizens of a third domain, the domain of abstract, or conceptual entities, of possibilities, essences, timelessly subsisting universals, numbers, truths, falsities, values and meanings. This idea enabled its holders to continue to say that philosophy was the science of something, while denying that it was the science of any ordinary subject-matter; to champion its autonomy as a discipline, while denying that it was just one science among others; to give it the standing of a science while admitting its unlikeness to the sciences. Thus the question "What are philosophy and logic the sciences of?" received a new answer, though one with a disquietingly dreamlike ring. It was the answer given by Frege and by Russell.

In Vienna thinkers were facing much the same question, though from an opposite angle. Whereas here it had been widely assumed that philosophy was Mental Science, and therefore just a sister-science to physics, chemistry, zoology, etc., in the German-speaking world it was widely assumed that philosophy stood to the other sciences not as sister but as mother—or even governess. Somehow professors of philosophy there enjoyed such a pedagogic domination that they could dictate even to the scientists. *Of course* philosophers were the right people to decide whether the teachings of Darwin, Freud and Einstein were true.

Late in the nineteenth century Mach had mutinied against this view that metaphysics was a governess-science. By the early 1920's this mutiny became a rebellion. The Vienna Circle repudiated the myth that the questions of physics, biology, psychology or mathematics can be decided by metaphysical considerations. Metaphysics is not a governess-science or a sister-science; it is not a science at all. The classic case was that of Einstein's Relativity principle. The claims of professors of philosophy to refute this principle were baseless. Scientific questions are soluble only by scientific methods, and these are not the methods of philosophers.

Thus, in England the question was this. What are the special virtues which the natural and the mathematical sciences lack but logic and philosophy possess, such that these must be invoked when the former find themselves in quandaries? In Vienna the question was this. Given that philosophers cannot decide scientific questions, what are the logical virtues which scientific procedures possess, but philosophical procedures lack? The contrast between philosophy and science was drawn in both places. In Vienna, where the autonomy of the sciences was actually challenged the object was to expose the pretensions of philosophy as a governess-science. Here, where, save for psychology, the autonomy of the sciences was not seriously challenged, it was drawn in order to extract the positive functions of logic and philosophy. Philosophy was regarded in Vienna as a blood-sucking parasite; in England as a medicinal leech.

To Wittgenstein the question came in its English form. And so he could not be called one of the Logical Positivists. Their polemics were not his; and his quest for the positive function of logic and philosophy was not, until much later, theirs. He was influenced by Frege and Russell, not by Mach. He had not himself felt the dead hand of professorial philosophy which cramped, and still cramps, even scientific thought in Germany and Austria. He, conversely, himself helped to fix the logical lifelines for the mathematicians.

I want to show how Wittgenstein transformed and answered what was all the time his master-question, "What can philosophers and logicians do, and how should they do it?"

I have said that after a long imprisonment in psychological idioms, philosophy was, for a time, re-housed in Platonic idioms. But this was only a temporary asylum. For after a short period during which philosophers tried not to mind the dreamlike character of the new asylum, something awoke them from the dream. Russell, in his enquiries into the logical principles underlying mathematics, found that he could not well help constructing statements which had the logically disturbing property that they were true only on condition that they were false, and false only on condition that they were true. Some of these self-subverting statements seemed to be inherent in the very basis which was to make mathematics secure. There was a major leak in the dry dock which Frege and he had built for mathematics.

Russell found a patch for the leak. Underlying the familiar distinction between truth and falsehood, there is a more radical distinction between significance and meaninglessness. True and false statements are both significant, but some forms of words, with the vocabulary and constructions of statements, are neither true nor false, but nonsensical—and nonsensical not for reasons of wording or of grammar, but for logical reasons. The self-subverting statements were of this sort, neither true nor false, but nonsensical simulacra of statements. Notice, it is only of such things as complex verbal expressions that we can ask whether they are significant or nonsense. The question could not be asked of mental processes; or of Platonic entities. So logic is from the start concerned, not with these but rather with what can or cannot be significantly said. Its subject-matter is a linguistic one, though its tasks are not at all those of philology.

In Wittgenstein's *Tractatus* this departmental conclusion is generalised. All logic and all philosophy are enquiries into what makes it significant or nonsensical to say certain things. The sciences aim at saying what is true about the world; philosophy aims at disclosing only the logic of what can be truly or even falsely said about the world. This is why philosophy is not a sister-science or a parent-science; that its business is not to add to the number of scientific statements, but to disclose their logic.

Wittgenstein begins by considering how a sentence, a map, a diagram or a scale-model can represent or even significantly misrepresent the facts. The isolated words "London" and "south" are not true or false. Nor can a single dot on a sheet of paper be an accurate or inaccurate map. The sentence "London is north of Brighton" is true. The same words, differently arranged as "Brighton is north of London" make a false statement. Arranged as "South is London of Brighton" they make a farrago which is neither true nor false, but nonsense. For dots on paper to represent or misrepresent the direction of Brighton from London, there must be a dot for each town and they must be set out in accordance with some convention for points of the compass. For a statement, map or diagram to be true or false, there must be a plurality of words or marks; but, more, these bits must be put together in certain ways. And underlying the fact that the truth or falsity of the statement or map partly depends upon the particular way in which its bits are arranged, there lies the fact that whether a significant statement or map results at all depends wholly on the general way in which the bits are put together. Some ways of jumbling them together are ruled out. What rules rule them out?

In the *Tractatus* Wittgenstein came to the frustrating conclusion that these principles of arrangement inevitably baffle significant statement. To try to tell what makes the difference between significant and nonsensical talk is itself to cross the divide between significant and nonsensical talk. Philosophising can, indeed, open our eyes to these structural principles, but it cannot issue in significant statements of them. Philosophy is not a science; it cannot yield theories or doctrines. None the less it can be skilful or unskilful, successful or unsuccessful. It is in pursuing the activity itself that we see what we need to see. Rather like learning music or tennis, learning philosophy does not result in our being able to tell what we have learnt; though, as in music and tennis, we can show what we have learnt.

Now it is true that philosophical clarity is achieved in the acts of appreciating arguments rather than in propounding theorems. But it is false that all philosophical talk is nonsensical talk. Wittgenstein had himself said very effective things, and talking effectively is not talking nonsensically. What had brought him to this frustrating conclusion? When he wrote the *Tractatus,* he was, I think, over-influenced by his own analogies between saying things and making maps, diagrams and scale-models. Certainly, for marks on paper to constitute a temperature-chart, or for spoken words to constitute a significant statement, the dots and the words must be arranged according to rules and conventions. Only if the zigzag of dots on the nurse's graph-paper is systematically correlated with the thermometer-readings taken at successive moments of a day can it represent or even misrepresent the alterations in the patient's temperature. Only if words are organized according to a number of complex general rules does a true or false statement result.

Suppose we now asked the nurse to depict on a second sheet of graph-paper, not the course of the patient's temperature, but the rules for representing his temperature by dots on graph paper, she would be baffled. Nor can the rules and conventions of map-making themselves be mapped. So Wittgenstein argued in the *Tractatus* that the philosopher or logician is debarred from saying what it is that makes things said significant or nonsensical. He can show it, but not tell it. After the *Tractatus* he realised that though saying things does resemble depicting things or mapping things in the respect for which he originally drew the analogy, it does not resemble them in all respects. Just as the nurse can tell, though not depict, how the temperature-chart represents or misrepresents the patient's temperature, so the philosopher can tell why, say, a scientist's statement makes or does not make sense. What alone would be absurd would be a sentence which purported to convey a comment upon its own significance or meaninglessness.

The *Tractatus* has two distinct but connected aims. The first, which I have crudely sketched, is to show both what philosophy is not, namely any sort of a science, and what it is, namely an activity of exploring the internal logic of what is said, for example, in this or that scientific theory. The second, which I shall not even try to sketch, is to show what sort of an enquiry Formal Logic is. This brings me to a general point about the *Tractatus*. Wittgenstein's first interest had been in the logic of mathematics and thence in the logical paradoxes which were the big leak in the dry dock that Frege and Russell had built. He was, therefore, equipped and predisposed to squeeze whatever can be significantly said into the few statement-patterns with which the logic of mathematical statements operates. He used its terminology, its codes, and its abacus-operations in his task of exploring various philosophical issues, and, above all, his own master-issue, that of the nature of philosophising itself. In consequence, the *Tractatus* is, in large measure, a closed book to those who lack this technical equipment. Few people can read it without feeling that something important is happening; but few experts, even, can say what is happening.

But this is not the end of the story Maybe it is only the preface. For, after lying fallow for some years, Wittgenstein returned to philosophy. His teaching in this period differs markedly from that of the *Tractatus;* it even repudiates parts of the *Tractatus*.

First, he no longer forces all expressions into the favoured few patterns of the logic of mathematics. With this goes a revolt against moulds of any sorts. The rubrics of logical systems and the abstract terms of philosophical schools are like the shoes of Chinese ladies, which deformed their feet and prevented them from walking on them. Philosophical elucidation is still inspection of expressions, but it is no longer inspection through the slots of a logician's stencil or through the prisms of a scholastic classification-system. His diction has reverted from that of a Russell discussing esoteric matters with mathematicians to that of a Socrates discussing everyday ideas with unindoctrinated young men. Nor does he now elucidate only the propositions of the sciences. Like Moore, he explores the logic of all the things that all of us say.

Next, though I think that his master-problem is still that of the nature, tasks and methods of the philosophical activity, he no longer thinks that philosophers are condemned to trying to say the unsayable. But he now avoids any general statement of the nature of philosophy, not because this would be to say the unsayable, but because it would be to say a scholastic and therefore an obscuring thing. In philosophy, generalisations are unclarifications. The nature of philosophy is to be taught by producing concrete specimens of it. As the medical student learns surgery by witnessing and practising operations on dead and on live subjects, so the student of philosophy learns what philosophy is by following and practising operations on particular quandary-generating ways of talking. Thus Wittgenstein would rove, apparently aimlessly because without any statement of aim, from one concrete puzzle to its brothers, its cousins, its parents and its associates, demonstrating both what makes them puzzling and how to resolve them—demonstrating, but not telling; going through the moves, but not compiling a manual of them; teaching a skill, not dictating a doctrine.

One favourite procedure of his might be called the "tea-tasting method." Tea-tasters do not lump their samples into two or three comprehensive types. Rather they savour each sample and try to place it next door to its closest neighbours, and this not in respect of just one discriminable quality, but along the lengths of various lines of qualities. So Wittgenstein would exhibit the characteristic manner of working of a particular expression, by matching it against example after example of expressions progressively diverging from it in various respects and directions. He would show how striking similarities may go with important but ordinarily unremarked differences, and how we are tempted to lean too heavily on their similarities and hence to be tripped up by their latent differences.

For philosophers do not examine expressions at random. The quest for their internal logic is forced upon us by the fact that we find ourselves already caught up in unforeseen entanglements. Why do we slide into quandaries? Let me invent an example. We find ourselves talking as if like a train, so time itself might one day slow down and stop. We divide a train into coaches and coaches into compartments. We divide a month into weeks and weeks into days. When a train is passing me, some coaches are beyond me, some are still to come, and one compartment of one coach is directly abreast of me. I look at its occupants through the window. Surely time is like this. Last week has gone, next week is still to come, but I can exchange glances with the occupants of Now. So, as trains always slow down and stop somewhere, what makes time puff on so tirelessly? Might not Now be the last compartment of the last coach? Yet surely not; there would still be something behind it, if only the empty wind. You see that it is tempting, but also that it smells like nonsense to speak of the last compartment of time. Why may we say some things about time which are very much like some things that we legitimately say about trains, when to some of the proper corollaries of what we say about trains there correspond no proper corollaries about time? To answer this question, we should have to examine the functioning of whole ranges of things that we say about trains, rivers and winds; about moving shadows, rainbows and reflections; about perpetual motion machines, stars, clocks, sundials, and calendars; about the series of numbers, days of the week and minutes of the day. And then we may see why we slid and no longer incline to slide from the proper corollaries of familiar dictions about trains to corresponding corollaries of somewhat similar dictions about time. We see that we had overpressed certain analogies between ways of talking; and that we were so dominated by a favourite model, that we had gone on using it where it could no longer work. And now we know, in a way, what time is, though there is no shorter or better way of saying what time is than by going through again the same sort of process of linguistic tea-tasting.

I must conclude. Wittgenstein has made our generation of philosophers self-conscious about philosophy itself. It is, of course, possible for a person to be very thoughtful about the nature and methods of an activity, without being made any the better at performing it. The centipede of the poem ran well until he began to wonder how he ran. Maybe we have been made a bit neurotic about the nature of our calling. But Wittgenstein's demolition of the idea that philosophy is a sort of science has at least made us vigilant about our tools. We no longer try to use for our problems the methods of arguing which are the right ones for demonstrating theorems or establishing hypotheses. In particular we have learnt to pay deliberate attention to what can and cannot be said. What had, since the early days of this century, been the practice of G. E. Moore has received a rationale from Wittgenstein; and I expect that when the curtain is lifted we shall also find that Wittgenstein's concrete methods have increased the power, scope and delicacy of the methods by which Moore has for so long explored in detail the internal logic of what we say.

Magdalen College, Oxford

JOHN WISDOM

[1904–   ]

Arthur John Terence Dibben Wisdom is not a pseudonym but the actual name of an extraordinarily wise, witty, and wide-ranging philosopher whose cousin, J. O. Wisdom, is also a philosopher—and both men have risked their philosophical purity by delving deeply into psychoanalysis and even talking about it.

As a brilliant young student at Cambridge University in the 1920's, John Wisdom almost inevitably was drawn into the Russell-Wittgenstein position, with strict logic as his method and logical atomism as his goal. Indeed his long series of papers in 1931-1933 on "Logical Constructions" is said to be the last word in logical atomism both as to time and to wholehearted concentration.

However, in 1929 Wittgenstein returned to Cambridge and in 1930 he began to teach there. In 1934, 1935, 1936, and 1937 Wisdom attended his lectures and frequently talked with him about philosophical questions. The first startling result of this meeting of minds was Wisdom's article "Philosophical Perplexity" (1936), which showed his changed viewpoint and, according to J. O. Urmson, "is something of a landmark in the history of philosophy," as "the first manifesto of a new way of doing philosophy." Here and in subsequent papers Wisdom expressed his profound debt to Wittgenstein but added in his characteristic footnote that "Wittgenstein has not read this paper and I warn people against supposing it a closer imitation of him than it is." This warning was necessary because Wittgenstein disliked having his thought reported at secondhand and yet published nothing himself during this final amazingly influential period of his life. But at least some of the things that he was then saying to his ardent listeners appear in *Philosophical Investigations*, published in 1953, two years after his death.

But to return to "Philosophical Perplexity," Wisdom began

432

rather forbiddingly by saying that "A philosophical answer is really a verbal recommendation in response to a request which is really a request with regard to a sentence which lacks a conventional use whether there occur situations which could conventionally be described by it." Or to put the matter in his more colloquial style: "I want to stress the philosophical usefulness of metaphysical surprises such as 'We can never really know the causes of our sensations,' 'We can never know the real causes of our sensations,' 'Inductive conclusions are never really justified'. . . . Remember what Moore said about 1924—words to this effect. When a philosopher says that really something is so we are warned that what he says is really so is not so really. With horrible ingenuity Moore can rapidly reduce any metaphysical theory to a ridiculous story. For he is right, they are false—only there is good in them, poor things." What often appear to be "symptoms of linguistic confusion" may be interpreted as "symptoms of linguistic penetration." In short, Wisdom was refusing to dismiss metaphysical statements as meaningless or nonsensical because he was refusing to bow down before a single, inflexible Principle of Verifiability, and that is the thesis of his second important article, "Metaphysics and Verification" (1938). But "Philosophy, Anxiety and Novelty" is "perhaps the best short summary of Wisdom's whole position," as D. A. T. Gasking suggests.

Finally it may be pointed out that Wisdom does not use psychoanalysis as a meat ax or a torpedo but as a searchlight. He nowhere tries to reduce philosophy to psychopathology but he does say (following Wittgenstein) that the "confused tensions" of philosophers are much like the apparently inescapable dilemmas of neurotics—and something can be done about both situations.

Wisdom's longest and most ambitious work to date is a series of dialogues on *Other Minds,* which is by no means easy reading but it is rich, profitable, and often amusing reading.

His essay on "Gods," first published in 1944 and now included in his collection *Philosophy and Psychoanalysis* (1953), has aroused much cogitation, irritation, and admiration!

GODS

1. *The existence of God is not an experimental issue in the way it was.* An atheist or agnostic might say to a theist, "You still think there are spirits in the trees, nymphs in the streams, a God of the world." He might say this because he noticed the theist in time of drought pray for rain and make a sacrifice and in the morning look for rain. But disagreement about whether there are gods is now less of this experimental or betting sort than it used to be. This is due in part, if not wholly, to our better knowledge of why things happen as they do.

It is true that even in these days it is seldom that one who believes in God has no hopes or fears which an atheist has not. Few believers now expect prayer to still the waves, but some think it makes a difference to people and not merely in ways the atheist would admit. Of course with people, as opposed to waves and machines, one never knows what they won't do next, so that expecting prayer to make a difference to them is not so definite a thing as believing in its mechanical efficacy. Still, just as primitive people pray in a business-like way for rain so some people still pray for others with a real feeling of doing something to help. However, in spite of this persistence of an experimental element in some theistic belief, it remains true that Elijah's method on Mount Carmel of settling the matter of what god or gods exist would be far less appropriate to-day than it was then.

2. *Belief in gods is not merely a matter of expectation of a world to come.* Someone may say, "The fact that a theist no more than an atheist expects prayer to bring down fire from heaven or cure the sick does not mean that there is no difference between them as to the facts, it does not mean that the theist has no expectations different from the atheist's. For very often those who believe in God believe in another world and believe that God is there and that we shall go to that world when we die."

This is true, but I do not want to consider here expectations as to what one will see and feel after death nor what sort of reasons these logically unique expectations could have. So I want to consider those theists who do not believe in a future life, or rather, I want to consider the differences between atheists and theists in so far as these differences are not a matter of belief in a future life.

3. *What are these differences? And is it that theists are superstitious or that atheists are blind?* A child may wish to sit a while with his father and he may, when he has done what his father dislikes, fear punishment and feel distress at causing vexation, and while his father is alive he may feel sure of help when danger threatens and feel that there is sympathy for him when disaster has come. When his father is dead he will no longer expect punishment or help. Maybe for a moment an old fear will come or a cry for help escape him, but he will at once remember that this is no good now. He may feel that his father is no more until perhaps someone says to him that his father is still alive though he lives now in another world and one so far away that there is no hope of seeing him or hearing his voice again. The child may be told that nevertheless his father can see him and hear all he says. When he has been told this the child will still fear no punishment nor expect any sign of his father, but now, even more than he did when his father was alive, he will feel that his father sees him all the time and will dread distressing him and when he has done something wrong he will feel separated from his father until he has felt sorry for what he has done. Maybe when he himself comes to die he will be like a man who expects to find a friend in the strange country where he is going, but even when this is so, it is by no means all of what makes the difference between a child who believes that his father lives still in another world and one who does not.

Likewise one who believes in God may face death differently from one who does not, but there is another difference between them besides this. This other difference may still be described as belief in another world, only this belief is not a matter of expecting one thing rather than another here or hereafter, it is not a matter of a world to come but of a world that now is, though beyond our senses.

We are at once reminded of those other unseen worlds which some philosophers "believe in" and others "deny," while non-philosophers unconsciously "accept" them by using them as models with which to "get the hang of" the patterns in the flux of experience. We recall the timeless entities whose changeless connections we seek to represent in symbols, and the values which stand firm[1] amidst our flickering satisfaction and remorse, and the physical things which, though not beyond the corruption of moth and rust, are yet more permanent than the shadows they throw upon the screen before our minds. We recall, too, our talk of souls and of what lies in their depths and is manifested to us partially and intermittently in our own feelings and the behaviour of others. The hypothesis of mind, of other human minds and of animal minds, is reasonable because it explains for each of us why certain things behave so cunningly all by themselves unlike even the most ingenious machines. Is the hypothesis of minds in flowers and trees reasonable for like reasons? Is the hypothesis of a world mind reasonable for like reasons—someone who adjusts the blossom to the bees, someone whose presence may at times be felt—in a garden in high summer, in the hills when clouds are gathering, but not, perhaps, in a cholera epidemic?

4. *The question "Is belief in gods reasonable?" has more than one source.* It is clear now that in order to grasp fully the logic of belief in divine minds we need to examine the logic of belief in animal and human minds. But we cannot do that here and so for the purposes of this discussion about divine minds let us acknowledge the reasonableness of our belief in human minds without troubling ourselves about its logic. The question of the reasonableness of belief in divine minds then becomes a matter of whether there are facts in nature which support claims about divine minds in the way facts in nature support our claims about human minds.

In this way we resolve the force behind the problem of the

---

[1] In another world, Dr. Joad says in the *New Statesman* recently.

existence of gods into two components, one metaphysical and the same which prompts the question "Is there *ever any* behaviour which gives reason to believe in *any* sort of mind?" and one which finds expression in "Are there other mind-patterns in nature beside the human and animal patterns which we can all easily detect, and are these other mind-patterns super-human?"

Such over-determination of a question syndrome is common. Thus, the puzzling questions "Do dogs think?", "Do animals feel?" are partly metaphysical puzzles and partly scientific questions. They are not purely metaphysical; for the reports of scientists about the poor performances of cats in cages and old ladies' stories about the remarkable performances of their pets are not irrelevant. But nor are these questions purely scientific; for the stories never settle them and therefore they have other sources. One other source is the metaphysical source we have already noticed, namely, the difficulty about getting behind an animal's behaviour to its mind, whether it is a non-human animal or a human one.

But there's a third component in the force behind these questions, these disputes have a third source, and it is one which is important in the dispute which finds expression in the words "I believe in God," "I do not." This source comes out well if we consider the question "Do flowers feel?" Like the questions about dogs and animals this question about flowers comes partly from the difficulty we sometimes feel over inference from *any* behaviour to thought or feeling and partly from ignorance as to what behaviour is to be found. But these questions, as opposed to a like question about human beings, come also from hesitation as to whether the behaviour in question is *enough* mind-like, that is, is it enough similar to or superior to human behaviour to be called "mind-proving"? Likewise, even when we are satisfied that human behaviour shows mind and even when we have learned whatever mind-suggesting things there are in nature which are not explained by human and animal minds, we may still ask "But are these things sufficiently striking to be called a mind-pattern? Can we fairly call them manifestations of a divine being?"

"The question," someone may say, "has then become merely a matter of the application of a name. And 'What's in a name?'"

5. *But the line between a question of fact and a question or decision as to the application of a name is not so simple as this way of putting things suggests.* The question "What's in a name?" is engaging because we are inclined to answer both "Nothing" and "Very much." And this "Very much" has more than one source. We might have tried to comfort Heloise by saying, "It isn't that Abelard no longer loves you, for this man isn't Abelard"; we might have said to poor Mr. Tebrick in Mr. Garnett's *Lady into Fox,* "But this is no longer Silvia." But if Mr. Tebrick replied, "Ah, but it is!" this might come not at all from observing facts about the fox which we have not observed, but from noticing facts about the fox which we had missed, although we had in a sense observed all that Mr. Tebrick had observed. It is possible to have before one's eyes all the items of a pattern and still to miss the pattern. Consider the following conversation:

" 'And I think Kay and I are pretty happy. We've always been happy.'

"Bill lifted up his glass and put it down without drinking.

" 'Would you mind saying that again?' he asked.

" 'I don't see what's so queer about it. Taken all in all, Kay and I have really been happy.'

" 'All right,' Bill said gently. 'Just tell me how you and Kay have been happy.'

"Bill had a way of being amused by things which I could not understand.

" 'It's a little hard to explain,' I said. 'It's like taking a lot of numbers that don't look alike and that don't mean anything until you add them all together.'

"I stopped, because I hadn't meant to talk to him about Kay and me.

" 'Go ahead,' Bill said. 'What about the numbers.' And he began to smile.

" 'I don't know why you think it's so funny,' I said. 'All the things that two people do together, two people like Kay and me, add up to something. There are the kids and the house and the dog and all the people we have known and all the times we've been out to dinner. Of course, Kay and I do quarrel sometimes but when you add it all together, all of it isn't as bad as the parts of it seem. I mean, maybe that's all there is to anybody's life.'

"Bill poured himself another drink. He seemed about to say something and checked himself. He kept looking at me." [2]

Or again, suppose two people are speaking of two characters in a story which both have read [3] or of two friends which both have known, and one says, "Really she hated him," and the other says, "She didn't, she loved him." Then the first may have noticed what the other has not although he knows no incident in the lives of the people they are talking about which the other doesn't know too, and the second speaker may say, "She didn't, she loved him," because he hasn't noticed what the first noticed, although he can remember every incident the first can remember. But then again he may say, "She didn't, she loved him," not because he hasn't noticed the patterns in time which the first has noticed but because though he has noticed them he doesn't feel he still needs to emphasize them with "Really she hated him." The line between using a name because of how we feel and because of what we have noticed isn't sharp. "A difference as to the facts," "a discovery," "a revelation," these phrases cover many things. Discoveries have been made not only by Christopher Columbus and Pasteur, but also by Tolstoy and Dostoievsky and Freud. Things are revealed to us not only by the scientists with microscopes, but also by the poets, the prophets, and the painters. What is so isn't merely a matter of "the facts." For sometimes when there is agreement as to the facts there is still argument as to whether defendant did or did not "exercise reasonable care," was or was not "negligent."

---

[2] *H. M. Pulham, Esq.*, by John P. Marquand.
[3] E.g., Havelock Ellis' autobiography.

And though we shall need to emphasize how much "There is a God" evinces an attitude to the familiar[4] we shall find in the end that it also evinces some recognition of patterns in time easily missed and that, therefore, difference as to there being any gods is in part a difference as to what is so and therefore as to the facts, though not in the simple ways which first occurred to us.

6. *Let us now approach these same points by a different road.*

6.1. *How it is that an explanatory hypothesis, such as the existence of God, may start by being experimental and gradually become something quite different can be seen from the following story:*

Two people return to their long neglected garden to find among the weeds a few of the old plants surprisingly vigorous. One says to the other, "It must be that a gardener has been coming and doing something about these plants." Upon inquiry they find that no neighbour has ever seen anyone at work in their garden. The first man says to the other, "He must have worked while people slept." The other says, "No, someone would have heard him and besides, anybody who cared about the plants would have kept down these weeds." The first man says, "Look at the way these are arranged. There is purpose and a feeling for beauty here. I believe that someone comes, someone invisible to mortal eyes. I believe that the more carefully we look the more we shall find confirmation of this." They examine the garden ever so carefully and sometimes they come on new things suggesting that a gardener comes and sometimes they come on new things suggesting the contrary and even that a malicious person has been at work. Besides examining the garden carefully they also study what happens to gardens left without attention. Each learns all the other learns about this and about the garden. Consequently, when after all this, one says, "I still

---

[4] "Persuasive Definitions," *Mind*, July, 1938, by Charles Leslie Stevenson, should be read here. It is very good.

believe a gardener comes," while the other says, "I don't," their different words now reflect no difference as to what they have found in the garden, no difference as to what they would find in the garden if they looked further and no difference about how fast untended gardens fall into disorder. At this stage, in this context, the gardener hypothesis has ceased to be experimental, the difference between one who accepts and one who rejects it is now not a matter of the one expecting something the other does not expect. What is the difference between them? The one says, "A gardener comes unseen and unheard. He is manifested only in his works with which we are all familiar," the other says, "There is no gardener," and with this difference in what they say about the gardener goes a difference in how they feel towards the garden, in spite of the fact that neither expects anything of it which the other does not expect.

But is this the whole difference between them—that the one calls the garden by one name and feels one way towards it, while the other calls it by another name and feels in another way towards it? And if this is what the difference has become then is it any longer appropriate to ask "Which is right?" or "Which is reasonable?"

And yet surely such questions *are* appropriate when one person says to another, "You still think the world's a garden and not a wilderness, and that the gardener has not forsaken it," or "You still think there are nymphs of the streams, a presence in the hills, a spirit of the world." Perhaps when a man sings "God's in His heaven" we need not take this as more than an expression of how he feels. But when Bishop Gore or Dr. Joad writes about belief in God and young men read them in order to settle their religious doubts the impression is not simply that of persons choosing exclamations with which to face nature and the "changes and chances of this mortal life." The disputants speak as if they are concerned with a matter of scientific fact, or of trans-sensual, trans-scientific and metaphysical fact, but still of fact and still a matter about which reasons for and against may be offered, although no scientific reasons in the sense of field surveys for fossils or experiments on delinquents are to the point.

6.2. *Now can an interjection have a logic?* Can the manifestation of an attitude in the utterance of a word, in the application of a name, have a logic? When all the facts are known how can there still be a question of fact? How can there still be a question? Surely, as Hume says, ". . . after every circumstance, every relation is known, the understanding has no further room to operate"?[5]

6.3. When the madness of these questions leaves us for a moment *we can all easily recollect disputes which though they cannot be settled by experiment are yet disputes in which one party may be right and the other wrong* and in which both parties may offer reasons and the one better reasons than the other. *This may happen in pure and applied mathematics and logic.* Two accountants or two engineers provided with the same data may reach different results and this difference is resolved not by collecting further data but by going over the calculations again. Such differences indeed share with differences as to what will win a race, the honour of being among the most "settlable" disputes in the language.

6.4. *But it won't do to describe the theistic issue as one settlable by such calculation,* or as one about what can be deduced in this *vertical* fashion from the facts we know. No doubt dispute about God has sometimes, perhaps especially in mediaeval times, been carried on in this fashion. But nowadays it is not and we must look for some other analogy, some other case in which a dispute is settled but not by experiment.

6.5. *In courts of law* it sometimes happens that opposing counsel are agreed as to the facts and are not trying to settle a question of further fact, are not trying to settle whether the man who admittedly had quarrelled with the deceased did or did not murder him, but are concerned with whether Mr. A who admittedly handed his long-trusted clerk signed blank cheques did or did not exercise reasonable care, whether a

---

[5] Hume, *An Enquiry Concerning the Principles of Morals.* Appendix I.

ledger is or is not a document,[6] whether a certain body was or was not a public authority.

In such cases we notice that the process of argument is not a *chain* of demonstrative reasoning. It is a presenting and re-presenting of those features of the case which *severally co-operate* in favour of the conclusion, in favour of saying what the reasoner wishes said, in favour of calling the situation by the name by which he wishes to call it. The reasons are like the legs of a chair, not the links of a chain. Consequently although the discussion is *a priori* and the steps are not a matter of experience, the procedure resembles scientific argument in that the reasoning is not *vertically* extensive but *horizontally* extensive—it is a matter of the cumulative effect of several independent premises, not of the repeated transformation of one or two. And because the premises are severally inconclusive the process of deciding the issue becomes a matter of weighing the cumulative effect of one group of severally inconclusive items against the cumulative effect of another group of severally inconclusive items, and thus lends itself to description in terms of conflicting "probabilities." This encourages the feeling that the issue is one of fact—that it is a matter of guessing from the premises at a further fact, at what is to come. But this is a muddle. *The dispute does not cease to be* a priori *because it is a matter of the cumulative effect of severally inconclusive premises*. The logic of the dispute is not that of a chain of deductive reasoning as in a mathematic calculation. But nor is it a matter of collecting from several inconclusive items of information an expectation as to something further, as when a doctor from a patient's symptoms guesses at what is wrong, or a detective from many clues guesses the criminal. It has its own sort of logic and its own sort of end—the solution of the question at issue is a decision,

---

⁶ *The Times*, March 2nd, 1945. Also in *The Times* of June 13th, 1945, contrast the case of Hannah v. Peel with that of the cruiser cut in two by a liner. In the latter case there is not agreement as to the facts. See also the excellent articles by Dr. Glanville L. Williams in the *Law Quarterly Review*, "Language and the Law," January, and April 1945, and "The Doctrine of Repugnancy," October, 1943, January, 1944, and April, 1944. The author, having set out how arbitrary are many legal decisions, needs now to set out how far from arbitrary they are—if his readers are ready for the next phase in the dialectic process.

a ruling by the judge. But it is not an arbitrary decision though the rational connections are neither quite like those in vertical deductions nor like those in inductions in which from many signs we guess at what is to come; and though the decision manifests itself in the application of a name it is no more merely the application of a name than is the pinning on of a medal merely the pinning on of a bit of metal. Whether a lion with stripes is a tiger or a lion is, if you like, merely a matter of the application of a name. Whether Mr. So-and-So of whose conduct we have so complete a record did or did not exercise reasonable care is not merely a matter of the application of a name or, if we choose to say it is, then we must remember that with this name a game is lost and won and a game with very heavy stakes. With the judges' choice of a name for the facts goes an attitude, and the declaration, the ruling, is an exclamation evincing that attitude. But *it is an exclamation which not only has a purpose but also has a logic,* a logic surprisingly like that of "futile," "deplorable," "graceful," "grand," "divine."

6.6. *Suppose two people are looking at a picture or natural scene.* One says, "Excellent," or, "Beautiful," or, "Divine"; the other says, "I don't see it." He means he doesn't see the beauty. And this reminds us of how we felt the theist accuse the atheist of blindness and the atheist accuse the theist of seeing what isn't there. And yet surely each sees what the other sees. It isn't that one can see part of the picture which the other can't see. So the difference is in a sense not one as to the facts. And so it cannot be removed by the one disputant discovering to the other what so far he hasn't seen. It isn't that the one sees the picture in a different light and so, as we might say, sees a different picture. Consequently the difference between them cannot be resolved by putting the picture in a different light. And yet surely this is just what can be done in such a case—not by moving the picture but by talk perhaps. To settle a dispute as to whether a piece of music is good or better than another we listen again, with a picture we look again. Someone perhaps points to emphasize certain features and we see it in a different light. Shall we call this "field work" and "the last of observation" or shall we call it "reviewing the premises" and "the beginning of deduction (horizontal)"?

If in spite of all this we choose to say that a difference as to whether a thing is beautiful is not a factual difference we must be careful to remember that there is a procedure for settling these differences and that this consists not only in reasoning and redescription as in the legal case, but also in a more literal re-setting-before with re-looking or re-listening.

6.7. *And if we say as we did at the beginning that when a difference as to the existence of a God is not one as to future happenings then it is not experimental and therefore not as to the facts, we must not forthwith assume that there is no right and wrong about it,* no rationality or irrationality, no appropriateness or inappropriateness, no procedure which tends to settle it, *nor even that this procedure is in no sense a discovery of new facts.* After all even in science this is not so. Our two gardeners even when they had reached the stage when neither expected any experimental result which the other did not, might yet have continued the dispute, each presenting and re-presenting the features of the garden favouring his hypothesis, that is, fitting his model for describing the accepted fact; each emphasizing the pattern he wishes to emphasize. True, in science, there is seldom or never a pure instance of this sort of dispute, for nearly always with difference of hypothesis goes some difference of expectation as to the facts. But scientists argue about rival hypotheses with a vigour which is not exactly proportioned to difference in expectations of experimental results.

The difference as to whether a God exists involves our feelings more than most scientific disputes and in this respect is more like a difference as to whether there is beauty in a thing.

7. *The Connecting Technique.* Let us consider again the technique used in revealing or proving beauty, in removing a blindness, in inducing an attitude which is lacking, in reducing a reaction that is inappropriate. Besides running over in a special way the features of the picture, tracing the rhythms, making sure that this and that are not only seen but

noticed, and their relation to each other—besides all this—
there are other things we can do to justify our attitude and
alter that of the man who cannot see. For features of the picture may be brought out by setting beside it other pictures;
just as the merits of an argument may be brought out, proved,
by setting beside it other arguments, in which striking but
irrelevant features of the original are changed and relevant
features emphasized; just as the merits and demerits of a line
of action may be brought out by setting beside it other actions. To use Susan Stebbing's example: Nathan brought out
for David certain features of what David had done in the
matter of Uriah the Hittite by telling him a story about two
sheep-owners. This is the kind of thing we very often do when
someone is "inconsistent" or "unreasonable." This is what we
do in referring to other cases in law. The paths we need to
trace from other cases to the case in question are often numerous and difficult to detect and the person with whom we are
discussing the matter may well draw attention to connections
which, while not incompatible with those we have tried to
emphasize, are of an opposite inclination. A may have noticed
in B subtle and hidden likenesses to an angel and reveal these
to C, while C has noticed in B subtle and hidden likenesses
to a devil which he reveals to A.

Imagine that a man picks up some flowers that lie half
withered on a table and gently puts them in water. Another
man says to him, "You believe flowers feel." He says this although he knows that the man who helps the flowers doesn't
expect anything of them which he himself doesn't expect; for
he himself expects the flowers to be "refreshed" and to be
easily hurt, injured, I mean, by rough handling, while the
man who puts them in water does not expect them to whisper
"Thank you." The Sceptic says, "You believe flowers feel,"
because something about the way the other man lifts the
flowers and puts them in water suggests an attitude to the
flowers which he feels inappropriate although perhaps he
would not feel it inappropriate to butterflies. He feels that this
attitude to flowers is somewhat crazy *just as it is sometimes
felt that a lover's attitude is somewhat crazy even when this*

is not a matter of his having false hopes about how the person he is in love with will act. It is often said in such cases that reasoning is useless. But the very person who says this feels that the lover's attitude is crazy, is inappropriate like some dreads and hatreds, such as some horrors of enclosed places. And often one who says "It is useless to reason" proceeds at once to reason with the lover, nor is this reasoning always quite without effect. We may draw the lover's attention to certain things done by her he is in love with and trace for him a path to these from things done by others at other times[7] which have disgusted and infuriated him. And by this means we may weaken his admiration and confidence, make him feel it unjustified and arouse his suspicion and contempt and make him feel our suspicion and contempt reasonable. It is possible, of course, that he has already noticed the analogies, the connections, we point out and that he has accepted them —that is, he has not denied them nor passed them off. He has recognized them and they have altered his attitude, altered his love, but he still loves. We then feel that perhaps it is we who are blind and cannot see what he can see.

8. *Connecting and Disconnecting.* But before we confess ourselves thus inadequate there are other fires his admiration must pass through. For when a man has an attitude which it seems to us he should not have or lacks one which it seems to us he should have then, not only do we suspect that he is not influenced by connections which we feel should influence him and draw his attention to these, but also we suspect he is influenced by connections which should not influence him and draw his attention to these. It may, for a moment, seem strange that we should draw his attention to connections which we feel should not influence him, and which, since they do influence him, he has in a sense already noticed. But we do—such is our confidence in "the light of reason."

Sometimes the power of these connections comes mainly from a man's mismanagement of the language he is using. This is what happens in the Monte Carlo fallacy, where by

---

[7] Thus, like the scientist, the critic is concerned to show up the irrelevance of time and space.

mismanaging the laws of chance a man passes from noticing that a certain colour or number has not turned up for a long while to an improper confidence that now it soon will turn up. In such cases our showing up of the false connections is a process we call "explaining a fallacy in reasoning." To remove fallacies in reasoning we urge a man to call a spade a spade, ask him what he means by "the State" and having pointed out ambiguities and vaguenesses ask him to reconsider the steps in his argument.

9. *Unspoken Connections. Usually, however, wrongheadedness or wrongheartedness in a situation, blindness to what is there or seeing what is not, does not arise merely from mismanagement of language but is more due to connections which are not mishandled in language, for the reason that they are not put into language at all.* And often these misconnections too, weaken in the light of reason, if only we can guess where they lie and turn it on them. In so far as these connections are not presented in language the process of removing their power is not a process of correcting the mismanagement of language. But it is still akin to such a process; for though it is not a process of setting out fairly what has been set out unfairly, it is a process of setting out fairly what has not been set out at all. And we must remember that the line between connections ill-presented or half-presented in language and connections operative but not presented in language, or only hinted at, is not a sharp one.

Whether or not we call the process of showing up these connections "reasoning to remove bad unconscious reasoning" or not, it is certain that in order to settle in ourselves what weight we shall attach to someone's confidence or attitude we not only ask him for his reasons but also look for unconscious reasons both good and bad; that is, for reasons which he can't put into words, isn't explicitly aware of, is hardly aware of, isn't aware of at all—perhaps it's long experience which he *doesn't* recall which lets him know a squall is coming, perhaps it's old experience which he *can't* recall which makes the cake in the tea mean so much and makes Odette so fascinating.

I am well aware of the distinction between the question

"What reasons are there for the belief that S is P?" and the question "What are the sources of beliefs that S is P?" There are cases where investigation of the rationality of a claim which certain persons make is done with very little inquiry into why they say what they do, into the causes of their beliefs. This is so when we have very definite ideas about what is really logically relevant to their claim and what is not. Offered a mathematical theorem, we ask for the proof; offered the generalization that parental discord causes crime, we ask for the correlation co-efficients. But even in this last case, if we fancy that only the figures are reasons we underestimate the complexity of the logic of our conclusion; and yet it is difficult to describe the other features of the evidence which have weight and there is apt to be disagreement about the weight they should have. In criticizing other conclusions and especially conclusions which are largely the expression of an attitude, we have not only to ascertain what reasons there are for them but also to decide what things are reasons and how much. This latter process of sifting reasons from causes is part of the critical process for every belief, but in some spheres it has been done pretty fully already. In these spheres we don't need to examine the actual processes to belief and distil from them a logic. But in other spheres this remains to be done. Even in science or on the stock exchange or in ordinary life we sometimes hesitate to condemn a belief or a hunch[8] merely because those who believe it cannot offer the sort of reasons we had hoped for. And now suppose Miss Gertrude Stein finds excellent the work of a new artist while we see nothing in it. We nervously recall, perhaps, how pictures by Picasso, which Miss Stein admired and others rejected, later came to be admired by many who gave attention to them, and we wonder whether the case is not a new instance of her perspicacity and our blindness. But if, upon giving all our attention to the work in question, we still do not respond to it, and we notice that the subject matter of the new pictures is perhaps birds in wild places and learn that Miss Stein is a bird-

---

[8] Here I think of Mr. Stace's interesting reflections in *Mind*, January, 1945, "The Problems of Unreasoned Beliefs."

watcher, then we begin to trouble ourselves less about her admiration.

It must not be forgotten that our attempt to show up mis-connections in Miss Stein may have an opposite result and reveal to us connections we had missed. Thinking to remove the spell exercised upon his patient by the old stories of the Greeks, the psychoanalyst may himself fall under that spell and find in them what his patient has found and, incidentally, what made the Greeks tell those tales.

10. *Now what happens, what should happen, when we in-quire in this way into the reasonableness, the propriety of be-lief in gods?* The answer is: A double and opposite-phased change. Wordsworth writes:

> ". . . And I have felt
>   A presence that disturbs me with the joy
>   Of elevated thoughts; a sense sublime
>   Of something far more deeply interfused,
>   Whose dwelling is the light of setting suns,
>   And the round ocean and the living air,
>   And the blue sky, and in the mind of man:
>   A motion and a spirit, that impels
>   All thinking things, all objects of all thought,
>   And rolls through all things . . ." [9]

We most of us know this feeling. But is it well placed like the feeling that here is first-rate work, which we sometimes rightly have even before we have fully grasped the picture we are looking at or the book we are reading? Or is it misplaced like the feeling in a house that has long been empty that someone secretly lives there still. Wordsworth's feeling *is* the feeling that the world is haunted, that something watches in the hills and manages the stars. The child feels that the stone tripped him when he stumbled, that the bough struck him when it flew back in his face. He has to learn that the wind isn't buffeting him, that there is not a devil in it, that he was wrong, that his attitude was inappropriate. And as he learns

---

[9] *Tintern Abbey.*

that the wind wasn't hindering him so he also learns it wasn't helping him. But we know how, though he learns, his attitude lingers. It is plain that Wordsworth's feeling is of this family.

Belief in gods, it is true, is often very different from belief that stones are spiteful, the sun kindly. For the gods appear in human form and from the waves and control these things and by so doing reward and punish us. But varied as are the stories of the gods they have a family likeness and we have only to recall them to feel sure of the other main sources which cooperate with animism to produce them.

What are the stories of the gods? What are our feelings when we believe in God? They are feelings of awe before power, dread of the thunderbolts of Zeus, confidence in the everlasting arms, unease beneath the all-seeing eye. They are feelings of guilt and inescapable vengeance, of smothered hate and of a security we can hardly do without. We have only to remind ourselves of these feelings and the stories of the gods and goddesses and heroes in which these feelings find expression, to be reminded of how we felt as children to our parents and the big people of our childhood. Writing of a first telephone call from his grandmother, Proust says: ". . . it was rather that this isolation of the voice was like a symbol, a presentation, a direct consequence of another isolation, that of my grandmother, separated for the first time in my life, from myself. The orders or prohibitions which she addressed to me at every moment in the ordinary course of my life, the tedium of obedience or the fire of rebellion which neutralized the affection that I felt for her were at this moment eliminated. . . . 'Granny!' I cried to her . . . but I had beside me only that voice, a phantom, as unpalpable as that which would come to revisit me when my grandmother was dead. 'Speak to me!' but then it happened that, left more solitary still, I ceased to catch the sound of her voice. My grandmother could no longer hear me . . . I continued to call her, sounding the empty night, in which I felt that her appeals also must be straying. I was shaken by the same anguish which, in the distant past, I had felt once before, one day when, a little child, in a crowd, I had lost her."

Giorgio de Chirico, writing of Courbet, says: "The word yesterday envelops us with its yearning echo, just as, on waking, when the sense of time and the logic of things remain a while confused, the memory of a happy hour we spent the day before may sometimes linger reverberating within us. At times we think of Courbet and his work as we do of our own father's youth."

When a man's father fails him by death or weakness how much he needs another father, one in the heavens with whom is "no variableness nor shadow of turning."

We understood Mr. Kenneth Graham when he wrote of the Golden Age we feel we have lived in under the Olympians. Freud says: "The ordinary man cannot imagine this Providence in any other form but that of a greatly exalted father, for only such a one could understand the needs of the sons of men, or be softened by their prayers and be placated by the signs of their remorse. The whole thing is so patently infantile, so incongruous with reality. . . ." "So incongruous with reality"! It cannot be denied.

But here a new aspect of the matter may strike us.[10] For the very facts which make us feel that now we can recognize systems of superhuman, sub-human, elusive beings for what they are—the persistent projections of infantile phantasies— include facts which make these systems less fantastic. What are these facts? They are patterns in human reactions which are well described by saying that we are as if there were hidden within us powers, persons, not ourselves and stronger than ourselves. That this is so may perhaps be said to have been common knowledge yielded by ordinary observation of people,[11] but we did not know the degree in which this is so until recent study of extraordinary cases in extraordinary conditions had revealed it. I refer, of course, to the study of multiple personalities and the wider studies of psychoanalysts.

---

[10] I owe to the late Dr. Susan Isaacs the thought of this different aspect of the matter, of this connection between the heavenly Father and "the good father" spoken of in psychoanalysis.

[11] Consider Tolstoy and Dostoievsky—I do not mean, of course, that their observation was ordinary.

Even when the results of this work are reported to us that is not the same as tracing the patterns in the details of the cases on which the results are based; and even that is not the same as taking part in the studies oneself. One thing not sufficiently realized is that some of the things shut within us are not bad but good.

Now the gods, good and evil and mixed, have always been mysterious powers outside us rather than within. But they have also been within. It is not a modern theory but an old saying that in each of us a devil sleeps. Eve said: "The serpent beguiled me." Helen says to Menelaus:

> ". . . And yet how strange it is!
> I ask not thee; I ask my own sad thought,
> What was there in my heart, that I forgot
> My home and land and all I loved, to fly
> With a strange man? Surely it was not I,
> But Cypris there!"[12]

Elijah found that God was not in the wind, nor in the thunder, but in a still small voice. The kingdom of Heaven is within us, Christ insisted, though usually about the size of a grain of mustard seed, and he prayed that we should become one with the Father in Heaven.

New knowledge made it necessary either to give up saying "The sun is sinking" or to give the words a new meaning. In many contexts we preferred to stick to the old words and give them a new meaning which was not entirely new but, on the contrary, *practically* the same as the old. The Greeks did not

---

[12] Euripides: *The Trojan Women*, Gilbert Murray's Translation. Roger Hinks in *Myth and Allegory in Ancient Art* writes (p. 108): "Personifications made their appearance very early in Greek poetry. . . . It is out of the question to call these terrible beings 'abstractions.' . . . They are real daemons to be worshipped and propitiated. . . . These beings we observe correspond to states of mind. The experience of man teaches him that from time to time his composure is invaded and overturned by some power from outside, panic, intoxication, sexual desire."

> "What use to shoot off guns at unicorns?
> Where one horn's hit another fierce horn grows.
> These beasts are fabulous, and none were born
> Of woman who could lay a fable low."
> —*The Glass Tower*, Nicholas Moore, p. 100.

speak of the dangers of thwarting Dionysos, of neglecting
Cypris for Diana, of forgetting Poseidon for Athena. We have
eaten of the fruit of a garden we can't forget though we were
never there, a garden we still look for though we can never
find it. Maybe we look for too simple a likeness to what we
dreamed. Maybe we are not as free as we fancy from the old
idea that Heaven is a happy hunting ground, or a city with
streets of gold. Lately Mr. Aldous Huxley has recommended
our seeking not somewhere beyond the sky or late in time
but a timeless state not made of the stuff of this world, which
he rejects, picking it into worthless pieces. But this sounds to
me still too much a looking for another place, not indeed one
filled with sweets but instead so empty that some of us would
rather remain in the Lamb or the Elephant, where, as we
know, they stop whimpering with another bitter and so far
from sneering at all things, hang pictures of winners at Kemp-
ton and stars of the 'nineties. Something good we have for each
other is freed there, and in some degree and for a while the
miasma of time is rolled back without obliging us to deny the
present.

The artists who do most for us don't tell us only of fairy-
lands. Proust, Manet, Breughel, even Botticelli and Vermeer
show us reality. And yet they give us for a moment exhilaration without anxiety, peace without boredom. And those who,
like Freud, work in a different way against that which too
often comes over us and forces us into deadness or despair,[13]
also deserve critical, patient and courageous attention. For
they, too, work to release us from human bondage into
human freedom.

Many have tried to find ways of salvation. The reports they
bring back are always incomplete and apt to mislead even
when they are not in words but in music or paint. But they
are by no means useless; and not the worst of them are those
which speak of oneness with God. But in so far as we become
one with Him, He becomes one with us. St. John says he is in
us as we love one another.

---

[13] Matthew Arnold: *Summer Night.*

This love, I suppose, is not benevolence but something that comes of the oneness with one another of which Christ spoke.[14] Sometimes it momentarily gains strength.[15] Hate and the Devil do too. And what is oneness without otherness?

---

[14] St. John 16:21.
[15] "The Harvesters" in *The Golden Age,* Kenneth Graham.

JACQUES MARITAIN

[1882–1973]

Casual observers may be amazed by the widespread growth of Thomistic philosophy throughout the Western world—but there need be no great mystery about the matter. In his Encyclical Letter *Aeterni Patris, On the Restoration of Christian Philosophy in Schools* (commonly abbreviated as "On Christian Philosophy"), of August 4, 1879, Pope Leo XIII, in the second year of his long reign, discussed the usefulness of a sound philosophy in leading people back to the path of faith and salvation, and then went on to exhort his brethren "in all earnestness to restore the golden wisdom of St. Thomas, and to spread it far and wide for the defense and beauty of the Catholic faith, for the good of society, and for the advantage of all the sciences." This encyclical was implemented the following year by an apostolic letter establishing Thomas Aquinas as the common patron of *all* Catholic schools. "The remarkable revival of Thomism in modern times has found a powerful incentive in these documents," according to Etienne Gilson, the historian par excellence of Catholic philosophy.

This "remarkable revival" was accelerated by new research institutes such as that established by Désiré Mercier, later Cardinal Mercier, at Louvain University. The monumental Leonine edition of the complete works of Thomas Aquinas was published, periodicals were started, articles and books poured forth, and a school or subschool of Thomistic philosophers emerged, culminating for the present at least, one may safely say, in Jacques Maritain. One does not have to be a Thomist or a Roman Catholic or even a Christian to recognize in him a philosopher of great stature—profound, subtle, widely learned.

He was brought up as a liberal Protestant—not a common thing in France—went to the Sorbonne to study science, and there fell in love with a Russian Jewess, Raïssa Oumansoff, as intelligent and sensitive as himself. Together they made exhilarating friendships, but they were depressed by the bleak materialism, positivism, scepticism, of their science curriculum. They decided suicide would be the proper solution if they could not find a more meaningful answer to their deepest questions.

Liberation if not salvation lay just around the corner at the Collège de France in the lecture room and the seminar room of Professor Henri Bergson, scorned by the scientists of the Sorbonne but adored by his followers—all too popular in his own lifetime, too much neglected now. Trained in mathematics and the natural sciences himself, Bergson brought to his frontal attack on "scientism" a rich fund of knowledge with a marvelous gift of metaphor. He maintained that intelligence was only a tool for practical ends, that intellectual analysis "spatialized" time and distorted reality. He maintained that only intuition, a kind of subtle "intellectual sympathy," grasped "real duration" in consciousness with its independence and freedom. Here was vengeance indeed—vengeance on all those scientific materialists who had constructed an inflexible block-universe in which life was nothing but a physicochemical process, mind an epiphenomenon, and indeterminism an absurdity! Here were vitalism, dualism, mysticism, expressed with eloquent defiance.

In her charming memoir, *We Were Friends Together,* Raïssa Maritain devotes a chapter to their exciting encounter with Bergson and his teaching. "We went to Bergson's classes filled with curiosity and a sacred expectation. We returned, carrying our little bouquets of truths or of promises, as though vitalized by healthful air—exuberant, prolonging to greater and still greater lengths our commentaries upon the master's teachings. Winter was passing away; Spring was coming." "Bergson restored philosophy to its own domain by showing that science and the procedures belonging thereto are completely inapplicable to it, from the very fact that, today at least, science seeks its final explanations in pure quantity, in the homogeneous and the measurable." "At the time that we were attending his lectures, shortly before the publication of *Creative Evolution,* we received only the benefits of the horizons he opened to us—away from the empty and colorless world of universal mechanism and toward the universe of qualities, toward spiritual certainty, toward personal liberty."

Jacques Maritain and Raïssa Oumansoff were married in 1904.

Not long after, they came across, in the literary column of a newspaper, a quotation from a letter by Maurice Maeterlinck to a writer they had never heard of, one Léon Bloy: "If by genius one understands certain flashes in the depths, *La Femme Pauvre* is the only work of the present day in which there are evident marks of genius." They found a novel which was first published in 1897 but written in the spirit of a primitive Christian prophesying the fall of the Roman Empire, in a style "plumed with flames and ash, like Vesuvius in the last days of Pompeii." They could sense in the author one who had been steeped in degradation but who had emerged into a serene faith only this side of saintliness. Bloy, who had become the friend and inspirer of Rouault, might himself be called the Rouault of literature.

The young Maritains wrote a letter of gratitude to Bloy; they soon became fast friends with him and his family, who lived in poverty in Montmartre; and within a year they were baptized into the Roman Catholic Church, Bloy standing as godfather.

Mme. Maritain's account of their meeting with Bloy and of their conversion is followed by a final chapter, "Awaiting the Angel of the School," for at this point they were not familiar with the work of St. Thomas Aquinas. Philosophy apparently put aside, Maritain went on with advanced work in science, meanwhile keeping body and soul together as editor of a *Dictionary of Practical Life!* It was actually Mme. Maritain who first began the study of the *Summa Theologica* during a period of illness, but Maritain soon joined her and found that he could "erect no obstacle to its luminous flood." Bergson's obsession with intuition and his denigration of the intellect could not stand up against the Thomistic synthesis of Faith and Reason. It was not long before Maritain adopted as his motto: *"Vae mihi si non thomistizavero!"*—"Woe is me should I not Thomistize!" He was now ready to set out on his long and tireless crusade.

His first published book (1914), no doubt written in sorrow rather than in anger, was an elaborate criticism of the Bergsonian philosophy. Ten years later, in *Three Reformers*, with ruthless brilliance he castigated Luther as the pioneer of an inflated individualism, Descartes as "the incarnation of the angel," and Rousseau as "nature's saint," reserving his harshest words for the last. In somewhat the same spirit he wrote his essay on "Freud and Psychoanalysis" from the Thomist point of view. As to method, he found

Freud to be "a genius of investigation and discovery." Secondly he regarded Freud "as a very valuable psychologist, whose ideas, activated by an extraordinary instinct of discovery, are obscured by a radical empiricism, and an aberrant metaphysics, unconscious of themselves." The Freudian philosophy, Maritain maintained, was motivated by the spirit of resentment and based upon a prejudice, "the violent negation of spirituality and liberty." One may differ sharply with Maritain's interpretations of these four epoch-marking figures and yet not be able to return to one's old opinions with complacency.

On the positive side, it is probably well to begin with Maritain's *Introduction to Philosophy*, which was first published in French in 1920. From the historical sketch leading to the judgment that "Aristotle is as truly the philosopher par excellence as St. Thomas is the theologian," he went on to argue that in practically every major controversy in philosophy, where there have been battles between opposite extremes, "the philosophy of Aristotle and St. Thomas" has invariably taken the sound, moderate position. From this elementary text, Maritain branched out with studies in nearly every field of philosophy, culminating in *The Degrees of Knowledge* (1932), *True Humanism* (1936), and *Creative Intuition in Art and Poetry* (1953).

In his large volume on *The Philosophy of Jacques Maritain*, Charles A. Fecher reminds us that Maritain's interest in art does not derive solely from his many friendships with painters, musicians and writers. "If he had not become a philosopher he would probably have been a biologist; but if he had not become a biologist either, then the chances are he would have been a painter." One of Maritain's most readable and popular books, *Art and Scholasticism*, largely inspired by his friend Rouault, was published as early as 1920. Perhaps the crowning work of his life is *Creative Intuition in Art and Poetry*, which grew out of his six A. W. Mellon Lectures in the Fine Arts, given at the National Gallery of Art in Washington in the spring of 1952. The central part of the last chapter was originally published as a contribution to the special Dante Number of *The Kenyon Review*, edited by Francis Fergusson for the spring issue of 1952. And here it is.

DANTE'S INNOCENCE AND LUCK

PART I

1.

When we meditate upon the unique grandeur of the *Commedia*, its cosmic scope, and the joint superiority in it of the inner melody, the action, the theme and the number, our admiration goes out to the genius of Dante, of course, but also to his luck.

A Frenchman has said that genius is *a long patience*. He was probably right. But the "longue patience" and mad obstinacy in labor depend themselves on a deeper source. Complex as the obscure reality meant by this word may be, genius has essentially to do with the fact of poetic intuition taking shape in the inaccessible recesses of the soul at an exceptional degree of depth. When it comes to designating the particular quality which characterizes those creative regions, we are at a loss to find an appropriate name. The least defective term I am able to suggest is *creative innocence*. This creative innocence, which is one with unimpeded power and freedom of poetic intuition, is, I think, the most profound aspect of Dante's genius.

The word innocence has two connotations. The first is naïveté, that sort of total simpleness and confidence in gazing at things of which intelligence at the highest degree of its vitality or childish ignorance alone is capable, and which, like the charity spoken of by St. Paul, believes as one breathes, "believeth all things."

How could one utter if he did not believe? The native reliance consubstantial with his own being—*la bêtise,* Baudelaire said (because he hid himself in the ironical rebelliousness of nineteenth century dandyism)—with which any great poet *believes all things*—not only all things brought to him by poetic experience, but also everything in the world and in himself which is food or support for it, and every nod and wink that events give to him, and his own feeling, and his own urge to speak an unspeakable truth of his own—is carried in Dante to the point of an adamantine certitude. He has no doubt at all. He seems even immune from the doubt which troubles so many great poets about their own work.

And the feeling that every great poet has—be it in distressing obscurity—of a certain wound which has set free in him the creative source, and has separated him from other men (through the dreams and detachment of childhood, or some abiding despair) is carried in Dante to the point of a perfectly clear awareness. He knows his wound and believes in it; and cherishes it. Beatrice has made it. The best that we can do is to accept his testimony, just as it is given. Freudians may explain in their way the sublimation of the experience he underwent in seeing a girl of nine when he was nine. What matters to us is the fact that this trauma, penetrating to the very center of the powers of the spirit, has made of his relation to Beatrice the unshakable personal truth on which his poetic intuitivity will live, the nest of his creative emotion, the basic *belief* through which all realities of the visible and invisible world will awaken his creative subjectivity. If by virtue of the magic of imagination and the symbol, Beatrice was to become, while remaining herself, a constellation of supreme spiritual lights, it is because everything revealed to Dante in the night of poetic knowledge was revealed to him in and through his love for her—captured itself by imagination but still keeping its original impact—and in continuity with the primordial intuition which had obscurely disclosed womanhood and desire to him.

Symbolically transmuted as she may be, Beatrice is never a symbol or an allegory for Dante. She *is* both herself and what she signifies. Dante's blessed naïveté is so profound that—at the preconscious level of creativity, in the deepest nocturnal recess of poetic intuition—he actually believes in this one and multiple identity. Without this central belief all his poetry would have quit him. His naïveté is such that he believes his love for Beatrice to be in itself and in the face of all men as important a thing as heaven and earth. This naïveté, which "believes all things," has such brazen audacity that nothing seems more natural to him than to have a certain girl, by the original fact that his flesh burned for her, exalted in Paradise as the incarnation of theological knowledge, in whose eyes the humanity and the divinity of Christ are mirrored, and of faith illumined by the contemplative gifts, and of the inspired guidance in the regions of the beatific vision. Virgil and all the abysses of darkness and light were mobilized, the great voyage from Hell to Heaven was undertaken, the entire *Commedia* was written to glorify this woman. This was the first basic incentive. "Therefore," as he puts it in the last chapter of the *Vita Nuova*, "if it be His pleasure through Whom is the life of all things that my life continue with me a few years, it is my hope that I shall write yet concerning her what hath not before been written of any woman."

2.

I would call *integrity* or incorruption, untouched original purity, the second connotation of creative innocence. The regions where poetic experience and poetic intuition are born, when they are to possess the fullness of their nature, are regions of ontologic simplicity which are blissfully shielded from all the busy-ness of psychological interests. At the center of the Self self-research loses any sense. I need not insist here on the essential disinterestedness of poetic intuition. There is no merit in this disinterestedness. It is but an effect of the ontologic simplicity I just mentioned, some visible image of which the gravity of a child's gaze sometimes offers to us, who seems simply astonished *to be*, and condemns all our interests and their futility.

The creative emotion of minor poets is born in a flimsy twilight and at a comparatively superficial level in the soul. Great poets descend into the creative night and touch the deep waters over which it reigns. Poets of genius have their dwelling-place in this night and never leave the shores of these deep waters. Here are the regions of integrity of which I am speaking.

We have no sign of this deep-seated integrity, except the work itself, or perchance the presence, in the visible regions of the soul, of some pure and lasting feeling, which is like a reflection on moving clouds of the sun fallen below the horizon. "What is God?" Thomas Aquinas asked when he was five. This question born in the creative innocence of a child's astonishment developed into the multiform and single movement of his life-long research. It is not unwise to assume that in Dante something similar came about: not a prime question of nascent reason, but a prime wound of nascent sensibility and, in proportion as later on poetic experience developed, a more and more profound (as this wound itself) discovery by poetic intuition—an amazement without end before the face of love unveiling its miraculous and terrible ambiguity; and then, across all the weaknesses and failings of a human life, a pure abiding feeling of spiritual fidelity, an unbroken process of deeper knowing and purifying of love. Shelley states that Dante "understood the secret things of love" more than any other poet. And did he not say himself:

Tutti li miei penser parlan d'Amore.

He never idealized carnal love, whose tricks he also understood, and he never forgot that any evil can "color as love wills," as did the Siren's *smarrito volto*. He knew perfectly the difference in nature which distinguishes the various kinds of love, and especially divine love from human love. He is frightened and ashamed when, at the appearance of Beatrice in the Earthly Paradise, even before recognizing her he suddenly feels "the mighty power of ancient love," *d'antico amor la gran potenza*, "through hidden virtue which went out from her." But he also knew that the lowest forms of love bear in darkness and distortion the seal of a higher origin, and that purified human love can be redeemed by divine love, and serve it. While his love for God his Savior, for "Him Who is the lord of courtesy," transfigures the woman he once desired, his love for this transfigured woman is the medium through which divine love penetrates the creative center of his poetry. The entire *Commedia* was written to bear testimony to the purification of love in the heart of a man. This was the second basic incentive, and it was one with the first.

Now would this long movement itself of self-purification have taken hold of the soul of the poet without the basic integrity of his creative experience, in which the "secret things of love" were gradually discovered to him?

3.

Creative innocence is in no way moral innocence. It is, as I have indicated above, of an ontologic, not a moral nature. It has essentially to do with the intuition of the poet, not with his loves. And of the two things which alone make life worth living, love is more valuable than intuition when it transforms us into something better than we are, but intuition is not liable to all kinds of illusion and moral defilement as love is: because intuition deals with knowledge (creative knowledge in the case of the poet) and, *qua* intuition, never misses the mark.

In every great poet creative innocence exists to some degree. It has its plenitude in the greatest. It exists in a place which is so deep-seated that no impact of the troubles, splits, vices or failures which may undermine the domain of free will, passion and instinct, can spoil its ontologic integrity. In this place there is no conflict or break between senses and reason, because there is no division. All the powers of the soul are brought to unity in a state of habitual permanence, proper to a poetic experience which is not fleeting and transient, as it is usually, but lasting and steady, at least virtually. This place is the only one that is not wounded, I would say, by the old hereditary sin which wounds human nature. It is a kind of earthly paradise—but physical, not moral—concealed in nocturnal depths, in which nothing, to be sure, of the divine pageant described by Dante can be hoped for, but where the smile and the eyes of a Beatrice of beauty, not of sainthood, are mirrored in deep waters.

The inner world in the midst of which such a place exists may be filled with impurity; the moral experience of a great poet may be rotten; his thought and his passion may be stimulated by energies of illusion or perversity. When the things he has nourished in himself enter his earthly paradise of creative innocence, they keep their moral impurity—if they have any—which will also pass into the work. But they bathe in the ontologic purity of this place. In the waters of poetic knowledge they are dehumanized and made into mineral entities, transmuted into forms of the revelation of being through creative emotion; they receive a new nature, a poetic nature, a new principle of existence, which replaces in them the human one, and causes their moral impact and moral qualities, as well as the marks and stains upon them of a man's tics or vices, to become henceforth accidental and secondary in the particular sphere of this new state of existence, where only poetry and beauty are essential. To the extent to which moral deformity always involves some ontologic defect, some naught, there will be, if the things in question, the poet's intellectual and moral supply, are corroded by such naught, some lack or deficiency in their new nature as forms of the revelation of being through creative emotion. Yet inasmuch as they receive this new nature, and emerge from a poetic intuition proper to the great depths, this lack or deficiency entails only some comparative imperfection in the work into which they enter, and they are invested with the ontologic purity of creative innocence, they are possessed of a purity which is poetic purity.

Thus it is that a great poet can be corrupt, while his creative intuition never is. A purity remains in him, which of itself is of no avail for his soul, but which is a blessing for his work and for us. And if there are in this work poisonous human meanings and morally impure ferments, their impact on human minds will wear off in time, absorbed or superseded by another impact, more essential to the work, the impact of poetic purity and poetic energy. Time, as Shelley put it, will wash away all the sins of the poet in the eyes of those who

receive from him the pure gift of a more profound discovery
in the experience of beauty and the human soul.

4.

Dante was not corrupt, and nothing morally impure went
from his heart into his work. This is not, however, the fact
with which our present considerations are concerned. They
point to this other fact, that all things a poet puts in his work
must pass through the creative night of poetic intuition. Nowhere is Dante's great lesson clearer.

No poet has had to do with heavier equipment and ammunition. Not to speak of his perfect craftsmanship, he knew
everything his time knew and took to heart all the conflicts,
whether social, political or religious, in which his time was
engaged. His work is a *summa* laden with a world of divine
and human truths, yearnings, and violence. For ivory tower
he has the earth and heaven. He describes, he narrates, he
teaches, he preaches. Why such freedom? All his immense
materials, all the constellations of Christianity were carried in
the creative night of his poetic intuition to a state of impon-
derable poetic existence. All passed through this intuitive
night—by virtue of his extraordinarily profound creative innocence. For creative innocence is the paradise of poetic intuition, the existential state in which poetic intuition can reach
full power and liberty. (And another quality of the entire soul
concurred, but this is another point.)

In addition to the basic poetic incentives, all kinds of purposes, human, non-artistic in nature, played their part freely
in the productive effort of Dante. None entered his art and his
work as an extraneous element, interfering with or "bending"
them. Being integrated in poetic intuition, all were *in*, from
the start, at each creative instant on which each part of the
work depended. As to the final end, it was, so he wrote, "to
remove those living in this life from the state of misery and
lead them to the state of felicity."[1] In fact, while the poet intended such a final purpose, poetry was freer than ever, quick-

---

[1] *Epistola* X, to Can Grande della Scala.

ened from within in its very liberty, and it was to make of the work, if not the great instrument of salvation that the poet proposed, at least a self-sufficient creation mirroring the wanderings of sinful humanity in search of blessedness—simply a poem, in a word, in which a host of readers most often deaf to its preaching would look for the delights of beauty—not to speak of the supreme delights afforded to scholars by the puzzles of allegory, trope and anagogy.

Dante teaches a great deal. Everybody teaches in the *Commedia*. Why do we never feel the tedium of didacticism? Nothing is more boring in a poem than philosophy or allegory. Why are we never bored with the philosophical lectures of Dante, and all his allegorical apparatus? Not to speak of his geographical contrivances and cosmological devices? The answer is always the same. If all these things are deprived of their natural weight, and become light and transparent, and have been made themselves *innocent,* it is because, as a natural result of the poet's creative innocence, they have been seized hold of by his emotion, abstract as they may be, and have received from it an ingenuous soul, and an indefinite meaning which matters more than their own. May I suggest that Dante believes in his riddles and his cosmological and geographical sand-castles with the ambiguous seriousness of childhood's imagination? As to allegory, he invests it with such visual melody that we already receive some intuitive pleasure from it—even from it!—before understanding anything of it. As T. S. Eliot observes, it is enough for us to know that it has a meaning, without knowing yet what this meaning can be.

And perhaps it is not necessary to understand Dante's philosophical discourses either, to be allured by a pleasure of reason: so pure are their perfect economy and the intellectual sweep they delineate, like a dance movement, by virtue of some underlying music of emotion. Yet we enjoy them to the full, to be sure, when the marvelous precision of the intelligible meaning appears also to us, adding clarity to clarity. Thus, in the *Purgatorio*, we are instructed in the existence of free will by Marco Lombardo:

Voi che vivete ogni cagion recate
   pur suso al cielo, sì come se tutto
   movesse seco di necessitate.

Se così fosse, in voi fora distrutto
   libero arbitrio, e non fora giustizia
   per ben, letizia, e per male, aver lutto.

Lo cielo i vostri movimenti inizia;
   non dico tutti, ma, posto ch'io il dica,
   lume v'è dato a bene ed a malizia

e libero voler, che, se fatica
   nelle prime battaglie col ciele dura,
   poi vince tutto, se ben si nutrica.

A maggior forza ed a miglior natura
   liberi soggiacete, e quella cria
   la mente in voi, che il ciel no ha in sua cura.

"Ye who are living refer every cause up
to the heavens alone, even as if they swept
all with them of necessity.

"Were it thus, Freewill in you would be destroyed,
and it were not just
to have joy for good and mourning for evil.

"The heavens set your impulses in motion;
I say not all, but suppose I said it,
a light is given you to know good and evil

"and Freewill, which, if it endure the strain
in its first battlings with the heavens,
at length gains the whole victory, if it be well nurtured.

"Ye lie subject, in your freedom, to a greater power
and to a better nature; and that creates
in you mind which the heavens have not in their charge."

Finally a point made by T. S. Eliot may be discussed, I think, in the light of our present considerations. Eliot observes that although the *Divine Comedy* could not have been written without Dante's religious faith, it is not necessary to share in this faith to understand the poem and assent to its beauty. You must be instructed, of course, about the things in which Dante believed, but you are not required to believe in them yourself. In reading the poem, Eliot says, "you suspend both belief and disbelief." Moreover, while being perhaps as remote as possible from Dante's own belief, you do not feel hurt by that imposition of the personal belief of a man forcing its way into another which other poets, Goethe for instance, do not spare us.[2] I assume, as Eliot does, that the typical characteristics of the religious doctrine to which Dante adhered are not alien to the fact. "A coherent traditional system of dogma and morals like the Catholic . . . stands apart, for understanding and assent even without belief, from the single individual who propounds it." More precisely, with the objective system of reference of a public revelation conveyed to all through the testimony of a visible Church, there is no need for the poet to push himself forward in speaking of what he believes more than in speaking of what everyone sees.

I hasten to say, nevertheless, that not with all Catholic poets does a non-Catholic reader feel himself protected from any intrusive assertion of an individual's belief. The reason for the fact mentioned by Eliot lies in the very purity of Dante's poetic approach. It relates to the sovereign and native primacy of the poetic sense over the intelligible sense—even in a poetry which is splendidly clear. The ego of the man has disappeared in the creative Self of the poet. Theological faith itself, the most sacred belief, has entered the work through the instru-

---

[2] "His private belief becomes a different thing in becoming poetry. It is interesting to hazard the suggestion that this is truer of Dante than of any other philosophical poet. With Goethe, for instance, I often feel too acutely 'this is what Goethe the man believed,' instead of merely entering a world which Goethe has created; with Lucretius also; less with the *Bhagavad-Gita*, which is the next greatest philosophical poem to the *Divine Comedy* within my experience. . . . Goethe always arouses in me a strong sentiment of disbelief in what he believes: Dante does not. I believe that this is because Dante is the purer poet, not because I have more sympathy with Dante the man than Goethe the man."—T. S. Eliot, "Dante," in *Selected Essays*.

mentality of creative emotion and poetic knowledge, and passed through the lake of disinterestedness of creative innocence.

PART II

5.

It is not enough to speak of Dante's genius. We must also take his luck into consideration. The extraordinary luck of Dante the poet was a result of the coincidence of an extraordinary variety of good fortunes. It had to do with the grace of God and the virtues of Dante the man, with centuries of culture and with a unique moment in time.

There was, first, the innocence of his heart. The subtle naïveté of the medieval man was all the greater in him as it was brightened but not yet corrupted by the dawning ardors of modern consciousness. Full of violence as he was, his passions, angers and prepossessions, as well as the ventures of his life, all emerged from candor and ingenuousness. The purity of his eye made his "whole body lightsome." No fault leaves mud in a soul which knows itself in clarity and is steeped in the feeling of the mercy of its Redeemer. I do not believe that the creative innocence of Dante, and the transparency of his poetic experience, could have been so deep, had not the innocence of his heart established his entire soul in genuine connaturality with them.

Another luck for his poetry was the freedom of mind he received from the firmness of his religious faith. Because he was so perfectly sure of his faith, his poetry was able freely to play even with its tenets, and to fancy, without deceiving anybody, that condition of the "neither rebellious nor faithful," rejected both by Heaven and Hell, which theology does not know Because he was perfectly sure of his faith, he was eager for knowledge, whose consonance with his faith was for him divinely unquestionable, and he had such liberty in his appreciation of any effort of human reason, that he welcomed in his praise and paradise both Thomas Aquinas and Siger of

Brabant. He was not afraid, as the Jansenists were later on, to do justice to the natural virtues of the pagans. He had none of the fears and complexes which paralyze our modern literary martyrs of freedom from truth. His undivided intellect was established in a state of general security by the all-pervading security of his faith. It is hard for our modern mind to imagine the simplicity in belief and firmness in adherence which characterized the whole thought of Dante, however refined, subtle and learned, and his vision of the world and of himself. Here again a certain kind of innocence in man, an innocence of the intellect, which was in no way credulity, but integrity of the natural élan or eros, assisted creative innocence.

And so we are led to a different category of luck, which has to do not with a strengthening of the creative source itself, but rather with the prerequired conditions—depending on the general equipment of the mind and the harvest garnered in its granaries—which relate to creative intuition from the outside. I am thinking, here, of the heritage of culture received by Dante, and of the articulate universe of beliefs and values in which his thought dwelt. Dante wrestled with his time, which forced into exile the poet threatened with death. But as concerns the spiritual quality of the cultural heritage he was blessed by his time. Then the human mind was imbued with the sense of being, and nature appeared all the more real and consistent as it was perfected by grace. Being still turned toward wisdom, still permeated with rationality and mystery both of which descended from the Uncreate Word, still softened by the blood of the Incarnate Word, the universe of the late thirteenth century, with its ontological hierarchies of intellectual disciplines, ensured to the intelligence and emotion of a poet, despite all the evil fevers, discords, crimes and vices of the time, a state of integration and vitality that the modern man has lost. Dante participated with all his fibers in an organic order which already felt the first breaths of a newly born spring, and did not know it was already decaying.

I do not believe that the greater or less perfection in intrinsic truth of the universe of thought of a poet matters to his poetry save in quite a remote manner. The medieval universe,

true as its highest metaphysical principles may be, was, on
the other hand, lacking in a great many truths that the modern man has discovered at the price of his internal unity. Moreover, great poetry was to live in universes of thought quite
different from that of Dante—already the universe of Cer-
vantes, and still more that of Shakespeare, and still more that
of Goethe, and still more that of Dostoievski, not to speak of
what had been the universe of Homer or that of Sophocles,
or that of the Upanishads. What matters to poetry in a close
and direct manner are, I think, certain extremely simple but
basic *presences* or existential certainties, assured by the universe of thought which constitutes the vital environment of
poetic intuition: for instance a certitude both of the mysterious
irrefragable existence and the exigency of intelligibility
involved in things; a certitude of the *interiority* of the human
being, and of its importance; a certitude that between man
and the world there is an invisible relationship deeper than
any material interconnection; a certitude that the impact of
his freedom on his destiny gives his life a movement which is
oriented, and not lost in the void, and which has to do, in
one way or another, with the whole fabric of being. Such
existential certitudes, and many others no doubt, existed in
the mind of Baudelaire (at what cost—columns in what desert)
as in that of Dante. The absence of some of them is responsible for the narcissism of Mallarmé. I submit that without them
the prerequired conditions are lacking for any great poetry to
reach full stature. Natural as they may be, these certitudes
exist with greater force and stability if they are integrated in
an articulate universe of thought. They cannot exist in us
when the universe of thought that we have received—and accepted in anguish or complacency, revolt, pride or self-aban-
donment—from our age of culture is a disintegrated universe
which rejects or denies them, and has lost, together with the
intellectual sense of being and truth, what Waldo Frank called,
in his Introduction to the *Collected Poems* of Hart Crane, the
sense of the person (or of the interiority of the human being)
and the sense of Time (or of the oriented movement of human existence). Dante's luck was to have all the *presences,*

the existential certitudes which are the natural soil of poetry, integrated with absolute firmness in a consistent universe of thought rooted in reason and faith, and radiant to his emotion in the blissful innocence of the intellect. Never has creative innocence enjoyed so favorable a climate and such exceptional assistance. A whole cosmos could pass through the creative night of his poetic intuition.

6.

Finally we have also to consider the fleeting uniqueness of the moment of human history which was the moment of Dante. As Allen Tate has pointed out, the luckiest periods for art and poetry are those where a great civilization is on the verge of decline. Then the vital force of this civilization meets with historical conditions which cease being appropriate to it, but it is still intact, for one moment, in the sphere of spiritual creativity, and it gives its last fruit there, while the freedom of poetry avails itself of the decay of social disciplines and ethos. Nothing less than age-old Christendom was singing its last song in Dante.

Yet the point with which I am concerned is much more particular. It has to do with the proper time of Poetry itself. Considering the process of self-realization, through a work of words, of poetry as free creativity of the spirit, I would say that during the Middle Ages poetry (I mean in the vernacular) had remained in a pre-adult state. The diversity of generic forms (mystery-play, romance, lyric, etc.) in which it expressed itself had only to do with a condition imposed by art or *technè*. Medieval poetry had not reached the stage where the inner growth of poetry demands a division of poetry itself into certain basic forms by virtue of an essential difference in its approach to the work. In other words art was differentiated; poetry, in its own ways of using the activity of art, was not. The virtualities of its energy of self-realization through the work of words were still united in indistinctness. Dante arrived just at the instant when medieval poetry touched its ultimate point of growth—on the verge of differentiation, but still undifferentiated.

Thus it is that the *Divine Comedy* breaks open the classical framework of the epic (it is in no way a simple Christian *Aeneid*) and cannot be classed in any literary genus. Here we are confronted with the central fact on which I wish to lay stress. The *Commedia* embraces in its substantial unity forms of poetic creation which demand of themselves to be separate, and which will separate after Dante—I say as specific types of *poetry*, apart from the more external division of the work (even if it happens to lack any poetry) into artistic or literary genera. The *Divine Comedy* is at the same time and with the same intensive reality Poetry of the Song, Poetry of the Theater, and Poetry of the Tale; the three epiphanies of poetic intuition compose its single soul or entelechy.

The *Divine Comedy* is indeed a Song—a song to a woman who was loved (all poets think so) as no other woman ever was or will be, and a song to the purification of love in the heart of the poet. With its "lax and humble method of speech," as Dante put it, it is a sustained avowal, veiled under infinitely variegated external forms, of the subjectivity of the poet wounded by this woman, and through this wound awakened to its own depths and all things in the transparent night of poetic knowledge.[3] A long inner melody of feelings and meanings, running through the entire work, gives it its secret unity, and that pure freedom, satisfied only with being, which witnesses to the freedom in it of the poetic sense. The indefinitely vibrating echoes and overtones in intelligibility due to the multiplicity of allusive senses and to the "imaginative fusion of images and ideas" enigmatically convey in the tercets and sequences a singular impact of subjectivity in the act of intuitive emotion. The music of intuitive pulsions,[4] prevented as it may be from direct expression by the requirements of intelligibility, passes despite all into the very intelligibility of the

---

[3] "If we consider the method of speech the method is lax and humble, for it is the vernacular speech in which very women communicate."—*Epist.* to Can Grande.

[4] I beg permission to use this expression without further explanation. It refers to analyses which are part of a book in preparation.

lines—translated into the infallible *cadence* of the intelligible and imaginative élan, which loads with pure emotion each particular unit or episode. Speaking of the third canto of the *Inferno*, "in this canto," Coleridge said, "all the images are distinct, and each vividly distinct, but there is a total impression of infinity; the wholeness is not in vision or conception, but in an inner feeling of totality, and absolute being";[5] and he noted the fundamental importance of "inwardness or subjectivity" in Dante's poetry. Everywhere, but especially perhaps in the *Paradiso*, the freedom of the Song is a sign of the kind of "aseity" peculiar to the poetic sense or meaning.

> Però che tutte quelle vive luci,
> vie più lucenti, cominciaron canti
> da mia memoria labili e caduci.
>
> O dolce amor, che di riso t'ammanti,
> quanto parevi ardente in quei flailli
> ch'avieno spirto sol di pensier santi!
> *Paradiso* XX, 10-15.

"Because all those living lights, far brightlier shining, began songs which from my memory must slip and fall.

O sweet love, smile-bemantled, how glowing didst thou seem in those flute-holes breathed on only by sacred ponderings!"

But the Divine Comedy is also, indeed, a Drama. Scott Buchanan in *Poetry and Mathematics* and Francis Fergusson in *The Idea of a Theater*, have remarked that "the deepest and most elaborate development of the tragic rhythm is to be found in the *Divine Comedy*."[6] The whole work and its three

---

[5] "Dante," in *Selected Poetry and Prose*, ed. Stephen Potter, London and New York, 1933, p. 330.

[6] On page 39 of the book by Fergusson: "The *Purgatorio* especially, though an epic and not a drama, evidently moves in the tragic rhythm, both as a whole and in detail. The daylight climb up the mountain, by moral effort, and in the light of natural reason, corresponds to the first moment, that of 'purpose.' The night, under the sign of Faith, Hope and Charity, when the Pilgrim can do nothing by his own unaided efforts, corresponds to the moments of passion and perception. The Pilgrim, as he pauses, mulls over the thoughts and experiences of the day; he sleeps and dreams, seeing ambivalent images from the mythic dreaming of the race, which refer, also, both to his

parts, and the whole and detail of each part, are animated by
the intellectual élan, articulate and definite, proper to the Action; and the unitary power of the theme is the meaning of a
particularly powerful action. In the last analysis, it is by virtue
of that objectivization of creative intuition which is the action
that "the most wakeful reason" enjoys full freedom in the
poem without threatening (because action and poetic sense
are in perfect consonance) the spells of the night, and gently
interweaves its threads with those of the myth and the dream.
Thus could a theorist of the theater like Fergusson find in the
Divine Comedy, especially in the *Purgatorio,* an ideal exem-
plar of dramatic Action. The *Commedia* is for him—with the
drama of Sophocles and Shakespeare—one of the "cultural
landmarks in which the idea of a theater has been briefly
realized"; it shows us "not the contemporary possibility, but
the perennial idea of a theater of human life and action."

And the *Divine Comedy* is also, indeed, a Tale, or better, a
Novel of the beyond and the here below. It is a continuous
and complex narrative, in which the particular adventures of
the two protagonists serve to put into existence and motion a
world of adventures and destinies, so as to make of each human being involved a center of interest, looked at by the poet
in its own singular ineffable reality. Though their fates are
now sealed, and their lives have become only an object of
memory, all these characters have life and existential interiority, because their author knows them, as every novelist does,
from the inside, that is, through himself, or through connaturality. As the *Commedia* clearly shows, it is through his own
inclinations, but especially through his love, that Dante knew
his characters; love was the great medium, either pity or piety
or furor (the reverse face of love). And although he nowhere

own 'suppressed desires' and to his own deepest aspirations. These images
gradually solidify and clarify, giving place to a new perception of his situation. This rhythm, repeated in various forms, carries the Pilgrim from the
superficial but whole-hearted motivations of his childhood, in the Antipurga-
torio, through the divided counsels of the growing soul, to the new innocence,
freedom and integrity of the Terrestrial Paradise, the realm of *The Tempest*
or of *Oedipus at Colonos.* The same rhythmic conception governs also the
moment in its literal fiction yet essentially moving ahead and pointing to
deeper meanings."

indulged in any kind of connivance or complicity, he even loved, and even admired, certain of his sinners without being in any way hindered by their state of damnation—as in particular that master of his youth, his dear Brunetto Latini, who even in Hell "seemed like him who wins, and not like him who loses":

> Poi si rivolse, e parve di coloro
>   che coronno a Verona il drappo verde
>   per la campagna; e parve di costoro
> quegli che vince e non colui che perde.
>   *Inferno* XV, 121-124.

"Then he turned back, and seemed like one of those who run for the green cloth at Verona through the open field; and of them seemed he who gains, not he who loses."

At this point—just as the essence of the Song appears everywhere, but especially perhaps in the *Paradiso*, and that of Drama everywhere but especially perhaps in the *Purgatorio*—must we note that the essence of the Novel appears everywhere, but especially perhaps in the *Inferno?* Fergusson has said of Dante: "His eye is always directly upon the life of the psyche in its shifting modes of being, its thought, its sufferings and its contemplation." In other words, he has the eye of a genuine novelist.

PART III

7.

The *Divine Comedy* is Novel, Drama and Song in indivisibility, and with equal plenitude. This fact—unique, I think, in our culture—does not depend only on the genius of Dante, it depends also on his extraordinary luck. Thereafter the three types of poetry united in the *Commedia* divided from one another, by virtue of an irreversible process of differentiation— here again I do not speak of the differentiation (long since

achieved) of the art of writing into various literary genera, I
speak of the differentiation of poetry itself into three essentially distinct types: namely the Poem, the Drama and the
Novel, insofar as, in literary genera which often do without
poetry, or betray it, poetry demands to make the work into a
real, pure and genuine expression of poetry itself.

As regards the Poem, I believe that this process of differentiation was fully achieved only in modern times, together with
the self-awareness of poetry. During the classical age it did
not proceed without trouble. One may wonder whether the
example of Dante was always profitable to great poets anxious
to compete with him in greatness, and the fact is that neither
Milton nor Goethe completely escaped the kind of boredom inherent in any poetic work too big for its soul. As to *Faust*,
whose general movement, curiously enough ("From Heaven,
through Earth, down to Hell") is the opposite of that of the
Divine Comedy, the action in it is poor and cold, and the philosophical expression owes its richness and warmth only to
lyricism vivifying an alien matter, which comes from abstract
reason.

Be that as it may, it is surely fair for us, when we think of
poetry, to bear in mind the paradigm offered by Dante, but
we may be unfair to modern poets if we use this paradigm as
a too simple and univocal measure of comparison.

No poem, except for the unique case of the *Commedia*, can
be poem, drama and novel, at the same time. The poem, the
song, exists through its poetic sense, the first epiphany of
creative intuition. Obviously it must have action and harmonic
expansion, but appropriate to its nature. When we say that
the theme is weak in modern poetry, we are right in regard
to those poets whose theme is frail or evanescent because they
have nothing to say, even about an experience of their own.
But it would be nonsense to require from modern poets a
"greatness," an objective intellectuality and universality of
theme comparable to those in Dante. With respect to the nature of a poetry whose prime virtue is to convey purely the
intuitive night of subjectivity and the non-conceptualizable
meanings caught in things through this night, modern poetry

has shown that it is capable of greatness, as well as of any quality required in the action, the theme, and the harmonic expansion.

It has been observed that the modern poet is secluded in his own self: when it is a question of a great modern poet, this is true only on the condition that one adds that in this single self and its emotion unknown things grasped in the world are present, and some more than real reality is passing. Where in modern poems is that interest for a host of other human beings which fills the *Divine Comedy?* Is the modern poet unable to enter into creative communication with other selves than his own? As far as the Poem, or the Song, is concerned, it is not with other subjectivities, it is indeed with the world to be revealed together with his own subjectivity that all his creative knowledge has to be occupied. Yet modern poetry is capable of knowing through connaturality, and making live, a host of human beings. This is the business of the poetry of the Novel. Just as the Theater at the time of Lope de Vega and the Elizabethans, the Novel in modern times has allowed the Poem to free itself from functions which are alien to it and alienate it from its nature.

"A poem of any length," Coleridge said, "neither can be, nor ought to be all poetry." But the modern Poem is determined, and bound, to be all poetry. This is perhaps why Edgar Allan Poe considered a long poem "a contradiction in terms." If it relates to the length of a poem materially considered, the quantity of lines, this statement might be questioned. At least one would like to know from what number of lines on a poem starts to be long. St. John Perse's *Anabase*, which Poe would have admired, I assume, is a comparatively long poem. (As to Mallarmé, he could not finish *Hérodiade*, and I wonder whether greater length than that of "The Hound of Heaven," for instance, or of "The Wreck of the Deutschland," may be expected as a rule of a modern poem.) But Poe's statement is simply true, I believe, if it relates to the length of a poem in relation to its own inner measure, which is the poetic sense. The developed Narrative, the Description of characters, the Exposition of a system, appear from this point of view as invested with incurable length. A great modern poem can be philosophical—why not?—or in the form of a tale. It must always be contained within the span of a free and pure conveyance of anything intuitively caught in and through the night of subjectivity.

T. S. Eliot remarks, in his essay on Baudelaire, that "many people who enjoy Dante enjoy Baudelaire." There must be some reason for this. In the strict order of poetry, Baudelaire appears in modern times, with his extraordinary depth in poetic intuition, his creative innocence surrounded by all the demons of impurity, as the most significant counterpart of Dante's extraordinary depth in poetic intuition, but blessed and lucky.

Baudelaire was wounded and destroyed by his time, as Dante was served by his. He waged within himself a hopeless spiritual war against his time, as Dante assumed his in exultation. He revealed the eternal and supernatural in man in man's perversity as Dante revealed it in God's justice and mercy. He was torn between God and the devil in his love for Beauty the idol as Dante was carried along toward his Savior in his love for Beauty the sacrament. I am aware of his atrocious weaknesses. Yet in his frustrated dreams he also had his Muse and Guardian Angel, a poor Beatrice of his own, powerless to save him. If we assume that he had perceived what kind of hell is our modern universe, and had descended into this hell, and looked at everything from there, we realize that, in distortion and cruelty, his vision of human love was the most profound—I do not say true—that the corrupt eye of a lost epoch was capable of; in darkness and division, his sense of the reality of sin and of the transcendent destiny of the soul, and his assertion of the necessity of Christianity—so thoroughly serious and personal, as Eliot emphasized—were the most gravely pressing, I do not say well-balanced, that the corrupt heart of a lost epoch was capable of.

Be all that as it may, what matters over and above all is the fact that Baudelaire had intelligence, and the creative innocence proper to the depths of poetry, to such an exceptional degree that the comparison with Dante forces itself upon us; and that in his despairing struggle with inspiration and with style, he succeeded in giving the Poem, reduced to its pure essence, such inwardness and revealing power that what he did for poetry in concentration and intensity may be compared to what Dante did for it in sovereignty and immensity, while embracing in a unique work the joint virtues of a triple poetic essence.

When T. S. Eliot wrote that "in the adjustment of the natural to the spiritual, of the bestial to the human and the human to the supernatural, Baudelaire is a bungler compared with Dante," I wonder whether he did not forget that Baudelaire, in the place where he was, and from which he looked at things, was precisely required by poetry not to perceive the adjustment, but to feel the split and derangement.

Allen Tate and Waldo Frank are right in pointing out the inadequacy of the theme in Hart Crane's poetry, and the tragic solitude and disintegration of the world in which his intellect and sensibility moved. But (apart from his moral weakness with respect to this world) the error of Crane, it seems to me, was to attempt a disproportionate task, and to look for a cosmic greatness which was but a cerebral ambition, a dream of a poet unaware of the limits of his own poetry. There was more soundness of the theme—as a simple objective reflection of the poetic sense—there was more greatness, proportionate to the universe of the Song, in the admirable purity, less ambitious, and more deeply revealing, of Emily Dickinson's profound poetry. There was also more greatness, and genuine force, in Walt Whitman's verbal outpouring, because he innocently obeyed the impulse of a free fervor.

In quite another sense than when it was a question of Dante, the luck of the modern poet has to do with the time proper to poetry, and the moment at which he was born to poetry. The self-awareness, and the sense of its own freedom, that poetry has gained in modern times, place him from the very start at the center of the citadel.

His ill-luck has to do with the time proper to culture, and the moment at which he was born to the world.

ERNEST NAGEL

[1901–   ]

In reviewing Ernest Nagel's latest collection of essays, *Logic Without Metaphysics*, A. J. Ayer remarked that Professor Nagel is the most levelheaded of philosophers and one of the leading philosophers of science today.

As an undergraduate at the College of the City of New York, he was of course greatly stimulated by the teaching of the late Morris R. Cohen, as he was later by John Dewey and F. J. E. Woodbridge in graduate study at Columbia. He tells us that he owes "a comparable debt" to the writings of Charles S. Peirce, Bertrand Russell and George Santayana. His dissertation *On the Logic of Measurement* was followed by the splendid textbook which he wrote in collaboration with Cohen, *An Introduction to Logic and Scientific Method. Principles of the Theory of Probability* is a technical monograph in the Foundations of the Unity of Science series. *Sovereign Reason,* an earlier collection of essays and articles, and *Logic Without Metaphysics* are indications of his very wide interests and his very level head.

"Naturalism Reconsidered" was first presented as a presidential address before the Eastern Division of the American Philosophical Association in December, 1954.

* * *

NATURALISM RECONSIDERED

It is surely not the highest reach for a philosopher to be a combatant in the perennial wars between standardized "isms" which fill conventional handbooks of philosophy. Philosophy at its best is a critical commentary upon existence and upon our claims to have knowledge of it; and its mission is to help

482

illuminate what is obscure in experience and its objects, rather than to profess creeds or to repeat the battle-cries of philosophical schools aiming at intellectual hegemony. The conception of philosophy as a struggle between competing systems is especially sterile when the "ism" defended or attacked covers as miscellaneous an assortment of not always congruous views as fly the banner of naturalism. The number of distinguishable doctrines for which the word "naturalism" has been a counter in the history of thought, is notorious. Even among contemporaries who proclaim themselves to be naturalists in philosophy, there are not only important differences in stress and perspective, but also in specific doctrines professed and in intellectual methods used to support commitments made. I am aware, therefore, that in taking naturalism as my subject this evening, I run the risk of becoming involved in futile polemics—a risk made graver by the fact that although the stated title of my address may have aroused different expectations, it is not my intention to recant and to confess past errors. I must explain why, notwithstanding the hazards of my theme, I have elected to discuss it.

The past quarter century has been for philosophy in many parts of the world a period of acute self-questioning, engendered in no small measure by developments in scientific and logical thought, and in part no doubt by fundamental changes in the social order. In any event, there has come about a general loss of confidence in the competence of philosophy to provide by way of a distinctive intellectual method a basic ground-plan of the cosmos, or for that matter to contribute to knowledge of any primary subject-matter except by becoming a specialized positive science and subjecting itself to the discipline of empirical inquiry. Although the abysses of human ignorance are undeniably profound, it has also become apparent that ignorance, like actual knowledge, is of many special and heterogeneous things; and we have come to think, like the fox and unlike the hedgehog of whom Mr. Isaiah Berlin has recently reminded us, that there are a great many things which are already known or remain to be discovered, but that there is no one "big thing" which, if known, would make everything else coherent and unlock the mystery of creation. In consequence, many of us have ceased to emulate the great system-builders in the history of philosophy. In partial imitation of the strategy of modern science, and in the hope of achieving responsibly held conclusions about matters concerning which we could acquire genuine competence, we have tended to become specialists in our professional activities. We have come to direct our best energies to the resolution of limited problems and puzzles that emerge in the analysis of scientific and ordinary discourse, in the evaluation of claims to knowledge, in the interpretation and validation of ethical and esthetic judgments, and in the assessment of types of human experience. I hope I shall not be regarded as offensive in stating my impression that the majority of the best minds among us have turned away from the conception of the philosopher as the spectator of all time and existence, and have concentrated on restricted but manageable questions, with almost deliberate unconcern for the bearing of their often minute investigations upon an inclusive view of nature and man.

Some of us, I know, are distressed by the widespread scepticism of the traditional claims for a *philosophia perennis,* and have dismissed as utterly trivial most if not all the products of various current forms of analytical philosophy I do not share this distress, nor do I think the dismissal is uniformly perspicacious and warranted. For in my judgment, the scepticism which many deplore is well-founded. Even though a fair-sized portion of recent analytical literature seems inconsequential also to me, analytical philosophy in our own day is the continuation of a major philosophic tradition, and can count substantial feats of clarification among its assets. Concentration on limited and determinate problems has yielded valuable fruits, not least in the form of an increased and refreshing sensitivity to the demands of responsible discourse.

On the other hand, philosophers like other men conduct their lives within the framework of certain comprehensive if not always explicit assumptions about the world they inhabit. These assumptions color evaluations of major ideals and proposed policies. I also suspect that the directions taken by analyses of specific intellectual problems are frequently if subtly controlled by the expressed or tacit beliefs philosophers hold concerning the over-all nature of things, by their views on human destiny, and by their conceptions of the scope of human reason. But conversely, resolutions of special problems made plausible by recent philosophical analysis, as well as by the findings of various positive sciences, seem to me to support certain broad generalizations about the cosmos and to disconfirm others. It is clearly desirable that such basic intellectual commitments, which are at once the matrix and the outcome of inquiries into specific problems, be made as explicit as possible. A philosopher who is a reflective man by profession, certainly owes it to himself to articulate, if only occasionally, what sort of world he thinks he inhabits, and to make clear to himself where approximately lies the center of his convictions.

The discharge of the important obligation which is mine this evening, seems to me an appropriate occasion for stating as simply and as succinctly as I can the substance of those intellectual commitments I like to call "naturalism." The label itself is of no importance, but I use it partly because of its historical associations, and partly because it is a reminder that the doctrines for which it is a name are neither new nor untried. With Santayana, I prefer not to accept in philosophic debate what I do not believe when I am not arguing; and naturalism as I construe it merely formulates what centuries of human experience have repeatedly confirmed At any rate, naturalism seems to me a sound generalized account of the world encountered in practice and in critical reflection, and a just perspective upon the human scene. I wish to state briefly and hence with little supporting argument what I take to be its major tenets, and to defend it against some recent criticisms.

Claims to knowledge cannot ultimately be divorced from an evaluation of the intellectual methods used to support those claims It is nevertheless unfortunate that in recent years naturalists in philosophy have so frequently permitted their allegiance to a dependable method of inquiry to obscure their substantive views on things in general. For it is the inclusive intellectual image of nature and man which naturalism supplies that sets it off from other comprehensive philosophies. In my conception of it, at any rate, naturalism embraces a generalized account of the cosmic scheme and of man's place in it, as well as a logic of inquiry.

I hasten to add, however, that naturalism does not offer a theory of nature in the sense that Newtonian mechanics, for example, provides a theory of motion. Naturalism does not, like the latter, specify a set of substantive principles with the help of which the detailed course of concrete happenings can be explained or understood. Moreover, the principles affirmed by naturalism are not proposed as competitors or underpinnings for any of the special theories which the positive sciences assert. Nor, finally, does naturalism offer its general view of nature and man as the product of some special philosophical mode of knowing. The account of things proposed by naturalism is a distillation from knowledge acquired in the usual way in daily encounters with the world or in specialized scientific inquiry. Naturalism articulates features of the world which, because they have become so obvious, are rarely mentioned in discussions of special subject-matter, but which distinguish our actual world from other conceivable worlds. The major affirmations of naturalism are accordingly meager in content; but the principles affirmed are nevertheless effective guides in responsible criticism and evaluation.

Two theses seem to me central to naturalism as I conceive it. The first is the existential and causal primacy of organized matter in the executive order of nature. This is the assumption that the occurrence of events, qualities and processes, and the characteristic behaviors of various individuals, are contingent on the organization of spatiotemporally located bodies, whose internal structures and external relations determine and limit the appearance and disappearance of everything that happens. That this is so, is one of the best-tested conclusions of experience. We are frequently ignorant of the special conditions under which things come into being or pass away; but we have also found repeatedly that when we look closely, we eventually ascertain at least the approximate and gross conditions under which events occur, and we discover that those conditions invariably consist of some more or less complex organization of material substances. Naturalism does not maintain that only what is material exists, since many things noted in experience, for example, modes of action, relations of meaning, dreams, joys, plans, aspirations, are not as such material bodies or organizations of material bodies. What naturalism does assert as a truth about nature is that though *forms* of behavior or *functions* of material systems are indefeasibly parts of nature, forms and functions are not themselves agents in their own realization or in the realization of anything else. In the conception of nature's processes which naturalism affirms, there is no place for the operation of disembodied forces, no place for an immaterial spirit directing the course of events, no place for the survival of personality after the corruption of the body which exhibits it.

The second major contention of naturalism is that the manifest plurality and variety of things, of their qualities and their functions, are an irreducible feature of the cosmos, not a deceptive appearance cloaking some more homogeneous "ultimate reality" or transempirical substance, and that the sequential orders in which events occur or the manifold relations of dependence in which things exist are *contingent* connections, not the embodiments of a fixed and unified pattern of logically necessary links. The existential primacy of organized matter does not make illusory either the relatively permanent or the comparatively transient characters and forms which special configurations of bodies may possess. In particular, although the continued existence of the human scene is precarious and is dependent on a balance of forces that doubtless will not endure indefinitely, and even though its distinctive traits are not pervasive throughout space, it is nonetheless as much a part of the "ultimate" furniture of the world, and is as genuine a sample of what "really" exists, as are atoms and stars. There undoubtedly occur integrated systems of bodies, such as biological organisms, which have the capacity because of their material organization to maintain themselves and the direction of their characteristic activities. But there is no positive evidence, and much negative evidence, for the supposition that all existential structures are teleological systems in this sense, or for the view that whatever occurs is a phase in a unitary, teleologically organized, and all-inclusive process or system. Modern physical cosmology does indeed supply some evidence for definite patterns of evolutionary development of stars, galactic systems, and even of the entire physical universe; and it is quite possible that the stage of cosmic evolution reached at any given time causally limits the types of things which can occur during that period. On the other hand, the patterns of change investigated in physical cosmogony are not patterns that are exhaustive of everything that happens; and nothing in these current physical speculations requires the conclusion that changes in one star or galaxy are related by inherent necessity to every action of biological organisms in some remote planet. Even admittedly teleological systems contain parts and processes which are causally irrelevant to some of the activities maintained by those systems; and the causal dependencies known to hold between the parts of any system, teleological or not, have never been successfully established as forms of logically necessary relations. In brief, if naturalism is true, irreducible variety and logical contingency are fundamental traits of the world we actually inhabit. The orders and connections of things are all accessible to rational inquiry; but these orders and connections are not all derivable by deductive methods from any set of premises that deductive reason can certify.

It is in this framework of general ideas that naturalism envisages the career and destiny of man. Naturalism views the emergence and the continuance of human society as dependent on physical and physiological conditions that have not always obtained, and that will not permanently endure. But it does not in consequence regard man and his works as intrusions into nature, any more than it construes as intrusions the presence of heavenly bodies or of terrestrial protozoa. The stars are no more foreign to the cosmos than are men, even if the conditions for the existence of both stars and men are realized only occasionally or only in a few regions. Indeed, the conception of human life as a war with nature, as a struggle with an implacable foe that has doomed man to extinction, is but an inverted theology, with a malicious Devil in the seat of Omnipotence. It is a conception that is immodest as well as anthropomorphic in the importance it imputes to man in the scheme of things.

On the other hand, the affirmation that nature is man's "home" as much as it is the "home" of anything else, and the denial that cosmic forces are *intent* on destroying the human scene, do not warrant the interpretation that every sector of nature is explicable in terms of traits known to characterize only human individuals and human actions. Man undoubtedly possesses characteristics which are shared by everything that exists; but he also manifests traits and capacities that appear to be distinctive of him. Is anything gained but confusion when all forms of dependence between things, whether animate or inanimate, and all types of behaviors they display, are subsumed under distinctions that have an identifiable content only in reference to the human psyche? Measured by the illumination they bring, there is nothing to differentiate the thesis that human traits are nothing but the properties of bodies which can be formulated exclusively in the language of current physical theory, from the view that every change and every mode of operation, in whatever sector of the cosmos it may be encountered, is simply an illustration of some category pertinent to the description of human behavior.

Indeed, even some professed naturalists sometimes appear to promote the confusion when they make a fetish of continuity. Naturalists usually stress the emergence of novel forms in physical and biological evolution, thereby emphasizing the fact that human traits are not identical with the traits from which they emerge. Nevertheless, some distinguished contemporary naturalists also insist, occasionally with overtones of anxiety, that there is a "continuity" between the typically human on the one hand, and the physical and biological on the other. But is man's foothold in the scheme of things really made more secure by showing that his distinctive traits are in some sense "continuous" with features pervasive in nature, and would man's place in nature be less secure if such continuity did not obtain? The actual evidence for a continuity of development is conclusive in some instances of human traits, however it may be in others. But I sometimes suspect that the cardinal importance philosophers assign to the alleged universality of such continuity is a lingering survival of that ancient conception, according to which things are intelligible only when seen as teleological systems producing definite ends, so that nature itself is properly understood only when construed as the habitat of human society. In any event, a naturalism that is not provincial in its outlook will not accept the intellectual incorporation of man into nature at the price of reading into all the processes of the cosmos the passions, the strivings, the defeats and the glories of human life, and then exhibiting man as the most adequate, because most representative, expression of nature's inherent constitution. No, a mature naturalism seeks to understand what man is, not in terms of a discovered or postulated continuity between what is distinctive of him and what is pervasive in all things. Without denying that even the most distinctive human traits are dependent on things which are non-human, a mature naturalism attempts to assess man's nature in the light of *his* actions and achievements, *his* aspirations and capacities, *his* limitations and tragic failures, and *his* splendid works of ingenuity and imagination.

Human nature and history, in short, are *human* nature and history, not the history and nature of anything else, however much knowledge of other things contributes to a just appraisal of what man is. In particular, the adequacy of proposed ideals for human life must be judged, not in terms of their causes and origins, but in reference to how the pursuit and possible realization of ideals contribute to the organization and release of *human* energies. Men are animated by many springs of action, no one of which is intrinsically good or evil; and a moral ideal is the imagined satisfaction of some complex of impulses, desires, and needs. When ideals are handled responsibly, they therefore function as hypotheses for achieving a balanced exercise of human powers. Moral ideals are not self-certifying, any more than are the theories of the physical sciences; and evidence drawn from experienced satisfactions is required to validate them, however difficult may be the process of sifting and weighing the available data. Moral problems arise from a conflict of specific impulses and interests. They cannot, however, be effectively resolved by invoking standards derived from the study of non-human nature, or of what is allegedly beyond nature. If moral problems can be resolved at all, they can be resolved only in the light of specific human capacities, historical circumstance and acquired skills, and the opportunities (revealed by an imagination disciplined by knowledge) for altering the physical and social environment and for redirecting habitual behaviors. Moreover, since human virtues are in part the products of the society in which human powers are matured, a naturalistic moral theory is at the same time a critique of civilization, that is, a critique of the institutions that channel human energies, so as to exhibit the possibilities and limitations of various forms and arrangements of society for bringing enduring satisfactions to individual human careers.

These are the central tenets of what I take to be philosophical naturalism. They are tenets which are supported by compelling empirical evidence, rather than dicta based on dogmatic preference. In my view of it, naturalism does not dismiss every other differing conception of the scheme of things as logically impossible; and it does not rule out all alternatives to itself on a priori grounds. It is possible, I think, to conceive without logical inconsistency a world in which disembodied forces are dynamic agents, or in which whatever happens is a manifestation of an unfolding logical pattern. In such possible worlds it would be an error to be a naturalist. But philosophy is not identical with pure mathematics, and its ultimate concern is with the actual world, even though philosophy must take cognizance of the fact that the actual world contains creatures who can envisage possible worlds and who employ different logical procedures for deciding which hypothetical world is the actual one. It is partly for this reason that contemporary naturalists devote so much attention to methods of evaluating evidence. When naturalists give their allegiance to the method of intelligence commonly designated as the method of modern empirical science, they do so because that method appears to be the most assured way of achieving reliable knowledge.

As judged by that method, the evidence in my opinion is at present conclusive for the truth of naturalism, and it is tempting to suppose that no one familiar with the evidence can fail to acknowledge that philosophy. Indeed, some commentators there are who assert that all philosophies are at bottom only expressions in different idioms of the same conceptions about the nature of things, so that the strife of philosophic systems is mainly a conflict over essentially linguistic matters. Yet many thinkers for whom I have a profound respect explicitly reject naturalism, and their espousal of contrary views seems to me incompatible with the irenic claim that we really are in agreement on fundamentals.

Although I do not have the time this evening to consider systematically the criticisms currently made of naturalism, I do wish to examine briefly two repeatedly voiced objections which, if valid, would in my opinion seriously jeopardize the integrity and adequacy of naturalism as a philosophy. Stated summarily, the first objection is that in relying exclusively on the logico-empirical method of modern science for establishing cognitive claims, naturalists are in effect stacking the cards in their own favor, since thereby all alternative philosophies are antecedently disqualified. It is maintained, for example, that naturalism rejects any hypothesis about transempirical causes or time-transcending spiritual substances as factors in the order of things, not because such hypotheses are actually shown to be false, but simply because the logic of proof adopted dismisses as irrelevant any evidence which might establish them.

This criticism does not seem to me to have merit: the logico-empirical method of evaluating cognitive claims to which naturalists subscribe does not eliminate by fiat any hypothesis about existence for which evidence can be procured, that is, evidence that in the last resort can be obtained through sensory or introspective observation. Thus, anyone who asserts a hypothesis postulating a transempirical ground for all existence, presumably seeks to understand in terms of that ground the actual occurrences in nature, and to account thereby for what actually happens as distinct from what is merely imagined to happen. There must therefore be some connection between the postulated character of the hypothetical transempirical ground, and the empirically observable traits in the world around us; for otherwise the hypothesis is otiose, and not relevant to the spatiotemporal processes of nature. This does not mean, as some critics of naturalism suppose the latter to maintain, that the hypothetical transempirical ground must be characterized exclusively in terms of the observable properties of the world, any more than that the sub-microscopic particles and processes which current physical theory postulates must be logical constructions out of the observable traits of macroscopic objects. But it does mean that unless the hypothesis implies, even if only by a circuitous route, some statements about empirical data, it is not adequate to the task for which it is proposed. If naturalists reject hypotheses about transempirical substances, they do not do so arbitrarily. They reject such hypotheses either because their relevance to the going concerns of nature is not established, or because, though their relevance is not in question, the actual evidence does not support them.

Nor does naturalism dismiss as unimportant and without consideration experiences such as of the holy, or divine illumination, or of mystical ecstasy, experiences which are of the greatest moment in the lives of many men, and which are often taken to signify the presence and operation of some purely spiritual reality. Such experiences have dimensions of meaning for those who have undergone them, that are admittedly not on par with the import of more common experiences like those of physical hunger, general well-being, or feelings of remorse and guilt. Yet such experiences are nonetheless events among other events; and though they may be evidence for something, their sheer occurrence does not certify *what* they are evidence for, any more than the sheer occurrence of dreams, hopes, and delusions authenticates the actual existence of their ostensible objects. In particular, whether the experience labelled as an experience of divine illumination is evidence for the existence of a divinity is a question to be settled by inquiry, not by dogmatic affirmations or denials. When naturalists refuse to acknowledge, merely on the strength of such experiences, the operation or presence of a divine power, they do so not because their commitment to a logical method prevents them from treating it seriously, but because independent inquiry fails to confirm it. Knowledge is knowledge, and cannot without confusion be identified with intuitive insight or with the vivid immediacy of profoundly moving experiences. Claims to knowledge must be capable of being tested; and the testing must be conducted by eventual reference to such evidence as counts in the responsible conduct of everyday affairs as well as of systematic inquiry in the sciences. Naturalists are therefore not engaged in question-begging when, through the use of the logic of scientific intelligence, they judge non-naturalistic accounts of the order of things to be unfounded.

There is, however, a further objection to naturalism, to the effect that in committing itself to the logic of scientific proof, it is quite analogous to religious belief in resting on unsupported and indemonstrable faith. For that logic allegedly involves assumptions like the uniformity of nature or similar principles which transcend experience, cannot be justified empirically, and yet provide the premises that constitute the ultimate warrant for the conclusions of empirical inquiry. But if naturalism is thus based on unprovable articles of faith, on what cogent grounds can it reject a different conception of the true order of governance of events which rests on a different faith?

I cannot here deal adequately with the complex issues raised by this objection. Its point is not satisfactorily turned by claiming, as some have done, that instead of being articles of faith, the alleged indemonstrable postulates of scientific method are simply rules of the scientific game which *define* what in that game is to be understood by the words "knowledge" and "evidence." As I see it, however, the objection has force only for those whose ideal of reason is demonstration, and who therefore refuse to dignify anything as genuine knowledge unless it is demonstrable from self-luminous and self-evident premises. But if, as I also think, that ideal is not universally appropriate, and if, furthermore, a *wholesale* justification for knowledge and its methods is an unreasonable demand and a misplaced effort, the objection appears as quite pointless. The warrant for a proposition about some specific inter-relations of events does not derive from a faith in the uniformity of nature or in other principles with a cosmic scope. The warrant derives exclusively from the specific evidence available for that proposition, and from the contingent historical fact that the special ways employed in obtaining and appraising the evidence have been generally effective in yielding reliable knowledge. Subsequent inquiry may show that we were mistaken in accepting a proposition on the evidence available earlier; and further inquiry may also reveal that a given inductive policy, despite a record of successful past performance, requires correction if not total rejection. Fortunately, however, we are not always mistaken in accepting various propositions or in employing certain inductive policies, even though we are unable to demonstrate that we shall never fall into error. Accordingly, though many of our hopes for the stability of beliefs in the face of fresh experience may turn out to be baseless, and though no guarantees can be given that our most assured claims to knowledge may not eventually need revision, in adopting scientific method as the instrument for evaluating claims to knowledge, naturalists are not subscribing to an indemonstrable faith.

The bitter years of cataclysmic wars and social upheavals through which our generation has been passing have also witnessed a general decline of earlier hopes in the possibilities of modern science for achieving a liberal and humane civilization. Indeed, as is well known, many men have become convinced that the progress and spread of science, and the consequent secularization of society, are the prime sources of our present ills; and a not inconsiderable number of thinkers have

made widely popular various revived forms of older religious
and irrationalistic philosophies as guides to human salvation.
Moreover, since naturalists have not abandoned their firm adherence to the method of scientific intelligence, naturalism
has been repeatedly charged with insensitivity toward spiritual values, with a shallow optimism toward science as an instrument for ennobling the human estate, and with a philistine
blindness toward the ineradicable miseries of human existence.
I want to conclude with a few brief comments on these allegations.

It is almost painful to have to make a point of the elementary fact that whatever may happen to be the range of special
interests and sensibilities of individual naturalists, there is no
incompatibility, whether logical or psychological, between
maintaining that warranted knowledge is secured only through
the use of a definite logical method, and recognizing that the
world can be experienced in many other ways than by knowing it. It is a matter of record that outstanding exponents of
naturalism, in our own time as well as in the past, have exhibited an unequaled and tender sensitivity to the esthetic and
moral dimensions of human experience; and they have been
not only movingly eloquent celebrants of the role of moral
idealism and of intellectual and esthetic contemplation in human life, but also vigorous defenders of the distinctive character of these values against facile attempts to reduce them to
something else.

It seems to me singularly inept, moreover, to indict naturalism as a philosophy without a sense for the tragic aspects of
life. For unlike many world-views, naturalism offers no cosmic
consolation for the unmerited defeats and undeserved sufferings
which all men experience in one form or another. It has never
sought to conceal its view of human destiny as an episode between two oblivions. To be sure, naturalism is not a philosophy
of despair. For one facet in its radical pluralism is the truth
that a human good is nonetheless a good, despite its transitory
existence. There doubtless are foolish optimists among those
professing naturalism, though naturalism has no monopoly in
this respect, and it is from other quarters that one usually re-

ceives glad tidings of a universal nostrum. But in any event, neither the pluralism so central to naturalism, nor its cultivation of scientific reason, is compatible with any dogmatic assumption to the effect that men can be liberated from *all* the sorrows and evils to which they are now heirs, through the eventual advances of science and the institution of appropriate physical and social innovations. Indeed, why suppose that a philosophy which is wedded to the use of the sober logic of scientific intelligence should thereby be committed to the dogma that there are no irremediable evils? On the contrary, human reason is potent only against evils that are *remediable*. At the same time, since it is impossible to decide responsibly, *antecedent* to inquiry, *which* of the many human ills can be mitigated if not eradicated by extending the operations of scientific reason into human affairs, naturalism is not a philosophy of *general* renunciation, even though it recognizes that it is the better part of wisdom to be equably resigned to what, in the light of available evidence, cannot be avoided. Human reason is not an omnipotent instrument for the achievement of human goods; but it is the only instrument we do possess, and it is not a contemptible one. Although naturalism is acutely sensitive to the actual limitations of rational effort, those limitations do not warrant a romantic philosophy of general despair, and they do not blind naturalism to the possibilities implicit in the exercise of disciplined reason for realizing human excellence.

Columbia University

BERTRAND RUSSELL
[1872–1970]

It is sometimes assumed that Russell did all of his solid, careful work before the First World War. Of course that is false, if one may point to *Introduction to Mathematical Philosophy, The Analysis of Mind, The Analysis of Matter, An Inquiry into Meaning and Truth* and *Human Knowledge,* not to mention the monumental *History of Western Philosophy,* which makes up for any lack of heavy erudition by its sheer scope, zest and brilliance. It is also suggested at times that Russell's books in social philosophy and history such as *Freedom versus Organization* and *Power: A New Social Analysis* were light, loose and easy works compared with his earlier masterpieces. But he himself says: "I have found my work on such subjects much more difficult and much less successful than my earlier work on mathematical logic. It is difficult because its utility depends upon persuasion, and my previous training and experience had not been any help toward persuasiveness."

There is much fresh and delightful information about Russell in his recent book, *Portraits from Memory and Other Essays.* It contains a broadcast which he did over the B.B.C. at the age of eighty-four and should serve as an ideal conclusion for this varied collection. It is good to hear him again just forty years after our first meeting with him in Boston in the spring of 1914.

•　　　•　　　•

KNOWLEDGE AND WISDOM

Most people would agree that, although our age far surpasses all previous ages in knowledge, there has been no correlative increase in wisdom. But agreement ceases as soon as we attempt to define "wisdom" and consider means of promoting it. I want to ask first what wisdom is, and then what can be done to teach it.

There are several factors that contribute to wisdom. Of these I should put first a sense of proportion: the capacity to take account of all the important factors in a problem and to attach to each its due weight. This has become more difficult than it used to be owing to the extent and complexity of the specialised knowledge required of various kinds of technicians. Suppose, for example, that you are engaged in research in scientific medicine. The work is difficult and is likely to absorb the whole of your intellectual energy. You have not time to consider the effect which your discoveries or inventions may have outside the field of medicine. You succeed (let us say), as modern medicine has succeeded, in enormously lowering the infant death-rate, not only in Europe and America, but also in Asia and Africa. This has the entirely unintended result of making the food supply inadequate and lowering the standard of life in the most populous parts of the world. To take an even more spectacular example, which is in everybody's mind at the present time: you study the composition of the atom from a disinterested desire for knowledge, and incidentally place in the hands of powerful lunatics the means of destroying the human race. In such ways the pursuit of knowledge may become harmful unless it is combined with wisdom; and wisdom in the sense of comprehensive vision is not necessarily present in specialists in the pursuit of knowledge.

Comprehensiveness alone, however, is not enough to constitute wisdom. There must be, also, a certain awareness of the ends of human life. This may be illustrated by the study of history. Many eminent historians have done more harm than good because they viewed facts through the distorting medium of their own passions: Hegel had a philosophy of history which did not suffer from any lack of comprehensiveness, since it started from the earliest times and continued into an indefinite future. But the chief lesson of history which he sought to inculcate was that from the year A.D. 400 down to his own time Germany had been the most important nation and the standard-bearer of progress in the world. Perhaps one could stretch the comprehensiveness that constitutes wisdom to include not only intellect but also feeling. It is by no means uncommon to find men whose knowledge is wide but whose feelings are narrow. Such men lack what I am calling wisdom.

It is not only in public ways, but in private life equally, that wisdom is needed. It is needed in the choice of ends to be pursued and in emancipation from personal prejudice. Even an end which it would be noble to pursue if it were attainable may be pursued unwisely if it is inherently impossible of achievement. Many men in past ages devoted their lives to a search for the Philosopher's Stone and the Elixir of Life. No doubt, if they could have found them, they would have conferred great benefits upon mankind, but as it was their lives were wasted. To descend to less heroic matters, consider the case of two men, Mr. A and Mr. B, who hate each other and, through mutual hatred, bring each other to destruction. Suppose you go to Mr. A and say, "Why do you hate Mr. B?" He will no doubt give you an appalling list of Mr. B's vices, partly true, partly false. And now suppose you go to Mr. B. He will give you an exactly similar list of Mr. A's vices with an equal admixture of truth and falsehood. Suppose you now come back to Mr. A and say, "You will be surprised to learn that Mr. B says the same things about you as you say about him," and you go to Mr. B and make a similar speech. The first effect, no doubt, will be to increase their mutual hatred, since each will be so horrified by the other's injustice. But, perhaps, if you have sufficient patience and sufficient persuasiveness, you may succeed in convincing each that the other has only the normal share of human wickedness, and their enmity is harmful to both. If you do this, you will have instilled some fragment of wisdom.

The essence of wisdom is emancipation, as far as possible, from the tyranny of the here and the now. We cannot help the egoism of our senses. Sight and sound and touch are bound up with our own bodies and cannot be made impersonal. Our emotions start similarly from ourselves. An infant feels hunger or discomfort, and is unaffected except by his own physical condition. Gradually, with the years, his horizon widens, and, in proportion as his thoughts and feelings become less personal and less concerned with his own physical states, he achieves growing wisdom. This is, of course, a matter of degree. No one can view the world with complete impartiality; and if anyone could, he would hardly be able to remain alive. But it is possible to make a continual approach towards impartiality: on the one hand, by knowing things somewhat remote in time or space; and, on the other hand, by giving to such things their due weight in our feelings. It is this approach towards impartiality that constitutes growth in wisdom.

Can wisdom in this sense be taught? And, if it can, should the teaching of it be one of the aims of education? I should answer both these questions in the affirmative. We are told on Sundays that we should love our neighbour as ourselves. On the other six days of the week, we are exhorted to hate him. You may say that this is nonsense, since it is not our neighbour whom we are exhorted to hate. But you will remember that the precept was exemplified by saying that the Samaritan was our neighbour. We no longer have any wish to hate Samaritans and so we are apt to miss the point of the parable. If you want to get its point, you should substitute "communist" or "anti-communist," as the case may be, for "Samaritan." It might be objected that it is right to hate those who do harm. I do not think so. If you hate them, it is only too likely that you will become equally harmful; and it is very unlikely you will induce them to abandon their evil ways. Hatred of evil is itself a kind of bondage to evil. The way out is through understanding, not through hate. I am not advocating non-resistance. But I am saying that resistance, if it is to be effective in preventing the spread of evil, should be combined with the greatest degree of understanding and the smallest degree of force that is compatible with the survival of the good things that we wish to preserve.

It is commonly urged that a point of view such as I have been advocating is incompatible with vigour in action. I do not think history bears out this view. Queen Elizabeth I in England and Henry IV in France lived in a world where almost everybody was fanatical, either on the Protestant or on the Catholic side. Both remained free from the errors of their time and both, by remaining free, were beneficent and certainly not ineffective. Abraham Lincoln conducted a great war without ever departing from what I have been calling wisdom.

I have said that in some degree wisdom can be taught. I think that this teaching should have a larger intellectual element than has been customary in what has been thought of as moral instruction. The disastrous results of hatred and narrow-mindedness to those who feel them can be pointed out incidentally in the course of giving knowledge. I do not think that knowledge and morals ought to be too much separated. It is true that the kind of specialised knowledge which is required for various kinds of skill has little to do with wisdom. But it should be supplemented in education by wider surveys calculated to put it in its place in the total of human activities. Even the best technicians should also be good citizens; and when I say "citizens," I mean citizens of the world and not of this or that sect or nation. With every increase of knowledge and skill, wisdom becomes more necessary, for every such increase augments our capacity for realising our purposes, and therefore augments our capacity for evil, if our purposes are unwise. The world needs wisdom as it has never needed it before; and if knowledge continues to increase, the world will need wisdom in the future even more than it does now.

D. T. SUZUKI
[1870–1966]

. . . Prophecy is rash but it may well be that the publication
of D. T. Suzuki's first *Essays in Zen Buddhism* in 1927 will
seem in future generations as great an intellectual event as
William of Moerbeke's Latin translation of Aristotle in the
thirteenth century or Marsiglio Ficino's of Plato in the fifteenth. But in Suzuki's case the shell of the Occident had been
broken through. More than we dream, we are now governed
by the new canon of the globe.

> —LYNN WHITE, J. R. *Machina Ex Deo*:
> *Essays in the Dynamism of Western Culture* (1968)

Daisetz Teitaro Suzuki was born in 1870 in the prosperous rice-
growing center of Kanazawa, two hundred miles northwest of
Tokyo. He received his training as a Buddhist disciple in the great
Zen monastery at Kamakura.

From 1897 to 1908 he lived near Chicago, translating from Japanese and Chinese for the Open Court Publishing Company. From
1921 to 1941 he was a professor of English and Buddhist philosophy at Otani University, Kyoto, until the thunder came. He was
a visiting professor at Columbia University from 1951 to 1957, and
he lectured extensively at many of the major American universities,
becoming the foremost interpreter of Eastern thought for Western
minds. Through the years he wrote more than a hundred works on
Zen and Buddhism in both Japanese and English and probably
traveled more than any other sage in history—Eastern or Western!
The aging seeker returned to Tokyo to die at the age of ninety-five.

EAST AND WEST

Many able thinkers of the West, each from his specific point of view, have dealt with this timeworn topic, "East and West," but so far as I know there have been comparatively few Far Eastern writers who have expressed their views as Easterners. This fact has led me to choose this subject as a kind of preliminary to what will follow.

Basho (1644-94), a great Japanese poet of the seventeenth century, once composed a seventeen-syllable poem known as *haiku* or *hokku*. It runs, when translated into English, something like this:

> When I look carefully
> I see the *nazuna* blooming
> By the hedge!

> *Yoku mireba*
> *Nazuna hana saku*
> *Kakine kana.*

It is likely that Basho was walking along a country road when he noticed something rather neglected by the hedge. He then approached closer, took a good look at it, and found it was no less than a wild plant, rather insignificant and generally unnoticed by passers-by. This is a plain fact described in the poem with no specifically poetic feeling expressed anywhere except perhaps in the last two syllables, which read in Japanese *kana*. This particle, frequently attached to a noun or an adjective or an adverb, signifies a certain feeling of admiration or praise or sorrow or joy, and can sometimes quite appropriately be rendered into English by an exclamation mark. In the present *haiku* the whole verse ends with this mark.

The feeling running through the seventeen, or rather fifteen, syllables with an exclamation mark at the end may not be communicable to those who are not acquainted with the Japanese language. I will try to explain it as best I can. The poet himself might not agree with my interpretation, but this does not matter very much if only we know that there is somebody at least who understands it in the way I do.

First of all, Basho was a nature poet, as most of the Oriental poets are. They love nature so much that they feel one with nature, they feel every pulse beating through the veins of nature. Most Westerners are apt to alienate themselves from nature. They think man and nature have nothing in common except in some desirable aspects, and that nature exists only to be utilized by man. But to Eastern people nature is very close. This feeling for nature was stirred when Basho discovered an inconspicuous, almost negligible plant blooming by the old dilapidated hedge along the remote country road, so innocently, so unpretentiously, not at all desiring to be noticed by anybody. Yet when one looks at it, how tender, how full of divine glory or splendor more glorious than Solomon's it is! Its very humbleness, its unostentatious beauty, evokes one's sincere admiration. The poet can read in every petal the deepest mystery of life or being. Basho might not have been conscious of it himself, but I am sure that in his heart at the time there were vibrations of feeling somewhat akin to what Christians may call divine love, which reaches the deepest depths of cosmic life.

The ranges of the Himalayas may stir in us the feeling of sublime awe; the waves of the Pacific may suggest something of infinity. But when one's mind is poetically or mystically or religiously opened, one feels as Basho did that even in every blade of wild grass there is something really transcending all venal, base human feelings, which lifts one to a realm equal in its splendor to that of the Pure Land. Magnitude in such cases has nothing to do with it. In this respect, the Japanese poet has a specific gift that detects something great in small things, transcending all quantitative measurements.

This is the East. Let me see now what the West has to offer in a similar situation. I select Tennyson. He may not be a typical Western poet to be singled out for comparison with the Far Eastern poet. But his short poem here quoted has

something very closely related to Basho's. The verse is as
follows:

> Flower in the crannied wall,
> I pluck you out of the crannies,
> Hold you here, root and all, in my hand,
> Little flower—but if I could understand
> What you are, root and all, and all in all,
> I should know what God and man is.

There are two points I like to notice in these lines:

1. Tennyson's plucking the flower and holding it in his
hand, "root and all," and looking at it, perhaps intently. It is
very likely he had a feeling somewhat akin to that of Basho
who discovered a *nazuna* flower by the roadside hedge. But
the difference between the two poets is: Basho does not pluck
the flower. He just looks at it. He is absorbed in thought. He
feels something in his mind, but he does not express it. He
lets an exclamation mark say everything he wishes to say. For
he has no words to utter; his feeling is too full, too deep, and
he has no desire to conceptualize it.

As to Tennyson, he is active and analytical. He first plucks
the flower from the place where it grows. He separates it
from the ground where it belongs. Quite differently from the
Oriental poet, he does not leave the flower alone. He must
tear it away from the crannied wall, "root and all," which
means that the plant must die. He does not, apparently, care
for its destiny; his curiosity must be satisfied. As some medical scientists do, he would vivisect the flower. Basho does not
even touch the *nazuna*, he just looks at it, he "carefully" looks
at it—that is all he does. He is altogether inactive, a good
contrast to Tennyson's dynamism.

I would like to notice this point specifically here, and may
have occasion to refer to it again. The East is silent, while
the West is eloquent. But the silence of the East does not
mean just to be dumb and remain wordless or speechless.
Silence in many cases is as eloquent as being wordy. The
West likes verbalism. Not only that, the West transforms the

word into the flesh and makes this fleshiness come out sometimes too conspicuously, or rather too grossly and voluptuously, in its arts and religion.

2. What does Tennyson do next? Looking at the plucked flower, which is in all likelihood beginning to wither, he proposes the question within himself, "Do I understand you?" Basho is not inquisitive at all. He feels all the mystery as revealed in his humble *nazuna*—the mystery that goes deep into the source of all existence. He is intoxicated with this feeling and exclaims in an unutterable, inaudible cry.

Contrary to this, Tennyson goes on with his intellection: "*If* [which I italicize] I could understand you, I should know what God and man is." His appeal to the understanding is characteristically Western. Basho accepts, Tennyson resists. Tennyson's individuality stands away from the flower, from "God and man." He does not identify himself with either God or nature. He is always apart from them. His understanding is what people nowadays call "scientifically objective." Basho is thoroughly "subjective." (This is not a good word, for subject always is made to stand against object. My "subject" is what I like to call "absolute subjectivity.") Basho stands by this "absolute subjectivity" in which Basho sees the *nazuna* and the *nazuna* sees Basho. Here is no empathy, or sympathy, or identification for that matter.

Basho says: "look carefully" (in Japanese "*yoku mireba*"). The word "carefully" implies that Basho is no more an onlooker here but the flower has become conscious of itself and silently, eloquently expressive of itself. And this silent eloquence or eloquent silence on the part of the flower is humanly echoed in Basho's seventeen syllables. Whatever depth of feeling, whatever mystery of utterance, or even philosophy of "absolute subjectivity" there is, is intelligible only to those who have actually experienced all this.

In Tennyson, as far as I can see, there is in the first place no depth of feeling; he is all intellect, typical of Western mentality. He is an advocate of the Logos doctrine. He must say something, he must abstract or intellectualize on his concrete experience. He must come out of the domain of feeling into that of intellect and must subject living and feeling to a series of analyses to give satisfaction to the Western spirit of inquisitiveness.

I have selected these two poets, Basho and Tennyson, as indicative of two basic characteristic approaches to reality. Basho is of the East and Tennyson of the West. As we compare them we find that each bespeaks his traditional background. According to this, the Western mind is: analytical, discriminative, differential, inductive, individualistic, intellectual, objective, scientific, generalizing, conceptual, schematic, impersonal, legalistic, organizing, power-wielding, self-assertive, disposed to impose its will upon others, etc. Against these Western traits those of the East can be characterized as follows: synthetic, totalizing, integrative, nondiscriminative, deductive, nonsystematic, dogmatic, intuitive, (rather, affective), nondiscursive, subjective, spiritually individualistic and socially group-minded,[1] etc.

When these characteristics of West and East are personally symbolized, I have to go to Lao-tse (fourth century B.C.), a great thinker in ancient China. I make him represent the East, and what he calls the multitudes may stand for the West. When I say "the multitudes" there is no intention on my part to assign the West in any derogatory sense to the role of Lao-tsean multitudes as described by the old philosopher.

Lao-tse portrays himself as resembling an idiot. He looks as if he does not know anything, is not affected by anything. He is practically of no use in this utilitarianistic world. He is almost expressionless. Yet there is something in him which makes him not quite like a specimen of an ignorant simpleton. He only outwardly resembles one.

The West, in contrast to this, has a pair of sharp, penetrating eyes, deep-set in the sockets, which survey the outside world as do those of an eagle soaring high in the sky. (In fact, the eagle is the national symbol of a certain Western

---

[1] Christians regard the church as the medium of salvation because it is the church that symbolizes Christ who is the savior. Christians are related to God not individually but through Christ, and Christ is the church and the church is the place where they gather to worship God and pray to him through Christ for salvation. In this respect Christians are group-minded while socially they espouse individualism.

power.) And then his high nose, his thin lips, and his general facial contour—all suggest a highly developed intellectuality and a readiness to act. This readiness is comparable to that of the lion. Indeed, the lion and the eagle are the symbols of the West.

Chuang-tze of the third century B.C. has the story of *konton* (*hun-tun*), Chaos. His friends owed many of their achievements to Chaos and wished to repay him. They consulted together and came to a conclusion. They observed that Chaos had no sense organs by which to discriminate the outside world. One day they gave him the eyes, another day the nose, and in a week they accomplished the work of transforming him into a sensitive personality like themselves. While they were congratulating themselves on their success, Chaos died.

The East is Chaos and the West is the group of those grateful, well-meaning, but undiscriminating friends.

In many ways the East no doubt appears dumb and stupid, as Eastern people are not so discriminative and demonstrative and do not show so many visible, tangible marks of intelligence. They are chaotic and apparently indifferent. But they know that without this chaotic character of intelligence, their native intelligence itself may not be of much use in living together in the human way. The fragmentary individual members cannot work harmoniously and peacefully together unless they are referred to the infinite itself, which in all actuality underlies every one of the finite members. Intelligence belongs to the head and its work is more noticeable and would accomplish much, whereas Chaos remains silent and quiet behind all the superficial turbulence. Its real significance never comes out to become recognizable by the participants.

The scientifically minded West applies its intelligence to inventing all kinds of gadgets to elevate the standard of living and save itself from what it thinks to be unnecessary labor or drudgery. It thus tries hard to "develop" the natural resources it has access to. The East, on the other hand, does not mind engaging itself in menial and manual work of all kinds, it is apparently satisfied with the "undeveloped" state of civilization. It does not like to be machine-minded, to turn itself into a slave to the machine. This love of work is perhaps characteristic of the East. The story of a farmer as told by Chuang-tze is highly significant and suggestive in many senses, though the incident is supposed to have taken place more than two thousand years ago in China.

Chuang-tze was one of the greatest philosophers in ancient China. He ought to be studied more than he is at present. The Chinese people are not so speculative as the Indian, and are apt to neglect their own thinkers. While Chuang-tze is very well known as the greatest stylist among Chinese literary men, his thoughts are not appreciated as they deserve. He was a fine collector or recorder of stories that were perhaps prevalent in his day. It is, however, likely that he also invented many tales to illustrate his views of life. Here is a story, which splendidly illustrates Chuang-tze's philosophy of work, of a farmer who refused to use the shadoof to raise water from his well.

A farmer dug a well and was using the water for irrigating his farm. He used an ordinary bucket to draw water from the well, as most primitive people do. A passer-by, seeing this, asked the farmer why he did not use a shadoof for the purpose; it is a labor-saving device and can do more work than the primitive method. The farmer said, "I know it is labor-saving and it is for this very reason that I do not use the device. What I am afraid of is that the use of such a contrivance makes one machine-minded. Machine-mindedness leads one to the habit of indolence and laziness."

Western people often wonder why the Chinese people have not developed many more sciences and mechanical contrivances. This is strange, they say, when the Chinese are noted for their discoveries and inventions such as the magnet, gunpowder, the wheel, paper, and other things. The principal reason is that the Chinese and other Asiatic peoples love life as it is lived and do not wish to turn it into a means of accomplishing something else, which would divert the course of living to quite a different channel. They like work for its own sake, though, objectively speaking, work means to accomplish something. But while working they enjoy the work and are not in a hurry to finish it. Mechanical devices are far more efficient and accomplish more. But the machine is impersonal and non-creative and has no meaning.

Mechanization means intellection, and as the intellect is primarily utilitarian there is no spiritual estheticism or ethical spirituality in the machine. The reason that induced Chuang-tze's farmer not to be machine-minded lies here. The machine hurries one to finish the work and reach the objective for which it is made. The work or labor in itself has no value except as the means. That is to say, life here loses its creativity and turns into an instrument, man is now a goods-producing mechanism. Philosophers talk about the significance of the person; as we see now in our highly industrialized and mechanized age the machine is everything and man is almost entirely reduced to thralldom. This is, I think, what Chuang-tze was afraid of. Of course, we cannot turn the wheel of industrialism back to the primitive handicraft age. But it is well for us to be mindful of the significance of the hands and also of the evils attendant on the mechanization of modern life, which emphasizes the intellect too much at the expense of life as a whole.

So much for the East. Now a few words about the West. Denis de Rougemont in his *Man's Western Quest* mentions "the person and the machine" as characterizing the two prominent features of Western culture. This is significant, because the person and the machine are contradictory concepts and the West struggles hard to achieve their reconciliation. I do not know whether Westerners are doing it consciously or unconsciously. I will just refer to the way in which these two heterogeneous ideas are working on the Western mind at present. It is to be remarked that the machine contrasts with Chuang-tze's philosophy of work or labor, and the Western ideas of individual freedom and personal responsibility run counter to the Eastern ideas of absolute freedom. I will not go into details. I will only try to summarize the contradictions the West is now facing and suffering under:

1. The person and the machine involve a contradiction, and because of this contradiction the West is going through great psychological tension, which is manifested in various directions in its modern life.

2. The person implies individuality, personal responsibility, while the machine is the product of intellection, abstraction, generalization, totalization, group living.

3. Objectively or intellectually or speaking in the machine-minded way, personal responsibility has no sense. Responsibility is logically related to freedom, and in logic there is no freedom, for everything is controlled by rigid rules of syllogism.

4. Furthermore, man as a biological product is governed by biological laws. Heredity is fact and no personality can change it. I am born not of my own free will. Parents give birth to me not of their free will. Planned birth has no sense as a matter of fact.

5. Freedom is another nonsensical idea. I am living socially, in a group, which limits me in all my movements, mental as well as physical. Even when I am alone I am not at all free. I have all kinds of impulses which are not always under my control. Some impulses carry me away in spite of myself. As long as we are living in this limited world, we can never talk about being free or doing as we desire. Even this desire is something which is not our own.

6. The person may talk about freedom, yet the machine limits him in every way, for the talk does not go any further than itself. The Western man is from the beginning constrained, restrained, inhibited. His spontaneity is not at all his, but that of the machine. The machine has no creativity; it operates only so far or so much as something that is put into it makes possible. It never acts as "the person."

7. The person is free only when he is not a person. He is free when he denies himself and is absorbed in the whole. To be more exact, he is free when he is himself and yet not

himself. Unless one thoroughly understands this apparent contradiction, he is not qualified to talk about freedom or responsibility or spontaneity. For instance, the spontaneity Westerners, especially some analysts, speak about is no more and no less than childish or animal spontaneity, and not the spontaneity of the fully mature person.

8. The machine, behaviorism, the conditioned reflex, Communism, artificial insemination, automation generally, vivisection, the H-bomb—they are, each and all, most intimately related, and form close-welded solid links of a logical chain.

9. The West strives to square a circle. The East tries to equate a circle to the square. To Zen the circle is a circle, and the square is a square, and at the same time the square is a circle and the circle a square.

10. Freedom is a subjective term and cannot be interpreted objectively. When we try, we are surely involved inextricably in contradictions. Therefore, I say that to talk about freedom in this objective world of limitations all around us is nonsense.

11. In the West, "yes" is "yes" and "no" is "no"; "yes" can never be "no" or vice versa. The East makes "yes" slide over to "no" and "no" to "yes"; there is no hard and fast division between "yes" and "no." It is in the nature of life that it is so. It is only in logic that the division is ineradicable. Logic is human-made to assist in utilitarianistic activities.

12. When the West comes to realize this fact, it invents such concepts known in physics as complementarity or the principle of uncertainty when it cannot explain away certain physical phenomena. However well it may succeed in creating concept after concept, it cannot circumvent facts of existence.

13. Religion does not concern us here, but it may not be without interest to state the following: Christianity, which is the religion of the West, talks of Logos, Word, the flesh, and incarnation, and of tempestuous temporality. The religions of the East strive for excarnation, silence, absorption, eternal peace. To Zen incarnation is excarnation; silence roars like thunder; the Word is no-Word, the flesh is no-flesh; here-now equals emptiness (*śūnyatā*) and infinity.

PAUL GOODMAN
[1911–1972]

Special to *The New York Times*:

North Stratford, N. H., August 3, 1973.
Paul Goodman, writer, therapist and social critic, who had
been called the Father Figure of the New Left, died here at
his farm last night, after suffering his third heart attack. He
was sixty.

He had planned to bring together nearly all of his poems for a
large collected edition but it was left for his friend Taylor Stoehr
to complete the second half. Another friend, George Dennison,
contributed an eloquent and illuminating Memoir and Appreciation, containing this triumphant sentence: "Until well into middle
age, Paul's work was produced in poverty and against a blank wall
of appalling neglect—and it poured out of him: poems, stories,
plays, novels, literary criticism, works of psychology, community
planning, social criticism, educational theory. He even composed
some music. In his forty-ninth year *Growing Up Absurd* made him
famous."

"His great masters, his fathers, were Aristotle and Kant," and
they must have contributed an underlying order to that apparently
chaotic and incredibly productive career.

In 1939 he began *Empire City*, his gigantic epic novel about the
New York he knew and loved, and "added to it at approximately
five-year intervals." He did not find a publisher until 1964, and it
has yet to find a public. In 1947 he and his architect brother Per-
cival published *Communitas: Means of Livelihood and Ways of
Life*, a gem in city planning—humane, learned, witty, philosophical.

Then came that explosive year with the success of *Growing Up
Absurd* in 1960 and the exhausting decade of lectures and conferences, forgotten books brought back into print, others printed for
the first time—and many courageous articles and essays.

514

THE PSYCHOLOGY OF BEING POWERLESS

People believe that the great background conditions of modern life are beyond our power to influence. The proliferation of technology is autonomous and cannot be checked. The galloping urbanization is going to gallop on. Our over-centralized administration, both of things and men, is impossibly cumbersome and costly, but we cannot cut it down to size. These are inevitable tendencies of history. More dramatic inevitabilities are the explosions, the scientific explosion and the population explosion. And there are more literal explosions, the dynamite accumulating in the slums of a thousand cities and the accumulating stockpiles of nuclear bombs in nations great and small. The psychology, in brief, is that history is out of control. It is no longer something that we make but something that happens to us. Politics is not prudent steering in difficult terrain, but it is—and this is the subject of current political science—how to get power and keep power, even though the sphere of effective power is extremely limited and it makes little difference who is in power. The psychology of historical powerlessness is evident in the reporting and the reading of newspapers: there is little analysis of how events are building up, but we read—with excitement, spite, or fatalism, depending on our characters—the headlines of crises for which we are unprepared. Statesmen cope with emergencies, and the climate of emergency is chronic.

I believe myself that some of these historical conditions are not inevitable at all but are the working out of willful policies that aggrandize certain interests and exclude others, that subsidize certain styles and prohibit others. But of course, *historically,* if almost everybody believes the conditions are inevitable, including the policy makers who produce them, then they are inevitable. For to cope with emergencies does not mean, then, to support alternative conditions, but further to support and institutionalize the same conditions. Thus, if there are too many cars, we build new highways. If administration is too cumbersome, we build in new levels of administration.

If there is a nuclear threat, we develop anti-missile missiles. If there is urban crowding and anomie, we aggravate it by stepping up urban renewal and social work. If there are pollution and slums of engineering because of imprudent use of technology, we subsidize Research and Development by the same scientific corporations working for the same ecologically irrelevant motives. If there is youth alienation, we extend and intensify the processing of youth in schools. If the nation-state is outmoded as a political form, we make ourselves into a mightier nation-state.

In this self-proving round, the otherwise innocent style of input-output economies, games-theory strategy, and computerized social science becomes a trap. For the style dumbly accepts the self-proving program and cannot compute what is not mentioned. Individual differences, belief and distrust, history, landscape, the available time, space, and energy of actual people—such things tend to be left out. Then the solutions that emerge ride even more roughshod over what has been left out. Indeed, at least in the social sciences, the more variables one can technically compute, the less likely it is that there will be prior thinking about their relevance to human life. Our classic example—assuming that there will be a future period to which we provide classic examples—is Herman Kahn on Thermonuclear War.

But what is the psychology of feeling that one is powerless to alter basic conditions? What is it as a way of being in the world? Let me list half a dozen kinds of responses to being in a chronic emergency; unfortunately, in America they are exhibited in rather pure form. I say unfortunately, because a pure response to a chronic emergency is a neurotic one; healthy human beings are more experimental or at least muddling. Instead of politics, we now have to talk psychotherapy.

By definition, governors cannot forfeit the symbol that everything is under control, though they may not think so. During President Kennedy's administration, Arthur Schlesinger expressed the problem poignantly by saying "One simply *must* govern." The theme of that administration was to be "pragmatic"; but by this they did not mean a philosophical pragmatism, going toward an end in view from where one in fact is and with the means one has; they meant turning busily to each crisis as it arose, so that it was clear that one was not inactive. The criticism of Eisenhower's administration was that it was stagnant. The new slogan was "get America moving."

This was rather pathetic; but as the crises have become deeper, the response of the present administration is not pathetic but, frankly, delusional and dangerous. It is to *will* to be in control, without adjusting to the realities. They seem to imagine that they will in fact buy up every economy, police the world, social-engineer the cities, school the young. In this fantasy they employ a rhetoric of astonishing dissociation between idea and reality, far beyond customary campaign oratory. For example, they proclaim that they are depolluting streams, but they allot no money; forty "demonstration cities" are to be made livable and show the way, but the total sum available is $1.5 billion (John Lindsay says we need $50 billion for New York alone); the depressed area of Appalachia has been reclaimed, but the method is an old highway bill under another name; poor people will run their own programs, but any administrator is fired if he tries to let them do it; they are suing for peace, but they despatch more troops and bombers. This seems to be just lying but, to my ear, it is nearer to magic thinking. The magic buoys up the self-image; the activity is either nothing at all or brute force to make the problem vanish.

In between the ideality and the brutality there occurs a lot of obsessional warding off of confusion by methodical calculations that solve problems in the abstract, in high modern style. A precise decimal is set beyond which the economy will be inflationary, but nobody pays any mind to it. Eighty-seven per cent of low income nations but only 48 per cent of middle income nations have had violent political disturbances. A precise kill-ratio is established beyond which the Vietcong will fold up, but they don't. Polls are consulted for the consensus,

like the liver of sheep, without noticing signs of unrest and
even though the administration keeps committing itself to an
irreversible course that allows for no choice. And they are
everlastingly righteous.

In more insane moments, however, they manufacture history out of the whole cloth, so there is no way of checking up
at all. They create incidents in order to exact reprisals; they
invent (and legislate about) agitators for demonstrations and
riots that are spontaneous; they project bogeymen in order to
arm to the teeth. Some of this, to be sure, is cynical, but that
does not make it less mad; for, clever or not, they still avoid
the glaring realities of world poverty, American isolation,
mounting urban costs, mounting anomie, and so forth. I do
not think the slogan "The Great Society" is cynical; it is
delusional.

Perhaps the epitome of will operating in panic—like a case
from a textbook in abnormal psychology—has been the government's handling of the assassination of John Kennedy. The
Warren Commission attempted to "close" the case, to make it
not exist in the public mind. Thus it hastily drew firm conclusions from dubious evidence, disregarded counter-evidence,
defied physical probabilities, and perhaps even accepted
manufactured evidence. For a temporary lull it has run the
risk of a total collapse of public trust.

Common people, who do not have to govern, can let themselves feel powerless and resign themselves. They respond
with the familiar combination of not caring and, as a substitute, identifying with those whom they fancy to be powerful.
This occurs differently, however, among the poor and the
middle classes.

The poor simply stop trying, become dependent, drop out
of school, drop out of sight, become addicts, become lawless.
It seems to be a matter of temperature or a small incident
whether or not they riot. In anomie circumstances, when people are left out and can't get in, it is hard to tell when riot
or other lawlessness is a political act toward a new setup and
when it is a social pathology. Being powerless as citizens,

poor people have little structure of meaning in which to express, or know, what they are after. The concrete objects of their anger make no political sense: They are angry at themselves or their own neighborhoods, at white people passing by, at Jewish landlords and shopkeepers. More symbolic scapegoats like "the capitalist system" or "communism" do not evoke much interest. One has to feel part of a system to share its bogeymen or have a counter-ideology, and by and large the present-day poor are not so much exploited as excluded.

But to fill the void, they admire, and identify with, what is strong and successful, even if—perhaps especially if—it is strong and successful at their own expense. Poor Spanish youth are enthusiastic about our mighty bombs and bombers, though of course they have no interest in the foreign policy that uses them. (If anything, the polls show that poor people are for de-escalation and peace rather than war.) Readers of the *Daily News* are excited by the dramatic confrontation of statesmen wagging fingers at each other. Negroes in Harlem admire the Cadillacs of their own corrupt politicians and racketeers. Currently there is excitement about the words "Black Power," but the confusion about the meaning is telling: In the South, where there is little Negro anomie, Black Power has considerable political meaning; in the Northern cities it is a frantic abstraction. Similarly, the contrary word "Integration" makes economic and pedagogic sense if interpreted by people who have some feeling of freedom and power; but if interpreted in an atmosphere of resentful hopelessness it turns into a fight for petty victories or spite, which are not political propositions, though they may be good for the soul.

The anomie of middle-class people, on the other hand, appears rather as their privatism; they retreat to their families and consumer goods where they still have some power and choice. It is always necessary to explain to non-Americans that middle-class Americans are not so foolish and piggish about their Standard of Living as it seems; it is that the Standard of Living has to provide all the achievement and value that are open to them. But it is a strange thing for a society to be proud of its Standard of Living, rather than taking it for granted as a background for worthwhile action.

Privacy is purchased at a terrible price of anxiety, excluding, and pettiness, the need to delete anything different from oneself and to protect things that are not worth protecting. Nor can they be protected; few of the suburban homes down the road, that look so trim, do not have cases of alcoholism, insanity, youngsters on drugs or in jail for good or bad reasons, ulcers, and so forth. In my opinion, middle-class squeamishness and anxiety, a kind of obsessional neurosis, are a much more important cause of segregation than classical race-prejudice which is a kind of paranoia that shows up most among failing classes, bankrupt small property owners, and proletarians under competitive pressure. The squeamishness is worse, for it takes people out of humanity, whereas prejudice is at least passionate. Squeamishness finally undercuts even the fairness and decency that we expect from the middle class.

The identification with power of the powerless middle class is also characteristic. They do not identify with brutality, big men, or wealth, but with the efficient system itself, which is what renders *them* powerless. And here again we can see the sharp polarity between those who are not politically resigned and those who are. Take the different effects of what is called education. On the one hand, the universities, excellent students and distinguished professors, are the nucleus of opposition to our war policy. On the other hand, in polls of general opinion there is always a dismaying correlation between years of schooling and the "hard line" of bombing China during the Korean War or bombing Hanoi now. But this is not because the educated middle class is rabidly anti-communist, and certainly it is not ferocious; rather, it is precisely because it is rational, it approves the technically efficient solution that does not notice flesh-and-blood suffering. In this style the middle class feels it has status, though no more power than anybody else. No doubt these middle-class people are influenced by the magazines they read, which explain what is efficient; but they are influenced because they are "thinking" types, for whom reality is what they read.

The bathos of the irresponsible middle class is the mighty TV newscast on our national networks. This combines commercials for the high Standard of Living, scenes of war and riot, and judicious pro-and-con commentary on what it all means. The scenes arouse feeling, the commentary provokes thought, the commercials lead to action. It is a total experience.

Let me illustrate the psychology of resignation with another example, for it has come to be accepted as the normal state of feeling rather than as pathological.

During the hearings on Vietnam before the Senate Foreign Relations Committee, Senator Dodd of Connecticut—who had been mentioned as Lyndon Johnson's favored choice for Vice-President in 1964—was asked what he thought of the sharp criticism of the government. "It is the price that we pay," he said, "for living in a free country." This answer was routine and nobody questioned it. Yet what an astonishing evaluation of the democratic process it is, that free discussion is a weakness we must put up with in order to avoid the evils of another system! To Milton, Spinoza, or Jefferson free discussion was the strength of a society. Their theory was that truth had power, often weak at first but steady and cumulative, and in free debate the right course would emerge and prevail. Nor was there any other method to arrive at truth, since there was no other authority to pronounce it than all the people. Thus, to arrive at wise policy, it was essential for everybody to say his say, and the more disparate the views and searching the criticism the better.

Instead, Senator Dodd seems to have the following epistemology of democracy. We elect an administration and it, through the intelligence service, secret diplomacy, briefings by the Department of Defense and other agencies, comes into inside information that enables it alone to understand the situation. In principle we can repudiate its decisions at the next election, but usually they have led to commitments and actions that are hard to repudiate. Implicit is that there is a permanent group of selfless and wise public servants, experts, and impartial reporters, who understand the technology, strategy, and diplomacy that we cannot understand, and therefore we must perforce do what they advise. To be sure, they continually make bad predictions, and, on the evidence, they are not selfless but partial or at least narrow in their commercial interests and political outlook. Yet this does not alter the picture, for if the President goes along with them, outside criticism is irrelevant anyway and no doubt misses the point, which, it happens, cannot be disclosed for reasons of national security. And surely irrelevant discussion is harmful because it is divisive. But it is the price we pay for living in a free country.

What can be the attraction of such a diluted faith in democracy? It is what is appropriate in a chronic low-grade emergency. In an emergency it is rational, and indeed natural, to concentrate temporary power in a small center, as the ancient Romans appointed dictators, to decide and act, and for the rest of us to support the *faits accomplis* for better or worse. But since we face a low-grade emergency—nobody is about to invade San Francisco—we like to go on as usual, including sounding off and criticizing, so long as it does not affect policy.

Unfortunately, this psychology keeps the low-grade emergency chronic. There is no way to get back to normal, no check on *faits accomplis*, no accountability of the decision makers till so much damage has been done that there is a public revulsion (as after a few years of Korea), or, as seems inevitable, one day a catastrophe. Worst of all there is no way for a philosophic view to emerge that might become effectual. Who would present such a view? In the classical theory of democracy, the electorate is educated by the clashing debate and the best men come forward and gain a following. But in Senator Dodd's free country, acute men are likely to fall silent, for what is the use of talk that is irrelevant and divisive?

The discussion in the Foreign Relations Committee, excellent as it was, was itself typical of a timid democracy. Not a single Senator was able to insist on basic realities that could put the Vietnam war in a philosophic light and perhaps work out of its dilemmas. (Since then, Senator Fulbright has become more outspoken.) In this context, here are some of the basic realities: In a period of worldwide communications and spread of technology, and therefore of "rising aspirations," nevertheless a majority of mankind is fast becoming poorer. For our own country, is it really in our national interest to come on as a Great Power, touchy about saving face and telling other people how to act, or else? In the era of One World and the atom bomb, is there not something baroque in the sovereignty of nation-states and legalisms about who aggressed on whom?

It will be objected that such anti-national issues can hardly be raised by Senators, even in a free debate. But the same limitation exists outside of government. In the scores of pretentious TV debates and panel discussions on Vietnam during the past two years, I doubt that there have been half a dozen —and these not on national networks—in which a speaker was invited who might conceivably go outside the official parameters and raise the real questions. Almost always the extreme opposition is himself a proponent of power politics, like Hans Morgenthau. (It usually *is* Hans Morgenthau.) Why not A. J. Muste, for instance? Naturally the big networks would say that there is no use in presenting quixotic opinions that are irrelevant. (The word "quixotic" was used by General Sarnoff of the National Broadcasting Company in his successful bid to Congress to deny to third party candidates equal free time.) By this response, the broadcasters guarantee that the opinions will remain irrelevant, until history, "out of control," makes them relevant because they were true.

This brings me back to my subject, how people are in the world when history is "out of control." So far I have noticed those who unhistorically will to be in control and those who accept their powerlessness and withdraw. But there is another possibility, apocalypse, not only to accept being powerless but to expect, or perhaps wish and hasten, the inevitable historical explosion. Again there are two variants, for it is usually a different psychology, entailing different behavior, to expect a catastrophe and beat around for what to do for oneself, or to wish for the catastrophe and identify with it.

To expect disaster and desert the sinking ship is not a political act, but it is often a profoundly creative one, both personally and socially. To do it, one must have vitality of one's own that is not entirely structured and warped by the suicidal system. Going it alone may allow for new development. For instance, when the youth of the Beat movement cut loose from the organized system, opted for voluntary poverty, and invented a morals and culture out of their own guts and some confused literary memories, they exerted a big and, on the whole, good influence. Also, the disposition of the powers-that-be to treat gross realities as irrelevant has driven many intellectual and spirited persons into deviant paths just to make sense of their own experience; thus, at present, perhaps most of the best artists and writers in America are unusually far out of line, even for creative people. They hardly seem to share the common culture, yet they are what culture we have. (According to himself, Dr. Timothy Leary, the psychodelics man, espouses the extreme of this philosophy, "Turn on, tune in, and drop out"; but I doubt that relying on chemicals is really a way of dropping out of our drug-ridden and technological society.)

We must remember that with the atom bombs there is a literal meaning to deserting the ship. This factor is always present in the background of the young. For instance, during the Cuban missile crisis I kept getting phone calls from college students asking if they should at once fly to New Zealand. I tried to calm their anxiety by opining that the crisis was only diplomatic maneuvering, but I now think that I was wrong, for eyewitnesses of behavior in Washington at the time tell me that there was a danger of nuclear war.

More generally, the psychology of apocalypse and the decision to go it alone are characteristic of waves of populism such as we are now surprisingly witnessing in the United States on the streets, in Sproul Hall, at meetings of City Councils, and so forth. The rhetoric of the agrarian populism of the Eighties and Nineties was vividly apocalyptic, and that movement brought forth remarkable feats of cooperation and social invention. The current urban and student populism has begun to produce its own para-institutional enterprises, some of which are viable.

The practice of civil disobedience also must often be interpreted in terms of the psychology of apocalypse, but even sympathetic legal analysts of civil disobedience fail to take this into account. It is one thing to disobey a law because the authorities are in moral error on some point, in order to force a test case and to rally opposition and change the law. It is another thing to disobey authorities who are the Whore of Babylon and the Devil's thrones and dominions. In such a case the conscientious attitude may be not respect but disregard and disgust, and it may be more moral for God's creatures to go underground rather than to confront, especially if their theology does not include an article on paradise for martyrs. As a citizen of the uncorrupted polity in exile, it might be one's civil duty to be apparently lawless. There is a fairly clear-cut distinction between civil disobedience in a legitimate order and revolution that may or may not prove its own legitimacy; but the politics and morality of apocalypse fall in-between and are ambiguous.

Quite different, finally, is the psychology of those who unconsciously or consciously wish for catastrophe and work to bring it about. (Of course, for the best youth to desert the sinking ship also brings about disaster, by default.) The wish for a blowup occurs in people who are so enmeshed in a frustrating system that they have no vitality apart from it; and their vitality in it is explosive rage.

Very poor people, who have "the culture of poverty," as Oscar Lewis calls it, are rarely so psychologically committed to a dominant social system that they need its total destruction. They have dreams of heaven but not of hellfire. A few exemplary burnings and beheadings mollify their vengeance. Their intellectual leaders, however, who are verbal and willy-nilly psychologically enmeshed in the hated system, might be more apocalyptic. For instance, Malcolm X once told me—it was before his last period, which was more rational and political—that he would welcome the atom bombing of New York to vindicate Allah, even though it destroyed his own community. James Baldwin is full of hellfire, but I have never heard much of it in popular religion.

On the whole, at present in the United States the psychology of explosive apocalypse is not to be found among rioting Negroes crying "Burn, baby, burn," nor among utopian beatniks on hallucinogens; it is to be found among people who believe in the system but cannot tolerate the anxiety of its not working out for them. Unfortunately, it is a pretty empty system and anxiety is widespread.

Most obviously there is the large group of people who have been demoted or are threatened with demotion, businessmen and small property owners who feel they have been pushed around; victims of inflation; displaced farmers; dissatisfied ex-soldiers; proletarians who have become petty bourgeois but are now threatened by automation or by Negroes invading their neighborhoods. Consciously these people do not want a blowup but power to restore the good old days; but when they keep losing out, they manifest an astounding violence and vigilantism and could become the usual mass base for fascism. In foreign policy, where imagination has freer rein, they are for preemptive first strikes, bombing China, and so forth. I do not think this group is dangerous in itself—I do not think there is an important Radical Right in the United States—but it is a sounding board to propagate catastrophic ideas to more important groups.

My guess is that, under our bad urban conditions, a more dangerous group is the uncountable number of the mentally ill and psychopathic hoodlums from all kinds of backgrounds. Given the rate of mental disease and the arming and training in violence of hundreds of thousands of young men, there is sure to be an increase of berserk acts that might sometimes amount to a reign of terror, and could create a climate for political enormities. Not to speak of organized Storm Troopers.

The most dangerous group of all, however, is the established but anomic middle class that I described previously. Exclusive, conformist, squeamish, and methodical, it is terribly vulnerable to anxiety. When none of its rational solutions work out, at home or abroad, its patience will wear thin, and then it could coldly support a policy of doom, just to have the problems over with, the way a man counts to three and blows his brains out. But this cold conscious acceptance of a "rational solution" would not be possible if unconsciously there were not a lust for destruction of the constraining system, as sober citizens excitedly watch a house burn down.

The conditions of middle-class life are exquisitely calculated to increase tension and heighten anxiety. It is not so much that the pace is fast—often it consists of waiting around and is slow and boring—but that it is somebody else's pace or schedule. One is continually interrupted. And the tension cannot be normally discharged by decisive action and doing things one's own way. There is competitive pressure to act a role, yet paradoxically one is rarely allowed to do one's best or use one's best judgment. Proofs of success or failure are not tangibly given in the task, but always in some superior's judgment. Spontaneity and instinct are likely to be gravely penalized, yet one is supposed to be creative and sexual on demand. All this is what Freud called civilization and its discontents. Wilhelm Reich showed that this kind of anxiety led to dreams of destruction, self-destruction, and explosion, in order to release tension, feel something, and feel free.

A chronic low-grade emergency is not psychologically static. It builds up to and invites a critical emergency. But just as we are able to overlook glaring economic and ecological realities, so in our social engineering and system of education glaring psychological realities like anomie and anxiety are regarded almost as if they did not exist.

The psychological climate explains, I think, the peculiar

attitude of the Americans toward the escalation of the Vietnam war. (At the time I am writing this, more bombs are being rained on that little country than on Germany at the peak of World War II, and there is talk of sending nearly a million men.) The government's statements of purpose are inconsistent week by week and are belied by its actions. Its predictions are ludicrously falsified by what happens. Field commanders lie and are contradicted by the next day's news. Yet a good majority continues to acquiesce with a paralyzed fascination. This paralysis is not indifference, for finally people talk about nothing else. One has the impression that it is an exciting attraction of a policy that it is doomed.

GEORGE SANTAYANA
[1863–1952]

In 1919 twelve or fifteen graduate students in philosophy at Columbia University took part in a memorable seminar led by Dean F. J. E. Woodbridge. Our basic reading throughout was Santayana's first magnum opus, the five volumes of *The Life of Reason,* published in 1905. The Dean had high respect for Santayana's work, but his Socratic interruptions were never stilled by that classic prose.

Ten years later I edited *The Book of Sonnet Sequences,* from Sir Philip Sidney to Edna St. Vincent Millay, and I included twenty sonnets by Santayana, written between 1883 and 1893. And some twenty years later I included in *Great Essays* what may be his most poignant piece of writing, "Tipperary," inspired by English veterans, cheerfully, confidently home from the war, unsuspicious of the future.

Indeed I suspect that neither *The Life of Reason* nor Santayana's second magnum opus, *Scepticism and Animal Faith* and *The Realms of Being* (five volumes written between 1923 and 1940) will endure as well as some of his essays, articles, and addresses, which are contained in four more or less miscellaneous collections: *Winds of Doctrine* (1913), *Character and Opinion in the United States* (1920), *Soliloquies in England and Other Later Soliloquies* (1922), and *Some Turns of Thought in Modern Philosophy* (1933).

One evening in the fall of 1923 I dropped into Frank Shay's Bookshop in Greenwich Village and noticed on the magazine rack the November issue of *The Dial* with a haunting title by Santayana, "A Long Way Round to Nirvana, or, Much Ado About Dying." I was shocked and delighted to find that the classic Spanish-American had been reading the questionable Freud! Now, more than fifty years later, that meditation provides an appropriate ending.

529

A LONG WAY ROUND TO NIRVANA
or, Much Ado About Dying

That the end of life is death may be called a truism, since the various kinds of immortality that might perhaps supervene would none of them abolish death, but at best would weave life and death together into the texture of a more comprehensive destiny. The end of one life might be the beginning of another, if the Creator had composed his great work like a dramatic poet, assigning some lines to one character and some to another. Death would then be merely the cue at the end of each speech, summoning the next personage to break in and keep the ball rolling. Or perhaps, as some suppose, all the characters are assumed in turn by a single supernatural Spirit, who amid his endless improvisations is imagining himself living for the moment in this particular solar and social system. Death in such a universal monologue would be but a change of scene or of metre, while in the scramble of a real comedy it would be a change of actors. In either case every voice would be silenced sooner or later, and death would end each particular life, in spite of all possible sequels.

The relapse of created things into nothing is no violent fatality, but something naturally quite smooth and proper. This has been set forth recently, in a novel way, by a philosopher from whom we hardly expected such a lesson, namely Professor Sigmund Freud. He has now broadened his conception of sexual craving or *libido* into a general principle of attraction or concretion in matter, like the Eros of the ancient poets Hesiod and Empedocles. The windows of that stuffy clinic have been thrown open; that swell of acrid disinfectants, those hysterical shrieks, have escaped into the cold night. The troubles of the sick soul, we are given to understand, as well as their cure, after all flow from the stars.

I am glad that Freud has resisted the tendency to represent this principle of Love as the only principle in nature. Unity

somehow exercises an evil spell over metaphysicians. It is admitted that in real life it is not well for One to be alone, and
I think pure unity is no less barren and graceless in metaphysics. You must have plurality to start with, or trinity, or
at least duality, if you wish to get anywhere, even if you wish
to get effectively into the bosom of the One, abandoning your
separate existence. Freud, like Empedocles, has prudently introduced a prior principle for Love to play with; not Strife,
however (which is only an incident in Love) but Inertia, or
the tendency towards peace and death. Let us suppose that
matter was originally dead, and perfectly content to be so,
and that it still relapses, when it can, into its old equilibrium.
But the homogeneous (as Spencer would say) when it is finite
is unstable: and matter, presumably not being coextensive
with space, necessarily forms aggregates which have an inside
and an outside. The parts of such bodies are accordingly differently exposed to external influences and differently related
to one another. This inequality, even in what seems most
quiescent, is big with changes, destined to produce in time a
wonderful complexity. It is the source of all uneasiness, of life,
and of love.

"Let us imagine [writes Freud [1]] an undifferentiated vesicle
of sensitive substance: then its surface, exposed as it is to the
outer world, is by its very position differentiated, and serves
as an organ for receiving stimuli. Embryology, repeating as it
does the history of evolution, does in fact show that the central
nervous system arises from the ectoderm; the grey cortex of
the brain remains a derivative of the primitive superficial layer. . . . This morsel of living substance floats about in an outer
world which is charged with the most potent energies, and it
would be destroyed . . . if it were not furnished with protection against stimulation. It acquires this through . . . a special
integument or membrane. . . . The outer layer, by its own

[1] The following quotations are drawn from *Beyond the Pleasure-Principle*,
by Sigmund Freud; authorized translation by C. J. M. Hubback. The International Psycho-Analytic Press, 1922, pp. 29-48. The italics are in the original.

death, has secured all the deeper layers from a like fate. . . .
It must suffice to take little samples of the outer world, to
taste it, so to speak, in small quantities. In highly developed
organisms the receptive external layer of what was once a
vesicle has long been withdrawn into the depths of the body,
but portions of it have been left on the surface immediately
beneath the common protective barrier. These portions form
the sense-organs. [On the other hand] the sensitive cortical
layer has no protective barrier against excitations emanating
from within. . . . The most prolific sources of such excitations
are the so-called instincts of the organism. . . . The child never
gets tired of demanding the repetition of a game. . . . He wants
always to hear the same story instead of a new one, insists
inexorably on exact repetition, and corrects each deviation
which the narrator lets slip by mistake. . . . According to this,
an instinct would be a tendency in living organic matter im-
pelling it towards reinstatement of an earlier condition, one
which it had abandoned under the influence of external disturbing forces—a kind of organic elasticity or, to put it another way, the manifestation of inertia in organic life.

"If, then, all organic instincts are conservative, historically
acquired, and directed towards regression, towards reinstatement of something earlier, we are obliged to place all the results of organic development to the credit of external, disturbing, and distracting influences. The rudimentary creature
would from its very beginning not have wanted to change,
would, if circumstances had remained the same, have always
merely repeated the same course of existence. But in the last
resort it must have been the evolution of our earth, and its
relation to the sun, that has left its imprint on the development of organisms. The conservative organic instincts have
absorbed every one of these enforced alterations in the course
of life, and have stored them for repetition; they thus present
the delusive appearance of forces striving after change and
progress, while they are merely endeavouring to reach an old
goal by ways both old and new. This final goal of all organic

striving can be stated too. It would be counter to the conservative nature of instinct if the goal of life were a state never hitherto reached. It must be rather an ancient starting point, which the living being left long ago, and to which it harks back again by all the circuitous paths of development. . . . *The goal of all life is death.* . . .

"Through a long period of time the living substance may have . . . had death within easy reach . . . until decisive external influences altered in such a way as to compel [it] to ever greater deviations from the original path of life, and to ever more complicated and circuitous routes to the attainment of the goal of death. These circuitous ways to death, faithfully retained by the conservative instincts, would be neither more nor less than the phenomena of life as we know it."

Freud puts forth these interesting suggestions with much modesty, admitting that they are vague and uncertain and (what it is even more important to notice) mythical in their terms; but it seems to me that, for all that, they are an admirable counterblast to prevalent follies. When we hear that there is, animating the whole universe, an *élan vital*, or general impulse toward some unknown but single ideal, the terms used are no less uncertain, mythical, and vague, but the suggestion conveyed is false, whereas that conveyed by Freud's speculations is true. In what sense can myths and metaphors be true or false? In the sense that, in terms drawn from moral predicaments or from literary psychology, they may report the general movement and the pertinent issue of material facts, and may inspire us with a wise sentiment in their presence. In this sense I should say that Greek mythology was true and Calvinist theology was false. The chief terms employed in psychoanalysis have always been metaphorical: "unconscious wishes," "the pleasure-principle," "the Oedipus complex," "Narcissism," "the censor"; nevertheless, interesting and profound vistas may be opened up, in such terms, into the tangle of events in a man's life, and a fresh start may be made with fewer encumbrances and less morbid inhibition. "The shortcomings of our description," Freud says, "would probably disappear if for psychological terms we could substitute physiological or chemical ones. These too only constitute a metaphorical language, but one familiar to us for a much longer time, and perhaps also simpler." All human discourse is metaphorical, in that our perceptions and thoughts are adventitious signs for their objects, as names are, and by no means copies of what is going on materially in the depths of nature; but just as the sportsman's eye, which yields but a summary graphic image, can trace the flight of a bird through the air quite well enough to shoot it and bring it down, so the myths of a wise philosopher about the origin of life or of dreams, though expressed symbolically, may reveal the pertinent movement of nature to us, and may kindle in us just sentiments and true expectations in respect to our fate—for his own soul is the bird this sportsman is shooting.

Now I think these myths of Freud's about life, like his old ones about dreams, are calculated to enlighten and to chasten us enormously about ourselves. The human spirit, when it awakes, finds itself in trouble; it is burdened, for no reason it can assign, with all sorts of anxieties about food, pressures, pricks, noises, and pains. It is born, as another wise myth has it, in original sin. And the passions and ambitions of life, as they come on, only complicate this burden and make it heavier, without rendering it less incessant or gratuitous. Whence this fatality, and whither does it lead? It comes from heredity, and it leads to propagation. When we ask how heredity could be started or transmitted, our ignorance of nature and of past time reduces us to silence or to wild conjectures. Something— let us call it matter—must always have existed, and some of its parts, under pressure of the others, must have got tied up into knots, like the mainspring of a watch, in such a violent and unhappy manner that when the pressure is relaxed they fly open as fast as they can, and unravel themselves with a vast sense of relief. Hence the longing to satisfy latent passions, with the fugitive pleasure in doing so. But the external

agencies that originally wound up that mainspring never cease
to operate; every fresh stimulus gives it another turn, until
it snaps, or grows flaccid, or is unhinged. Moreover, from time
to time, when circumstances change, these external agencies
may encrust that primary organ with minor organs attached
to it. Every impression, every adventure, leaves a trace or
rather a seed behind it. It produces a further complication in
the structure of the body, a fresh charge, which tends to repeat the impressed motion in season and out of season. Hence
that perpetual docility or ductility in living substance which
enables it to learn tricks, to remember facts, and (when the
seeds of past experiences marry and cross in the brain) to
imagine new experiences, pleasing or horrible. Every act initi-
ates a new habit and may implant a new instinct. We see people even late in life carried away by political or religious con-
tagions or developing strange vices; there would be no peace
in old age, but rather a greater and greater obsession by all
sorts of cares, were it not that time, in exposing us to many
adventitious influences, weakens or discharges our primitive
passions; we are less greedy, less lusty, less hopeful, less generous. But these weakened primitive impulses are naturally
by far the strongest and most deeply rooted in the organism:
so that although an old man may be converted or may take
up some hobby, there is usually something thin in his elderly
zeal, compared with the heartiness of youth; nor is it edifying
to see a soul in which the plainer human passions are extinct
becoming a hotbed of chance delusions.

In any case each fresh habit taking root in the organism
forms a little mainspring or instinct of its own, like a parasite;
so that an elaborate mechanism is gradually developed, where
each lever and spring holds the other down, and all hold the
mainspring down together, allowing it to unwind itself only
very gradually, and meantime keeping the whole clock tick-
ing and revolving, and causing the smooth outer face which
it turns to the world, so clean and innocent, to mark the time
of day amiably for the passer-by. But there is a terribly
complicated labour going on beneath, propelled with diffi-

culty, and balanced precariously, with much secret friction
and failure. No wonder that the engine often gets visibly out
of order, or stops short: the marvel is that it ever manages to
go at all. Nor is it satisfied with simply revolving and, when at
last dismounted, starting afresh in the person of some seed it
has dropped, a portion of its substance with all its concentrated instincts wound up tightly within it, and eager to repeat the ancestral experiment; all this growth is not merely
material and vain. Each clock in revolving strikes the hour,
even the quarters, and often with lovely chimes. These
chimes we call perceptions, feelings, purposes, and dreams;
and it is because we are taken up entirely with this pretty
music, and perhaps think that it sounds of itself and needs
no music box to make it, that we find such difficulty in conceiving the nature of our own clocks and are compelled to
describe them only musically, that is, in myths. But the in-
eptitude of our aesthetic minds to unravel the nature of
mechanism does not deprive these minds of their own clearness and euphony. Besides sounding their various musical
notes, they have the cognitive function of indicating the hour
and catching the echoes of distant events or of maturing inward dispositions. This information and emotion, added to
the incidental pleasures in satisfying our various passions,
make up the life of an incarnate spirit. They reconcile it to
the external fatality that has wound up the organism, and is
breaking it down; and they rescue this organism and all its
works from the indignity of being a vain complication and a
waste of motion.

That the end of life should be death may sound sad: but
what other end can anything have? The end of an evening
party is to go to bed; but its use is to gather congenial people
together, that they may pass the time pleasantly. An invitation to the dance is not rendered ironical because the dance
cannot last forever; the youngest of us and the most vigorously
wound up, after a few hours, has had enough of sinuous stepping and prancing. The transitoriness of things is essential to
their physical being, and not at all sad in itself; it becomes

sad by virtue of a sentimental illusion, which makes us imagine that they wish to endure, and that their end is always
untimely; but in a healthy nature it is not so. What is truly
sad is to have some impulse frustrated in the midst of its
career, and robbed of its chosen object; and what is painful is to have an organ lacerated or destroyed when it is still
vigorous, and not ready for its natural sleep and dissolution.
We must not confuse the itch which our unsatisfied instincts
continue to cause with the pleasure of satisfying and dismiss-
ing each of them in turn. Could they all be satisfied harmoniously we should be satisfied once for all and completely.
Then doing and dying would coincide throughout and be a
perfect pleasure.

This same insight is continued in another wise myth which
has inspired morality and religion in India from time immemorial: I mean the doctrine of Karma. We are born, it says,
with a heritage, a character imposed, and a long task assigned,
all due to the ignorance which in our past lives has led us
into all sorts of commitments. These obligations we must
pay off, relieving the pure spirit within us from its accumulated burdens, from debts and assets both equally oppressive.
We cannot disentangle ourselves by mere frivolity, nor by
suicide: frivolity would only involve us more deeply in the
toils of fate, and suicide would but truncate our misery and
leave us forever a confessed failure. When life is understood
to be a process of redemption, its various phases are taken up
in turn without haste and without undue attachment; their
coming and going have all the keenness of pleasure, the holi-
ness of sacrifice, and the beauty of art. The point is to have
expressed and discharged all that was latent in us; and to this
perfect relief various temperaments and various traditions
assign different names, calling it having one's day, or doing
one's duty, or realizing one's ideal, or saving one's soul. The
task in any case is definite and imposed on us by nature,
whether we recognize it or not; therefore we can make true
moral progress or fall into real errors. Wisdom and genius lie
in discerning this prescribed task and in doing it readily,

cleanly, and without distraction. Folly on the contrary imagines that any scent is worth following, that we have an infinite nature, or no nature in particular, that life begins without obligations and can do business without capital, and that the will is free, instead of being a specific burden and a tight hereditary knot to be unravelled. This romantic folly is defended by some philosophers without self-knowledge, who think that the variations and further entanglements which the future may bring are the manifestation of spirit; but they are, as Freud has indicated, imposed on living beings by external pressure, and take shape in the realm of matter. It is only after the organs of spirit are formed mechanically that spirit can exist, and can distinguish the better from the worse in the fate of those organs, and therefore in its own fate. Spirit has nothing to do with infinity. Infinity is something physical and ambiguous; there is no scale in it and no centre. The depths of the human heart are finite, and they are dark only to ignorance. Deep and dark as a soul may be when you look down into it from outside, it is something perfectly natural; and the same understanding that can unearth our suppressed young passions, and dispel our stubborn bad habits, can show us where our true good lies. Nature has marked out the path for us beforehand; there are snares in it, but also primroses, and it leads to peace.

•   •   •

Daniel Cory met George Santayana in Rome in 1927 when the latter was sixty-three years old. He became Santayana's secretary and closest friend and was with him the day he died in 1952.

Daniel Cory to the dying Santayana:
"Are you suffering? Are you suffering?"

Santayana:
"Yes, my friend, but my anguish is entirely physical; there are no moral difficulties whatsoever."

FOR FURTHER READING

A comparatively short, lucid, and up-to-date reference is here given for nearly all of the writers in this collection. The longer volumes are indicated.

J. A. Passmore: *Hume's Intentions*. Cambridge. 1952.

Ernst Cassirer: *The Question of Jean-Jacques Rousseau*. Columbia. 1954. Original German edition, 1932.

Richard Kroner: *Kant's Weltanschauung*. Chicago. 1956. Original German edition, 1914.

Mark Schorer: *William Blake—The Politics of Vision*. Holt. 1946.

> Especially Chapter VII: "The Broken Mold: Toward Restatement."

David Baumgardt: *Bentham and the Ethics of Today*. Princeton. 1952. 584 pages.

John Henry Newman: *An Essay in Aid of a Grammar of Assent*. Image Books (Doubleday). 1955.

> Introduction by Étienne Gilson.

I. Berlin: *Karl Marx—His Life and Environment*. Home University Library. 1939.

James W. Lane: *Whistler*. Crown. 1942.

Walter A. Kaufmann: *Nietzsche: Philosopher, Psychologist, Antichrist*. Princeton. 1950. 409 pages.

W. B. Gallie: *Peirce and Pragmatism*. Penguin. 1952.

Ralph Barton Perry: *The Thought and Character of William James*. Little, Brown and Company. 1935. 2 volumes, 1,594 pages.

> A companion for winter or summer; a treasure for a lifetime.

Alan Wood: *Bertrand Russell: The Passionate Skeptic*. Simon and Schuster. 1958.

Helen Huss Parkhurst, Ralph Barton Perry, and others: On William Pepperell Montague in *The Journal of Philosophy*. October 14, 1954.

Calvin S. Hall: *A Primer of Freudian Psychology*. Mentor Books. 1955.

Paul Arthur Schilpp, editor: *The Philosophy of Alfred North Whitehead*. Tudor. 2nd edition, 1951.

This monumental volume contains "Autobiographical Notes" by Whitehead and nineteen chapters by others on practically every phase of his thought.

Sidney Hook: *John Dewey—An Intellectual Portrait*. John Day. 1939.

Ruth L. Munroe: *Schools of Psychoanalytic Thought*. Dryden. 1955. 670 pages.

A massive work covering the whole field including Fromm and the other "revisionists."

Alfred J. Ayer, and others: *The Revolution in Philosophy*. Macmillan (London). 1956.

Introduction by Gilbert Ryle.

J. O. Urmson: *Philosophical Analysis—Its Development Between the Two World Wars*. Oxford. 1956.

G. J. Warnock: *English Philosophy Since 1900*. Oxford. 1958.

Charles A. Fecher: *The Philosophy of Jacques Maritain*. Newman. 1953. 361 pages.

On Existentialism, see Walter Kaufmann, editor: *Existentialism from Dostoevsky to Sartre*. Meridian. 1956.

On Western philosophy from the Middle Ages to the present time see "The Mentor Philosophers," six volumes, each one under distinguished editorship.

THE METAPHYSICAL COMPASS

From *The Ways of Things*, by William Pepperell Montague

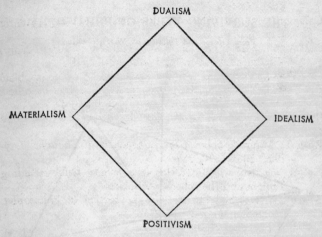

DUALISM

MATERIALISM

IDEALISM

POSITIVISM

". . . Neither in metaphysics nor in epistemology will you find any actual philosophy which could be located on the chart at the exact 'North' or 'South' or 'East' or 'West.' Take, for example, the metaphysics of ordinary theistic religion. We can best locate it about halfway between dualism and idealism." Montague's own position, which he called "animistic materialism" or "modified dualism," would fall, of course, between materialism and dualism.

The "Compass" might also be thought of as a baseball diamond, in which case, it might be suggested that the antimetaphysical positivist never reaches first base! Other positions, such as dialectical materialism, pragmatic pluralism, creative or emergent evolutionism, organic mechanism, and critical naturalism might be located helpfully, although not solemnly, within the diamond.

THE THREE-DIMENSIONAL DIAGRAM

OF

THE SURVIVING TYPES OF PHILOSOPHY

From *Process and Polarity*, by W. H. Sheldon

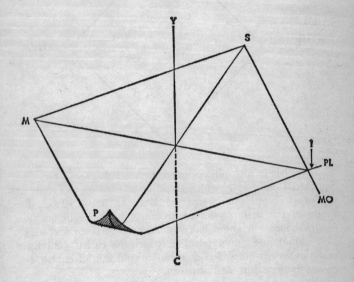

M—materialism
I—idealism
PL—pluralistic idealism
MO—monistic idealism
S—scholasticism
P—process-philosophy

YC—irrationalism
Y—extreme mysticism or
    superrationalism
C—scepticism or anti-
    rationalism